D1627439

venice | the city and its architecture

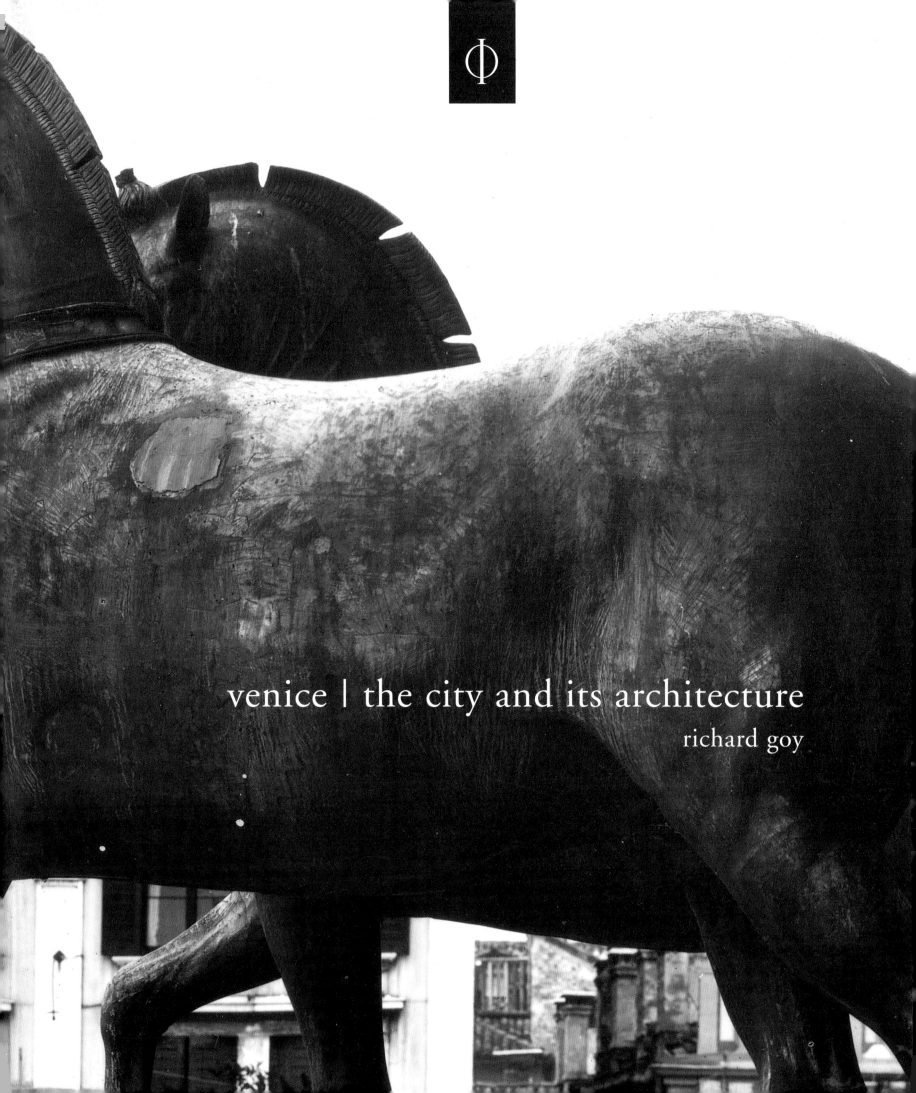

venice | the city and its architecture

richard goy

Contents

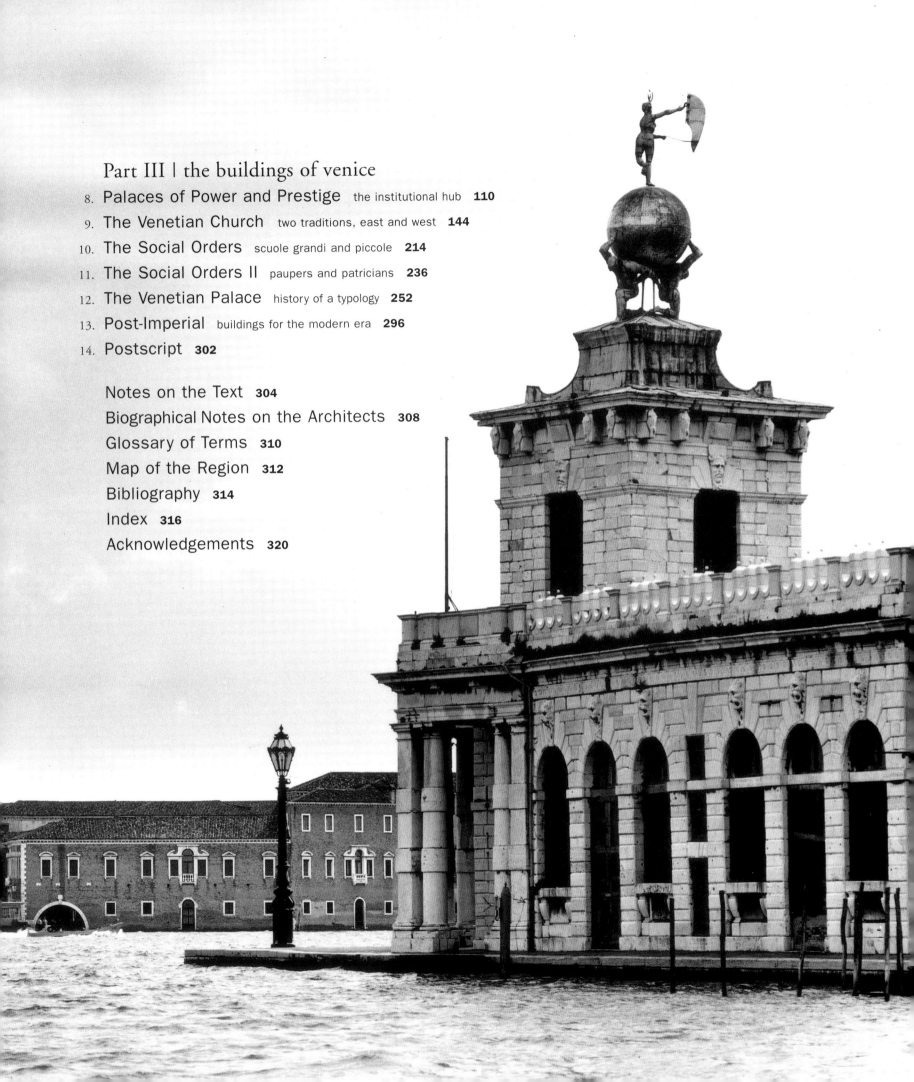

To Barbara and Catherine

Foreword

Countless books are written about the Serenissima, and I seem to have contributed forewords to a good many of them; but it has seldom been my good fortune to introduce a work as remarkable as that which you now hold in your hands. The author is not content to describe the Stones of Venice; he roots them firmly in their historical context, discussing not just the buildings themselves but why and how they came to be built, the purposes for which they were intended and even the degree to which those purposes were fulfilled.

He stresses, first of all, the paramount importance of the lagoon, that fundamental *raison d'être* without which the city would never have come into being: for had not the barbarians of the fifth and sixth centuries obliged the populations of the coastal cities to flee for their lives to the shoals and sandbanks of its mercifully shallow water – far more effective as a defence than deep – who in their senses would have settled in so bleak and inhospitable an environment, marshy, malodorous and malarial, the plaything of current and tide? The lagoon, in a very real sense, gave birth to Venice; and it also made it the place that it is. First, it provided the city with a degree of physical security that was the envy of all other cities in Italy. (For proof we have only to compare their palazzi pubblici – fortresses every one – with the delicate filigree of the Doge's Palace, to whose creators the concept of defence can never have occurred.) Then the lagoon directed Venice's energies towards the sea, and thence to the trade which was soon to make it the richest and most powerful state in the Mediterranean. Finally, it enabled Venice to turn its back on the strife-torn Terraferma and to look to the East, not only for its commercial promise but for its cultural inspiration: not for nothing is St Mark's modelled on the Church of the Holy Apostles in Constantinople, possessing a wealth of Byzantine mosaics unmatched anywhere in the world.

He understands, too – and would that more of his fellow architects understood with him – that just as no man is an island, nor is any building either. This realization has led him to focus, in the second part of his book, on what he calls the four nuclei of the city: the Piazza, the Arsenale, the Ghetto and the Rialto. Each of them is in its way a product of Venice's unique way of government and outlook on life; each casts its own revealing light on the city and its people. Only after their lessons have been learnt does he turn his spotlight on to the individual buildings themselves – the palaces, churches and scuole that give Venice its splendour and its opulence, that make it the breathtaking architectural treasure-house it is.

This book is, in short, a work of scholarship, of perception, of discernment – and, above all, it is a testament to the author's love for Venice. But love also means concern; and in the Postscript he warns of the two fundamental threats to the modern city: the increasing danger of serious flooding and the dramatic decline in population, now less than half what it was at the end of the Second World War. Indeed, I would add a third menace: that of uncontrolled tourism, which can bring in well over 150,000 visitors in a single summer's day. For the Venice in Peril Fund, Save Venice Inc., and the twenty-odd other private organizations which have been at work for the past quarter-century, problems such as these are assuming ever greater importance. We shall continue, with the Italian authorities (who have, incidentally, been responsible for some 90% of all restorations) to work on bricks and mortar; but we have no wish to see some of the most dazzlingly beautiful buildings in the world becoming part of a waterlogged museum, the thinking-man's Disneyland. Surely, if Venice is to survive at all, it must be as a living, working city, in which ordinary Venetians will still be proud and happy to make their homes.

John Julius Norwich

Preface

Polo: 'Sire, now I have told you about all the cities I know.' / 'There is still one of which you never speak.' / Marco Polo bowed his head. / 'Venice,' the Khan said. / Marco smiled. 'What else do you believe I have been talking to you about ?' / The emperor did not turn a hair. 'And yet I have never heard you mention that name.' / And Polo said 'Every time I describe a city I am saying something about Venice.' **Italo Calvino**, *Invisible Cities*, 1972.

There have been as many images, analyses and opinions of Venice down the centuries as there have been footfalls on the Rialto. Many have been romantic, idealized; a few have been cynical, world-weary; others practical, perceptive, shrewdly analytical; still others have been frankly self-congratulatory, laudations by devoted patriotic citizens.

By the fifteenth century, Venice's fame was universal. It derived from a number of different sources, and it was essentially their cumulative effect that made the city the focus of such attention and praise. One of its most outstanding features was its prodigious wealth, derived from its role as one of the great international hubs of European trade; what made Venice particularly unique, though, was its position as the nucleus of trade between western Europe and the Middle East. With this trade went the Venetians' internationally famed skills in banking and insurance. Another remarkable feature was its location, and its extraordinary site, with the Grand Canal as its artery, and the great basin of San Marco as its natural harbour. Still another was its role as a religious centre, and this role itself consisted of two related elements. Firstly, Venice was the chief port of embarkation for Western pilgrims to the Holy Land, and Venetian fleets dominated – indeed monopolized – this extensive (and lucrative) trade for centuries. The other was the city's role as a pilgrimage site in itself: the shrine of San Marco attracted millions of pilgrims over the centuries, as indeed it still does today. And the wealth that derived from all these activities itself was re-invested into the building of an evermore splendid city to attract more and more visitors.

To Philippe de Commynes, a French traveller, writing in 1494, for example, she was 'the most triumphant city' that he had ever seen, and the Grand Canal was 'the fairest and best-built street, I think, in the whole world'. To an Englishman, Thomas Coryat, a little later, his first sight was 'the most glorious and heavenly shew upon the water that any mortal eye beheld'. And to another English visitor, Sir Richard Guylforde, the spectacle was quite overawing: 'The rychesse, sumptuous buyldynge, the relygyous houses … make a cytie glorious, surmounteth in Venyse above all places yt ever I sawe…'

At even the very highest social level, the city has always had a dazzling effect on its visitors. When King Henri III of France visited Venice in 1574 he was presented with such an extraordinary display of pageantry, spectacle, music, feasting and ritual that it is said that the visit remained the most overwhelming experience of his life, and he confessed that 'if I were not King of France … I would choose to be a citizen of Venice'. The king may have been young and impressionable, and the spectacles carefully organized to achieve precisely that effect, but even a much travelled, and highly sophisticated intellectual prelate, such as Cardinal Bessarion, concluded in 1469 that Venice was 'almost another Constantinople', then perhaps the greatest metropolis in the world.

A few visitors were less easily impressed; Sir Dudley Carleton, English ambassador to the Republic, wrote in 1612 that 'in matter of trade, the city's decay is so manifest that all men conclude that within twenty years space here is not one part left of three'. Carleton's view was a rare one, though, as much a political and moral judgement as a mercantile one; as a prophecy it was to be singularly inaccurate, too, since the Venetian Republic had two centuries of life left in it, when he wrote, during which time many of its greatest artistic achievements were to be created. Other observers gave a more political interpretation of the unique city in the sea, and its equally unique form of government. To Pope Pius II the Venetians were 'the most powerful people both on land and sea … and seem not unfitted to the larger empire to which they aspire': the most triumphant city is here coldly evaluated in the context of Italian realpolitik.

All great cities, of course, were praised by their own inhabitants; in Florence Leonardo Bruni had claimed that the Tuscan capital was the rightful heir of the mantle of Republican Rome, and Pier Candido Decembrio made a virtually identical claim for Milan. However, there was little that was republican about the government of the latter city, as it was ruled in turn by the Visconti and the Sforza families, essentially as a feudal city state. In Florence, too, the political struggles of the Guelf and Ghibelline factions hardly presented an image of stability and continuity to the world, and in the early fifteenth century, Florence also became more and more clearly identified with one-family rule by the Medici. Only in Venice was there a government that was truly stable, not a democracy, of course, but an oligarchy based on the rule of law and justice, with an elected prince.

Praise of the city by its own inhabitants was often unashamed; at the end of the quattrocento Bernardo Bembo claimed grandiloquently and dogmatically that 'the Venetians are called new Romans', and this Renaissance image was invoked on countless occasions in the sixteenth century, both to commend Venice's wise, stable government, and to evoke the physical image of the 'new Rome' as put into practice by Jacopo Sansovino, Andrea Palladio and Michele Sanmicheli.

Admiration for Venice's 'democracy', too, went back at least as far as Petrarch, who in 1364 praised 'the one home today of liberty, peace and justice, the one refuge of honourable men', a phrase with which Sansovino himself undoubtedly concurred as he fled the horrors of the Sack of Rome to make his own home there 160 years later.

His compatriot, Pietro Aretino, similarly found tolerant sanctuary there for his often forthright views, and wrote to Doge Andrea Gritti that he was 'bound to praise Venice and revere you; the former for having accepted me, you for having defended me against the persecution of others'. Not only a uniquely wealthy and beautiful city, therefore, on many occasions Venice also secured an honourable role as a place of refuge, where in times of bigotry and persecution, minorities of many kinds were often accepted with considerably greater tolerance and equanimity than elsewhere.

In the broader cultural sense, too, Venice was always a comparatively open city, one that absorbed influences from elsewhere freely and flexibly; that gave self-expression to many artists from other cities and other cultural backgrounds. The institutions of the Republic itself, circumspect, traditional and often reluctant to change, at the same time often welcomed and encouraged the Republic's own self-glorification by the nurturing of skills both from within the state's borders and from elsewhere. Andrea Palladio and Jacopo Sansovino, Titian and Paolo Veronese, were all drawn to the capital on the lagoon and found there the means to develop their own creative identities, while at the same time adding further lustre to the image of the city in the sea, the Dominante, ruler of the Adriatic.

To Calvino, as to many others, Venice holds an inimitable place in our collective memory. More than simply a city, Venice has become a globally recognized symbol of our common cultural inheritance. It has become a paradigm, representing many vulnerable but invaluable historic cities, scattered in time and space; paradoxically, however, it is a city which remains uniquely itself: the richest example of man's collective creativity, his genius for building triumphant order out of what was once a marshy, reed-choked wilderness.

Introduction

The Most Serene Republic of Venice was perhaps the most extraordinary and arguably the longest-surviving independent state that has ever existed in Europe. Having emerged at the dawn of the Middle Ages, the Republic survived the countless wars, religious upheavals, revolutions, alliances and counter-alliances that have characterized Europe's history. Apparently immutable, she became an anachronism, a small oligarchical 'statelet' in an era of emerging modern superpowers and great land empires. Finally, she was brusquely consigned to history, without a struggle, by Napoleon.

The built legacy of the city today is a mirror of that millennium of continuity, unique not only in its historical value and extraordinary profusion and quality, but because so many of its characteristics are exclusively Venetian. The difficulties of the topography, the changing light, the reflective qualities of the waters, the nature of the government of the Republic and of Venetian society, all contributed to an architecture developing and responding to an environment quite unlike any other. Since the thirteenth century, when the rest of Italy, indeed most of Europe, was governed by powerful despots from great, impregnable fortresses, the Venetian aristocracy, secure within its natural moat, was building palaces with airy logge, open balconies, large fully glazed windows, and decorated with refined marble reliefs and complex capitals. Medieval Venice is epitomized by these dignified palaces: the patriciate is here transmuted into stone tracery and colonnades. The later architectural history of these palaces, too, forms a long, extended metaphor for the rise, the power, the changing fortunes and the final decline and extinction of the nobility and of the Republic itself.

The purpose of this book is twofold: to provide a comprehensive discussion of the principal paths of architectural development, but also to put the buildings into their physical, historical and social context. Venice's architectural history is incomprehensible without some appreciation of its political and historical origins and its urban development. The question that I am asked far more frequently than any other, in discussing Venice's architectural history, is 'Why was the city built here at all?'. The second question, equally invariably, is 'How was it built?'

In an attempt to answer both of these questions the book is divided into three major parts. In Part 1, the site is described, and its historical development surveyed. A brief opening chapter introduces Venice's physical context and outlines the emergence of the Republic, its chief characteristics and lines of development. In the second chapter, the overall form of the city itself is then analysed, its essential features and characteristics identified. This chapter is the key to those that follow, and traces the general evolution of the city's structure, and the nuclei that developed into its key organs. This evolution is charted against the chief events of the Republic's history, and by discussion of historic plans and other surviving visual records. The third chapter attempts to answer the second of the two questions posed above: how the city was built, by whom, and with what materials and techniques. It is clear that special considerations have to be applied when constructing a great city on a scattering of small islands and here these are discussed, and examples given of the various solutions to building in the environment of the lagoon.

Part 2 looks more closely at the evolution of the city's most important cultural and historical nuclei. All of these represent both physical and metaphysical expressions of the institutions of the Serene Republic, and as such, they have become metaphors or symbols in themselves. The first of these centres is the Arsenale, a great complex of specialized industry, employing thousands, and symbolizing the Venetian Republic's overseas empire. The second is the Ghetto, the heart of an alternative, minority culture, and representative of the international component of the city's cultural make-up, the name itself now universally linked with Jewry's pain and persecution. The third is the Rialto, the financial and commercial hub, as well as the city's retail core, the name very redolent of banks, spice-dealers and markets. Finally there is San Marco itself, the Piazza as the hub of a great and wealthy empire, with the shrine at its heart, a glistening cavern that links the Western

Catholic Church with its most profound Eastern origins. These were the nuclei that shaped a capital city.

The third and longest part of the book discusses the key buildings that occupy and have for centuries given daily life to this urban matrix. The first are the palaces of power and administration that surround the Piazza of San Marco. The chief of these is the Palazzo Ducale, administrative hub of Empire, but over a long period it became surrounded by a number of 'satellite' palaces, all of them developed not only for practical functions but to enhance the image of the Republic. The Venetian church is then discussed, from its origins in the ruins of Roman Aquileia to Baldassare Longhena's Baroque masterpiece, Santa Maria della Salute. This is the history of the first of the two most widespread and important building types in the city's fabric, tracing a long continuous thread of stylistic development, from the two early churches at Torcello, through San Marco and beyond, to the great Gothic monasteries, to the Renaissance churches of Codussi and Palladio, and the rich diffusion of the Venetian Baroque, epitomized in the work of Longhena. The Scuole Grandi are considered next, a group of uniquely Venetian institutions, lay brotherhoods that met for devotional purposes and developed extensive philanthropic activities; the most generous and influential of all the patrons of the arts in the sixteenth century, whose strong rivalries characterized their building programmes. The breadth of the city's social scale is further analysed, firstly by a summary of the pious and charitable institutions, hospitals, hospices and housing that provided a safety net for the underprivileged; and then, in sharp contrast, the building types that were developed to serve the nobility: the theatre, opera, *ridotti* and coffee houses.

Finally, the last major chapter discusses perhaps the most dominant building type of all, the palace of the Venetian merchant-noble, from its origins as a Byzantine warehouse, through the great era of medieval palace building to the imposing Renaissance palaces of Codussi and Sansovino, and the Baroque masterpieces of Longhena. If the development of the Venetian church represents a pragmatic, shifting response to influences from East and West, the evolution of the Venetian palace is the clearest development of all in its continuous representation of the rise and self expression of a single clearly identifiable class, serving a particular purpose in a highly specific physical context.

It is hoped, then, to trace the development of these building types and to outline the ways in which social, cultural and political influences served to determine the very particular direction that Venetian architecture has taken. It is neither feasible nor desirable to render the book comprehensive by embracing every significant historic building in the city. There are simply too many of them, and such a 'universalist' approach would confuse far more than it clarified. In discussing the city's numerous churches and palaces, therefore, I have concentrated on key examples and on key stages in stylistic development. For more encyclopedic surveys of these buildings the reader is referred to the introductory section of the bibliography. The illustrations are intended to complement the text throughout, and to be largely self-explanatory. The images are primarily informative; by a combination of photographs, historic plans, drawings and paintings, it is hoped to give a comprehensive survey of the extraordinarily rich variety of Venice's architectural heritage. Venice remains a compact but extremely complex urban form, with strong, even violent contrasts of scale. It is a city of great swathes of water, of vistas, of skylines; but it is also, of course, a uniquely well-preserved historic organism, one of the world's great medieval cities, intensely crowded, a dense matrix of overlaid networks, from the tangled roofscapes with their characteristic chimneys and terraces down to the Byzantine maze of *campi*, *calli* and *corti*, and finally to the labyrinth of its canals, the water from which the city emerged. The architecture that developed here remains, in its rich stylistic profusion, Venice's unique contribution to the cultural history of the West.

Part I | the form of the city

1 **Origins**

'Far as the eye can reach, a waste of wild sea-moor, or a lurid ashen-grey; not like our northern moors with their jet-black pools and purple heath, but lifeless, the colour of sackcloth, with the corrupted sea water soaking through the roots of its acrid weeds, and gleaming hither and thither through its snaky channels. No gathering of fantastic mists, nor coursing of clouds across it; but melancholy clearness of space in the warm sunset, oppressive, reaching to the horizon of its level gloom.' **John Ruskin**, *The Stones of Venice*, London, 1851–3.

Desolate, flat, marshy and indefinable: the Venetian littoral in the last days of the Roman Empire was indeed much as Ruskin described it, rather melodramatically, a place of indeterminate form and colour. Here the Italian mainland almost imperceptibly slid into the swampy fringes of the shallow, irregular expanses of water that were themselves barely divided from the great gulf of the Adriatic Sea.[1] The lagoon has always been marginal, a place on the physical limits of Italy; and as Venice herself grew, she, too, remained marginal, half within and half out of the water, half Eastern and half Western, poised in that elusive zone between sea and sky.

Around the great arc of the north-eastern shores of Italy, this same topography prevailed, from the extensive, ragged delta of the Po as far as the rocky peninsula of Istria. The lagoon's hinterland was the eastern part of the great plain of northern Italy, one of the most fertile and densely populated regions of the Roman Empire. It was watered by several major rivers, the Adige, Brenta, Piave and Tagliamento, all of which descended from the eastern Alps and Dolomites, meandered across the plain and finally reached the Adriatic through a chain of lagoons and marshes. This long chain of lagoons was divided from the Adriatic by narrow, precarious barriers, strips of land later known in the Venetian dialect as *lidi*.

The Roman settlement of this important region was defined by trunk roads, the Via Annia and the Via Popilia, which skirted this marshy fringe, linking a number of substantial towns together, from Ravenna in the south, via Adria, Altino and Concordia, to Aquileia in the north-east, a large, sprawling and populous city, the administrative capital of the Roman Tenth Region of 'Venetia et Histria'. Other arteries connected Patavium (Padua), Vicetia (Vicenza), Opitergium (Oderzo) and Verona. On the mainland, the 'Roman' side of the coastal trunk road, were rich farms and villas; on the other, the scattered huts and hamlets of the poor fishermen at the lagoon's margins.[2]

The city of Aquileia was to play an important role in the early history of the Venetian Republic. Not only the regional capital, it was the strategic key to Italy from the mountainous terrain to the north and east; many Roman remains still attest to the city's size and significance. Equally well-established were the routes northwards, through the Alpine passes into Germany, routes which were later to form a vital element in Venice's continental trading network.[3]

When the long disintegration of the Roman Empire finally began, this region was left on the margins between the original Western Empire and the new Empire of the East, with its capital at Constantinople. The territory was ceded to the Eastern Empire, but its marginality remained, and was to have a profound effect on Venice's culture; a city between two civilizations, in the West but, at least partly, of the East.

During the acutely unstable fifth century, when there were waves of invasions from the north across the Alps, the lagoons were primarily regarded as a place of safety *in extremis*; a difficult region mostly composed of water, but with scatterings of islands and sand bars. Ideal, perhaps, as a temporary haven from mainland aggressors such as the Goths and Visigoths, who had no means of attacking by water, but hardly an attractive site for the permanent establishment of a

VERONA: THE PORTA BORSARI, 1ST CENTURYAD.

Verona was one of the chief Roman cities of northern Italy; many monuments and remains attest to its importance. In 1404 it became Venice's most important mainland possession.

substantial town, still less of a great city. On 21 March 421, as the *Altino Chronicle* and other early sources tell us – with singular conviction and remarkable precision – Venice herself was founded. No documentary evidence whatsoever supports such accuracy, although the date has become part of the tangle of truth, part truth and pure legend that is an inescapable element of early Venetian history; the city's oldest church, San Giacometto at the Rialto, is said to have been founded on that very day.

The ferocious campaign of Attila in the region thirty years later gave rise to still further migrations from the insecurity of the open plain to the comparative safety of the margins of the lagoon, and led to the establishment of 'tribunes' or assemblies of leading citizens to govern the lagoon's settlements; they also began to take over some of the functions of the nominal and ineffectual long-distance government from the Eastern imperial capital. In this manner began the long, halting progress towards independence.

Most importantly of all, a distinct pattern could now be discerned in these migrations from the Roman mainland towns, southwards and eastwards towards the arc of the Gulf: from Aquileia to Grado; from Concordia to Caorle; from Oderzo to Eraclea and Iesolo; from Altino to Torcello, Murano and Rivo Alto; from Padua to Malamocco; and from Este and Padua to Clodia (Chioggia). Settlement was now becoming more definitive.

In 552, Narses, the Emperor Justinian's general, succeeded in driving the Goths out of northern Italy with the help of the lagunar peoples. Narses was appointed Governor of Ravenna, and in this manner Italy became a 'Greek' province of the Eastern Empire. With this new stability, an era of outstanding cultural achievement was established, particularly at Ravenna itself, where the reign of Theodoric (493–526), created the magnificent mosaics of San Vitale and Sant'Apollinare. These masterpieces established a tradition of mosaic decoration in north-east Italy that was later to reach further heights at San Marco.[4]

Nevertheless, the mainland plains remained highly vulnerable to attack. The marshy coastal zone, heartland of the emergent Republic, marked the extent of the lands notionally subject to the Eastern emperor, beyond which was the northern Italy of the Lombard conquerors. The religious independence of this coastal zone – the future Dogado – had been established by the honorific title of patriarch bestowed by the emperor on Aquileia, but the patriarchate was transferred to the safety of the Lido of Grado in 568. Shortly afterwards, this transfer was rendered permanent by the construction of Grado's new cathedral, which survives to this day. These events reflected the fundamental division between mainland and the maritime littoral, with the latter still under the ecclesiastical authority of Byzantium. In this way, therefore, the Venetian church itself developed under the long-distance sovereignty, not of the pope, but of the emperor of the East.

In 697, the same chronicles claim, Paoluccio Anafesto was the first man elected *dux* of the confederation of the lagoons; with this authority these lands took the name of the Dogado. Anafesto is an elusive figure, although his honorific was to survive the centuries, and the classical title of 'dux' (prince or ruler) was transformed into 'doge' by the lagoon's dialects.[5]

This tentative ducal system survived only briefly until it was overthrown by violent conflict between Eraclea and Iesolo, but was re-established five years later, when the doge's seat was transferred to a new site at Malamocco in an attempt to avert future rivalries. These early decades were marked by frequent clashes between the twelve members of the inappropriately titled 'confederation', and a further civil war erupted in 803. As a result, in 810 this still somewhat notional capital was moved for a second time, to a place known as Rivo Alto, an archipelago of islets in the largest, southernmost lagoon on the littoral. From this date we might justifiably claim that Venice herself was officially born, since Rivo Alto became Rialto, and then Venetia, capital of

GRADO

The cathedral, above, was begun in 569, after the transfer of the bishopric from nearby Aquileia.

the Dogado, and future metropolis of what came to be known as the Most Serene Republic of Venice.[6]

The name of Rivo Alto, 'high bank', was at first applied to the whole of the archipelago that was to become the future Venice. The lagoon in which it lay was a long, crescent-shaped body of water, around 40 kilometres (25 miles) in length and perhaps five or six across, studded with numerous clusters of islets; the Realtine complex itself lay in the centre of this lagoon. Between the lagoon and the Adriatic was a chain of narrow strips of land, the lidi; today there are only three true lidi, but in this early period they probably numbered six or seven, with gaps between them through which the tidal, salt waters of the Adriatic mingled with the freshwater run off from the streams of the Terraferma.[7]

At this lagoon's southernmost corner was the ancient Roman town of Clodia (now known as Chioggia), standing on its own island, and again protected from the sea by a lido, the littoral of Sottomarina. Chioggia had been a very important producer of salt in the Roman era, an invaluable specialization that it retained under the Republic; the town was also later to become the dominant fishing port on the whole Adriatic. Closer to Rivo Alto was Malamocco, short-lived seat of the confederation; its original site, on the seaward side of the vulnerable lido, was later lost below the waters of the Adriatic, following the fate of many of these earliest settlements; its see, too, was transferred to Chioggia.[8] But a second little nucleus with the same name was established on the lee shore of the precarious littoral, where a hamlet still remains today.

In the northern waters of the same lagoon stood the sites of Torcello and Murano, both to become important satellites of the new, growing capital. Torcello was the religious hub of the northern lagoon, its own bishopric transferred here from the abandoned Roman town of Altino in 636; in time, it attracted several satellite settlements of its own, including Mazzorbo, Ammiana and Burano. Murano, Venice's closest major satellite, was to achieve wealth and fame as a producer of glass, particularly after 1292, when all of Venice's furnaces were transferred there to reduce the danger of fire in the capital.[9]

Much of the lagoon was extremely shallow, but it was traversed by a complex network of deeper, navigable channels, their courses known only to the inhabitants, and impenetrable to a potential aggressor. It was a source of at least some of the staples of life: fish and seafood were naturally abundant; some of the islands were also extremely fertile, while Chioggia's saltpans, spread over the shallows of the southern lagoon, became one of the chief sources of the Republic's early wealth.

With Rivo Alto now established as the capital, in 829 two enterprising travellers from the lagoon, Rustico from Torcello and Bono from Malamocco, variously recorded as merchants, sailors or pirates, voyaged to Alexandria, the great hub of Middle Eastern trade. They returned with an unusual cargo in their ship, the preserved body of Mark the Evangelist, hidden, so the legend relates, in a barrel of pork to escape detection by the Muslim authorities.[10] The first patron of Rivo Alto, the Greek saint Theodore or Todaro, had symbolized Venice's intimate links with the Eastern Empire, but he was now joined by this far greater prize, who was laid in the little ducal chapel while a more fitting shrine was begun. This famous and evocative story encapsulates several vital features of Venice's early history: the importance of trading and cultural links with the Middle East; the desire to enhance wealth and status, and thereby to develop political and theological hegemony; and the legitimization of such an act by moral justification. This last claim was supported by an ancient legend that Mark himself had visited the lagoons in the year 42 AD, when it was said that he had established the first Christian church at Aquileia. The 'translation' of his body, therefore, 800 years later, was seen as the affirmation of this early witnessing of God's word, the fulfilment of the prophecy that His Church and that of His Evangelist should flourish in Venice.

THE VENETIAN LAGOON (above and right)

Torcello, in the lagoon, was formerly a wealthy town and is now a mere hamlet in the marshes.

A watery maze of creeks, sandbanks and shallows; this was the environment in which the first Venetian settlements arose in the early Middle Ages.

VENICE (overleaf)

The northern part of the city from the campanile of San Marco; in the centre is the campanile of Santa Maria Formosa, and directly beyond it is the great monastic church of Santi Giovanni e Paolo. Beyond again is the cemetery island of San Michele, and further still the glassmaking island of Murano.

The symbol of Mark was a winged lion, and it was adopted by the emergent Republic as its insignia; as the Republic grew in power and wealth, it became one of the most respected (and feared) symbols over the entire Mediterranean. The lion traditionally carried an open book between its paws; on it was inscribed the divine message given to Mark when stranded in the lagoons: *Pax Tibi Marce, Evangelista Meus* (Peace to thee, Mark, my Evangelist). The invocation was adopted down the centuries as a divinely directed guide to the actions of the Republic's captains and senators, its prelates and doges; in Venetian iconography, too, when the book was depicted closed, then this message of peace was replaced by that of war.

In 840 the Eastern Emperor, Lothario, established the definitive boundaries of the Dogado, a territory which was thus formally recognized as Venetian land. In so doing he also established the Republic as a clearly defined and at least partly independent political entity.[11] Nevertheless, Rivo Alto's history was still far from settled. Doge Pietro Tradonico was assassinated in a civil uprising in 864, and we have very little detailed knowledge of the later ninth and tenth centuries. The institution of the doge survived, however, and in 962 the establishment of the Holy Roman Empire in the West once again ratified Venice's independent status, this time 'in perpetuity'. The growing population and naval skills of the people of the lagoons were illustrated thirty years later when Pietro Orseolo II commanded a Venetian fleet against the Croats, who lay claim to the peninsula of Istria, directly across the Gulf from the lagoon. The Croats were defeated, and Istria became Venetian territory, the first strategic expansion beyond the confines of the original Dogado. As a result of this conquest, Venice now controlled the waters of the Gulf, and the doge instigated the annual ritual of his 'Marriage to the Sea', a symbolic union between the doge and the waters that they now controlled. The *Sposalizio* (Marriage) was celebrated on Ascension Day every year thereafter until the fall of the Republic, and on several occasions the ritual was further elaborated and enriched with symbolism. In practice, Venice's control already extended down much of the Dalmatian coast, a direct reflection of the need to protect the city's essential trading routes towards the eastern Mediterranean.

Already, therefore, all the defining elements of the Most Serene Republic were established: the patronage of Mark the Evangelist; the institution of the doge; the Dogado and Istria, the heartlands of the state; and its mainstay, commerce. (For the future wealth of the Republic was essentially to be based on trade with the East, and the consolidation of that trade through the conquest of vital strategic islands and fortresses.) On these fundamental principles the fortunes of the next seven centuries were to be founded.

'So we advanced into this ghostly city, continuing to hold our course through narrow streets and lanes, all filled and flowing with water. Some of the corners where our way branched off, were so acute and narrow, that it seemed impossible for the long, slender boat to turn them …On we went, floating towards the heart of this strange place – with water all about us where water never was elsewhere – clusters of houses, churches, heaps of stately buildings growing out of it – and everywhere the same extraordinary silence.' **Charles Dickens**, *Pictures from Italy*, 1844.

The site of the city

The Realtine archipelago lies in the very centre of the Venetian lagoon, with the mainland shore three or four kilometres (two miles) safely away to the west, and with the protective littoral of the Lido to the east. Direct access to the Adriatic Sea was provided by a broad, meandering channel that threaded its way through the archipelago and across the lagoon to discharge into the sea at the Porto di Lido. This channel itself divided the Realtine archipelago into two roughly equal parts, and its form was a sinuous inverted 'S'. It was slowly to be transformed into the Grand Canal, the most magnificent waterway in Europe.

The islands forming Rivo Alto, though, were a scattered, heterogeneous collection, some large and firm, others smaller, and all interspersed with mudbanks (*barene*) and reed-clogged marsh. The overall size of this archipelago of perhaps a hundred islets was about 4 kilometres (2½ miles) in length and around half of that in breadth. The network of watercourses that traversed this archipelago also extended beyond it into the shallow lagoon, with an intricate pattern of navigable channels over much of its surface, although on the landward perimeter it petered out into a treacherous maze of marshes and shallows, as indeed it still does today, impassable for boats and wheeled vehicles alike.

In addition to the great channel that was to become the Grand Canal, there were other larger channels that were to have considerable importance in the city's development. One was the Cannaregio Canal, which led directly north-westwards towards the mainland shore near the little fort-village of Mestre. Another was the Rio di Noale, which cut through the archipelago at its narrowest point and provided a direct route to Murano and the islands of the northern lagoon: Torcello, Burano and Mazzorbo. Other navigable channels led east and southwards towards Pellestrina and Venice's furthest major satellite, Chioggia. All of these routes, though, focused on the Rialto archipelago, and more particularly, on two districts, the Rialto itself and the basin of San Marco.

The islets forming the future city varied considerably in size and shape, but most were separated only by the narrowest of channels or *rii*, their courses tortuous and random, and navigable only by small boats of shallow draught. A couple of dozen islets were larger and firmer, and were sufficiently high to avoid the flooding of spring and autumn tides. These were naturally the most attractive to the earliest settlements. A handful were to be of fundamental importance in defining the form, extent and nature of the future Venice. Among them were two firm, substantial islets that straddled the Grand Canal about halfway down its course, and where the canal was particularly narrow: a natural site for a bridgehead, therefore, and the location of the Rivo Alto or high bank, the Rialto itself.[1] Nearby was another large island, site of the early parish foundation of Santi Apostoli, which was reputedly established by St Magnus in the seventh century. According to tradition, near the church stood the house of Angelo Partecipazio, doge during the momentous period from 811 to 827, when the capital was transferred here from Malamocco; he was, therefore,

THE PONTE DEI TRE ARCHI

Built by Andrea Tirali in 1688, the bridge spans the Cannaregio Canal, one of the city's chief arteries, joining the Grand Canal with the route to the mainland near Mestre.

the first doge to preside over the confederation from this new capital, and the site of his fortified house is said to be recorded in the Campiello della Cason, just behind the church. Santi Apostoli itself became an important parish at the junction of several routes, as it remains today.[2]

The islet at San Marco, facing the great natural basin of water, was early established as the spiritual heart of the city; firstly, with the chapel dedicated to San Todaro, the original patron, and then, after the translation of the Evangelist's remains in 827, with that dedicated to St Mark. With the Realtine archipelago now the new capital, it was necessary to provide the doge with an administrative base, and this was built immediately adjacent to the original chapel of San Todaro, and the rather larger chapel of his successor, Mark. This first ducal 'palace' was almost certainly more of a castle, and its site commanded the great basin of water.

Further afield, at the eastern extremity of the archipelago, was the islet known as Olivolo, perhaps because an olive grove flourished there, perhaps in recognition of its olive-like shape. It was fortified at an early date, since it lay close to the strategic route to the sea. Olivolo was also the site of the bishopric established in these islands in 775; significantly, the see was not located centrally, at Rialto, for example, but in this rather isolated outpost, a reflection of the carefully established distance between the Republic and the established church that was to be such a feature of Venetian political and ecclesiastical history.

Early growth: island-parishes

These fairly scattered nuclei formed the most fundamental primary skeleton on which the city's secondary structure of communities was to be built. These secondary elements were to take two basic forms: some were lay, parochial foundations, essentially urban social nuclei, while the others were monastic establishments. These early monasteries were of great importance in defining the city's extent and the pattern of its growth; the Benedictine houses of San Zaccaria (founded in 827) and San Giorgio Maggiore (982) were the most notable, and over time also became the wealthiest. They served to define further the pattern of settlement around the great basin of San Marco, bounded to the north as it already was in the ninth century by the castle-palace of the doge and the shrine of the patron. Its eastern extremity was similarly delimited by the bishop's island of Olivolo. Further towards the south-east, the Benedictine monastery island of San Servolo was founded in 800, defining the great body of water on the other side, where the basin widened out into the lagoon. These monastic institutions, therefore, together established the southern aquatic limits of the city, much as the scattering of island parishes slowly came to define its internal structural form.[3]

As in the cases of Rialto, San Marco and Olivolo, some of these latter islands were settled for specific reasons: almost all of them lay on the banks of the larger watercourses. Within the more central parts of the archipelago, therefore, a pattern can be discerned in the establishment of the earliest parish nuclei. These nuclei were essentially lay settlements, hamlets built around an independent parish church. Some had been founded before the transfer of the ducal seat to Rialto in 810; they numbered around fourteen in all, and included, in the west, San Nicolo, the Angelo Raffaele, San Pantalon, San Trovaso and Santa Croce; in the central Realtine districts were Santi Apostoli, Santa Maria Formosa and San Salvador; and towards Olivolo in the east were San Martino, Sant'Antonin, Santa Giustina and San Giovanni in Bragora. Eight of them were said by tradition to have been founded by St Magnus, bishop of Oderzo, in the seventh century.

The transfer of the seat of the doge and his tribunes, together with the translation of San Marco's remains a few years later, naturally gave a great impetus to the foundation of additional settlements. Among those established in the immediate aftermath of these two momentous events were San Zulian or Giuliano (829), Santa Margherita (837), San Bartolomeo (840), Santa Sofia (866) and San Silvestro (884).[4]

CHIOGGIA: THE CANALE VENA

Chioggia was Venice's most important satellite town, an important producer of salt and the largest fishing port on the Adriatic.

The location of both of these earliest groups of parish foundations has some significance in the structure of the Realtine archipelago. San Nicolo and San Pantalon, for example, both lie on routes that join the Grand Canal with the surrounding lagoon, while several others lie on the course of the Grand Canal itself, among them the last four noted above. And on the eastern side of the city, Santa Maria Formosa, San Martino and Bragora all lie on canals that join the basin of San Marco with the Rialto and the northern lagoon. Indeed, every one of these first and second generation foundations lies on a watercourse that has an important role in the archipelago's communications network, and beyond it, into the lagoon as a whole. By the end of the ninth century these island-parishes already numbered more than thirty in all.[5]

The island-parish was thus the primary building-block in the city's urban fabric. At first scattered, and with many patches of marsh and unsettled islets between them, these settlements slowly multiplied, such that by the end of the millennium a further twenty-five had been added to the thirty first- and second-generation parishes. They now formed a fairly well-distributed network over much of the Realtine archipelago; among the later ninth-century foundations were the important local nuclei of San Giacomo dell'Orio, San Fantin and Sant'Angelo. Expansion continued, though, throughout the following century, with the establishment of a further thirteen parishes; by now the city had reached a certain degree of equilibrium and was, by the standards of the time, a very large settlement indeed. Some estimates of Venice's population have ranged as high as 100,000, although a more realistic (though still impressive) figure is perhaps 60–70,000.[6]

The original communities had steadily expanded to fill the islets on which they stood; the second- and third- generation parishes had then been established on the larger, adjacent islets, although still leaving some mudbanks and unsettled smaller islets between them. Finally, though, after nearly all of these more attractive sites had been occupied, a fourth generation was established, some in distinctly peripheral zones, such as San Lunardo and Santa Maria Maddalena (although both are still adjacent to the Grand Canal), while still others filled in the remaining interstices in the more central districts, such as San Luca, Sant'Aponal and San Giovanni Crisostomo. After about 1100, though, there were few new foundations, and the most characteristic process in this period was the consolidation and further urbanization of the existing nuclei.

Land and water

Many island-parishes contained features in common, although all of them remained unique in some aspect of their size or shape. They were focused on the church, in front of which was the community's village square. This was (and still is) known as a *campo* (literally, a field), because they were originally grassed, like a village green. Adjacent to the church was its freestanding *campanile* (bell tower), to regulate the religious life of the community; a handful of early *campanili* survive today, including the twelfth-century tower of San Nicolo, and that of San Giacomo dell'Orio, of similar date. In virtually all parishes there was direct water access from the campo to one of the surrounding canals. Around the square stood the houses of the parish's leading citizens, one or two of whom were members of the nobility, the class that was to emerge to rule the Republic. In the centre of the campo was a well, or, more accurately, an underground storage cistern, since the city had no natural supplies of fresh water, and rainwater was carefully collected in these cisterns for re-use. Hundreds of these characteristic 'wellheads' can still be seen today, the oldest of them Byzantine survivors from the eleventh and twelfth centuries, others spanning the styles from Gothic to the Baroque.[7]

The parish squares, like the islands on which they stand, vary considerably in size and shape, although certain broad categories can be identified. The largest islets had a spacious campo with the church on one side, and these squares are often still enclosed by particularly fine houses: San Polo and Santa Maria Formosa are perhaps the most imposing parish squares in the city. More

RIO DEI BARCAROLI (above)

near San Fantin; the canals in the city centre are all very narrow, and since land was scarce, there are no quays, the buildings rising directly from the water.

CORTE BOTTERA (right)

near Santi Giovanni e Paolo: a characteristic courtyard, with the remains of a fine 13th century Byzantine arch, and typical Venetian open staircase and wellhead.

typical, though, are small, more compact, rectangular *campi*, with a canal down one side, the church on another, and housing occupying the remaining two. San Barnaba and San Moisè are examples of this type. Still others, though, have a more organic, less well-defined form, such as the squares of Santi Apostoli and San Giacomo, while the parishes in the most crowded central districts have very restricted squares, little more than public courtyards, like those of San Zulian and San Giovanni Novo.[8]

The larger, oldest-established parish-islands still retain a distinctive and clearly-defined street pattern, with a central axial 'spine' street, at the end of which is the parish square, and from either side of which parallel secondary streets run out towards the surrounding canals. Parishes such as San Lio and San Barnaba retain this 'fishbone' pattern with great clarity, and in both examples the main street maintains its ancient role as the social and retail axis of the community.

The terminology given to the Venetian street system is unique to the city, and reflects the vigorous independence of Venetian culture through the centuries. Although Latin was used as a formal language for legal documents and by the Church, the language of the Republic, from senators to stonemasons, was (and to a large extent remains) the Venetian dialect. Italian in its basic structure, Venetian is highly individualistic in its vocabulary, in pronunciation and in verb declensions; it still remains largely incomprehensible to mainland Italians. The Venetian street is therefore not a *via*

CALLE DEL PARADISO (below, left)

One of the most complete surviving medieval streets in Venice, it was developed in the 13th century.

RIO DI SAN BARNABA (below)

Dividing the parishes of San Barnaba, right, with Santa Margherita, left. Beyond the city centre, canals often have quays down each side.

or a *strada*, but a *calle*, from the Latin *callis*, a path or track. Other terms are used more sparingly and specifically; for example, a *salizzada* is a street that was paved from an early date, a reflection of its importance in the city's street network; these *salizzade*, too, often retain this importance today, fulfilling the function of a local 'high street', such as those of San Lio, San Samuele, Sant'Antonin and San Polo. The term *ruga*, too, is occasionally found (from the French *rue*), and again indicates a street of particular importance, usually lined with shops or workshops, such as Ruga Giuffa at Santa Maria Formosa, and the Ruga dei Oresi (goldsmiths) at Rialto. A *ramo* (branch), by contrast, is a minor alley, usually a cul-de-sac, while a *fondamenta* is a public quay along a canal.

While the urban texture of each individual island is often fairly clear, the relationship between neighbouring island-parishes was, and is, quite random, and it is this randomness that slowly gave rise to the complex, often tortuous pedestrian routes linking parishes with each other. We may recall the directions given to Gobbo by Launcelot in *The Merchant of Venice*, when asked how to find Shylock's house: 'Turn up on your right hand at the next turning, but, at the next turning of all, on your left; marry, at the very next turning, turn of no hand but turn down indirectly to the Jew's house.' Gobbo's heartfelt reply – 'By God's sonties, 'twill be a hard way to hit' – has been echoed by countless visitors to the city down the centuries as they attempt to comprehend the maze of calli, salizzade, campi, campielli, rami and cortili that represents one of the most complete and complex medieval urban forms in the world, but which equally defies all rational orientation.[9]

The islands are divided by narrow canals, but are today linked to each other by around 400 bridges. Most were traditionally built of timber, and from time to time required repair or reconstruction; even the famous bridge at Rialto was of timber until the late sixteenth century. Most bridges today are of stone and brick, although their parapets are comparatively modern, and in the past most had no protection at the sides; only two such bridges survive today, one of which is the well-known Ponte del Diavolo at Torcello. The bridges were built with large ramped steps to allow the passage of horses, the chief means of terrestrial communication for the wealthy until the later Middle Ages; thereafter horses fell into disuse and Venetians travelled by boat or on foot, with goods transported

25

CAMPO SANTA MARIA FORMOSA

Dominated by Mauro Codussi's church of
the 1490s, the square is surrounded by fine
palaces, including Manopola's Palazzo
Ruzzini, of the 1580s, at the far end.

on carts and barrows of various specialized types, to traverse the bridges, much as they still do today. The bridges still have a high-arched profile, to permit small vessels to pass beneath them in different tidal conditions; boats have always been rowed *ala valesana*, with the oarsman standing upright, facing the prow. Many bridges, though, are comparatively modern, including the large number added in the nineteenth century; in the medieval period, when there were fewer, and it was a good deal more difficult, even tortuous, to traverse the city on foot than it is today. Many canals, too, have been lost over the centuries; around forty were reclaimed in the eighteenth and nineteenth centuries, and are today identifiable as *rii interrati* (reclaimed canals) or, more commonly, as a *rio terà*.[10]

The Most Serene Republic

While the city's form itself became more distinct and better defined in the eleventh and twelfth centuries, the institutions of the Republic, too, were evolving in important ways. In 1026, Doge Ottone Orseolo was deposed, and the following years saw important modifications to the role of the doge, who became less of a *dux* and more the elected representative of a *de facto* ruling class, the nobility, with significant curbs on his personal power. The nobility itself was somewhat heterogeneous, some claiming direct descent from the Roman nobles of Venetia and Istria, others simply wealthy leading citizens and traders; this process, however, also divided the doge and nobility more clearly from the common people. To reinforce this modified role, a few years later again, in 1032, there was initiated a process by which the doge was required to formally consult with the other nobles before making any important political decisions; this process itself evolved into the establishment of the Senate or Pregadi, one of the central pillars of the Republic's constitution.[11]

The increasing population and wealth of the capital in this era is epitomized by the definitive construction of the church of San Marco, on a considerably larger scale than its predecessor; in 1053 the pope, Leo IX, visited the lagoons, to pray at the shrine of the patron, and to consecrate two new churches, Santa Caterina and San Lio. Ironically, however, in view of this gesture of recognition, only a year later the Church of Rome formally split from the Eastern Church, whose spiritual heart remained at Constantinople. Henceforth the Western and Eastern Churches took decisively different courses, the latter developing into the Orthodox rite, while the West remained Roman and Catholic. Venice itself continued to claim at least some degree of subjection to the East, although the city's own rite was to some extent Romanized; in many practical and political matters, however, the Republic was to pursue a robustly independent middle course.

The twelfth century was a period of consolidation of Venice's role as capital of its subject territories and of increasing trade with (and piracy in) the East. Links with Constantinople remained extremely close, and there was a substantial quarter of the metropolis that was legally defined as a Venetian 'city within the city', where Venetian laws, language and customs prevailed. Venetian sea power now extended as far as the Holy Land, where in 1125 their fleet assisted in the recovery of Tyre for the Crusaders.[12]

As was to be the case a century later with the infamous Fourth Crusade, these earlier expeditions were characterized by a mixture of spiritual piety and realpolitik. In the aftermath of the taking of Tyre, for example, Doge Domenico Michiel, who had captained the fleets himself, took Rhodes from the Greek Emperor, as well as many islands in the Aegean on the journey homeward. On the same voyage, Michiel gained the Dalmatian coastal forts of Spalato, Trau and Sebenico. Two decades later again, the inhabitants of Istria, for a time subject to the Hungarians, volunteered their subjection to Venice once more and, despite later struggles with the Greek Emperor, these territories were held, as was Zara, after an unsuccessful rebellion in 1171.

The purpose of such conquests was consistent: these towns and forts were not acquired with the intention of expanding an empire based on territory, but rather for their essentially strategic and commercial value. From the very first establishment of footholds in Istria and the later fort-ports in the Peloponnese (southern Greece), the Republic's wealth rested on trade, on its position as a conduit between East and West. It saw its uniquely close relationship with Byzantium as a means of developing and even monopolizing the importation of various luxury goods from the Middle East, and their distribution throughout western Europe; similarly, it exported from Germany and northern Europe to the same regions. The Republic was not without its bitter opponents, as its protracted naval rivalry with Genoa epitomizes, but its concentration on certain goods (peppers, spices and luxury fabrics in particular) ensured great profits if the ships reached port safely. This maritime trade was developed in a uniquely Venetian manner, not by individual merchants but by the Republic itself; ships were built in the Serenissima's own yards, and their regular voyages (*viazij*) were auctioned to the Venetian nobility by those same nobles in the role of the Republic's government.[13]

The maturation of the city's form

Soon after the completion of the new San Marco in its definitive form, the turn of the new century saw the establishment of the first state naval dockyards, the Arsenale, in 1104. In the eastern part of Venice, near the bishop's island of Olivolo, these were strategically located for ease of access to the sea through the Porto di Lido, the gap between the two littoral sandbanks. A few decades later, it had become necessary to reorganize the administration of what was by now a great and populous city. In 1171, Doge Vitale Michiel divided the capital into six districts, to enforce law and order and to impose taxation. These 'sixth parts' or *sestieri*, three on each bank of the Grand Canal, have survived to our own day as elements of the city's government. On the west bank were established San Polo, Santa Croce and Dorsoduro, and on the east bank San Marco, Cannaregio and Castello. San Marco, San Polo and Santa Croce all represented important religious foundations, while Castello records the ancient fortifications that once stood at Olivolo. Dorsoduro (literally 'hard back') refers to the chain of firm islands that constitute this part of the city, while Cannaregio is said to derive either from 'canal regio' (royal canal) or from the *canne* (reeds) that flourished there.[14]

The following year, 1172, saw a key stage in the evolution of the Republic's form of government, with the institution of the Maggior Consiglio, or Great Council. Its establishment, and the definition of those nobles who formed its membership, effectively closed off the government of the Republic to all but this newly defined patriciate of 480 members. Henceforth only those adult male nobles whose names were inscribed in the *Libro d'Oro* (*Golden Book*) were permitted to participate and to vote. It was a time of great political tension, therefore, and Doge Vitale Michiel was assassinated in May 1172 by disaffected factions; however, he was replaced by the remarkable Sebastiano Ziani, and the Maggior Consiglio was retained as the chief legislative and debating chamber for the remaining six centuries of the Republic. Its members also voted for the 'inner cabinet' or Signoria of eleven men who themselves were to elect the new doge.[15]

Ziani was reputedly the wealthiest man in Venice; his reign was marked (partly for this reason, no doubt) by the first ritual scattering of coins to the people in the Piazza on the occasion of his coronation, a practice borrowed from that of the Eastern Emperors, and followed by all future doges. His reign, although brief, was highly eventful, and was triumphantly crowned by the almost legendary summit conference held in Venice in 1177, between the pope, Alexander III, and the Holy Roman Emperor, Frederick Barbarossa. As the catalyst for this historic peace and reconciliation, Venice was now firmly established as one of the most influential powers in Italy, its reputation for international trade and diplomacy unrivalled. The same historic meeting further enhanced the importance of the Sposalizio, the wedding of the doge to the sea on Ascension Day,

ARCO DEL PARADISO (above)

This fine early 15th century arch closes one end of Calle del Paradiso. Depicting the Virgin of Misericordia (Charity), it bears the arms of the Foscari and Mocenigo clans.

THE STONE FIGURE IN CAMPO DEI MORI (right)

known as Sior Antonio Rioba is an eastern merchant, symbol of Venice's trading links with the 'Moors'.

when the pope blessed this union by giving the doge a gold ring with which to symbolize this 'wedding', and which the doge then cast into the sea.

The establishment of the Maggior Consiglio, turbulent though its early history was, again proved to be a defining moment in the government of the Republic. Its foundation made it necessary to house the council in a great new chamber within the seat of government, and to this end Sebastiano Ziani began the reconstruction of the 'ducal palace' to take account of this newly-defined requirement, at the same time transforming the seat of government into a better ordered and far less defensive structure.[16]

Indeed, the remarkable Ziani went much further and, reinforcing his role as head of state after the turbulent demise of his predecessor, instigated a series of key works of urban improvement. Among them was the enlargement of the Piazza in front of the church, the reclamation of the Piazzetta, and the erection of the two patronal columns on the waterfront next to the ducal palace; these all served to further emphasize the role of the nucleus of San Marco as the spiritual and administrative heart of the city. They also added greatly to its civic dignity.

Ziani also reinforced the important axis that joined San Marco with the market district at the Rialto. Markets had been established on the island in the eleventh century, on land that had been given to the Republic by two wealthy merchants; it is traditionally claimed that Ziani built the first timber bridge at the Rialto, thus creating a direct link between the markets on one bank of the Grand Canal and the hub of San Marco on the other bank. The direct route between these key nuclei was destined to develop into the chief commercial axis of the city.

The consolidation of the empire

Enrico Dandolo, Ziani's successor in 1192, was the first doge to draft and sign the Promissione, a declaration of his faith, loyalty and duties to the Republic, and of his intention to uphold peace and justice. The Promissione was closely examined after his death, and judgement passed by his fellow nobles on his reign. Dandolo's reign was also marked by a decisive further stage in the development of Venice's maritime empire, which thus far had consisted almost exclusively of sheltered harbours, strategic islands and fortresses, the *raison d'etre* of which was to protect and support vital trading routes. However, in 1204, the Fourth Crusade began, the inital object of which (like the earlier campaigns) was the recapture of the Holy Land from the 'infidel'. But Dandolo succeeded in diverting the great Christian fleet to Constantinople instead; the Eastern metropolis was taken by the Western fleets and was comprehensively pillaged and sacked. Countless treasures were looted, and many of them taken back to Venice, including the four bronze horses of San Marco, which were relocated on the facade of the basilica. Baldwin, King of Flanders, was installed as the new emperor, and Doge Dandolo, for his part, was declared 'lord of a quarter and half of a quarter' of the Eastern Empire. In this way Venice added Crete, Negroponte, the Cyclades and the important forts of Modon and Coron (both in the Peloponnese) to the overseas empire, the empire 'da Mar'. The Most Serene Republic was now no longer an Adriatic sea-trading city but had become one of the great political powers of the eastern Mediterranean.[17]

The first part of the fourteenth century saw the Republic's consolidation of this scattered constellation of settlements, some of them simply isolated harbours, others, such as Crete, extensive territories that had to be absorbed within the Republic's system of government. In general the Serenissima developed and operated a carefully balanced 'arm's length' policy in governing its subject lands, by allowing the continuation of a significant amount of local self-government in secondary matters and the retention of local titles and privileges; at the same time it ensured that the colony as a whole remained loyal by the appointment of a Venetian noble as governor, who in different colonies was variously known as a *podestà*, *luogotenente* or *rettore*, supported by his own militia.

PAOLINO'S MAP OF 1346 (above)

The oldest surviving map of the city; over 100 churches are indicated, as are the main channels of navigation. Murano is on the left, the Giudecca to the right, and the Lido at the top. (Biblioteca Nazionale Marciana, Venice.)

ISTRIA: THE TOWN CENTRE OF PIRANO (left)

The rocky peninsula of Istria was one of the Republic's earliest possessions; it remained Venetian territory until the fall of the Republic in 1797. Almost all the towns on the Istrian and Dalmatian coasts remain strongly Venetian in character, particularly their churches and campanili.

Venetian commercial hegemony in the eastern Mediterranean, however, was increasingly threatened in the fourteenth century by the rival trading networks of the Genoese; the first direct conflict between them arose in 1256, over a clash of mercantile interests, and although on this occasion the Serenissima was victorious, there were further encounters in 1294 at Pera, near Constantinople, and again in 1298 at Curzola in Dalmatia. This last was a great naval encounter, the scale of the conflict (eighty to ninety vessels on each side) reflecting the nautical power of the two combatants. The Venetians were defeated, although there were no further conflicts until 1324.

The first image of Venice: Paolino's map

Shortly after this latter skirmish, a man recorded simply as 'Paolino' affixed his name to a map of the city of Venice. Today kept in the Biblioteca Marciana, the Library of St Mark, and dated 1346, this map is the oldest depiction of Venice in existence. In origin, however, it is certainly considerably earlier than the mid fourteenth century, since the plan depicts certain aspects of the city's form that by then were already long obsolete; among them are Paolino's depiction of the buildings on the Piazza of San Marco enclosed by a great defensive wall, demolished by the fourteenth century. Nevertheless, the map remains a unique record of the medieval city, clearly delineating not only the highly developed *urbs* itself but also Venice's role as a hub, a metropolitan core surrounded by satellite communities. Considerable emphasis is given to the navigable waterways surrounding the city, as far as the fort of San Nicolo at the northern tip of the Lido. The most prominent and closest satellite is the Giudecca, which Paolino depicts as a single island, although in fact it consisted (and still does) of a chain of islets facing the city across the broad, deep Giudecca Canal. It was built-up only along this northern shore, with a mixture of monastic houses and the cottages of fishermen and boatbuilders.[18]

Murano was the most populous, distinctly separate satellite community, an important town in its own right, governed by a *podestà* appointed by the Republic, and with its own elected citizens' assemblies. It was also home to several wealthy monastic houses, including San Cipriano. Equally important, and by now well established, were the numerous glassworks that had been transferred here from Venice in 1291, and which now underpinned the local economy. Murano, too, was built along its own Grand Canal, a broad, meandering waterway dividing the island into two parts, although the glassworks were all concentrated on one of the secondary canals, the Rio dei Vetrai, as they remain today.

The capital was also surrounded by a constellation of smaller islets, most of them monastic houses: San Giorgio, San Michele, San Servolo, Sant'Elena. Others, though, had been designated by the Republic as isolation hospitals in an attempt to curb the spread of leprosy and the plague. San Lazzaro, for example, was established in the twelfth century as an asylum, later becoming a leper colony or 'lazzaretto'. Other islets were allocated by the Republic as hostels for pilgrims en route to the Holy Land, among them La Grazia or Cavanella and San Clemente. Most of the perimeter of the city itself was occupied by monasteries, orchards and market gardens.[19]

Despite the distortions of the city's canal pattern, Paolino's plan is in many other ways remarkably precise. He records the existence and the names of some ninety churches, both parochial and monastic, fifty-seven on the San Marco side of the Grand Canal, and thirty-three on the other.[20] By now Venice was indeed a metropolis, and all the essential features of its form were well established. The Grand Canal formed the central highway or artery of the city, lined with a mixture of palaces, monasteries, parish churches and an assortment of warehouses and other more mercantile functions. It bisected the city with its sinuous form, terminating at the west end in the monastic islet of Santa Chiara, facing the lagoon and the mainland shore, while at the other it broadened out into the great basin of San Marco. Paolino also represented the naval base and dockyards of the Arsenale, although here, again, they are anachronistically depicted solely by the

MAP OF MODON

Modon (modern Methoni), in southern Greece, was known as the 'eye of the Republic', a vital fort and harbour for the merchant fleets. (16th century Turkish source.)

small enclosed basin that had formed the original nucleus when the Arsenale had been established back at the beginning of the twelfth century. By the mid fourteenth century it had already been expanded significantly beyond this original core, and was now several times larger.

Since the establishment of the Rialto markets in the eleventh century, and the first crossing of the Grand Canal, the district between the Rialto and San Marco had seen the development of the highest concentration of commercial activity in the city. The two poles were linked by a group of streets, collectively known as the Mercerie, which had been lined with mercers' shops and other crafts probably since well before the time of Paolino. A number of other specialized groups of crafts were also concentrated in these most central districts, and their locations survive today in the street names: the Frezzeria (street of arrow-makers); Calle dei Fabbri (smiths); Spadaria (sword-makers); Casselleria (makers of chests and boxes); and Calle dei Specchieri (mirror-makers).[21] Other, more essential day-to-day crafts, however, were scattered all over the city; almost every parish had its own *pistor* (baker), and many streets still record other widely distributed activities: *taiapiera* (stonemason); *spezier* (pharmacist or spice-dealer); and numerous *magazeni*, warehouses. Although the chief retail and wholesale markets were at the Rialto, there was also a meat market at San Marco, near the quay on the edge of the Bacino, while a few of the larger parish squares also had local markets, among them San Polo and Santa Maria Formosa. The greatest concentration of specialist crafts was at the Arsenale, representing the various operations that contributed to the shipbuilding process, from ships' carpenters to caulkers and rope- and oar-makers. Smaller, private boatyards or *squeri*, however, could still be found scattered in all parts of the city, particularly in the outlying districts of Cannaregio, Dorsoduro and the Giudecca. The famous boatyard at San Trovaso is today a rare survivor of these formerly numerous traditional yards for the building and repair of smaller lagoon craft, of *gondole* and *sandoli*.

War, plague and recovery

The fourteenth century was divided in half by the devastating spread of the plague, the 'Black Death', which reached Venice from the east in 1348, and thereafter spreading with terrifying rapidity over western Europe. It carried off probably half of the city's population, and its effects were equally disastrous in every other major city in Europe. As a result, therefore, in the second half of the century most of the West took several decades to recover numbers, to rebuild trade and to re-establish military and diplomatic networks. Venice's own final confrontation with the ancient enemy, Genoa, in 1379–80, was still conditioned by the after-effects of the plague, although the conflict brought the Republic closer to military defeat than at any other time in its history. The Genoese formed an alliance with the Carrara, lords of nearby Padua, in an attempt to encircle the hitherto impregnable lagoon. They succeeded in taking Chioggia, Venice's southern key, and only a bitterly fought seige and counter-attack by the Republic resulted in the retaking of Chioggia and thus preventing the launch of a direct assault on the capital.[22]

If there was a single guiding principle in the Republic's policy towards the Italian mainland throughout these centuries, it was one of carefully balanced neutrality between the many disparate elements of which the peninsula was still composed: the Papal States, the despotic fiefdoms of the Carrara, the Scaligeri in Verona, the d'Este in Ferrara, the Visconti in Milan, and the Doria in Genoa. Venice's own Terraferma possessions were still confined to the ancient coastal Dogado, together with the Marca Trevigiana, the lands of Treviso, which voluntarily ceded itself to the Republic in 1338.

Venice's supreme interest still lay in the continuation and furtherance of Mediterranean trade by almost any means available, including (on many occasions) trading directly with the Muslim 'infidel', despite papal condemnation. It was only at the very end of the fourteenth century that Venice became drawn further into the complex jigsaw of mainland politics.[23] Alliances with Milan

against the Carrara brought Venice the territorial prizes of Vicenza, Feltre and Bassano in 1403, and the Polèsine in the following year. In 1405 the acquisition of both Padua and Verona marked a decisive break with the Republic's ancient policy of non-intervention in peninsular affairs. Both were wealthy, important cities, and with their subjection, the Most Serene Republic had now become an important mainland power as well as capital of an extensive maritime trading empire. Henceforth the Republic comprised these two distinct and in many ways quite diverse and disparate elements; this profound territorial shift was further strengthened and consolidated by the aggressive foreign policies of Doge Francesco Foscari, in whose reign (1423–57) westward expansion spread still further to embrace the Lombard cities of Brescia and Bergamo, for centuries considered a natural part of Milan's own *contado* or home territory.[24] The middle decades of the fifteenth century saw a protracted struggle with the Visconti of Milan to retain these new lands, although by 1441, when peace was negotiated, Ravenna and Cervia had also been added to the Republic's list of mainland subject cities.

The fifteenth century, therefore, was one of growth and expansion in almost every sphere of activity: territorial, commercial and in building works. The acquisition and expansion of the Terraferma empire was paralleled by a great increase of numbers in the city itself, such that it became not only almost certainly the wealthiest city in Europe, but also one of the largest and most populous.[25] The middle and later decades of the century mark an era of outstanding cultural achievement in Venice as the nobility expressed its own confidence in this epoch of expansion by a great programme of palace building, reiterated only a little later by a 'golden age' of native artistic flowering, the era of Vittore Carpaccio and the Bellini.

Nevertheless, the new mainland territories had to be fortified (at enormous cost), while the overseas empire, too, had to be maintained and defended against the ominous advances of the Turks in the Balkans. The climactic political event of the era was the fall of Constantinople in 1453 to the Turkish invaders. The great metropolis, the original 'new Rome', and symbol of the Christian East, had finally fallen to the Muslims, and with it the continuity of Venice's role as direct representative of the East in the West. The Republic, too, clashed directly with the Turks, at Rhodes in 1465, and in Negroponte two years later. The latter territory fell in 1470 after 265 years of Venetian suzerainty.[26] Although the Republic continued to make sporadic territorial advances in the East, gaining Zante (Zakinthos), Zeffalonia (Keffalinia), and above all, in 1489 the great prize of Cyprus, the Ottoman Empire continued its inexorable landward advances through the Balkans; the twin forts of Modon and Coron in southern Greece, way stations for the Venetian fleets, were both lost to the Turks before a general peace was concluded in 1503.[27]

The fifteenth century was remarkable for the way in which the Republic itself played an ever more prominent part in determining the city's form and directions of development. The government department known as the Piovego had been founded (or perhaps re-established) as early as 1282 to control and record building activity and to maintain the urban fabric, its streets and canals; but in the fifteenth century a series of laws and decrees was enacted with the clear intention of enhancing the dignity of the city, and in particular of the Grand Canal. Boatyards were banished from its banks in 1433, for example, while in 1462 stonemasons' yards were similarly removed an acceptable distance from its quays.[28]

The wealth and confidence that derived from the Terraferma empire and from the rapid re-establishment of trading links over much of the Mediterranean gave rise to an unprecedented era of construction of new noble palaces in the fifteenth century, particularly from the 1450s to the 1480s, transforming the appearance of the city: fine new palaces rose on almost every parish square, and down the entire course of the Grand Canal. Much of this late medieval character has survived today, and the Church, too, was equally active in the completion of the great new monastic houses

PADUA: THE CLOCKTOWER (left)

Padua became a Venetian city in 1405, and remained subject to the Republic until 1797. The clock was the model for Venice's own, built in the 1490s.

of the Frari and Santi Giovanni e Paolo, together with several other fine late-Gothic churches, notably Santo Stefano and the Madonna dell'Orto. Towards the end of the century, a further decisive contribution was made to the architectural dignity of the city by the building activities of the Scuole Grandi. These unique institutions, lay brotherhoods dedicated to prayer and charitable works, all embarked on ambitious programmes of reconstruction of their own premises, which, when completed, were also decorated by the finest artists of the day. In the Piazza of San Marco, too, the last decade of the century saw the beginning of a long, staged process of redevelopment, beginning with the new Clock Tower, which was to culminate in the great works of Jacopo Sansovino more than half a century later, at the Library of San Marco and the Mint.

Mid-millennium: Jacopo de'Barbari and Marin Sanudo

At the end of the fifteenth century the image of Venice was recorded twice for posterity, once in words and again visually, on both occasions with extraordinary precision and detail. We have no records of the city's appearance for a century and a half after Paolino, other than a handful of small, inaccurate or stylized pictographs. But now, in the mid-millennial year of 1500, a unique depiction of the hub of an empire appeared, proudly displayed on six great woodcut blocks (still preserved in the Correr Museum), and surmounted by the bold legend 'VENETIE MD', VENICE 1500. That Jacopo de'Barbari's work was intended as a triumphant display of imperial splendour is undeniable; it was a definitive statement of the size, wealth, power and population of the maritime capital, an almost precise visual parallel to the chronicle 'Laus urbis venetae' (Praise of the city of Venice), written by Marin Sanudo only a few years earlier. Sanudo, a nobleman whose higher political ambitions were thwarted, nevertheless made his own unique contribution to history with his diaries, in which every significant event in the city and its colonies was painstakingly recorded, on a daily basis, over a period of more than thirty years. In his unpublished 'Praise of the city of Venice', drafted in 1493, the city's many marvels are carefully listed, from the bones and relics in its churches to the ferries that traversed the Canalazzo (the Grand Canal), from proud ducal procession to the species of fish taken from the lagoon.[29]

De'Barbari's image is equally accurate, building up the picture of the capital through a vast amount of precisely delineated detail, down to the level of chimneypots and wellheads. His Venice was one of the greatest cities in Europe, and one of the most populous; with up to 130,000 inhabitants, only Paris, Milan and Naples were comparable in size, and none was wealthier.[30] Venice now extended as a mature urban form from Santa Chiara in the west to the furthest monastic islets of Castello. De'Barbari naturally places San Marco physically and symbolically in the very centre of his panorama, which is drawn, with immense skill, as a bird's-eye view from the south, from an imaginary point several hundred metres into the sky. The Piazza of San Marco was paved with brick, as were a number of the other important streets and squares. Adjacent to it, the waterfront to the Bacino was dominated by the great mass of the Palazzo Ducale, which had reached its definitive form following a long rebuilding process begun in the 1340s, and which had culminated in the construction of the Porta della Carta, the new state entrance from the Piazzetta; this in turn was followed by the rebuilding of the east wing after a serious fire in 1483. San Marco, too, had reached its final external appearance (which is almost unchanged today), with the addition of a complex array of high level pinnacles and decorations in the early fifteenth century.

All the city's central districts were now precisely defined and fully built-up, the only open spaces being the *campi*, *calli* and *corti* and the network of canals. Not a blade of grass can be detected between the Carità monastery (the present Accademia) and San Zaccaria, and perhaps for some way beyond both.

The city's perimeter, however, remained far from fully built-up even at this time, and if de'Barbari's great work had been rendered in colour, a green fringe of orchards, gardens and vineyards would be clearly identifiable to the west, north and east, where a crescent of monastic houses encircled the city's heart – Santa Croce, San Girolamo, the Madonna dell'Orto, Santi Giovanni e Paolo, San Francesco della Vigna, Le Vergini, San Domenico, Sant'Anna and San Antonio – a great arc of cloisters and herb gardens. Beyond them still, in several districts the city still petered out into reeds and mud flats.

Other concentrations, too, were prominent. On the north shore, behind the great monastic church of Santi Giovanni e Paolo, was a zone exclusively devoted to timber-yards; its axis was formed by a street still known as the Barbaria delle Tole (*tole* are planks of timber), and its shoreline was filled with rafts of timber brought down from the mountain forests and floated across the lagoon for processing into beams and floorboards for the building industry. Further east, the Arsenale had by now expanded to cover much of the sestiere of Castello and was surrounded by a dense matrix of dockyard workers' housing and ancillary activities such as bakeries for ships' biscuits and sail-making yards.

The Grand Canal

The city's internal structure remained entirely dominated by the course of the Grand Canal, the Canalazzo; the lifeline of the metropolis, its chief artery served many functions, both practical and symbolic. At the former level, it was the main highway of the city, down which vessels of every type sailed, from the humble sandoli of the lagoon's fishermen to barges carrying building materials and produce to market, to the gilded ducal Bucintoro, the state barge, to the trading ships of the Empire. It was primarily, therefore, an axis of commerce at every level; but it was naturally also very much more. As a 'street', albeit an unconventional one, it was far more spacious and imposing than any of the more conventional streets in the other great European cities. None of them, not Paris, Rome, Milan, Naples or Florence, could claim such a fine thoroughfare, such a fit setting for the building of noble palaces; and none made remotely comparable use of their own rivers. In the narrow streets of medieval cities elsewhere it was rarely, if ever, possible to appreciate the whole facade of any major building except at a very acute angle. The exceptions, of course, were the public and civic buildings and the cathedrals in the central piazza, such as the Campo in Siena and the Piazza della Signoria in Florence. But Venice could not only boast a civic square at least as fine as these; it could also proclaim this great three-mile-long highway for the proud display of private wealth. No sumptuary laws were ever imposed by the Republic to moderate such displays; here, one could admire tranquilly a palace facade in its finely-balanced symmetrical entirety, reflected in the waters, rather than attempting to appreciate its proportions from a narrow alley, constantly threatened by horses, carts and other traffic, as one was constrained, for example, to admire the palaces of the Strozzi and the Medici in Florence.[31] This unique advantage was exploited to the full by Venice's patriciate as they developed and refined the design of their own palaces. By the time that de'Barbari depicted the city, many exceptionally fine, new late-Gothic palaces had been built down the course of the Canalazzo, among them Cà Foscari and the extraordinarily richly-carved Cà d'Oro. Although not all of the houses on the Grand Canal were patrician palaces (there were still many more modest structures between them), the status of a site on the Grand Canal was strongly emphasized by Sanudo; in 1493 he wrote that:

all around, on both banks, are the houses of the nobility, and other beautiful palaces, worth 20,000 ducats or more … [among them are] those of Zorzi Corner … and Francesco Foscari [the late doge], and so many others that it would take a great deal of time to list them. Those on the Grand Canal are highly prized and are more valuable than those elsewhere; the most valuable of all are those near Rialto and San Marco …[32]

VERONA: THE PORTA NUOVA (above, top)

Begun in 1533, it is one of many works of fortification that Michele Sanmicheli designed for the Republic's subject cities in the 16th century.

MURANO (above)

One of Venice's chief satellites, it has been the centre of glass production since 1291.

GIOVANNI MANSUETI, *Miracle at San Lio*, 1494 (right)

One of a cycle of paintings commissioned by the Scuola Grande di San Giovanni Evangelista. Mansueti depicts a location still identifiable today, with typical Venetian roof-terraces and gothic windows. (Gallerie dell' Accademia, Venice.)

'The new Rome'

The Venice of Sanudo and de'Barbari was essentially an organic, medieval capital, with little evidence yet of the rationalizing influence of the Renaissance in its urban structure. Nevertheless, by 1500 we can see the first signs of Renaissance design and town planning ideas; the new Land Gate to the Arsenale had already been built in a revolutionary classical Roman style, while on the Piazza of San Marco the new Clock Tower, prominently shown by de'Barbari, is further evidence that Renaissance concepts of urban renewal had begun to make their presence felt in the city's appearance.

For some time to come, however, these philosophies of rational, formal planning had a somewhat limited impact on this dense organic urban matrix. Soon after de'Barbari's view was completed there was a disastrous fire at the Rialto in 1514; the Republic's response to this catastrophe, like their cautious, stage by stage works of improvement at San Marco, reflects the inherently conservative attitudes of the government towards more radical (and disruptive) changes to the city's form. As we will see in more detail in later chapters, urban renewal was often piecemeal, slow and fragmented, and many of the more radical proposals put forward during the sixteenth century came to nothing.

The concept of Venice as 'the new Rome' gained widespread currency in the Renaissance, although often promoted rather more eagerly by its own citizens and nobility than by others in the peninsula. On the more abstract level it reflected a belief in the serene, just, stable and orderly

government that had now characterized the Republic for so long, particularly and acutely evident since much of Italy had recently reverted to domination by individual families of varying degrees of despotism and tyranny. On the other, the same concept was advanced (again most enthusiastically by the Venetians themselves) in a more practical sense: Venice was epitomized as a great, glorious and wealthy capital city, a rather belated successor to the glories of classical Rome.[33] Although the Venetians were naturally the most enthusiastic promulgators of this concept, there were others, too, who admired greatly the Venetian system

of government. The Florentine Francesco Guicciardini, for example, one of the foremost theorists of the time, wrote in his 'Dialogue' (written in c1524, but set in 1494) that, 'the Venetian government is as fine perhaps as that which any free republic has ever had'. Against Guicciardini's scholarly analysis, though, we should set the less considered views of another Florentine, Benedetto Dai, who wrote in 1472 some of the harshest invective ever committed to paper on the 'foul traitors of a thousand sets of gallows', the Venetians who, 'falsified the laws and ordinances' and who, 'imprisoned and tortured the pope's sister…' Inaccurate and chauvinistic though Dai was, his views were held by many others who feared Venice's wealth and power. On a purely literal plane, it is difficult to find two cities less alike in their natural topography than Venice and Rome, one built on islets in the marshes and surrounded by lagoons, the other poised on its legendary seven hills, overlooking a narrow river, and some distance from the sea. Even Constantinople, Byzantium, the first 'new Rome', had a closer topographical claim, standing on a promontory with its own seven hills, overlooking the Golden Horn. But the concept was intended to bring into the debate Venice's inheritance of the spiritual, cultural and Republican mantle of Rome, as much as its physical grandeur: Mark as the successor to Peter, both founding spirits of the true Church; the just and sagacious Venetian Senate as the heir to its Roman namesake. Venice now had a further claim: as the spiritual successor of Constantinople, which since 1453 had been in Muslim control; the Christian beacon continued to shine in the venerable patriarchate of the Republic, and in the basilica dedicated to Mark the Evangelist. As far as Venice's physical succession to Rome was concerned, it was achieved symbolically rather than through the physical execution of dramatic

GENTILE BELLINI, *Miracle at San Lorenzo*, 1500 (below, left)

From the same cycle as Mansueti's painting, Bellini's is another richly detailed example of 15th century Venetian life, with a newly built Renaissance palace on the left. (Gallery Accademia, Venice.)

HOUSING

A terrace of characteristic working-class housing in eastern Castello, a district where many of the hundreds of workers in the Arsenale lived.

DETAILS FROM A PANORAMIC VIEW OF
THE CITY by Erhard Reuwich, 1486 (below).

On the left is the Punta della Dogana, with
the old customs-house. On the right is the
eastern district of Castello, with the great
church of Santi Giovanni e Paolo.

urban transformations. One early example of this spirit of urban renewal was the new gate to the Arsenale, a clear manifestation of the ways in which classical imagery – in this case the triumphal arch – could be reused to considerable effect. It was also singularly appropriate since the Arsenale epitomized the martial might of the Venetian navy.

The works of civic improvement in the Piazza of San Marco were another expression of Renaissance pride and imperial display; the first such work being the Torre dell'Orologio, the Clock Tower, built in the 1490s, and soon followed by the new building for the Procurators of San Marco, which occupies the north side of the square. Later still came a series of improvements begun by Jacopo Sansovino in the 1530s, and which continued for several decades. They collectively represent clearly the ways in which the Republic sought to enhance the heart of the city and its Republic; the three classical concepts of urban harmony, civic dignity and architectural grandeur were all embraced in these works. Sansovino remodelled the shape of the Piazza itself, isolating the Campanile and banishing the quotidian markets, and in this way executing the first of these three concepts, the improvement of the spaces themselves. The construction of the Biblioteca Marciana, the Library of San Marco, itself a work redolent with cultural importance and symbolism, and again to designs by Sansovino, marks the apogee of both civic dignity and architectural richness.[34]

In political terms, however, there was a serious crisis in the early sixteenth century, as a direct result of the Republic's Terraferma expansion. The difficulties in defending a diverse two-part empire

became acutely apparent with the short-lived League of Cambrai, a grand alliance of Western mainland powers, which was intended to break the maritime interloper on the Terraferma. The alliance resulted in the rapid loss of almost all of the mainland empire to the French at the debacle of Agnadello. Venice's lands were largely restored by treaty, however, as the grand alliance itself quickly crumbled, and new accommodations were made; with only minor modifications, these lands were to remain the territorial limits of the Terraferma empire until the final fall of the Republic itself in 1797. Thenceforth, Venice's mainland policies reverted, through force of economic necessity, to carefully balanced, circumspect neutrality.

The sixteenth century is almost universally regarded as the Republic's greatest era of artistic and cultural achievement. The wealth and opportunities offered by this great city attracted a remarkable influx of skilled masters in painting, sculpture and architecture that was without parallel in any other period, with perhaps the exception of the flourishing of native Venetian art in the immediately preceding decades. The magnetic strength of Venice in this century directly reflected its cultural dominance, not of all Italy, but certainly of virtually all of the peninsula north of the Apennines. And it was not solely in the visual arts that the city flourished; in the intellectual sphere, in the dissemination of literature and philosophy, the city quickly became by far the most important centre of printing in Europe. The presses of Aldo Manuzio (the Aldine Press), in particular, printed accessible editions of Greek and classical Roman authors in much greater numbers than any other presses; by the middle of the sixteenth century there were 125 publishers in the city.[35] Like so many other aspects of the city's culture, the Renaissance in Venice was modelled in an intellectual climate that interpreted the new humanistic philosophies in ways that made them distinctly Venetian; the innate cultural liberalism of many individual nobles was balanced by the caution and pragmatism that could be considered the watchwords not only of the native instincts of the Venetian people, but equally of the policies and politics of the Republic itself.

The city defined

The sixteenth century also saw no shortage of other ambitious plans for urban renewal, in many and various forms, some feasible, others clearly not. Cristoforo Sabbadino, for example, the chief surveyor to the Savii alle Acque (the government agency responsible for the maintenance of the lagoon, its channels and sea defences), produced several schemes for major hydraulic works, including new canals. His contemporary, Alvise Corner (Cornaro), a wealthy citizen who had made a fortune in land reclamation on the nearby Terraferma, produced even more ambitious and daunting proposals for the city's defence, including a completely new circumference of walls to be built directly out of the lagoon. None of them was executed. More intellectually based was Corner's proposal for the redevelopment of the great basin of San Marco, which envisaged its classicization with a Greek theatre built on a new islet in the water between the island of San Giorgio and the Customs House point at the end of the sestiere of Dorsoduro; he also proposed another artificial island with a hill, to be reclaimed from the basin just off the shoreline near the Doges' Palace, and which was to be planted with trees and landscaped, to provide a glimpse of Arcadia from the heart of the city.[36]

GIOVANNI BELLINI, *Doge Leonardo Loredan,* c.1501

Loredan was a reticent, puritanical figure but his portrait emphasizes the ducal qualities of sagacity, tranquility and permanence. (National Gallery, London.)

Many other visionary proposals for the city were put forward during the sixteenth century, some the result of intense intellectual and humanistic debate, in which such notable figures as Daniele Barbaro took a prominent role. Barbaro, Patriarch of Aquileia, and his brother MarcAntonio, were outstanding patrons of the arts, and in the later 1550s commissioned Andrea Palladio and Paolo Veronese to design and decorate their new villa at Maser. The Republic also sometimes encouraged such debate by the sponsorship of architectural competitions. After a serious fire in the Palazzo Ducale, for example, in 1577, alternative proposals were sought from several leading architects, including Palladio; and the debate over the form of the new stone bridge proposed for the Rialto, to replace the ancient timber structure, was to continue for decades. Frequently, however, although these debates were often lively (or acrimonious), conservatism in design tended to prevail over more radical solutions; such was the course finally taken at the Palazzo Ducale, where the fire-damaged south wing was eventually repaired, rather than rebuilt to a modern design. The extraordinarily protracted debate over the design of the Rialto Bridge indicates how finely balanced some of these discussions were over stylistic matters; it is notable, however, that despite the boldness of the great sweep of the single arch that was finally built by Antonio da Ponte in the 1580s, in some ways his scheme was less monumental and radical than some of the other proposals, such as that of Palladio.

Later in the sixteenth century a further series of works of urban improvement was undertaken, all of them practical and pragmatic in nature, urbanistic rather than architectural. Pressure of increasing numbers in this period and shortage of land gave rise to large-scale government-funded reclamation projects. The first of several such works was the construction of the Fondamente delle Zattere, the long quay facing the Giudecca, which was begun after a Senate decree in 1520 and when completed, extended from Santa Marta to the Punta della Dogana, the Customs House at the eastern end of Dorsoduro. Once in use, the *zattere* or rafts of timber from the mainland forests had to be brought here before distribution in the city, rather than to their earlier location on the north shore. The Zattere marks an important stage in defining the physical limits of the city, and was followed by similar projects elsewhere.

The even more radical reclamation of the Fondamente Nuove (the New Quays), which began in 1546, again had a twofold purpose. On a practical level it extended the city's physical limits by around 200 metres into the lagoon along the north shore, and provided new land for development; but it also provided a more dignified, fitting termination to the city's form and defined its northern shore much as the Zattere had done on the south side, with a long new quay facing San Michele

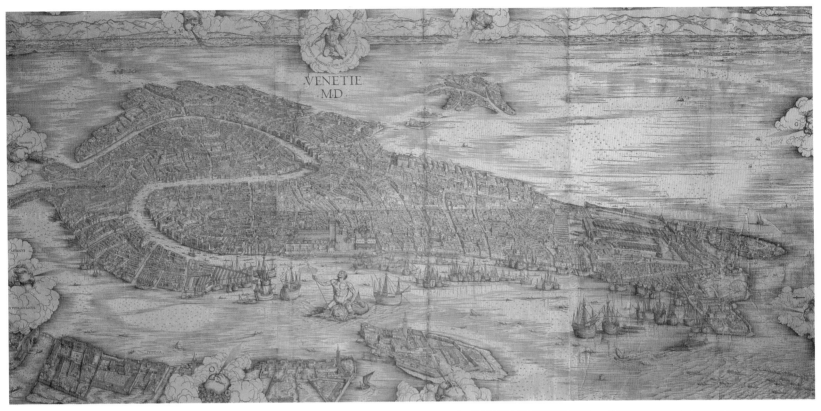

JACOPO DE'BARBARI'S *VENETIE MD*,
1500 (above)

The woodcut is the most famous and
accurate historical depiction of Venice ever
made. Hundreds of individual buildings can
still be identified. The original woodblocks
still survive. (Museo Civico Correr, Venice.)

FRANCESCO GUARDI, *Pope Pius VI Blessing
the Multitude in Campo SS Giovanni e
Paolo*, 1782 (left)

The square, one of the largest in the city,
was the site for numerous processions and
events. Many doges were buried in the
adjacent church. (Ashmolean Museum,
Oxford.)

in Isola and Murano. With the completion of these works Venice's northern and southern limits were established as they remain today.[37]

Further reclamation, though, took place in eastern Castello, while another, more remarkable project was that of the *Tereni Nuovi* (the 'New Lands') at Santa Maria Maggiore. This large but remote district lay to the west of the historic centre, between Santa Croce and the peninsula of Mendigola; in 1500 de'Barbari had rendered its unimportance by condensing his representation of it to a few muddy creeks and sandbanks, but the extensive Tereni Nuovi were reclaimed and planned in a fully rational manner, with a group of rectangular islets (separated by parallel canals), which were then slowly built up over the next two centuries. All of these works thus combined the practical relief of congestion with the enhancement of the dignity of the *civitas*, the exertion of control by the city over its natural environment, and the adaptation of that natural environment to the Republic's will.[38]

During the second half of the sixteenth century, the nobility built ever more imposing palaces for themselves, all of them now in the Renaissance style which had finally supplanted the indigenous Venetian Gothic. The first were the palaces built by Mauro Codussi, a young architect from Bergamo, for the Lando, Zorzi and Loredan families, but the era culminated in the great monumental palaces designed by Jacopo Sansovino for the Corner family and by Michele Sanmicheli, the Republic's military architect, for the Grimani, all of them on the Grand Canal. Such palaces were unprecedented in their size and imposing grandeur. Although in purely numerical terms Venice remained a city of predominantly Byzantine and Gothic houses, these great new structures decisively altered the scale of parts of the city, and their effect was to render even the finest medieval palaces comparatively less prominent.

Many large-scale, high-density housing developments were also constructed in the sixteenth century, again a reflection of increasing population and an awareness on the part of the nobility that such works provided useful long-term investments and regular rental income. In the Church, too, the period was active in the reconstruction and modernization of churches, particularly parochial foundations, some of which were already ancient. Here again, Codussi made his mark with the new architectural language of the Renaissance, at the rebuilt Santa Maria Formosa and with the revolutionary facade of San Michele in Isola. San Salvador, by the architect Giorgio Spavento, is the most imposing of the earlier Renaissance churches, and it was followed a generation or so later by the outstanding works of Andrea Palladio: the facade of San Francesco della Vigna, the Redentore and San Giorgio Maggiore, the last two making vital contributions to the form and image of the city. The Redentore is particularly significant as another direct reflection of the power of the Republic itself as a patron, and marks a deliberate attempt to further extend, enhance and define the heart of the metropolis. Spatially less radical, but even more prominent, was the new San Giorgio Maggiore, whose role as a counterbalance to the political hub of the capital across the Bacino represents a further defining moment in the evolution of the Bacino as an open space, not beyond but within the fabric of the city; to this end, too, its campanile was closely modelled on that of San Marco, an echo across the water.

By the end of the sixteenth century, Piazza San Marco was largely complete, in the shape that it takes today; Jacopo Sansovino's radical but sensitive interventions had now resulted in three new structures, the Mint, the Loggetta and the Biblioteca Marciana, while work was now also almost complete on the second great range of procuracy buildings that was to occupy the whole south side of the Piazza. After two centuries of slow and careful renovation, therefore, the hub of the Empire had almost reached its definitive form.

A marked shift in the attitude of the Venetian nobility towards their palaces in the city centre and their increasingly luxurious design had a corollary in the development of the suburban villa as a

SABBADINO'S MAP, c.1557

Cristoforo Sabbadino was chief surveyor of the Magistrato alle Acque, and responsible for the maintenance of the lagoon and the littoral; he produced many detailed maps, several of which have survived. (Archivio di Stato, Venice.)

CAMPO SANTI GIOVANNI E PAOLO

Andrea Verrochio's superb equestrian statue of the condottiere Bartolomeo Colleoni, of the 1480s, stands in the square.

distinct building type. Positive considerations, such as a humanist education and the development of the garden, offset against the more negative aspects of noise, pollution and congestion in the city centre provoked the nobility into developing both Murano and the Giudecca as places for retreat. Once there, gardens could be laid out and admired, poetry and philosophy could be debated and affairs of state and business briefly left behind.[39] By 1600 the quays of both of these satellite communities were lined with such houses, many with large gardens behind them, extending to the edge of the lagoon. But their popularity was to be comparatively short-lived; already by the middle of the sixteenth century the wealthiest patricians, and those with an eye to long-term investments were turning to the Terraferma, which had now been Venetian territory for well over a century. Here they could build truly noble country seats, as well as developing considerable tracts of land for farming and investment. As the countryside of the Veneto became dotted with Palladian villas, so the Giudecca and Murano declined; although a number of their villas survived into the eighteenth century, many were later abandoned, and the majority at Murano were destroyed with the nineteenth-century industrial expansion of the glassworks. By now, too, many noble clans were themselves extinct. Today, very few such houses survive.[40]

The sixteenth century remained Venice's truly golden age; in almost all of the arts, but especially in architecture and painting, the city exerted its irresistible magnetic influence over creative masters from elsewhere, many of whom settled permanently in the capital: Jacopo Sansovino from Rome; Mauro Codussi, Pietro Lombardo and many others from Bergamo and Lombardy; Antonio Rizzo from Verona; Andrea Palladio from Padua and Vicenza; Veronese again from Verona; Giorgione from Castelfranco and Titian from Cadore. They were all drawn to the lagoons where much of their finest work was produced.

Venice attracted foreign communities from further afield equally irresistibly. There had been foreigners resident in the city for centuries, of course, but by the latter part of the sixteenth century most of the resident foreign settlements were clearly defined, their places of residence established and in some cases codified into law. The Jewish Ghetto, for example, had been established in 1516, and by the end of the century was one of the largest and most important centres of Jewish culture in Europe. Most of the other foreign communities directly reflected the Republic's trading links and cultural connections. The Greeks, too, had had ancient links with Venice for centuries, although their numbers increased markedly after the Fall of Constantinople to the Turks in 1453. In 1526 a site was allocated to them by the government in the parish of Sant'Antonin, and around their church grew a largely self-sufficient Greek enclave. Albanians and Dalmatians also both retained their own cultural identity in the city, the former's community centred on the church of San Maurizio, while the Dalmatians (known to the Venetians as Slavs) were located just inland from the quay that still bears their name, the Riva degli Schiavoni. There was also a small Armenian enclave established near San Zulian. The other foreign communities were based not on a district of the city's fabric but rather on their trading base, their *fondaco* or *fontego*. The most important and numerous were the Germans, whose own trading base, the Fondaco dei Tedeschi, stood at the foot of the Rialto Bridge. Its reconstruction on an imposing scale, after a disastrous fire in 1506, well illustrates their vital role in the Venetian trading economy. Other trading bases were held by the Persians and the Turks, the former almost next door to that of the Germans, the latter further down the Grand Canal beyond the markets.

The later history of the maritime component of the Most Serene Republic is a story of slow, piecemeal retreat. The *impero da mar* was simply too dispersed, and too far away, to remain defensible. In 1566 the Turks had gained Naxos and the Cyclades, while four years later, Cyprus became the object of Ottoman attack, and Nicosia fell. In the following year, the Western powers formed another grand alliance, this time led by the Venetian Republic's still formidable navy, to engage the Turks at the great battle of Lepanto. Although it was one of the largest naval engagements ever fought in European waters, and nominally a Western victory, Venice still ceded its claims to Cyprus to the Turks, by way of a peace agreement negotiated in 1573.[41]

During the early seventeenth century, while mainland Europe was being more clearly defined by the great land empires of the French, the Hapsburgs and (in the East) the Ottomans, the Republic attempted to maintain its vital sea-trading routes, and to defend them against both the numerous pirates in the Adriatic and against the Ottoman Turks. The tenacious defence of the remaining empire overseas is the most remarkable feature of the Republic's history in the late seventeenth century, exemplified and symbolized by the twenty-four-year struggle over Crete. Despite resounding victories at the Dardanelles in 1656, and two years of all-out seige at Candia (Eraklion), the Venetians finally again ceded the island to the Turks in 1669.[42]

Even now, though, the Republic had not yet renounced complete control of the Ionian Sea, the farther nucleus of the impero da mar, and in four years, from 1683, Francesco Morosini regained the Peloponnese and most of the Ionian islands. A general peace was finally concluded with the Turks at Passarowitz in 1718, after which the Republic made no further territorial gains or losses until its final extinction in 1797. The Most Serene Republic's sea empire had retreated once more to its original territories and Venice had reverted to its previous status as 'lord of the gulf', dominating the Istrian peninsula, the coastline of Dalmatia and Corfu.

The Baroque era

The seventeenth and eighteenth centuries were periods of consolidation of the urban structure of the city, since its overall form was by now effectively sealed and defined. The most dramatic new contributions to the city's appearance were the buildings of Baldassare Longhena, the greatest Baroque architect of Venice, whose magnificent Santa Maria della Salute dominates the western end of the Bacino of San Marco. The Salute marks the second outstanding direct intervention by the Republic in the vicinity of the Bacino, following Palladio's Redentore church.

One of the most striking features of seventeenth-century Venice was the divergence in the extremes of wealth and poverty, as epitomized on one hand by the sumptuous interiors of the palaces built by Longhena and others, and on the other by the expansion of orphanages and charitable foundations. A further, disastrous outbreak of the plague in 1630 had drastically reduced the city's population once more, including significant numbers of the nobility. Partly as a result of this calamity, the Republic allowed a number of wealthy citizen families to buy their way into the patriciate, a reflection not only of the extraordinary wealth of this 'new money' but also indicative of the decline of many of the older patrician clans. As well as producing much-needed revenue, the practice attempted to inject new life into the Republic's government, as it also tried to come to terms with the decrease of its importance in a changing world. These 'new men' not only built some imposing new palaces but they also endowed many parish churches, sometimes on a prodigious scale, and some of which were refaced or indeed completely rebuilt in rich Baroque and Neoclassical styles.[43]

The seventeenth century was thus a period of reinforcement of the urban form. Many palaces on the Grand Canal were, like the churches, refaced and modernized or sometimes reconstructed, following (though rarely surpassing) the earlier examples left by Codussi, Sanmicheli and Sansovino. These palaces are notable for the almost universal use of stone for the entire facade, now virtually *de rigueur* for a new palace of any consequence. The city's population experienced little overall change between 1600 and 1700, although to a significant extent this reflects the devastation of the 1630 plague; from around 150,000 in 1600 numbers fell to barely 100,000 survivors, to recover only slowly to reach perhaps 140,000 by the century's end. Nevertheless, building activity was extensive in all fields, particularly churches and palaces, and urbanization slowly continued in the 'new zones' that had been reclaimed in the previous century. Outlying districts, such as

THE GRAND CANAL FROM RIALTO TOWARDS CÀ FOSCARI (above)

Doge Foscari's palace dominates this section of the Canal, and was the largest in the city when built in the 1450s.

CANAL GRANDE (right, above)

The finest waterway in Europe: the Grand Canal from the Accademia Bridge, with Baldassare Longhena's church of Santa Maria della Salute dominating the entrance to the Canal from the Basin of San Marco beyond.

CANALE DELLA GIUDECCA (right, below)

The broad canal divides the district of Dorsoduro from the Giudecca beyond. In the foreground is the Dogana (customs-house), its beacon marking the entrance to the Grand Canal.

northern Cannaregio, traditionally sparsely populated, were slowly developed more intensively, as were the Giudecca and the backwaters of Dorsoduro. This expansion helped to relieve acute overcrowding in the centre, and gave the wealthier patricians more space to build palaces with gardens, such as those of the Savorgnan and Surian, both in Cannaregio, the first of which had a famous and extensive garden. In the seventeenth century, too, Longhena's vast palaces set new standards of massive grandeur that epitomized the self-image of the nobility, and in some cases, of the newly ennobled citizenry.

The period is also notable for the rise of the theatre and the opera house, flourishing in Venice as nowhere else in Europe, with many new buildings both for the Baroque theatre and for the slightly different requirements of lyric opera. They were also, in a sense, paralleled by an increasing Baroque theatricality in architecture itself, nowhere more pronounced than in the great palaces built by Longhena for the Bon and Pesaro families. Church facades, too, became ever more deeply moulded and three-dimensional, backdrops to an almost endless succession of carnivals, processions and festivals. None rivalled Longhena's Santa Maria della Salute, the influence of which extended to incorporate the rebuilding of the Customs House at the Punta della Dogana, another element of urban theatre on the edge of the Bacino.

More modest housing developments were also extensive, particularly in the latter half of the century, as numbers were slowly regained. Large new apartment blocks for rent were built in the Tereni Nuovi, on Rio della Sensa in Cannaregio, at San Basilio on the Zattere, and elsewhere. More humble terraces of cottages for the city's craftsmen were similarly built in almost all outlying zones, from the Giudecca to San Nicolo, from Castello to the Ghetto.[44]

THREE DETAILS FROM LUDOVICO UGHI'S PLAN OF THE CITY IN 1729 (right)

Left: The Tereni Nuovi, reclaimed from the lagoon in the 16th century; centre: northern Cannaregio, with its long, parallel canals; right: the ancient island parish of San Barnaba, with its 'fishbone' street-pattern.

The somewhat self-conscious aggrandizement of the city's fabric in the seventeenth century was paralleled by fundamental changes in the place of the Republic in the world economy, and Europe's political systems; equally, too, in the world's perception of the Republic. The Grand Tour was undertaken by increasing numbers of visitors from northern Europe (particularly from Britain), broadening the familiarity of the city. Here, though, rather than bringing European trade to Venice, the visitor exported from Venice the city's self-image as a great centre of culture, music, learning and the arts. Plans, views, maps and guides were published (in many different languanges) to accommodate this booming market. Francesco Sansovino's seminal guide, *Venetia, città nobilissima*, for example, first published in 1580, was comprehensively modernized (for a second time) by Giustiniano Martinioni in 1663, to cater for newer generations of visitors.

Ironically, while the city welcomed ever greater numbers to its festivals and carnival, the Republic's economy was battered on several fronts: by a slump in Germany which badly damaged trans-Alpine trade; by the 1630 plague and the slow recovery from it; by the battle for the Mantuan succession, in which the Venetian army was decisively routed by Imperial troops outside the Terraferma city; and later, by the debilitating twenty-four-year struggle with the Turks, finally resulting in the loss of Crete.[45]

The eighteenth century: the fall

The eighteenth century is still regarded as the period of Venice's final terminal decline as an independent political entity, with all the associations of enfeeblement, emasculation and decadence that accompany this over-familiar (and by no means wholly accurate) image. In fact, for almost all of her last century, the Republic was at peace. The European political map had changed dramatically and irrevocably, and with the seemingly permanent establishment of large, monarchical land empires, the Republic's ancient constitution appeared increasingly anachronistic. Nevertheless, its traditional position, once again at the very edge of the realpolitik of mainland western Europe, gave Venice considerable advantages. Despite undeniable enfeeblement as a political and military force, cultural life of all kinds flourished in this rather belated second golden age. The city's attractions to

Grand Tourists began to slowly transform the world's perception of Venice from the reality of a rather unimportant anachronistic city-state into a final metaphysical version, an apotheosis, of the myth of the Republic, uniquely preserved, free, stable and apparently immutable.

The familiar image of political diminution must be balanced by the outstanding creativity of many native-born masters; it was, after all, the century of the playwright Carlo Goldoni, of the composers Benedetto Marcello and Antonio Vivaldi, of the painters Antonio Canaletto, Francesco Guardi, Sebastiano Ricci and Giambattista Tiepolo, the last and finest Baroque artist in Europe. It is true that in architecture the eighteenth century produced no new Longhena, but there were in the city gifted groups of followers of Longhena as well as representatives of the new Neoclassical movement.[46] What is particularly remarkable is that none of these masters was a foreigner attracted to the city by hope of advancement, as many of Venice's outstanding artists had been in earlier centuries, but all were native Venetians who remained in the city, where their skills were encouraged and developed by the Republic and its nobility.

Venice's population remained broadly static over the whole century, with around 140,000 inhabitants; there were no devastating plagues to drastically curtail numbers. Given the extensive 'filling in' operations of urban consolidation that had already occupied much of the previous

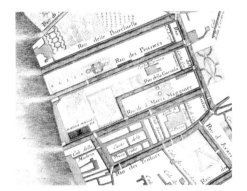 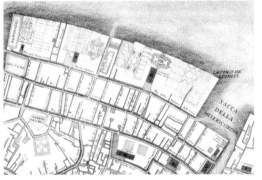 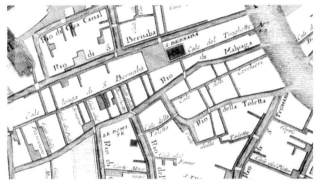

century, most building works in the eighteenth century took the form of restorations or re-constructions on the same sites, rather than new buildings on new land.

The theatre's importance continued to increase. Many were built or reconstructed to accommodate developing tastes and dramatic styles, both of prose and lyric opera, culminating in the Gran Teatro alla Fenice of 1792, one of the finest opera houses in Italy. The period thus marked the process of the completion of the urban fabric; its street pattern and canal network had long been fully defined, but the urban 'grain' was further refined and completed. Some of the more ambitious projects of the previous century were finally completed, among them Cà Rezzonico (begun by Baldassare Longhena for the Bon family, but completed by Giorgio Massari), while others were built anew to imposing dimensions. A few, however, such as Palazzo Venier dei Leoni, the present home of the Peggy Guggenheim Collection, were simply too grandiose for their patrons to sustain them, and were never completed. After the more dramatic Baroque facades of the seventeenth century, the re-paving of the Piazza San Marco in stone and marble (to replace the traditional brick) marks one symbolic 'civilizing' intervention, while the cool Neoclassical churches of Tommaso Temanza and others mark another.

The Republic's political and economic role in the world was becoming almost yearly more enfeebled; finally, the crumbling political edifice was summarily demolished by Napoleon Bonaparte in 1797 as, after a millennium of independence, the new world order finally reached the lagoons. From this time on, Venice's cultural destiny became ever more closely interlinked with that of the European mainland. The nineteenth-century saw many changes in the city's physical form and in its architectural development; these will be returned to in the final chapter.

3   **Constructing a City** | Materials, Craftsmen and Techniques

'... A beautiful and marvellous building material is the hard stone which is brought from Rovigno and Briani, a citadel on the Dalmatian coast. It is white in colour, and like marble, but sound and strong, of a kind that resists frost and sun for a long time ...' **Francesco Sansovino**, *Venetia, città nobilissima*, Venice 1581

Materials to build a city

Few cities have been built in a physical environment quite so comprehensively lacking in the basic materials of building construction as Venice. The lagoon has no building timber, no stone and no clay for brick-making. The islands of the lagoon, by their nature fragmented and isolated, are built on clay, and it was necessary to develop a range of sometimes highly ingenious solutions to the unique difficulties of the city's site. Fortunately, though, the all-enveloping waters offered two distinct advantages in Venice's development. One was that they provided unparalleled physical security, which in turn meant that the city's architecture could develop in a manner quite different to that on the Terraferma, where mass and security remained primary considerations. It was thus possible to develop an architecture based on a 'minimalist' approach to the question of mass and loads, which in turn minimized the difficulties in forming foundations. The other great advantage of the city's aquatic site was that the delivery of bulk building materials was rendered very much easier than it was in the case of a Terraferma city with inadequate water access, and reliant on muddy, potholed roads. Stone from Istria, bricks from the mainland, timber from the Friuli, all could be delivered in barges by water very much more easily than was possible by using the mainland road network.

The earliest houses built in the Venetian lagoons were of timber. They were simple, almost hut-like structures, with timber frames, pitched roofs and a covering of osier thatch from the margins of the lagoon. Slowly, though, as the city grew in size and substance, naturally more permanent materials were sought, and considerable effort and ingenuity was necessary, not solely in procuring the materials, but equally in the slow development of building techniques that were appropriate for the difficult terrain.[1]

Although in the lagoon there were no materials suitable for the construction of permanent buildings, during the Roman period there had developed on the adjacent Terraferma a flourishing brick-making industry, based on the fine clay with which the great eastern Po plain is particularly well supplied. Many Roman remains in the Venetian hinterland evince the extensive use of brick, and the earliest surviving post-Roman structures of the lagoons (such as the sixth-century baptistery at Grado) indicate that the skill had been early revived, if indeed it had ever been lost.

For some time after the collapse of the Western Roman Empire it had been possible to pillage the Roman cities of Aquileia, Altino and the rest for recycling building materials; Altino was a particularly convenient site since it is only a mile or two from Torcello. Reused Roman bricks are characterized by their small size and flat tile-like proportions, and can be seen in a number of early buildings in Venice. Indeed, brickwork proved to be the ideal permanent building material in such an environment. It is far less heavy than stone, and the small elements of which a brick wall is composed, together with the use of fairly soft mortar (always with a high proportion of lime) ensured that walls could withstand and accommodate a significant amount of structural movement and settlement.

Venice thus became an essentially brick-built city, as it is today, a fact that still often surprises those whose chief impression remains the imposing stone and marble facades of so many churches and palaces. Almost all of these facades are backed by stout walls of fairly soft orange-pink brick, and even in such august monuments as Palladio's churches of the Redentore and San Giorgio Maggiore, much of the fabric beyond the facade is clearly visible, unashamed brickwork.

THE BUILDING CRAFTS (above and right)

Two of a series of watercolours by Giovanni Grevembroch, showing the city's trades and guilds. Above: the terrazzo-layer, with the tools of his craft. Right: Two pile-drivers, using a heavy timber drop-hammer (*mazzuolo*) to drive the stakes. (Museo Civico Correr, Venice.)

For many centuries, therefore, bricks for the city were manufactured in brickfields around the nearby fort-town of Mestre, just across the lagoon on the Terraferma, which (although a mile or so inland) had been directly connected to the lagoon by the Canale Salso, cut through the margins of the lagoon in 1361. Barges could thus be laden at or near the kilns and brought directly to the site in the city, each barge typically carrying a load of 4–5,000 bricks. The almost universal 'Roman' roof tiles were produced in the same kilns, from the same clay. With such local, large-scale production, too, transport costs were minimized. On occasion, though, particularly in times of shortage, bricks were obtained from Treviso and even Ferrara, a source of high quality brick clay, and itself a quintessentially brick built city.[2]

Slowly, however, as the city grew in size, wealth and dignity, it became necessary to find a source of stone with which to decorate and give greater prestige to its chief monuments. For a time, again, the Roman cities of the Terraferma (particularly Altino) provided a rich quarry, especially of more specialized elements such as columns and capitals, which could be reused in a similar manner to their original function. But Altino was not inexhaustible, and Venice's extensive trading networks and colonial territories led to the importing of stone from many Eastern sources.

The closest and by far the most important source of building stone was Istria, the rocky peninsula directly across the Venetian Gulf, which had been confirmed as a Venetian possession by the Greek Emperor as early as 1085. Its extensive quarries stood directly on the coast, chiefly in the neighbourhoods of Rovigno (Rovinj), Brioni and Orsera (Vrsar), and over the centuries specially developed cargo vessels (marani) ferried great quantities of stone the short distance across the gulf back to the capital. Often mistaken for marble, Istrian stone is a fairly hard, durable white limestone, comparatively easy to work and suitable for a wide variety of uses. The best stone came from Rovigno, and was that generally used for fine sculpture or detailed carving, while that from further south (from the island of Brioni and near Pola) was more suitable for more mundane purposes, such as sills, gutters and simple door frames. With a range of qualities, therefore, Istrian stone became the stone of Venice, and the overwhelming majority of all the stone in the city today originated from this one shoreline. The Palazzo Ducale, the Salute church, the great Baroque palaces of Longhena, all are primarily constructed of (or faced with) this one material. Its bright colour is generally described as white, although it sometimes verges towards pink; its dramatic contrast with the soft orange-red bricks is perhaps the most characteristic and widespread combination of materials in the city.[3]

For prestigious buildings and for more specialized works such as funerary chapels and monuments, however, marble was used, although sparingly, from a very early date. Marble was brought into Venice from a wide range of sources, from both East and West. From the West, that is from the Italian mainland, a prodigious variety of marbles was available, although in practice most were imported from the Republic's Terraferma territories. The most widely used was the orange-red broccatello from Verona, again a Venetian city. Broccatello was often used to create a contrast with Istrian limestone, particularly in paving where it is frequently seen in a chessboard pattern on the floors of churches, such as the great Dominican church of Santi Giovanni e Paolo. Although hard and rather difficult to work, it was also sometimes used for more sculptural pieces, such as wellheads, and in funerary monuments.

Brescia on the western border of the Venetian Terraferma, was also an important producer of marble (as it remains today), notably of the fine white breccia aurora. Occasionally, too, the famous white Carrara marble was imported across the Apennines from Tuscany, particularly for important works of sculpture. In the later medieval period and into the Renaissance – and despite several ordinances from the Palazzo Ducale – marble was taken from the abandoned and decaying monasteries of the northern lagoon, particularly those around Torcello, since there was now little left to pillage from the Roman ruins of Altino and Aquileia. Both malaria and the silting of the canals had led to the dramatic decline of these previously wealthy, populous islands, and there was much material there for reuse; the famous nunnery church of San Zaccaria, rebuilt after 1456, was one of many new projects that incorporated recycled stone from these sources in the later fifteenth century.

Venice's extremely close links with Constantinople and its own colonies in the Aegean Sea provided another source of fine marble. Not only was the cultural and stylistic influence of Byzantium extremely strong, therefore, but some of the materials themselves, too, were imported into Venice: the famous Pentelicon marble from Greece can occasionally be identifed, as can that from Paros, one of the Cyclades islands. The rich green of verde antico was highly regarded for its colour and figuring, and was used (sparingly) on monuments, and on the rich facades of such characteristic early Renaissance buildings as Palazzo Dario and Santa Maria dei Miracoli.

Timber was the third essential building material and, like brick, was required in very large quantities by two important industries; building construction and the shipbuilding activities of the Arsenale. Both were almost insatiable devourers of timber throughout the later medieval and Renaissance eras. In the earliest centuries, the natural pinewoods of the sandy coastal littoral were exploited, but it soon became clear not only that their extent was very limited, but that they also served an essential ecological function in preventing coastal erosion. Thereafter, stocks were carefully conserved and, instead, building timber was obtained from two principal sources; the inland hills of Istria and the extensive upland forests of the northern Veneto and the Friuli, much of which territory again (after around 1400) lay within the lands of the Republic. From these last sources, great rafts of logs were guided down the Terraferma rivers, especially the Piave and Tagliamento, and these rafts were then floated through the lagoons to the city. Here they were brought ashore along the northern edge of the city, to the extensive timber-yards of the Barbaria delle Tole, where the rafts were broken up and sawn down into beams and planks. Later, after the Zattere was reclaimed in the early sixteenth century, such activities were transferred there.[4]

The species of timber generally used for the more durable and exposed elements of a new building were larch, fir and oak, and sometimes elm; the first was particularly important for piles and foundations, while oak was frequenty used for the large floor beams of palaces, and for roof trusses. The transport of timber was a substantial large-scale commercial activity, in which a number of noble families played a significant role.

Brick, stone and timber were thus the three primary building materials. But there were several other even more basic materials essential before work could begin on any building site: chief among these were sand, lime and water, all essential for making mortar and plaster. Lime was generally obtained from the hills near Padua and Treviso, and then fairly easily transported by boat down the rivers and canals to the lagoon; lime kilns were often found on the nearby Terraferma, around Mestre, where it was processed in conjunction with brick-making. Sand was not taken from the coastal littoral, because, like deforestation, this would have exacerbated erosion of the lidi; instead it was dredged from the lower courses of the mainland rivers, chiefly the Brenta, where its removal also assisted in deepening the channels and aided navigation.

The provision of water, the most fundamental commodity of all, frequently proved difficult. Despite the great proliferation of the city's cisterns, they were still unable to cope with the demand in times of drought, and the building industry required considerable quantities for making mortar. Doge Francesco Foscari had dug thirty large, new wells to ease a particularly acute shortage in 1425, but in emergencies fresh water had to be brought to the city by barge, again usually from the lower Brenta.[5]

ANTONIO AVERLINO (FILARETE) *DE ARCHITECTURA*, 1488–9

The title-page of Filarete's influential treatise on architecture, with details of contemporary building works in the lower corners. (Biblioteca Nazionale Marciana, Venice.)

STONEMASONS' STATUTES, 1517

The guild of stonemasons was founded in 1307. Their statutes were altered several times later; this is the title-page of the 1517 revision. (Biblioteca Civica Correr, Venice.)

Building technology in the lagoons

Venetian architecture has evolved a number of special responses to the exigencies of its unique environment, and certain basic practical principles can be identified in the way that Venice's architecture has evolved over the centuries. The difficult nature of the subsoil meant that it was necessary to minimize the load of a building on to the foundations, and this was achieved chiefly by building in brick and timber. Only later did the use of large quantities of stone become widespread; very few palaces, for example, had facades all of stone until the sixteenth century.[6]

The second principle was to ensure that the design of the building incorporated flexibility, so that if settlement did take place, it could do so without endangering the basic stability of the structure as a whole. To this end, for example, brick walls were always built with soft-lime mortar, and timber was universal for the upper floors of houses.

Thirdly, it was necessary to distribute loads as evenly as possible, to avoid high localized stresses that might lead to uneven settlement; thus, for example, we find the large, closely-spaced floor beams that are so typical of the Venetian palace. These beams were themselves supported on continuous wall plates, beams set into the wall so that their load was spread evenly over the wall's entire length.

Although many historic buildings in Venice show considerable evidence of cracking and settlement, this rarely results in serious instability. A number of severe earthquakes over the centuries have resulted in comparatively little damage, certainly far less than would have arisen in a city with more rigid forms of construction. The severe earthquake in the Friuli in 1968, for example, produced only minimal damage in the city, as a result of the inherently absorbent nature of both the buildings and their foundations.

Nevertheless, certain forms of construction always remained problematic, and to some extent risky, in the environment of the lagoon. The construction of palaces gave little difficulty, but much more challenging were the requirements of large churches. Vaults and domes posed specific problems, since they rely on an essentially rigid system of supports for their integrity, and uneven settlement could easily result in high stresses and perhaps in collapse. Domes therefore remain comparatively rare in Venice, and (with a few notable exceptions) are usually quite small. Even those of San Marco are of modest diameter, as are the early Renaissance domes of San Giobbe and Santa Maria Formosa. The extraordinary feat of Brunelleschi's great dome at Florence cathedral, for example, spanning 40 metres (140 feet), would have been quite impossible to achieve in Venice without the most elaborate of precautions and secondary restraints. It was only in the mid seventeenth century, with Longhena's great dome for Santa Maria della Salute, that Venice was able to boast a dome of the same degree of magnitude as that of early fifteenth-century Florence. Even here, its span of around 18 metres (60 feet) is still considerably less than Brunelleschi's masterpiece.

The vaulting of the naves of churches gave rise to similar difficulties; many of the earliest basilical churches of the lagoons had open timber truss roofs, a prudent and suitable form of construction in this environment; but in the Gothic period, after around 1300, churches began to be vaulted. There are some imposing examples in Venice, including those of the two great monastic churches of the Frari and Santi Giovanni e Paolo, but here, too, prudence intervened and dictated the incorporation of stout timber tie-beams across the nave, directly above the main column capitals and again at a higher level, at the springing of the vaults. The ties were a form of structural insurance, should there develop uneven settlement of one of the great nave columns. There are very few vaults elsewhere in the city; most of the great halls, such as those in the Palazzo Ducale and the Scuole Grandi, have flat ceilings of timber, often elaborately coffered and richly decorated.

But perhaps the most striking example of the special difficulties of building in such an environment arose in the case of church bell towers, campanili. Venetian campanili, like those

BUILDING THE TOWER OF BABEL (above)

Detail of a mosaic from the atrium of San Marco. The 13th century mosaic depicts contemporary construction techniques.

VITTORE CARPACCIO, *Miracle of the True Cross*, 1494 (left)

The timber roof terraces and forests of chimneys at the Rialto were characteristic features of the city's skyline. Few of the latter survive unaltered today. (Gallerie dell' Accademia, Venice.)

elsewhere in Italy, were traditionally freestanding, adjacent to the church but detached from it. Here it was impossible to avoid highly concentrated loads on top of the foundations, and the difficulties of providing a solid, even base led to widespread problems of settlement over the centuries. Many towers have collapsed, some have been rebuilt on more than one occasion, and today several of them graphically illustrate the structural challenge that they present by their dramatic inclination from the vertical. The towers of Santo Stefano and San Giorgio dei Greci are among the more remarkable examples, as is that of San Martino at Burano, all three apparently defying the laws of statics. The great tower of San Marco itself, having stood for a millennium, finally succumbed to the ravages of time and structural deterioration on 14 July 1902 when, without warning, it collapsed into a great pyramid of rubble, narrowly missing the facade of San Marco itself. It was faithfully reconstructed, however, to its original form (but with new foundations), and was completed on St Mark's Day ten years later.

Venetian architecture thus developed a number of characteristic features in order to minimize the dangers that arose from building in such a context. The first and literally most fundamental difficulty was naturally the design of adequate footings. The Venetian islands are themselves fairly firm, but they rise only slightly above the level of the highest normal tides, and they are (and always have been) flooded from time to time by exceptional tides. Needless to say, the topsoil is incapable of supporting a considerable load, but building in such inpropitious surroundings is made possible by a layer of firm clay, known as the *caranto*, from three to five metres (ten to fifteen feet) down, and it is this stratum that makes possible the construction of most of the city's important buildings.[7]

Foundations were originally fairly simple, and took the form of a raft of timber planks, buried in the clay, known as a *zattaron*, and from which the walls were directly built. Such a raft, however, was too shallow to be directly supported by the firm layer of caranto further down, and it effectively 'floated' on the upper layer of softer clay. More complex foundations were necessary for larger, heavier structures, and so a system of timber piling was developed; after about the fourteenth century (and probably earlier) all substantial buildings were supported on forests of such piles, millions of which were required over the succeeding centuries. Most were of larch or oak, both extremely durable timbers, and were pointed at the end to assist driving them into the clay. This was traditionally carried out by two men using a heavy wooden drop hammer, the *mazzuolo*, and chanting to maintain a rhythm of blows. These piles (known as *tolpi* in Venetian) remain preserved almost indefinitely provided they are not exposed to the atmosphere; when the piles supporting the facade of the Palazzo Ducale were comprehensively examined in 1874, they were still perfectly sound after 530 years of service, and remain so today. Since piling was an expensive, labour-intensive operation, piles were frequently reused in the successive rebuilding of structures on the same site: at the Cà d'Oro, for example, Marin Contarini's reuse of most of the piles of the earlier palace determined to a large extent the essentially asymmetrical configuration of the new palace; in the same period, the Santa Maria della Carità also made use of the foundations of the earlier church.

The piles were usually driven in rows, two or three abreast, under major structural walls, and were typically from ten to fifteen feet long. On top of them was constructed a thick timber decking or raft, from which the main walls of the building rose. The lowermost part of these walls was usually formed of large, squared, coursed blocks of Istrian stone, which formed a strip foundation, and also acted as a damp-course, preventing water from rising into the brickwork above. Only in rare examples are these principal walls themselves built entirely of stone; the Palazzo dei Prigioni, the Republic's prison next to the Palazzo Ducale, offers one of the few examples, but the majority of the walls of palaces, for example, are of brick with a comparatively thin 'veneer' of stonework.[8]

The type of finish to the ground floor varied considerably, and depended on the nature of the building: from simple beaten earth in the humblest cottages to brick paving in larger houses, and to marble and stone in the most prestigious churches and palaces. Brick paving was widespread, and only with the great wealth of the sixteenth century can we trace the introduction of stone floors. Walls of brick were always bedded in a soft sand-lime mortar, and to minimize the load onto the foundations, the walls generally decreased in thickness towards the top of the building. A substantial palace, for example, would have walls two bricks thick on the ground floor, but narrowing to only one brick in thickness on the top floor.

The upper floors and the roofs of almost all Venetian buildings are of timber, again generally larch or oak. Typical floors consisted of large, parallel, squared beams, set very closely together. If the spans were particularly great, for example in the great halls of the Palazzo Ducale, then the floor beams were sometimes supported on timber brackets known as *barbacani*. These brackets were either built out from the side walls or stood on a row of columns, in both cases reducing the effective span of the beams themselves. Barbacani were often carved into complex decorative shapes.

The most typical form of Venetian ceiling consisted of the exposed underside of these closely spaced beams, which were then painted and decorated. Sometimes a more elaborate version can be seen, in which smaller transverse timbers are fixed between the main beams to form a square, coffered pattern, which again was usually decorated. This form became known as the 'Sansovino' ceiling since it was developed by Jacopo Sansovino in the sixteenth century, sometimes with very rich, elaborate decoration and gilding. The most opulent ceilings of all were those in the halls of state in the Palazzo Ducale and the great chapter halls of the Scuole Grandi, where, in the later sixteenth century, there was developed a complex, early Baroque style with deep coffering and large, elaborate scrollwork, usually with paintings set inside carved, gilded frames.[9]

The ceilings or roofs to churches had rather different forms, with considerable variation. Other than the vaulting discussed above, many churches retained an open timber truss roof which, again, like the open timber ceiling, was painted and decorated. A few, though, have more complex soffits in the form known as a 'ship's keel', from their resemblance to the inverted hull of a sailing ship, and which perhaps derived from shipbuilding techniques. Santo Stefano retains a particularly fine roof of this type.

The upper floors of the Venetian palace were traditionally finished with timber boarding, on which terrazzo was laid. This is a characteristic Venetian technique, many centuries old, and which was formed from a 'paste' of lime mortar, containing large quantities of chippings of marble or Istrian stone. This was laid and compacted by the specialized craft of terrazzo-layers, who then polished the surface with linseed oil to obtain a high lustre. Sometimes, too, decorative patterns or borders of marble were worked into the surface. The resulting floor was extremely attractive and durable, but was also very heavy. This frequently led to the deformation of the beams below it, although since the terrazzo contained a high proportion of lime, it remained flexible and cracked comparatively rarely.[10]

Venetian roofs are again all built of timber, with traditional trusses supporting a covering of interleaved 'Roman' clay tiles. Roofs always have a fairly steep pitch, since Venice has a comparatively high (and often exceptionally heavy) rainfall, and the city's lack of fresh water meant that run-off from roofs was carefully gathered for reuse. Rainwater was therefore collected in stone gutters, descending in large pipes built into the walls, and was then fed by drains into the underground cisterns that occupied almost every campo in the city; larger houses, too, had their own cistern, standing in the centre of the courtyard.[11]

WINDOW-MAKERS (below)

An engraving by Gaetano Zompini, one of a collection published in 1753 as *Le arti che vanno per via* ('the street trades of the city').

WALL CONSTRUCTION (right)

From Andrea Palladio's *Quattro libri dell' architettura*, 1570 (Book One, p13): the page illustrates three different wall-building techniques.

Remoto lastre, e veri a chi me chiama,
Comodo le fenestre, e pò a botega,
Ghe le fazzo da niovo a chi le brama.
50

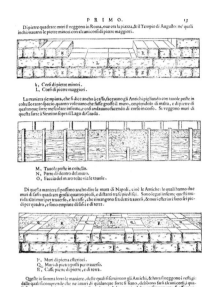

The fundamental principle of minimizing the loads of a building, together with the essentially framed construction of the Venetian palace, and the security of the city's site, gave rise to the use of extensive glazing, particularly in the later medieval palaces. In this characteristic aspect of Venetian architecture, the city was able to exploit fully the one building material that was produced within the lagoon: glass. The numerous furnaces of Murano produced window glass not only in extremely large quantities, but also very cheaply so that, as Francesco Sansovino proudly recorded in his guide to the city, *Venetia città nobilissima et singolare*, in 1580, every Venetian (except, probably, the extremely poor) could afford to have his house fully glazed, at a time when window glass was still considered a luxury in all the other great cities of Europe.

A number of features of building construction in the city are a direct reflection of the acute shortage of land, and the need to maximize available space. The roof-terrace or *altana* is a particularly prevalent feature; it was usually approached by a dormer in the roof, and was constructed on brick columns built directly off the main walls below. It was constructed entirely of timber, to minimize its load, and many dozens of examples survive, particularly in the innermost parts of the city.

Particularly Venetian, too, was the development of a specific design for chimneys. The risk of fire in Venice was always extremely high, and the city's history is scarred by numerous conflagrations over the centuries. The unique form of the Venetian chimney took the shape of an inverted cone or pyramid, and incorporated a cinder trap to reduce the risk of fire from flying embers. Comparatively few survive today, although in the fifteenth and sixteenth centuries they were almost universal, and the paintings of Vittore Carpaccio and others show veritable forests of these characteristic forms.[12]

Extremely high densities of development led to the use of other devices to increase valuable space within houses. One was the use of oversailing jetties for the upper stories, similar to the timber jetties seen in late medieval houses in England, Germany and France. Like the brackets that support beamed floors, these jetties are also known as barbacani, and again they are most prevalent in the innermost quarters, particularly around the Rialto and San Marco. Further, more substantial gains in space were achieved by building accommodation on colonnades above a public street, producing a covered way known as a *sottoportego*. The department of the Piovego exerted fairly stringent controls over this form of development, though, and an open public right of way always had to be maintained below the new building.[13]

The facades of the majority of Venetian buildings are constructed of brick. Bricks are soft, and so to protect them from the weather, the walls were often finished with a render, traditionally formed with brick dust mixed with lime mortar, to produce a pinkish-red surface, which again contrasts strongly with the white stonework. Many palace facades were once decorated with frescos, although the salty air of the lagoon has led to the loss of almost all but a few faded fragments. The great Fondaco dei Tedeschi, the German trade centre at Rialto, for example, was once decorated with frescos by Titian and Giorgione, but only a few isolated fragments survive, now kept in the Accademia galleries.[14]

Craftsmen and guilds: masons, builders, carpenters; the proto and the architect

Just as there were three fundamental building materials with which the city was constructed – brick, stone and timber – so, too, there were three principal guilds whose members transformed these materials into the city's churches, palaces and warehouses: the stonemasons (in Venetian dialect *taiapiera*), the builders (*muratori* or *mureri*) and the carpenters (*marangoni*). The last were sometimes distinguished as marangoni da casa, rather than the marangoni da nave, the shipwrights of the Arsenale. All three crafts were incorporated into Venice's guild system at an early date; the carpenters and builders were both registered in 1271 and the stonemasons a little later, in 1307.

As well as these three 'primary' guilds, there were several lesser crafts whose members provided ancillary functions and skills necessary for the completion of any sizable building project. They included glaziers and window-makers; smiths to provide ironwork, nails, hinges and other fittings for doors and windows; painters to decorate walls and ceilings; and terrazzo layers, representatives of a typically Venetian speciality.

All the city's many dozen trade guilds were registered with (and subject to the authority of) the government agency known as the Giustizia Vecchia, which was also responsible for many other regulatory roles, such as weights and measures. The Giustizia Vecchia maintained records of the guilds' statutes or articles of association (*mariegole*), and had to approve any amendment or variations to them.[15] It also ensured that certain universal principles applicable to all guilds were enforced; these included such matters as ensuring that no guild members worked on feast days or, of course, on a Sunday.[16]

The members of all of these guilds were bound not only by the guild system in general, but also by the specific rules of their own individual guild. They were known in Venice as *arti*, and they served two rather different, though complementary and interwoven functions. On the practical level, the guilds' statutes determined their organization, the methods, standards and duration of the training of apprentices, the nature and quality of materials that the members were permitted to use, and other similar matters. Fines could be levied for breaches of the statutes, while regular income was raised by charging membership fees and raising special levies for the guilds' annual festival. As well as these duties, concerned with the maintenance of professional standards, the members had a number of rights, reflecting the other function of the guild, a quasi-religious Christian brotherhood, responsible for the spiritual welfare of its members.

In the large number of building projects of average size and complexity, the chief master responsible for building the basic fabric was the *murer*, literally the 'wall-builder', but more accurately described as the general contractor. He would coordinate the activities of all the lesser crafts, but had to work particularly closely with the *marangono*, the carpenter responsible for building floors and the roof. The builder himself organized scaffolding and erected the basic 'shell' of a building, including its walls, and executed most of the finishing trades such as plastering and the laying of brick flooring. Many building projects, particularly simple terraces of housing or charitable almshouses, required only a small amount of stone, chiefly for door and window frames, cornices and gutters. The builder could not carve these himself, but he would 'buy them in' from a mason, and fix them in place.

On larger, more prestigious projects such as a palace or an important church, the quantity of stone was considerably higher, and the mason naturally played a more prominent part in the building process. Nevertheless, even a fairly large project, such as the reconstruction of the Carità church in the 1440s, was primarily a brick construction; the stonemason in this case was the outstanding local master Bartolomeo Bon. Even here, though, he had no general responsibility for the basic fabric, but simply supplied a large quantity of stone (windows, portals, capitals, the pinnacles for the facade) from his yard at San Marziale, for fixing in place by the master builder.[17] Indeed, the career of Bon, outstanding though it was, marks, in a sense, the end of the *ancien régime* in terms of the organization of the building process. Despite his prestigious output, which included the Porta della Carta and the portals of Santi Giovanni e Paolo and the Madonna dell'Orto, Bon remained a master mason, in charge of a flourishing shop, but never in complete charge of a major building project.

Only on the very largest and most generously funded projects do we find a more complex hierarchical system of organizing the building process. Such projects were almost always institutional in character and were sponsored by the Republic itself, by the Procurators of San

SCHOOL OF PIETRO LONGHI, *The Blacksmith's Shop*, mid-18th century (above)

Such workshops were scattered over all parts of the city, but there was a concentration in the centre, in the street still known today as Calle dei Fabbri (smiths). (Museo del Settecento, Venice.)

CANALETTO, *The Stonemason's Yard*, c.1720 (right)

The yard is on site during the construction of the church of San Vidal; masons' yards had hardly changed since the building of Santa Maria della Carità (in the background), 300 years earlier. (National Gallery, London.)

Marco, by a wealthy monastic house, or by one of the Scuole Grandi, the great charitable confraternities. In such cases, in the later fifteenth century, we find the introduction of a man known as the *protomaestro* (literally 'chief master'), usually abbreviated to *proto*. He was a permanent salaried master who had overall responsibility for coordinating all of the building crafts, including the masons, builders and carpenters. He was often, though not necessarily, the chief designer or architect of the building as well, and thus corresponds to the role in England of 'chief surveyor of the fabric'. The Republic itself was almost certainly the first body to employ men on this basis, and the most important proti were those employed by the Procurators of San Marco, the senior nobles who administered the shrine and the Republic's other buildings around the Piazza. The procurators were responsible for the maintenance and occasional restoration or reconstruction of a substantial estate of buildings; it is not surprising, therefore, to find this office the first to employ a master of this nature. The Provveditori al Sal, the Salt Commissioners, also employed a proto on a regular basis. By the later fifteenth century, the Provveditori had become effectively the Republic's executive agency for major public works projects, and decrees promulgated by the Senate or the Council of Ten were delegated to them to fund and supervise. Later, when the large-scale rebuilding of the east wing of the Palazzo Ducale was begun after the 1483 fire, the chief mason at the palace was promoted to the status of proto, recognizing the importance of the task.

THE STONEMASON AT WORK

Detail of one of the capitals on the Palazzo Ducale, copy of a late 14th century sculpture.

With the increasing richness and complexity of some of the new Renaissance buildings in the later fifteenth century, too, other bodies began to employ proti, such as the nunnery of San Zaccaria in the 1450s, whose church was reconstructed on an ambitious and elaborate scale. In such projects the institution itself generally established a board or *banca* to monitor progress and disburse funds; sometimes, too, like the Scuola di San Marco, they appointed their own commissioner or provveditore to direct the works and to instruct their proto. It is revealing to note the contrast between San Zaccaria and the only slightly earlier rebuilding of the Carità church (itself still largely of brick), which had been executed in the traditional manner by a master builder. At San Zaccaria, Antonio Gambello was appointed as a permanent, salaried proto on a project that was clearly to take many years to complete. According to the accounts of the project, in 1458 he also had to produce a wooden model of his proposals for the nunnery's approval, perhaps the earliest record of an architectural model in the Venetian archives, and an equally clear indication that he was the architect as well as the chief master responsible for its construction. After Gambello's death, the nunnery appointed Mauro Codussi (on almost the same terms) to complete the works.

The ambitious reconstruction of the Scuola di San Marco in the 1480s also bridges this transitional period in its site organization. Pietro Lombardo was initially employed here purely as a master mason, alongside Griguol, the chief master builder, but when Lombardo was abruptly dismissed and replaced by Mauro Codussi in 1490, Codussi was again given the role (and benefits) of the proto, clearly – in this instance – in an attempt to rationalize and provide better control over the building process. As at San Zaccaria, he again took on the difficult task of completing a project already designed by another, which was already well advanced on site.

Many of Venice's most outstanding Renaissance architects were employed on this basis at some time in their careers; Antonio Rizzo, for example, was proto at the Palazzo Ducale in the 1480s, while Giorgio Spavento was proto at San Marco in the 1490s and early 1500s. The role of proto in the service of one of the departments of government, however, was no guarantee of a significant architectural career. The first few proti in the service of the Procurators, for example, were all fairly obscure figures, and it was only on the occasions when a proto's career coincided with a government decision to embark on major building works that there was the opportunity for personal advancement and for association with a major new work of architecture. The most remarkable record of service in such a role was that of Jacopo Sansovino, who was in the service of

THE SCUOLA DEI TAIAPIERA

Detail from the facade of the stonemasons'
guildhall, showing the four patron saints.

the Procurators for no less than forty-one years; he was appointed only two years after his arrival in Venice in 1527, and remained in his post until his death in 1570. In all such cases, however, the proto had the security of a regular monthly salary, and was usually given free lodgings by his employer. The latter, of course, had the advantage of knowing that their project was under permanent, regular supervision by a master who had the most intimate knowledge of the project.[18]

In retrospect we can identify the latter part of the quattrocento as the decisive period in which this figure emerged more and more clearly as the one man with overall responsibility for the entire building process: as the chief designer, producing drawings (and sometimes models); ordering all of the necessary materials; coordinating all trades on site, and (in almost every case) also taking the role of chief master mason.

In this role he therefore becomes what we now understand to be the architect. The pivotal figure in this process is undoubtedly Mauro Codussi, whose first revolutionary work in Venice, San Michele in Isola, was the result of the appreciation of his exceptional skills as a designer by his illustrious intellectual patrons; among them the Abbot Maffeo Girardo, who was later Patriarch, and such outstanding humanist scholars as Pietro Donà, Pietro Dolfin and Andrea and Lorenzo Loredan. All of these men patronized Codussi's career, some of them on several occasions; Pietro Donà, for example, and Lorenzo Loredan both furthered his development later by sponsoring him at San Zaccaria. Donà was again one of Codussi's patrons at Santa Maria Formosa, while Andrea Loredan commissioned one of his last and greatest works, Palazzo Loredan (later Vendramin-Calergi) on the Grand Canal. Throughout Codussi's life, therefore, we can identify a network of patronage, of commissions specifically given, not to a master mason, or even a proto, but to an architect known for his skills in design, as well as his accepted skills in construction. In this respect Codussi is the precise forerunner of Andrea Palladio, and in Venice at least, was unique in his time.

Several decades after Mauro's death, Palladio's earlier career in Vicenza echoes Codussi's closely. Like Mauro, he was taken under the wing of a wealthy and influential local noble, Count Gian-Giorgio Trissino, who (again rather like Girardo at San Michele) aspired to the practice of architecture himself, and became his mentor. Palladio later developed a similar network of noble patrons in Vicenza, among them the Thiene and Valmarana. Later, of course, his patronage spread further to include the Venetian nobility, among them the Corner, Pisani and Foscari, and, most importantly of all, Daniele and his brother Marc-Antonio Barbaro, who were particularly closely involved with architectural patronage.

Part II | the nuclei of the city

'Between those pillars (at the end of the Piazza) there opens a great light, and, in the midst of it, as we advance slowly, the vast tower of St Mark seems to lift itself up visibly forth from the level field of chequered stones; and, on each side, the countless arches prolong themselves into ranged symmetry, as if the rugged and irregular houses that pressed together above the dark alley had been struck back into sudden obedience and lovely order …' **John Ruskin**, *The Stones of Venice*, 1851–3.

The nucleus of power: Church and Palace

The Piazza San Marco is the heart of Venice, and was for centuries the symbol of the Republic's wealth and stability. Every important event in the Serenissima's thousand-year history was celebrated (or mourned) here, from ducal coronations to state funerals, from great naval victories to the rituals of the Christian calendar and the festivals of the patron saint. Concentrated at San Marco were the national shrine, the seat of power of the Empire and the official residence of the head of state, the doge.

The development of the Piazza over several centuries was a direct reflection of the evolution of the Republic itself, of its institutions, its self-image, its administration. From the first strategic choice of site, the Piazza and its buildings have combined the functions of a national pilgrimage site with the seats of government and justice. The widely differing architectural styles of the buildings by which the Piazza and the adjacent Piazzetta are surrounded reflect the stage-by-stage evolution of the Republic's development; so too do the spaces themselves. These two great squares reflect a long process of refinement of the image and function of the state.[1]

The choice of the location for the earliest ducal castle, and that of the chapel dedicated to the Republic's first patron, was essentially strategic. The islet was fairly large and firm, and it faced the deep body of water that became known as the Bacino or Basin of San Marco, a safe, and very extensive anchorage for shipping. Towards the east, the *Bacino* was continued by a deep channel that led through the Porto di Lido to the Adriatic Sea, while to the west lay the opening of the Grand Canal and the broad Canale della Giudecca.

The first ducal castle overlooked this basin of water; it was probably fortified by towers at the corners, and was flanked on one side by a small inlet of water (a *cavanna*) that provided a sheltered dock for small ships. At the back of the inlet was the chapel dedicated to San Todaro, the first patron, while nearby stood its freestanding bell tower. Although we know nothing of the appearance of this first 'palace', it already contained several functions within one building or group of buildings: the residence of the doge; halls for magistracies and accommodation for prisons; a large assembly hall for the nobility; and facilities for military defence – armouries, stables and guardhouses. All of these varied functions were to be retained in its later reconstructions.

An open space or *campo* spread out in front of the patronal chapel, which was bound on the far side by a narrow canal, the Rio di Batario; beyond the canal was an orchard owned by the wealthy and ancient nunnery of San Zaccaria. Next to this orchard was another small church, one of the earliest parochial foundations, dedicated to San Gemignano which had been established, according to tradition, in the sixth century. The embryonic form of what were to become the Piazza and Piazzetta was already established, although the latter square had not yet been reclaimed from the lagoon. The two spaces formed an inverted 'L', with the church bell tower forming a 'hinge' at the angle, the shorter arm being the future Piazzetta and the longer one the Piazza itself. This was the fundamental configuration of the city's heart that was to be slowly refined over the following centuries.[2]

PROCURATIE VECCHIE

Detail of the repetitive rhythms of the windows of the Procuracy, begun by Bartolommeo Bon in c.1517.

In 829, the Greek patron Todaro was joined by the new patron saint, Mark the Evangelist, and work began almost immediately on a larger, more fitting shrine to house his body. Despite his much greater prestige, Mark's role in relation to the emergent Republic remained the same: his shrine was to be the ducal chapel, and the system that evolved to administer this shrine was to be quite distinct from the Church hierarchy and the bishopric based at San Pietro in Castello. San Marco was to be in the charge of a primate (*primicerio*), nominated directly by the doge; affiliated to the primate were the Procurators of San Marco, who administered the chapel and the adjacent properties on the Piazza. The primate himself was to be housed north of the chapel, on the site of the present Palazzo Patriarcale.

The church of San Todaro was joined firstly by a small new chapel dedicated to San Marco, which was rebuilt after serious damage by fire in 976. Finally, though, in around 1060 the definitive form of the new shrine was begun, and the basic structure of this church is that which survives today. It was considerably larger than its predecessor; although of fairly imposing size, the church was all of brickwork, and was initially very simple, even severe in appearance. It was separated from the castle by a narrow canal, where the later Porta della Carta was to rise, and which joined the Rio di Palazzo so that the castle was surrounded by a natural 'moat' on all four sides.[3]

Doge Ziani's transformations

The seat of government remained in this condition until a pivotally important series of works was begun by Doge Sebastiano Ziani in the 1170s. In 1172 the extremely wealthy and influential Ziani initiated a fundamental reorganization of the spaces at the hub of what was now a great, populous city; arguably the most important was the extension of the length of the Piazza by filling in the Rio di Batario, and the acquisition of the orchard that lay beyond it. San Gemignano was demolished and rebuilt further west, so that it now faced San Marco at the far end of what was now a great rectangular square some six hundred feet in length, more than twice its earlier size. In this dramatic way Ziani defined the overall length of the Piazza that has remained to this day.

The northern side of this imposing square was then occupied by a long block of colonnaded buildings that housed the Procurators of San Marco, the officials in charge of the shrine. The Procuratie were built in a characteristic Venetian-Byzantine style, with a long colonnade on the ground floor and apartments and offices for the Procurators on the first floor; they were to survive in this form for more than three centuries.

Doge Ziani's works at the Palazzo Ducale were equally revolutionary, and can be characterized as the transformation of what was still a rather random collection of fortified structures, a *castrum*, into a *palatium*; that is, their residual defensive functions were removed, and the buildings, now rationalized into three wings, were redesigned in much the same manner as the contemporary private palaces along the Grand Canal, with spacious ground-floor colonnades or *logge* and the principal accommodation on the first floor.[4] The building on the waterfront was to contain the meeting halls for the nobility, chiefly that of the newly-defined Maggior Consiglio, while the wing facing west was to contain the Palace of Justice; to the east, along the Rio di Palazzo, were the ducal apartments and other facilities, including prisons and stables.

To further enhance the dignity of this hub of power, Ziani effected another work of great significance to the Palazzo Ducale. The inlet of water next to the palace was now reclaimed to form a second square, the Piazzetta of San Marco, and a broad quay, the Molo, was reclaimed in front of the Palazzo to provide a more fitting approach to the city from the Bacino. And finally, to add still further prestige to this approach, Ziani erected the two great monolithic columns of granite, which still stand today, to form a symbolic gateway into the city. (According to legend, there was also a third column, that fell into the water and was never recovered.) They were crowned by figures representing the Republic's two patrons, the Greek Todaro and the winged lion of San Marco.

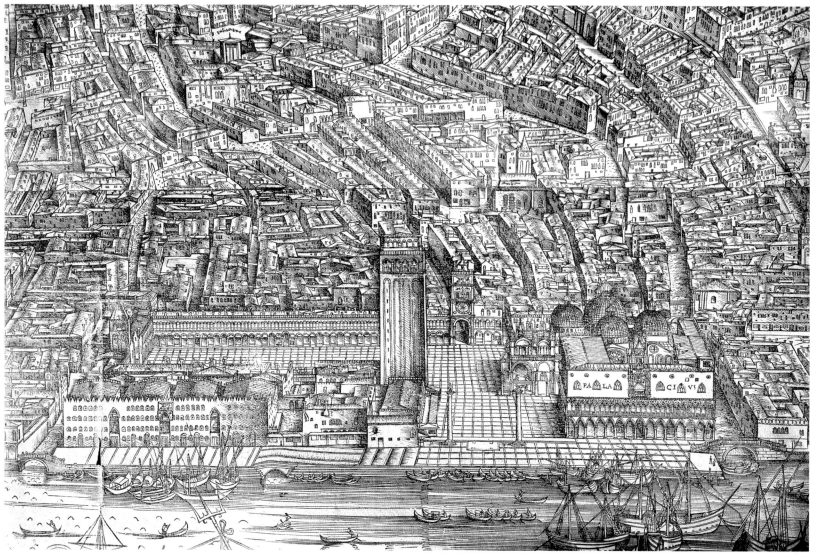

SAN MARCO IN 1500 (above)

Detail from Jacopo de'Barbari's view of the city; the church and Palazzo Ducale remain almost unchanged today. The Torre dell'Orologio, just right of the campanile, had only just been completed. In the left foreground are the great state grain warehouses, demolished by Napoleon.

PLAN OF PIAZZA SAN MARCO AND SURROUNDING BUILDINGS IN 1853

The west end is now occupied by the Ala Napoleonica, and the granaries replaced by the Giardinetti Reali, the public gardens.

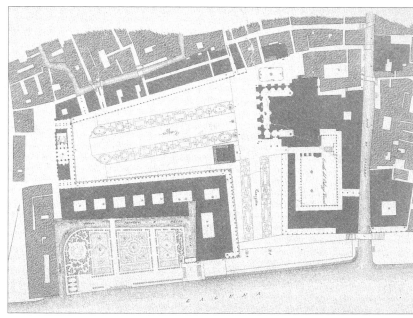

SAN MARCO IN 1486

Detail of Erhard Reuwich's panorama of the city; the Piazzetta is still occupied by an accretion of shops, inns and market stalls.

Todaro stands on top of a dragon or crocodile, since he is traditionally associated (like St George) with the slaying of such a creature; the famous lion of San Marco, on the other hand, is in fact an ancient bronze oriental chimera of unknown date and imprecise origin, to which wings were added by Ziani to form the definitive symbol of the Republic of St Mark.[5]

The reclamation of the inlet removed the element of water from any direct contact with the church and the Piazza, which was henceforth effectively landlocked. However, it also created an important new public space, the Piazzetta, which was developed with a rather different, though complementary role, to that of the Piazza itself. The primary purpose of the Piazza was to provide a setting for the pilgrimage shrine of San Marco, whose importance was thus enhanced, its setting dignified. Ziani's great achievement in extending the length of the Piazza was that the church's facade could now be seen in its entirety from some distance, and a great public space for ceremonies and processions was thereby created. In contrast the Piazzetta became an essentially civic, political space. With the Molo as the symbolic point of arrival in the city, and the palace of government on one side, it was the logical place to receive important foreign visitors, and for embarking and disembarking: hence the symbolic importance of the twin columns and their proud announcement of the Republic's patron saints.

Naturally, there was a close correlation between the Piazza and the Piazzetta; the two spaces were mutually complementary. The approach to the shrine by water could now only be made by landing at the Molo, passing the patrons on their columns and approaching the flank wall of the church. Nevertheless, the later history of the Piazzetta confirms, with increasing clarity, its role as the square of the Republic, while the Piazza remained the square of the ducal shrine.

At the south-east corner of the Piazza stood the Campanile of San Marco. The first bell tower had been built in the ninth century, but it had been restored, enlarged and repaired on numerous occasions. In appearance it resembled many other campanili in the Dogado, particularly the surviving eleventh-century tower at Torcello, although, fittingly, it is more massive than any of them. With the Piazzetta now reclaimed, its function as a visual 'hinge' between the two spaces had become much clearer, and it too was restored by Ziani. But it was still attached to other buildings on two faces; to the west stood the Ospizio Orseolo, a famous hostel for pilgrims en route to the Holy Land, which survived until the sixteenth century – it can be seen on Gentile Bellini's great painting, *Miracle of the Holy Cross in the Piazza San Marco* of 1496. However, down the west side of the newly reclaimed Piazzetta, there accumulated a miscellaneous accretion of shops, inns and market stalls, providing useful facilities for both citizens and pilgrims, but detracting from the emergent dignity of the heart of the city. It seems certain that, just as San Marco itself took several decades to construct, so also the ambitious programme of civic improvements begun by Doge Ziani must have taken a considerable time to complete, certainly longer than his own brief six-year reign.[6]

The Piazza and Piazzetta remained in this new form for more than three centuries. During much of this period the long, staged reconstruction of the Palazzo Ducale continued, begun in 1340, but not concluded until more than a hundred years later. This rebuilding is discussed in more detail in Chapter 8, but it commenced with the reconstruction of the Molo wing, followed in turn by that of the second wing, with its facade on to the Piazzetta, and finally by the new state entrance, the Porta della Carta, in the 1440s. The great mass of the new Palazzo served to define the Piazzetta and the Molo and dominated the whole of this side of the Bacino. The style of the Palazzo, too, represented an affirmation of Venetian culture and civilization in this period of great wealth and power. It epitomizes the later Venetian Gothic, with its two storeys of stone colonnades surmounted by the great volume of the hall of the Maggior Consiglio, the Great Council that formed the heart of government.

The last stage of this programme, the richly carved Porta della Carta, symbolically and physically united the Palazzo and San Marco, while at the same time finally providing the seat of government with a formal state entrance. It remained the only official approach to the Palazzo and was therefore imbued with great symbolic and iconographic importance.

The Renaissance: Jacopo Sansovino's interventions

In the 1490s there began a further stage in the enhancement of the image of the Piazza as the heart of the Republic. By now Renaissance theories of urban improvement were beginning to affect the government's philosophies towards the fabric of the capital, and the first of these late-fifteenth-century works was the new Clock Tower, the Torre dell'Orologio, the design of which is usually attributed to Mauro Codussi. The Torre is a distinctly triumphant element in the fabric of the Piazza, marking the point at which the Merceria, the chief commercial street linking San Marco with the banks and markets of the Rialto, enters the great square. The arch and tower above it formed important new landmarks, and the role of the Torre in the developing sophistication of the Piazza's spatial relationships is considerable. It terminates the vista from any approach to the Molo by water, creating a rich backdrop to the urban composition.[7]

Shortly after the completion of the Torre in the 1490s, in 1512 a fire damaged the Old Procuracy building that still occupied almost all of the north side of the Piazza. It was reconstructed in a manner very similar to the old Byzantine structure, although with a second storey above the first. Like its predecessor, its ground floor was characterized by a continuous colonnade, and the additional storey not only provided much more spacious accommodation, but gave the Piazza a considerably stronger sense of dignity and enclosure.

The minor, but significant contribution made by the three tall bronze standards in front of the basilica formed part of this same phase of urban improvements. They may have been planned by Codussi in conjunction with the Torre dell'Orologio, and they were cast in bronze by Alessandro Leopardi in 1505. The standards were carefully located to frame the axis from the Molo towards the Clock Tower, and the great banners of San Marco that proudly flew from them added a colourful and powerfully patriotic element to the urban ensemble.

By the early 1520s, therefore, the northern side of the Piazza had been reconstructed in the new Renaissance style, and a new sense of civic dignity was beginning to be imposed on the heart of the Republic. At the end of the decade, though, there began the most radical reordering of the Piazza since that of Doge Ziani, nearly four centuries earlier. The appointment of Jacopo Sansovino as *proto* to the Procurators of San Marco in 1529 was to lead to the most notable example of Renaissance urban design in the city. Although many plans were made, and much aesthetic debate took place both inside and outside the Palazzo Ducale, the modernization of the Piazza after the 1530s is the clearest example of how far the government of the Republic was prepared to go in rationalizing the city centre and turning it into 'a new Rome'.

Sansovino was approached to design a new, second building for the Procurators, the numbers of whom had now increased significantly beyond the original nine. It was to face the earlier one on the opposite side of the Piazza, and his radical proposal, illustrated by a model, envisaged the complete realignment of the south side of the Piazza, dramatically widening it at the east end, and in the process freeing the Campanile from the accretion of structures around its base, including the ancient Ospizio Orseolo. The bell tower would become a far more dramatic element in its own right, while the broadened shape of the Piazza considerably enhanced the setting of the basilica. Sansovino also envisaged that these new buildings would incorporate a continuous colonnade which would begin down the west side of the Piazzetta, running along the whole of the south side of the Piazza and returning at the far end, to abut the church of San Gemignano.

CANALETTO, *The Molo Looking West*, c.1730 (right, above)

To the right are the Biblioteca Marciana, the Mint and the Granai, while the entrance to the Grand Canal is dominated by Longhena's great church of Santa Maria della Salute. (Tatton Park, Cheshire, The National Trust.)

CANALETTO, *Piazza San Marco Looking North*, c.1730 (right, below)

Sansovino's Loggetta (left foreground) is shown now augmented with a terrace. The side wings of the Torre dell'Orologio were added in the early 16th century. (Nelson Atkins Museum of Art, Kansas City.)

Sansovino himself began, but did not complete, this ambitious programme. He was, however, directly responsible for the design of the new Biblioteca Marciana, the Library of San Marco. Once completed, the exceptionally fine Library finally replaced the squalid collection of hostelries and market stalls that had still defaced this most important civic location. It was begun in 1537, although the southernmost bays were added after Sansovino's death by Vincenzo Scamozzi. The richly modelled Library forms a sharp contrast with the Palazzo opposite, in materials, in style and in function. It represented the Republic as the home of learning and culture, directly facing the embodiment of the Republic as the seat of justice and wise government. The completion of the Biblioteca Marciana thus marks an important stage in the enhancement of the Piazzetta as the civic square, which was now raised to the same level of architectural dignity as the Piazza itself. The alignment of the Library, however, is not precisely regular in its relationship to the Palazzo Ducale; Sansovino's planning again resulted in a trapezoidal form, like that of the Piazza, with the Piazzetta widening from the Molo towards the church, once more enhancing its setting and increasing the sense of space.[8]

Sansovino also designed the little loggia at the base of the Campanile, built at the same time as the Library. Although less significant as a work of architecture, the Loggetta also plays a role in the urban development of the Piazza, as it terminates the axis which begins inside the Porta della Carta of the Palazzo Ducale. It was thus intended to reinforce this important ceremonial route, down which the doge processed at his coronation. Small in scale, the Loggetta is rich in detail, and was to function as a meeting place for the nobility before going in to sessions of the Maggior Consiglio.

Although he did not live to see the completed construction of the new procuracy buildings on the Piazza itself, Sansovino made one final contribution to the urban ensemble, with a new facade for San Gemignano, which faced San Marco from the far end of the Piazza. The facade, of two superimposed orders, was intended to relate to both the existing procuracy on the north side (which he had completed) and that which he had designed for the south side.[9]

The important programme of works executed by Sansovino was extended beyond the strict confines of the Piazza itself with the reconstruction of the State Mint, the Zecca. Mints for both gold and silver coins had been located at San Marco since the tenth century, but by the sixteenth century these modest premises could no longer cope with the volume of coinage now required. Although it does not have a facade directly onto the Piazzetta, the Zecca nevertheless further raised the dignity of the complex of buildings now assembled at San Marco. Its site was severely restricted, since it stood facing the Bacino, hemmed in by Sansovino's own new Library on one side, and with a narrow canal and the huge mass of the medieval state granaries on the other. Sansovino's original two-storey design was later extended with a second floor, and although its style is appropriately quite different from the rich classicism of the Library, its powerful stone facade maintains the dignity of its context and reflects the building's important symbolic function.

The last works of construction in the Piazza itself were the New Procuracy (Procuratie Nuove) buildings that were eventually to occupy the whole of the south side, broadly following Sansovino's original intentions. In 1582, twelve years after his death, the crumbling Ospizio Orseolo was finally demolished and work begun on the New Procuracy. The architect, Vincenzo Scamozzi, based the design closely on Sansovino's Library, although it was to be one storey higher. Construction was extremely protracted, though, and the New Procuracy was only finally concluded in around 1640 under Baldassare Longhena's direction. Once completed it established a formidable and imposing enclosure to the Piazza's south side. The spatial complex at San Marco had now finally reached its last stage of maturity and completion: all the institutions of the Republic were now housed in appropriate style and in a relationship that directly reflected their role in the governance of the Serenissima.

GABRIELE BELLA, *Festa della Sensa*, mid-18th century (right)

The Ascension Day Fair was marked by an elaborate construction of temporary stalls. (Galleria Querini Stampalia, Venice.)

FRANCESCO GUARDI, *Piazza San Marco looking west, with San Gemignano* (right, centre)

The painting is a record of the appearance of the church before its destruction by Napoleon.

CANALETTO, *The Molo and Piazzetta from the Bacino*, c.1732, (far right)

The classic formal approach to the heart of the city by water, with Doge Ziani's twin columns forming the gateway to the hub of the Empire. (The Royal Collection.)

CANALETTO, *The Basin of San Marco on Ascension Day*, c.1740 (overleaf)

The painting illustrates the role of the Basin as a great natural harbour in the centre of the city. (National Gallery, London.)

Function and symbolism

Throughout this centuries-long process, the Piazza remained primarily an atrium for the patronal church. This purpose is rendered particularly clear when we appreciate the functions of the buildings that immediately surround the square, as finally completed by Longhena. None are directly concerned with the government of the Republic; almost all are related to the shrine. The two long sides are entirely occupied by the procuracy buildings, structures built not for the government but for the functionaries who administered San Marco, its income and interests. The Procurators too, as an institution, collectively controlled the land on which these buildings stood (as, indeed, they still do to this day).

The Piazzetta, by contrast, was essentially a civic space, the square of the Republic. This distinction has been clear to the Venetians themselves for centuries; in 1493, Marin Sanudo, lauding the praises of his capital, described 'two great paved squares', one that of the church, the other the 'piazza dil Palazzo'. A century later, Francesco Sansovino, Jacopo's son, identifed four 'piazze' or spaces in all, as we can today. Two served the Palazzo Ducale: the broad quay or Molo at the front and the Piazzetta at the side. San Marco also had two 'piazze', the great square itself and the little flanking square, that of the Leoncini, where the primate resided.[10] The Piazzetta, remaining distinctly civic and political in character, was where nobles met and talked (and occasionally conspired) under the arcades of the Palazzo Ducale and in Sansovino's Loggetta; the Library is

equally a governmental building, as is the Mint. The wing of the Palazzo Ducale abutting the Piazzetta contained the department of Justice, and on the Piazzetta, too, was this justice all too publicly executed, for all Venetians to see. After their conviction, malefactors were traditionally put to death either between Doge Ziani's two great columns, or were hanged between two smaller columns, symbolically coloured red (now bleached to pink), on the upper loggia of the Palazzo Ducale, overlooking the Piazzetta.[11]

The interdependence and interconnection of these two spaces is one of the reasons for the uniqueness of the San Marco complex. Such an arrangement is rarely found in any other historic city centre in Italy, where the two poles of ecclesiastical focus (usually the cathedral) and the civic focus (the Palazzo Comunale or the castle of the city's lord) almost always have distinctly separate identities, standing some little distance apart. Thus, for example, at Florence, the cathedral square is some way from the Palazzo Vecchio, which stands on its own square, the Piazza della Signoria; very similar patterns can be seen at Siena (again with its cathedral square and the Piazza del Campo) and at Vicenza, Treviso and Verona, the three most important cities in Venice's own home territories, other than Padua. At Padua the cathedral also dominates its own square, the Palazzo della Ragione another, and the great shrine of the Santo yet another. At Venice, though, the cathedral, San Pietro di Castello, remained comparatively insignificant (and distant): the real spiritual heart was San Marco, the state shrine and ducal chapel, which, together with the civic, administrative core are essentially one group of buildings and one spatial complex; in this they reflect the inseparable nature of the two elements within the Republic's constitution; and, of

course, the result is a far greater concentration not only of outstanding works of architecture, but also of civic and urban identity.

Despite the connotations of Doge Ziani's columns, the chief ceremonial approach to the city was always by water, disembarking at the Molo. Approaching in this way, we can still appreciate the splendour of this ceremonial vista. The Piazzetta becomes dramatically foreshortened when seen from a vessel approaching the Molo, and the assemblage has the appearance of an elaborate perspective theatre set. Beyond the columns are the flanks of the Palazzo on one side and the ornate Biblioteca Marciana on the other; beyond again is the south facade of San Marco, which was originally approached by a large portico. San Marco is balanced on the left by the simple contrasting mass of the Campanile, beyond which again are the three standards, while the entire vista is closed by the screen of the Procuratie Vecchie and the vertical focus of the Torre dell'Orologio. Encompassed within this 'stage set', therefore, are all the chief elements, both spiritual and political, of the Most Serene Republic.

Within this complex spatial assembly the Campanile plays a pivotal role. Not only is it a powerfully simple vertical feature among the other rich architectural forms, but it also united the two worlds, the spiritual and the temporal. The tower (traditionally known as 'el paron de la caxa', the father of the household), contained the bells that regulated the city's life; besides ringing the ecclesiastical offices, the bells had other specific functions. That known as the *marangona* defined the working day for the crafts of the city, the *nona* and *mezza terza* rang the hours; the *trottiera* summoned nobles to the Palazzo to vote; and the *maleficio* announced a public execution. The bells were also rung to announce important news, military victories and other events.[12]

The square of San Marco remains the only space in Venice always dignified with the title of Piazza; all the other city squares, even those as impressive as Santi Giovanni e Paolo and Santa Maria Formosa are simply *campi*. Even today it is always known to Venetians simply as 'la Piazza'. The events which it hosted during the Republic's thousand-year history were countless in number and diverse in character; some were purely political, others spiritual, while many others combined the two; still others were more domestic and commercial in character. They varied from the coronation of doges to the Ascension Day fairs, to bullfights and tournaments.[13]

Pageant and procession

Ritual and procession permeated the very fabric of the Republic, and the Piazza was its natural setting. Many rituals were an essential expression of Republican philosophy; by definition they were collective rather than individualistic, and although there was always a rigid hierarchy of protocol, many different orders of men participated, followed the same route and shared at least some of the same experience. Such rituals and processions were thus, in a somewhat contradictory manner, both 'levelling' and hierarchical. In this they reflected the essentially oligarchical nature of the Republic, with its three clearly-defined orders of inhabitants: the nobility, the citizenry and the common people. Although by no means despotic, as were most of its contemporary states, the Venetian Republic could not be described by the modern mind as democratic; in practice the Serenissima was ruled by a comparatively benevolent oligarchical gerontocracy. Procession and ritual maintained for all levels of society the appearance of continuity that they all desired. Such rituals were timeless, codified, repetitive and reassuring, epitomizing the Republic's own stability, much as the Piazza in which they took place epitomized these same qualities in stone and marble. Even the slow measured steps of the processions on the great days of the Venetian calendar came to be echoed in the rhythmic, repetitive arcades by which the Piazza was surrounded.

The square fulfilled its highest function at the election and coronation of a new doge. The ceremony was rich and complex, but at its core was a celebratory Mass in the basilica, at which the doge assumed his spiritual mantle as the protector of the Evangelist. He was then carried aloft in

THE LION OF SAN MARCO

The lion sits on top of one of the two columns erected by Sebastiano Ziani after 1172. Despite its universal fame as the symbol of the Republic, it is oriental; the wings were added later by Ziani.

THE ALA NAPOLEONICA

Begun in 1807, the Ala occupies the site of
Sansovino's San Gemignano. A detail of the
upper order and attic is also shown below.

a chair in procession around the Piazza, scattering gifts of newly minted ducats to the people. The practice incorporated the symbolic elements of both meeting and being greeted and accepted by the people, even though, after the 'locking' of the Maggior Consiglio in 1297, they no longer took part in the electoral process.[14] Finally, the doge returned to the Palazzo Ducale where he was again presented to the people (this time as head of state), with the formulaic incantation, 'Here is your doge, if it please you.' On this occasion, too, the doge's *Promissione* was formally read out to the Venetians, a statement of the aims and principles of his coming reign. At this, the rite concluded with the firing of mortars and the ringing of bells.[15]

The life-cycle of the doge was ritually drawn to a close in a similar manner in some respects. After his death, his body was lain in state in the Palazzo Ducale for three days; he was by no means resting in peace yet, however, since three state inquisitors were carefully analysing his reign and passing judgement as to whether he had fulfilled his ducal oath. If his reign was deemed satisfactory (it almost always was, although the Inquisition was no mere formality), a Mass was sung at San Marco, followed by a solemn procession in the Piazza. The conclusion of the rite, though, was markedly different, since, having left this world, the doge had also relinquished his title and spiritual duty. He was then usually taken to the family parish church for a simple private burial service, although a number of doges chose to be buried in the more imposing surroundings of the great Dominican church of Santi Giovanni e Paolo.[16]

Several festivals during the year were celebrated with sometimes dazzling displays of pomp and circumstance in the great square. St Mark's Day (25 April) was naturally one of them, again with a great procession around the Piazza, embracing the population of the city as well as the participants. In recognition of the universality of this festival to all Venetians, the procession was

remarkably egalitarian, with representatives of almost all elements in society from the doge and Procurators to the numerous trade guilds, all proudly displaying their treasures, relics and banners.[17] Other central events in the Christian cycle were treated as rather more purely religious occasions: Palm Sunday, for example, and Holy Thursday, just before Easter. By contrast, though, 'Fat Thursday' (Giovedi Grasso), the day marking the end of Carnival and the forty-days' austerity of Lent, was marked by a raucous public fair in the Piazza, with bullfights, acrobats, jugglers and other distinctly secular entertainments. There were also spectacular firework displays, at which the Venetians were famously skilled.[18]

The one great festival that best represents the way in which the Republic skilfully fused together the spiritual and the patriotic, the symbolic and the pragmatic, was Ascension Day, which combined political, civic and religious elements in equal measure. The festival of the annual marriage of the doge to the sea had been greatly enhanced in 1177, when the pope had given Doge Ziani a ring with which to 'marry the sea' and thereby reinforce the Republic's dominion over the waters. A great fleet of boats left the Molo and proceeded to San Nicolo at the northern tip of the Lido, where the ceremony took place. Although the day itself was a deeply symbolic Christian event, representing the supreme truth of the Resurrection, the Venetian ceremony can also (perhaps more accurately) be read as a pagan rite of union between the Republic and the water, the element from which Venice was born.[19] The Serenissima did not neglect the temporal advantages that could be derived from this notable occasion. For fifteen days the Piazza hosted a great international trade fair, crammed with stalls and thronged with merchants from all over Europe, bargaining, negotiating and exchanging news and information. In later centuries, the square was filled with temporary stalls, tents and marquees to house the fair.

All of these events were largely fixed, cyclical festivities. The Piazza, however, also hosted countless other national celebrations. For example, in 1364 after Venice's victory over the rebels in Candia (Crete), Petrarch, who was living in the city at the time, praised highly the lavish scale of the festivities. The defeat of the Genoese at Chioggia in 1381 was celebrated in a similar manner. Finally, there were special receptions for illustrious visitors, one of the most remarkable of which was that given to the French king, Henri III, in July 1574. On this occasion Andrea Palladio's skills were enlisted to enhance the approach to the city from the Lido. Since there were few permanent structures on the littoral, a 'triumphal arch with three portals' was built at San Nicolo, together with an adjacent 'beautiful and spacious loggia, with ten classical columns'; their appearance survives in a contemporary etching although they stood for only a few days before being dismantled. The lavish reception given to the king in the city was said to have been one of the most outstanding experiences of his life.[20]

GABRIELE BELLA, *Coronation of the Doge on The Scala dei Giganti*, mid-18th century

The painting depicts the climactic moment when the new doge was presented to the nobles and citizenry on taking his oath of office. (Galleria Querini Stampalia, Venice.)

The Piazza San Marco thus reached its definitive form as the slightly belated result of Sansovino's sensitive and highly skilful replanning. The only further significant alteration to the square's appearance until the fall of the Republic was the repaving of its surface. Until as late as the early eighteenth century the Piazza was still floored with the traditional, almost domestic Venetian paving of red brick, divided into squares by strips of stone. In 1723, though, Andrea Tirali, then proto to the Procurators of San Marco, began its comprehensive repaving in more dignified materials: grey trachite from the Euganean Hills near Padua, with a pattern of white Carrara marble. The expensive operation took twelve years to complete, but while it was in progress, Tirali also enhanced the dignity of the little square north of San Marco; this Piazzetta, formerly known as that of San Basso, after the adjacent parish church, was also repaved, given a new wellhead, and the two marble lions were added by Giovanni Bonazza in 1722. Henceforth it became known as the Piazzetta dei Leoncini (little lions).[21]

Napoleon and the new order

Throughout the centuries, the Piazza had served as the nucleus of the city, at every level – social, spiritual and patriotic. After 1797, however, its role, and to a significant extent its appearance, was decisively altered.

Events other than ducal coronations took place in the Piazza in 1797, after Napoleon achieved the final capitulation of the Republic. A 'Tree of Liberty' was erected in the square, and on Whit Sunday the victors organized a festival at which the former doge, Ludovico Manin, in a final act of humiliation, witnessed the ritual burning of his *corno* (cap of office), the Libro d'Oro (the register of the Venetian nobility) and other symbols of the now extinguished Republic.

Napoleon's conquest was followed by a brief Austrian occupation, followed again in 1805 by the incorporation of the former Terraferma empire into Napoleon's Italian Kingdom or Regno Italico. Venice was designated the 'second capital' of this new kingdom, (the first being Milan), and to enhance this new status, many grandiose plans were produced for reordering the Piazza, thereby expunging it of its Republican past. To this end, Napoleon intended turning the Procuratie Nuove into a new palace for his Italian viceroy, the most dramatic element of which was the construction of the Ala Napoleonica, the Napoleonic Wing, initiated in 1807. It necessitated the demolition of the whole west end of the Piazza, including Sansovino's San Gemignano; the new wing contained a monumental ceremonial staircase rising to a great ballroom on the first floor (neither of them facilities that had been required by the Procurators), and executed to a design by Giuseppe Soli in

GENTILE BELLINI

Miracle of the Holy Cross in the Piazza San Marco, 1496

On countless occasions the Piazza hosted processions such as this one, celebrating the feast day of St Mark, 25 April. The painting was commissioned by the Scuola Grande di San Giovanni Evangelista, whose members figure prominently. (Gallerie dell' Accademia, Venice.)

1810. The exterior of the Ala was based on the two lowermost orders of the Procuratie Nuove, but instead of a third order, the wing was surmounted by a tall attic screen, decorated with friezes and figures of Roman emperors, more literal representatives of 'the new Rome' than the Republic had ever permitted. In the centre there was to have been a giant figure of Napoleon, which was (perhaps mercifully) never installed. Despite the jarring effect of the attic, though, the colonnade on the ground floor of the new wing opened the Piazza to the west and created new spaces linking the city's heart with the traditional urban texture beyond, as well as forming a dramatic new approach to the basilica. The interior was cool, refined and Neoclassical; the imposing ballroom was completed by Lorenzo Santi in 1822.[22]

The alterations to the function of the Procuratie Nuove also led to the demolition of the great medieval granaries on the waterfront, the Granai di Terranova. Napoleon's intention was to open the vista from the Procuratie to the Bacino, and clad the palace with a new monumental southern facade, for which various proposals were drawn up, but none executed. The vista was retained, though, and the little Public Gardens (Giardinetti Reali) were laid out on the site of the Granai. The elegant little Neoclassical pavilion at the west end, built as a café, is again the work of Santi, the most prominent of this last generation of Neoclassical architects in the city.

Santi was also responsible for the very last building constructed at San Marco until modern times; this was the remodelling of the Palazzo Patriarcale, which dominates the Piazzetta dei Leoncini. Many alternatives were produced for this sensitive site next to the basilica, but the adopted scheme is a rather reticent Neoclassical facade, with a giant order of columns on a tall base. The completion of these works in 1843 brought the Venetian Patriarch's residence into the Piazza for the first time, and this symbolic relocation marked the final reconciliation between the established Church and the state that the Republic had for so long and so successfully kept apart.[23]

The Piazza regained something of its traditional and symbolic dignity in 1848, however, during the brief period of Venice's rebellion against the Austrians who had occupied the city since 1814. The rebellion, led by Daniele Manin, was fuelled by early success. In March 1848, the Venetians tore up the pavings in the Piazza and threw them at the occupying soldiers; Italian flags were run up the three standards, and eight Austrians were killed. The Arsenalotti, the craftsmen of the Arsenale, also rebelled, and a few days later Manin himself declared a new Republic from one of the café tables in the Piazza. There followed an extraordinary seige of the city by the Austrians, during which Venice was cut off from all supplies for five months, until the city finally capitulated on 23 August 1849.

Although Manin's was therefore a short-lived success, the final act in the history of the 'new Republic' really took place twenty years later, when in 1866 a universal plebiscite was balloted from the Palazzo Ducale, the overwhelming result of which was the Venetians' decision to join the newly unified Italy.

5   **The Arsenale** | Trading Power and Naval Supremacy

'As in the Arsenal of the Venetians / boils in winter the tenacious pitch / To smear their unsound vessels over again / For sail they cannot; and instead thereof / One makes his vessel new, and one recaulks / The ribs of that which many a voyage has made / One hammers at the prow, one at the stern / This one makes oars and that one cordage twists / Another mends the mainsail and the mizzen ...' **Dante Alighieri,** *'L'inferno', La Divina Commedia,* canto XXI, c1309–20.

The first nucleus

The Venetian Arsenale was one of the wonders of the medieval world, a vast, sprawling industrial complex, greater than any other in Europe. It was the key to the power and prosperity of the Most Serene Republic, source of its naval supremacy and its trading pre-eminence. In 1509 the Senate had described the Arsenale as 'the heart of the Venetian state', and if we take this metaphor as literally as it was perhaps intended, then it was indeed true that from the powerful pump of this great naval base there flowed the life-blood of empire: the firepower, the nautical skills, above all, the ships themselves that sailed the imperial sea passages and enforced the rule of the Republic of San Marco from the rocky shores of nearby Istria to the farthest coasts of Cyprus.

The Arsenale grew by a series of stages to become the largest single industrial complex in the West, at its peak employing several thousand highly-trained men within the daunting confines of its great three-mile-long perimeter walls. It became as much a symbol of the Republic as the Piazza of San Marco, and none in the Palazzo Ducale ever doubted its key role in keeping the peppers and silks flowing into the city, and the gold ducat circulating from London to Baghdad. The term 'Arsenale' itself, which later spread among the world's languages, is said to derive from the Arabic *darsina'a*, a place of industry, and its adoption in Venice directly reflects her intimate links with the Muslim world.[1]

The original nucleus of the Arsenale was very modest in extent; it was established in 1104, on a pair of islets (*zimole* or twins) in the eastern part of the city, in the *sestiere* of Castello, immediately to the north of the present principal water gate. Here, two rows of covered shipbuilding sheds were constructed, each with twelve bays, and facing each other across a central basin; this basin had itself been dredged from a natural pond, which was then connected by a short channel with the great Basin of San Marco. This first small nucleus was built by the Republic to construct its own war galleys, and specifically for the crusading fleets, although there were still at this time many other, private shipyards in various parts of the city, notably on the northern shores of Cannaregio; there was another at San Marco, on the site known as Terranova (perhaps because it had been reclaimed), later to be occupied by the state granaries, and later still by the Napoleonic Public Gardens.[2]

By 1298 this first compact nucleus in Castello had become too small, particularly in the light of the recent war against the Genoese; the Republic had by now taken over the Terranova yards at San Marco to build fifteen new great galleys or *galere grosse*, and so it was decided to undertake a major expansion in Castello, thus establishing the pre-eminence of these yards as the central shipbuilding facility of the Republic. This enlargement began in 1303 with an eastward extension to incorporate the adjacent sites of the ropeworks and oar-making yards. In 1325 this stage was completed by the enclosure of the Lago di San Daniele, a large natural pond directly to the east of the original nucleus. This great basin thus became the Arsenale Nuovo and its surrounding walls more than quadrupled the extent of the complex. It was during this period of expansion, in 1312, that Dante Alighieri visited Venice, and was so impressed by the spectacle of the activities of the Arsenale that he wrote the famous lines that opened this chapter.[3]

THE ARSENALE VECCHIO

The original basin from which the great naval complex developed. Many of the original sheds remain here, some from the 15th century, although the oldest are now roofless.

CANALETTO, *The Arsenale: the Water Entrance*, c.1732

This view shows the Land Gate and the oratory of the Madonna dell'Arsenale. The wooden drawbridge has now been replaced by a fixed bridge. (Woburn Abbey, Bedfordshire.)

THE ARSENALE IN 1500 (left)
Detail of de'Barbari's view of Venice. At left centre are the Water Gate, with its twin towers, and the recently-built Land Gate. To the right are the largest basins, the Arsenale Nuovo and Nuovissimo; today joined as one.

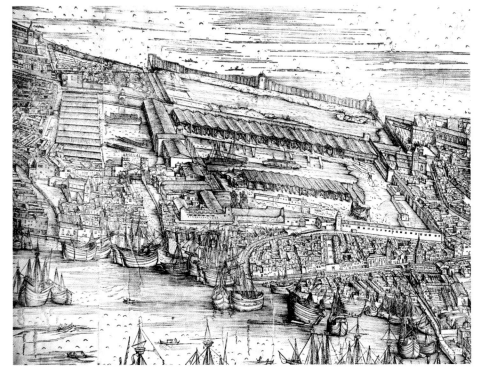

In many ways the site was a natural one for the establishment and development of the Republic's chief naval base. It lay between the heart of the city and the Porto di Lido, the entrance into the sea from the enclosed lagoon; it lay close to the deep-water channel, the Canale di San Marco, that formed a direct continuation of the Grand Canal as it opened into the Bacino. The Bacino itself offered sheltered anchorage for a sizable battle fleet without interrupting the normal trading activities of the port; such a fleet could be quickly deployed to repel an invasion fleet, and equally easily despatched to sea. The Arsenale became a self-contained fortress, almost a town within the city, and the only part of Venice that remained fully fortified throughout the Republic's history. Its only potential point of vulnerability was the Porto di Lido, the vital gate to the sea; this was initially defended by the fort of San Nicolo, on the southern bank, but San Nicolo was later reinforced by Michele Sanmicheli's massive and imposing new fort of Sant'Andrea, on the northern bank, in 1543.[4]

The location of the Arsenale also allowed space for future expansion if necessary, since this was a comparatively underdeveloped district of the city, much of the perimeter of which was occupied by monastic houses with their extensive gardens and orchards. The only other significant urban feature lay in the far north-eastern corner, the isolated community on the islet of San Pietro in Castello (the ancient Olivolo), where the cathedral was sited. Much of the remainder of the city's eastern perimeter, though, dissolved into marshes and mud flats.

By the mid fourteenth century the Arsenale had become the sole significant state-funded shipyard in the city. Although considerably larger, in some ways it was comparable with similar facilities elsewhere, notably the naval bases at Pisa and Genoa. The closest analogy can be made with the former, since it also occupies one corner of the city, just inside its walls, with direct access to the river Arno, again forming a large, specialized self-contained community.[5]

Expansion and rationalization

Concurrent with the fourteenth-century expansion of the Arsenale, a radical reorganization took place within its new walls; the unique Venetian 'production line' process originated in this period. New shipbuilding sheds were built around the Arsenale Nuovo, but only the keels and hulls were constructed here; the hulls were then launched and floated around to the covered docks for completion. Here they proceeded through all the fitting-out stages and were equipped firstly with masts, then with ropes, sails, oars and weaponry. To support these processes, to the south of the large new basin a specialized zone was developed exclusively for these fitting-out activities; all the departments had water access to the ships on the northern side, while at the back, along their southern flank, an internal street provided vehicular connections.

The shipbuilding sheds and covered docks were all built to precise, standardized dimensions to accommodate the forms of the ships produced, the design of which was equally standardized and fully rationalized. The entire process was organized very much like the sequential, staged production lines that grew out of the Industrial Revolution, although this even more revolutionary development took place here some four centuries earlier. With all this specialized, compartmentalized production there also grew an increasingly complex mechanism of state control of supplies, of men and of materials; it was a pure state monopoly in every respect, with a rigorous hierarchy of officials to monitor every stage of production.[6]

This industrial complex was further enlarged in 1390, when the foundries were transferred here from their previous site across the city in Cannaregio, later to become the Jewish Ghetto. This represented yet another stage in the centralization process, bringing the manufacture of the weapons of war (cannons, balls and firearms) all into the same organizational system. Despite several fires and explosions, chiefly the result of the inadvisable proximity of the powder stores, the foundries remained in this location, at the south-eastern end of the Arsenale Nuovo; in 1539,

THE ARSENALE, PISA (above)

Part of the fortifications of the Arsenal on the banks of the Arno; the Pisan Arsenale was extended by the Medici in the 16th century.

THE LAND GATE (left)

Built in 1460 under the patronage of doge Pasquale Malipiero, it is the first fully Renaissance work in the city, and based on the classical Roman arch at Pola in Istria. It was further enriched in 1571 and again after the reconquest of the Morea in 1687.

though, it was prudently, if rather belatedly, decided to transfer the powder store to a remote island in the lagoon near Fusina, which thus became known as Sant'Angelo della Polvere. The island itself was later struck by lightning and exploded.

THE LAND GATE AND THE WATER GATE

The Water Gate (below, left) was enlarged twice to allow the passage of steadily increasing sizes of ships.

The Land Gate

Thus the Arsenale remained until a new land gate was constructed in 1460. This work marked a key stage in the Arsenale's development since it was the first attempt to introduce dignified, civic architecture to this most symbolic feature of the great naval base. The Gate is often attributed (although without documentation) to Antonio Gambello, sometime military architect to the Republic, and is generally recognized as the first fully Renaissance structure in the city. It was built chiefly as the result of the enlightened classical scholarship of Doge Pasquale Malipiero, and the coincidence of his brief reign with further works of expansion within the Arsenale itself, brought about by the renewed Turkish threat, and their conquest of Constantinople in 1453. The Gate is modelled on the ancient Roman arch at Pola, across the Venetian Gulf in Istria, one of the Republic's long-established possessions.

The revival of the classical form of the Roman triumphal arch, never yet seen in Venice, was entirely appropriate for such a location, and for the first time gave the Arsenale an important role

in the civic fabric of the city. Its original form was comparatively simple, although it is richly detailed; its triumphant arch was to be embellished on several later occasions, as its symbolic possibilities were further developed into the form that we see today. After the great 'allied' victory of Lepanto in 1570, when the Western powers defeated the great Turkish fleets, two winged victories were added to the spandrels above the arch, and since the battle had taken place on Santa Giustina's Day, the figure of the saint was placed on top of the Gate. Later again, in 1682, a terrace was added at the front, with a series of allegorical figures on the balustrade; finally, in 1687, the two large flanking lions were installed as trophies, the result of Admiral (later Doge) Francesco Morosini's victories in the Peloponnese, one of the lions having once guarded the harbour of Piraeus.[7]

The greatest naval base in Europe

Shortly after the completion of the Land Gate, another major stage of expansion was undertaken, beginning in 1473; it was again triggered by concern over the Turkish menace, and in particular by the Venetians' loss of Negroponte to them in 1470, and the consequent threat to Cyprus. This expansion consisted of the enclosing of a further large basin, directly north of the Arsenale Nuovo and covering about the same area; it became known, inevitably, as the Arsenale Nuovissimo, and it, too, was enclosed by a further considerable length of high brick wall. This marked the extent of the great naval complex illustrated by de'Barbari in 1500; by now the main basin, the Arsenale Nuovo, was lined with eighteen large sheds on the northern side and a dozen or so on the southern quay. The western side of the original Arsenale Vecchio was also lined with sheds, which had probably been rebuilt in the early fifteenth century, and the massive roofless remains of some of which survive today. In the same period as de'Barbari's woodcut, the Arsenale was described by Marin Sanudo as being:

79

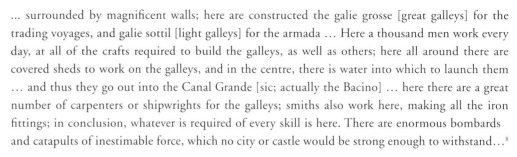

... surrounded by magnificent walls; here are constructed the galie grosse [great galleys] for the trading voyages, and galie sottil [light galleys] for the armada … Here a thousand men work every day, at all of the crafts required to build the galleys, as well as others; here all around there are covered sheds to work on the galleys, and in the centre, there is water into which to launch them … and thus they go out into the Canal Grande [sic; actually the Bacino] … here there are a great number of carpenters or shipwrights for the galleys; smiths also work here, making all the iron fittings; in conclusion, whatever is required of every skill is here. There are enormous bombards and catapults of inestimable force, which no city or castle would be strong enough to withstand…[8]

The Arsenale Nuovissimo was probably built to house the reserve fleet; only recently enclosed, it still appears distinctly underused in Jacopo de'Barbari's view. But it, too, was later surrounded by shipbuilding, storage and repairing sheds. Initially it formed a self-contained basin with its own new gate at the north-east corner, which was later filled in as it was thought too vulnerable to attack; it was then joined directly to the Arsenale Nuovo, with just a small spur of land separating the two basins.[9]

In the sixteenth century, two further, smaller extensions brought the Arsenale up to its maximum extent under the Venetian Republic. In 1539, the Reparto delle Galeazze was added, just north of the original nucleus, and then in 1564 it was further extended by the Vasca delle Galeazze, with additional space for building six new ships simultaneously. Both works were built as a direct result of new developments in ship design, and in particular the introduction of the new 'great galley' or *galeasse*, which was larger than the traditional galleys, and could not be built in the older sheds. These two basins filled in the angle on the west side, and were once again enclosed by a high brick wall.

THE ARSENALE: WALLS AND TOWERS

The eastern perimeter walls are the oldest sections surviving, reaching their final appearance in the 16th century.

The sixteenth century also saw the construction of several buildings that still survive and which, like the Land Gate, served to enhance the architectural dignity of this great industrial complex. The Arsenale's vital importance to the Republic ensured that, by the sixteenth century, a certain quality of building was now considered appropriate to some of its activities. The principal Water Gate was clearly one such element; although of ancient origin, it had had to be rebuilt on two occasions to accommodate the increasing size of the Republic's ships. In the early sixteenth century, the Gate still consisted of two simple, stocky brick towers, with the Venetian lion on the face of each one, and with a drawbridge in front to permit pedestrian communications across the canal in front. The chief enlargement took place in 1574, although further work was necessary in 1686, and it is this latter restoration that survives today. The Water Gate combined both ceremonial and purely practical functions, and for most of the Republic's history it was the only water access into the whole vast complex. The two imposing towers had not only a traditional symbolic and defensive role, but they also supported the stout timber gates that secured the Arsenale at night. From this gateway there were manoeuvred not only the countless sailings of the regular merchant fleets, but the gilded ducal barge, the Bucintoro, on the great occasions of state, as well, of course, as the Republic's impressive fleets of war.

The great Water Gate is still flanked by the daunting perimeter wall of the Arsenale. The present wall is of various dates, broadly corresponding to the stages of the naval base's successive enlargements. The oldest surviving walls are probably those to the east and south-east, along the Rio della Tana and the Rio di San Daniele; the towers along these walls were built in the fifteenth century, in the same period as the reclamation of the Arsenale Nuovissimo, although they were restored in the sixteenth, and some bear stone coats of arms from the 1520s and 1530s.[10]

Within the walls several important building works took place in the sixteenth century, most of them identifiable as conscious elements in the urban renewal that shaped so many diverse parts of the city in this period.[11] In the ancient nucleus of the Arsenale Vecchio, for example, Michele

PAOLO VERONESE,
The Battle of Lepanto, 1571 (left)

The painting celebrates the 'allied' victory over the Turks in 1571. Over half of the western fleet of 208 ships were built in the Venetian Arsenale. (Gallerie dell' Accademia, Venice.)

VITTORE CARPACCIO, *The Arrival in Cologne*, from the Saint Ursula cycle, 1490 (above)

The depiction of heavily-fortified Cologne is closely based on the Venetian Arsenale, and his ships are Venetian vessels. (Gallerie dell' Accademia, Venice.)

Sanmicheli, the Republic's chief military architect, built a new shed to house the Bucintoro. Its style is simple but monumental, rusticated and Doric, a variation of the design of his fortress of Sant'Andrea; it was completed in 1555. Equally massive is the Artillery Gate, from the same period and to a similar design; it, too, is attributed to Sanmicheli.[12] The great size and scale of so many of the Arsenale's buildings resulted in works which (like the Bucintoro shed) are part architecture and part engineering; into this category fall the two slightly later wet docks built at the east end of the Arsenale Nuovissimo, and often attributed to Jacopo Sansovino. They were known as the '*volti acquei alle canne*', literally 'wet vaults in the reeds', and they represent an almost Piranesian monumental fusion of military architecture and engineering, their massive stone piers supporting great brick arches and imposing timber truss roofs. Completed in 1573, they are roughly contemporary with the equally imposing sheds of the Vasca delle Galeazze, originally three on each side of the central basin. In the same period, too, was built the extraordinary structure known as the Corderia or Tana, the ropeworks. Designed by Antonio da Ponte, architect of the Rialto Bridge, and completed in 1583, it consists of a great aisled hall, no less than 315 metres (around 1,000 feet) long and 20 metres (66 feet) wide. It was specifically designed for the large-scale production of rope for the fleet, with its central hall roofed by large timber trusses, supported on two rows of robust stone columns. The Corderia still occupies the whole length of the south-east flank of the Arsenale, along the Rio della Tana.[13]

Also forming a part of this general renovation of some of the key functions of the Arsenale in the mid sixteenth century was the rebuilding of the ancient fourteenth-century oar-making shed. It was reconstructed in 1562, to a design by Andrea Pisano, in the south-west corner of the Arsenale Nuovo, its traditional location, since it contributed to the final fitting-out stages of ship production. The Officina Remi (oarworks) was so extensive and imposing that after a disastrous fire in the Palazzo Ducale in 1577, it was considered capacious enough to house temporary assemblies of the Maggior Consiglio until repairs were completed.

The Arsenale probably reached its absolute peak of activity in 1570, when it is said that no less than a hundred galleys were completed in barely two months to join the great Christian fleet that was being coordinated to fight the Turks at Lepanto. Over half of this entire fleet, one of the largest ever assembled until modern times, was built by the Venetian Arsenale, and 110 of the 208 'allied' vessels were under Venetian command, more than the combined forces of the Papacy, Naples, Genoa, Spain and Sicily. Even though the nominal Western victory proved to be far from decisive, the battle was the most spectacular individual military event of the era, and illustrates well the might and resources of the Venetian navy at the time.[14]

By this period, all state shipbuilding activities were concentrated here, and the only yards left elsewhere in the city were small-scale private operations. The Arsenale now occupied most of eastern Castello, and its employees and dependents formed virtually the whole population of this part of the city. Despite his unorthodox etymology, Francesco Sansovino was fully justified in writing, in the immediate aftermath of Lepanto, that:

> The base and foundation of the greatness of this Republic, rather the honour of all Italy, and to say it better and with more honesty, of all Christendom, is the house of the Arsenal, which derives from Ars Senatus, that is, the fortress, the bastion, the defensive line, and the supporting wall of the Senate and of our faith against the arms of the Infidel.[15]

Foreign visitors were equally impressed, although a degree of security was not surprisingly imposed on their carefully-monitored guided tours. Thomas Coryat, in the early seventeenth century, thought it: 'the richest and best-furnished storehouse for all manner of munition, both by Sea and Land … in so much that all the strangers whatsoever are moved with great admiration when they contemplate the situation, the greatnesse, the strength, the incredible store of provision thereof.'[16]

AVVERTIMENTO

CANAL DELLE CALEVIZE

CANAL DI NOVISSIMA GRANDE

DICHIARAZIONE
DEGLI USI E DESTINAZ
DI TUTTI QUESTI FABB

CAVAL DI ARSENAL VECCHIO

CANAL DI ARSENAL NUOVO

DICHIARAZIONE DEGLI USI E DESTINAZIONI DI TUTTI QUESTI FABBRICATI

ALLA
AVGV.CES REG AP MAESTA
DI
FRANCESCO. II
PRESENTA QUESTO
DISEGNÒ PRIMO
DELL IMPER. REG. ARSENALE
DI VENEZIA
ANDREA QVERINI
CONS. INT ATT DI STATO
PRESIDENTE
PER LA PRELODATA MARINA
DELL ARSENALE MEDESIMO
E DELLA VENETA TERESTINA
TVTTA MILITARE MARINA
MDCCIIC

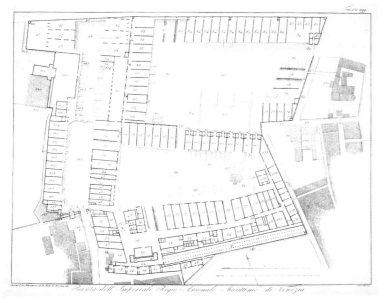

ANTONIO NATALE, PLAN OF THE ARSENALE,
17th century (far left)

(Museo Civico Correr, Venice.)

G.M. MAFFIOLETTI, PLAN OF THE ARSENALE
IN 1798 (above)

This is the definitive form of the naval base
at the fall of the Republic, with four
principal basins of water, all surrounded by
sheds and other specialized facilities. (Museo
Storico Navale, Venice.)

PLAN OF THE ARSENALE IN 1853 (left)

This is the extent of the Arsenale after the
fall of the Republic, but before Italian
unification. After 1867 the two large eastern
basins were joined together, and a further
eastern extension added.

John Evelyn was almost as generous in his admiration; he saw 'a court full of cannon, bullets, chains, grapples, grenadoes Etc., and over that arms for 800,000 [sic] men … together with weapons of offence and defence for sixty two ships'.[17] Finally, Peter Munday reported that 'they are able in a few dayes to build, rigg, furnish, arme and sett forth a good fleete of gallies'.[18]

The final extent of the Arsenale under the Venetian Republic was now established, and comparatively few developments took place within the walls after the end of the sixteenth century. One of the very last was begun only a few years before the fall of the Republic, when in 1778 work began on the Sala dei Squadratori, designed by Giuseppe Scalfarotto, and which occupies the east side of the Canale delle Galeazze. This monumental structure was originally 150 metres (nearly 500 feet) long and divided into thirteen bays; it was built for the storage of baulks of oak, for seasoning and for sawing into the main frames of sailing ships.

Arsenalotti

By around 1700, the great Arsenale had long been the source of dominant activity in the eastern city. But rather as the departments of the government of the Republic eventually spilled beyond the confines of the Piazza, so too did the activities associated with the Arsenale extend beyond its forbidding walls. On the Riva (quay) nearby were the cereal warehouses (built in 1322), and the bakeries for making ships' biscuits, reputedly of excellent quality; the former survive today as the Museo Storico Navale, the Museum of Naval History, while the facade of the bakery also still stands, with its rich portal constructed in 1473.

THE BUCINTORO BOATSHED (below, left)

The imposing shed to house the ducal state barge was designed by Michele Sanmicheli in 1555, in a characteristically robust Doric style.

HOUSING ON THE RIO DELL'ARSENALE (below)

Most of eastern Castello was occupied by the modest housing of the dock-workers.

Almost all of Castello east of the Rio della Pietà was given over to the homes of the Arsenalotti, the shipyard workers, and in particular the four parishes of San Martino, San Biagio, Santa Ternita and San Pietro in Castello. The most densely populated quarters were those immediately west and southeast of the walls, notably the zone around the present Via Garibaldi, formerly a canal, the Rio di Castello. This canal formed the focal axis of the whole district, and today it still retains much of its original character, that of a fairly poor, largely self-contained district, quite distinct from the city centre, and largely orientated towards the Arsenale and the Bacino. Some of the local concentrations of trades are recalled in the surviving street names, *ancore* (anchors), *vele* (sails) and *bombardieri* (bombardiers).[19] There are no noble palaces in this quarter, and the only part of eastern Castello where we can identify a slightly more *signorile* (noble or upper class) character is immediately adjacent to the Land Gate of the Arsenale where the Republic provided forty houses for the Arsenale's *patroni*, or senior craft managers. A pair of them are built into the south wall of the Arsenale itself, originally fifteenth-century Gothic, but modernized in the sixteenth century. They are approached by their own bridges, and were named Palazzo dell'Inferno and Purgatorio, in recognition of Dante's visit to the city; the main timber drawbridge in front of the Water Gate was known as the Ponte del Paradiso. The broad square in front of the Land Gate thus represents the focus of this small class of citizen managers, and was the hub of the whole district, channelling the movements of the thousands of Arsenalotti through the Land Gate each working day.

Associated with the Arsenale were several charitable housing developments; the most prominent is the Marinarezza, a state-built almshouse for sailors who had given particularly distinguished service to the Republic. Still standing today on the quay facing the Bacino, the Marinarezza originally contained fifty-five dwellings in three parallel terraces of accommodation, built before 1500. An additional wing was built across the front in 1645, with large archways to the terraces.[20]

THE MARINAREZZA (below)

A charitable housing development, built by the Republic in the late 15th century, to accommodate retired mariners who had given outstanding service to the navy.

THE NAVAL BAKERIES ON THE RIVA DEGLI SCHIAVONI, 1473 (below, right)

Support facilities for the great naval base spilled out into much of the surrounding district.

Despite their comparative security of employment, many Arsenalotti were not highly paid; the men were formed into their own specialized guilds or *arti*, the chief and most numerous of which were those of the *marangoni da nave* (ships' carpenters), and the *calafati* or caulkers. As well as the smiths, oar-makers and others noted by Sanudo above, there were also seamstresses to make sails, although many were also made in charitable hospitals under 'sub-contract' to the Republic. The Arsenalotti acquired a number of privileges over the centuries, including generous wine allowances, and the (frequently abused) use of supposedly 'scrap' material from the yards; their posts were often effectively lifetime sinecures. But they also played a special and honourable role in the civic life of the city; they executed public policing duties over the whole of Castello east of Bragora, a direct reflection of the Arsenale's influence in this part of the city. The guard at the Palazzo Ducale was formed from their ranks, as was the doge's own personal guard. The Arsenalotti also participated directly in the ceremony of the 'Marriage to the Sea' on Ascension Day, when they rowed the ducal Bucintoro; and they formed a guard of honour at ducal funerals. Their loyalty to the institutions of the Republic was considered beyond question.[21]

The Arsenale after 1797

The history of the Venetian Arsenale was by no means brought to an end with the fall of the Republic, and the great naval base has retained its strategic importance to the present day. In 1797

it was divested of all its arms and equipment by the French, but in 1810 the north-eastern access gate was reopened and newly fortified with a great new tower, the Porta Nuova, which still stands. After 1814, the whole Arsenale was extensively restored by the Austrians, although in 1849, after the unsuccessful rebellion of Daniele Manin, it was effectively abandoned again until 1866, the year of the Unification of Italy. Restoration then began once more, and the Arsenale again became an important naval base for the new Italy. Works undertaken to modernize the base in this period included the joining together of the two large eastern basins, the Arsenale Nuovo and Nuovissimo, to form a single great body of water, and a further eastward extension made possible by the demolition of the nunnery of Le Vergini. Finally, the dry docks (*bacini di carenaggio*) were built in the far north-eastern corner in 1875–8.

The Arsenale was used an an active naval base in 1915–18, and again in 1940–5, and has been occupied by the Italian navy until very recently. Today, though, after nearly nine centuries of shipbuilding, the quays and sheds of the Arsenale are silent. There are many proposals for its future; the buildings that survive, though, collectively represent an unparalleled heritage of 'pre-modern' industrial buildings, and their sensitive restoration and re-use presents a challenge of great scope but of daunting extent.[22]

'Be it determined that, to prevent such grave disorders and unseemly occurrences, the following measures shall be adopted, ie that all the Jews who are at present living in different parishes within our city … shall be obliged to go at once to dwell together in the houses in the court within the Geto [sic] at San Hieronimo, where there is plenty of room for them to live.'

Decree of the Venetian Senate, 29 March 1516.[1]

The Jews in Venice: the establishment of the Ghetto

We have no knowledge of the earliest Jewish communities in Venice, although there were undoubtedly Jews in the city from a very early date. In general, the Republic was a good deal more tolerant of Jews than were many other European states, with the result that the Venetian Hebrew population was itself mixed, containing Jews from a number of other countries and regions.[2] It is often traditionally recorded that in the thirteenth century the Jews were granted permission to settle on the chain of islets known as Spinalonga, as a result of which (it is said) its name was changed to Judaicha (the earliest spelling), or Giudecca, the place of the Jews or of those 'adjudged to be different'. Other chronicles record that two synagogues were established here, and survived until the eighteenth century.

However, this Republican tolerance came to an abrupt halt in 1298, when the Jewish community was accused of the serious crime of usury, and was expelled from the capital. They were not expelled from the Republic itself, though, and were permitted to resettle at Mestre on the nearby Terraferma, and a little further, at Chirignago, Mogliano and Conegliano. From this acceptable distance, they continued their traditional activities of trading and moneylending; slowly, too, at least some returned to the capital. The most decisive point in Venetian Jewish history, though, came with the decree of the Senate, quoted above, which not only formally allowed the Jews to return to the city, but required them to settle in a precisely defined place.[3]

This place was an islet in the parish of San Geremia; since the early fourteenth century the Republic's iron and brass foundries had been located here, and we have knowledge of their establishment at least as early as 1306, when the islet was already referred to as the *Ghettum*, a place where metals were *gettate*, cast or founded. The foundries' principal purpose was to provide the Arsenale with metal artefacts and weapons of war, their isolation in this remote quarter chiefly in order to reduce the risks of fire and to maintain security. The islet was not large, but compact, an irregular kite-shaped rectangle, surrounded on all sides by narrow canals which greatly enhanced its security; it was connected to the rest of the city by a single bridge. The fact that this islet was known as the Ghetto Nuovo indicates that the foundries had already been expanded or transferred here from an adjacent, original site, the Ghetto Vecchio. The Ghetto Nuovo was perhaps annexed to build additional furnaces, which numbered at least twelve in all, or perhaps as a site for the deposit of waste products from them.

In the early fifteenth century, though, the Republic decided that, despite the fire risk, the foundries were to be relocated within the walls of the Arsenale itself; a record of 1458 notes that thay had been transferred there some time earlier. After this removal, the islet was taken over for housing, and by the end of the fifteenth century (as de'Barbari records), its redevelopment was already clearly defined: there was a two-storey 'ring' of modest housing around the perimeter, and a large spacious square in the centre. Access was still confined to a single bridge. It resembled a typical island-parish, therefore, in many respects, although no new church was established here.

The decree of 1516 changed the history of Venetian Jewry. It allowed Jews to settle in the city and to participate in the social and economic life of the capital; it also provided an atmosphere

SCHOLA SPAGNOLA

The spiritual heart of the Ghetto lay in the synagogue. This fine interior dates from 1655.

THE GHETTO (right)

Detail of Ludovico Ughi's plan of the city in 1729. The Ghetto Vecchio lies to the south-west of the original island-ghetto.

SCHOLA TEDESCA (overleaf)

Situated in the Ghetto Nuovo, the schola was built in 1528, but much elaborated in the 17th century.

considerably more tolerant than that in most other European cities, and it permitted the development of a clear focus for religious and cultural identity. To a degree, therefore, the Ghetto resembled the other foreign enclaves in the city, particularly that of the Greeks. On the other hand, the Republic imposed considerable restrictions on the Jews' movements and activities, including the requirement to wear a badge of identity; the form of this 'badge' varied over time, but was usually a yellow *berretta* (cap) or a figure 'O' fixed to clothing.[4] There were also strict limits to the working activities in which the Jews were permitted to engage; they were forbidden to exercise any of the noble business or professional pursuits (except medicine), to labour manually or to indulge in sexual activity across the religious divide. They could not buy real estate, and were confined to the islet of the Ghetto, where they rented accommodation; the island was locked under curfew at night.

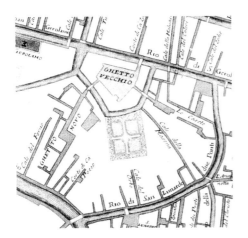

The 1516 decree summarizes these humiliating restrictions, which in some respects turned the Ghetto into a kind of open prison; the two sides of the island which were not at the time occupied by housing were to be enclosed by 'two high walls' onto the adjacent canals, while the two sides that were built-up with apartments were to have their quays walled-in. The Collegio, or cabinet, was to provide two boats to patrol the surrounding canals, 'by day and by night', paid for (it is no surprise to read) by the Jews themselves. They also had to pay for the 'four Christian guards' who were to impose the curfew and control the points of access, of which there were now two. Any Jew found outside the walls after curfew would be instantly arrested. Finally, and in a sense most significantly, the location of the Hebrew community in this 'geto' gave to the world a new word and concept of physical identification with which to isolate and suppress Jews down the centuries, on countless occasions far more ruthlessly than the Venetians themselves ever did.[5]

Growth and expansion

Despite all these severe limitations and restrictions, the Jewish community in Venice prospered and multiplied. Although heavily circumscribed, they were equally protected, and were never persecuted or expelled from their new home, half sanctuary and half prison. By 1534, the Jews of Venice had formed themselves into three distinct groups, collectively known by the Republic as the Università degli Ebrei. The first consisted of Ashkenazy or 'German' Jews, many of whom were in fact Italian in origin, and who had entered the city in large numbers after the 1509 crisis of the League of Cambrai, when a brief alliance of France, the Papacy, Spain and the Hapsburg Emperor had resulted in the temporary loss of almost all of Venice's mainland empire. The result was that several hundred Jews fled the Terraferma and swelled the city's Hebrew population, forming the nucleus of the inhabitants of the Ghetto island. The second group of Jews consisted of émigrés from Spain and Portugal, and were generally known as the Ponentine or Western Jews. Finally, there were the Levantine or Oriental Jews, who were recognized as a distinct category by the Republic in 1541, when the Ghetto had to be expanded to take account of their numbers.[6]

The heart of the Ghetto remained the large campo of the original islet, still today known, rather confusingly, as the Ghetto Nuovo. Circumscribed by water on all sides, its housing developed, as numbers increased, in the only possible direction – upwards – with the result that we see today: crowded tenements up to seven or eight storeys high, in sharp contrast to the three or four storeys of most of the rest of the city's historic centre. To supplement the original bridge on the south side, a second bridge had been built on the east side of the islet, to which access was gained by a dark, narrow, *sottoportego* or covered passageway under the towering tenements. Both of these original restricted points of access still survive, together with a more recent third one, across the Rio di San Girolamo on the north side. Below the square a large cistern provided fresh water, and was marked by the typical Venetian wellhead, while around the perimeter were the other essential facilities of the community: butchers, bakeries and three banks or loan offices.

The great block of tenements of the Ghetto Nuovo remains its dominant and most distinctive feature; occupying the whole of the south-east and south-west faces of the islet, from the exterior its form is almost fortress-like in appearance and massing. Simple in the extreme, the buildings are devoid of any ornamentation, all the door and window openings simple rectangles of white Istrian stone. It seems highly likely that these great blocks were developed directly out of the much lower rows of housing shown on de'Barbari's view of 1500, since their ground plan remains almost identical. It was extremely expensive to form new foundations in Venice, after all, and the Jewish communities that first settled here, those from Italy and Germany, were by no means wealthy. Unfortunately, the fact that Jews were not allowed to purchase land means that all such records are comparatively scarce. The Scuola di San Rocco, one of the great religious confraternities, owned one of the blocks in the sixteenth century, while another was owned by the noble Venier family; the rented accommodation often seems to have remained in the same Jewish families for two or three centuries.[7]

Cultural life and social limitations

The spiritual heart of the Ghetto lay in the synagogue, which was known in Venice as a 'schola' (with a distinctive spelling), partly because its function in some ways resembled that of the Venetian Christian scuola (or confraternity) of devotion, and also because one of the essential roles of the synagogue is as a place of learning (*scuola* generally means school in Italian). There were three schole in the original nucleus of the Ghetto Vecchio, eventually rising to a total of nine. These first three were small, and were discreetly located on the upper storeys of the great tenement blocks; in part, this reflected an early concern with the threat of physical persecution. Such a concern proved to be more imagined than real, and the Jews were never physically attacked here, although this location also reflects a liturgical requirement to have no accommodation directly above the hall itself, part of which for certain ceremonies was opened to the sky. These schole are thus barely identifiable from the street below.

The first of these three major surviving original schole is that of the Tedeschi or Germans, built in 1528, as the inscription above the doorway records; it is one of the oldest synagogues in Europe. It was probably followed by the building of the Schola Canton (*canton* is Venetian for a corner) in 1553, and finally by the Schola Italiana in 1575, although this last may have succeeded an earlier synagogue elsewhere.[8]

At first, the Jewish community was decisively isolated, both literally and metaphorically, from the life of the capital. Slowly, though, numbers rose and the community became wealthier, more numerous, more self-confident and more influential. The incorporation of the second-stage Ghetto, therefore, the so-called Ghetto Vecchio, marks the expansion of the Jewish presence beyond these metaphorical and physical confines of their circumscribed islet, and out into the general fabric and cultural life of the city.

On 2 June 1541, twenty-five years after the first decree, the Venetian Senate again debated the Ghetto; a petition had been put forward by the Levantine Jews stating that, 'because the Ghetto is [already] so cramped they can find nowhere to stay in it … they want a place to be provided for their [own] lodging'. This was to be the second Ghetto, which, since it was to occupy the sites of the very earliest foundries, was identified as the Ghetto Vecchio. The Levantines, however, were still 'always to be enclosed and guarded in the same way as those of the [original] Ghetto and they may not engage in banking or the second-hand trades or in any employment other than pure mercantile activity …'[9]

This newer Ghetto occupied a large rectangular plot, extending from the original 'drawbridge' south-westwards as far as the Cannaregio Canal, although it was not defined by canals on the two

SCHOLA SPAGNOLA (above)

Also known as the Ponentina, and lying in the Ghetto Vecchio, it is the largest surviving synagogue, and is attributed to Longhena.

SCHOLA LEVANTINA (right)

The richly-carved woodwork is by Andrea Brustolon, the outstanding master of the 17th century.

roughly parallel longer sides. It was to be largely occupied by Spanish and Oriental Jews, both of which groups built their own new synagogues here, and both of which survive today. The Oriental or Levantine Jews were the wealthiest and most influential of the Jewish groups, a fact reflected in the strongly distinctive form of their schola which, uniquely in the Ghetto, is expressed as an elegant, clearly defined architectural statement, rather than forming an almost indistinguishable part of the general residential fabric of the Ghetto. Originally built in the sixteenth century, soon after the new Ghetto's establishment, it was completely remodelled in a rich Baroque style in the seventeenth century.[10]

Finally, nearly a century later, it was found necessary to expand the Ghetto for a second and last time. In 1633, this third and smallest stage of development was begun, the Ghetto Novissimo, an irregular plot of land to the east of the original islet. Again a response to acute shortages of space, it was constructed specifically to house twenty Sephardic families. The Ghetto Novissimo is again built to a very high density, and is almost entirely occupied by five-storey apartment blocks. The most distinctive of them is the very large seventeenth-century building on the corner of the Rio di San Gerolamo, known as Palazzo Treves since it was funded by the wealthy Jewish banking family of that name. Reminiscent of the large apartment block next to the Scuola Grande di San Rocco known as the Castelforte, which was built a century earlier, the Palazzo Treves was built around a T-shaped intersection of two streets, with superimposed apartments on a highly rationalized plan to maximize space.[11]

The Venetian Jewish community reached a peak of numbers and importance in the seventeenth century, when it was estimated to contain up to 5,000 members. Nevertheless, the Republic's attitude towards the different Jewish groups varied, and they retained their clearly separate identities. The Jews of the original Ghetto, the Germans and Italians, remained the least liberated of the groups with the tightest controls over their commercial activities; some of the Levantines, by way of contrast, such as those from Corfu and Crete (both Venetian territories) enjoyed full rights as Venetian citizens with few, if any, restrictions on their activities. Still different again were the Marranos, Jews of Spanish origin who had converted to Christianity; persecuted in Spain, they moved to Portugal, and then, when the Inquisition followed them there too, some migrated to Venice. Here reaction was ambivalent, and wealthy Marrano traders aroused the enmity of the Republic; as a result, for a short time, overt anti-Semitism made a rare appearance in the city, exacerbated by political alliances between the Marranos and the Turks. Although the Senate voted

EXTERIOR OF THE ORIGINAL GHETTO
(above, left)

There were only two points of access, one of which was this timber bridge.

THE CAMPO DEL GHETTO NUOVO
(above, centre)

Still the heart of the remaining Jewish community in Venice. With steadily increasing numbers, a great wall of high-density housing developed around the perimeter of the island, reaching seven or eight storeys in places.

ENTRANCE TO THE SCHOLA LEVANTINA
(above)

The doorway is reputed to be by Longhena.

THE GHETTO NOVISSIMO (above)

To the right of the canal, the third stage of
expansion took place after 1633.

to expel all of Venice's Jews in 1571, the decree was quickly revoked before it could be implemented. Thereafter relations between the Jews and the Republic were generally cooperative, and the Levantine and Ponentine Jews (from Spain and Portugal) were given the right to security of residence for ten years, and to engage in international trade, otherwise the exclusive prerogative of the nobility.[12]

Henceforth the community enjoyed a long period of peace and prosperity, with a considerable degree of mutual self-interest deriving from this condition of equilibrium and stability. According to rabbis and Christian prelates alike, Jews were exceptionally well treated in Venice, with a great deal of cross-cultural activity, including concerts and other festivals. Jewish physicians, too, were particularly highly regarded. In 1580, Francesco Sansovino wrote that 'Here, as a result of trade, they are extremely opulent and wealthy, and they prefer to live in Venice rather than in any other part of Italy …'[13] Thirty years later, Thomas Coryat remarked on the 'many Jewish women … so elegant in their dress, adorned with gold chains and rings, ornamented with precious stones …' The city's permanent Jewish population rose from 1,700 in 1586 to 2,600 by 1640, and it was in this period of prosperity that most of the synagogues of the Ghetto were rebuilt or modernized, with rich Baroque and Rococo decoration.

'The Duke [doge] cannot deny the course of law: For the commodity that strangers have / With us in Venice, if it be denied, Will much impeach the justice of his state / Since that the trade and profit of the city, Consisteth of all nations.'   **William Shakespeare**, *The Merchant of Venice*, III. iii, c1596–7.

Origins and early history

The Rialto district gained its pre-eminence as a market and a trading centre, among the many other islets of the archipelago, through the merits of its site. This primacy was in time to become so remarkable that a simple recitation of the word by an Elizabethan playwright on the other side of Europe could immediately conjure up in the minds of his London audience an image of glittering jewels, piles of rare spices and the complex dealings of international banking.

The island of Rialto (the original 'Rivo Alto' of the city) lies at the very heart of the Venetian archipelago, where all of the city's principal routes converge. Not only does the waterway network meet here, but so do all the principal pedestrian routes, from San Marco, San Polo, Santi Apostoli and San Giacomo dell'Orio. Here, at its midpoint, the course of the Grand Canal makes a sharp turn; it is also narrower here than at any other place in its length: a natural site, therefore, for a potential bridgehead, and rendered even more attractive to settlement by the two firm, substantial islets on either side. That of San Bartolomeo was reputedly established in the ninth century, while San Giacometto, on the west bank, is said by tradition to be the oldest parish foundation in Venice, established in 421, the legendary date of the foundation of the city itself.[1]

A site destined for notable significance since these earliest settlements, the Rialto's market functions seem to have followed as a natural result of its centrality. They were already established by 1097, when a considerable area of land, with shops and stores, was bequeathed to the Republic by two wealthy citizens, Tiso and Pietro Orio; this was to prove a vital factor in the Rialto's development as it established the Republic's direct ownership of the site, and ensured its further development by the Venetian government down the centuries.[2] To improve communications between the two banks, a bridge, probably of boats, was first constructed in around 1175, to be replaced in about 1265, by a more permanent bridge of timber. In this form it survived until 1310, when it apparently fell victim to the serious civil unrest later known as the Baiamonte Tiepolo plot, an attempt by a noble faction to overthrow the government, but which ended in confusion and the rout of the rebels. Rebuilt and restored on a number of later occasions, it was constructed with two inclined ramps, flanked by small shops or booths, and with a drawbridge in the centre to allow the passage of larger ships. The early importance of the Rialto district of the emerging metropolis can be gauged today by the nearby grouping on the quays of the Grand Canal, on both banks, of a number of notable surviving Byzantine palaces: Cà da Mosto in one direction and Cà Loredan, Cà Farsetti and Palazzo Donà in the other. All of them, and others, represented important patrician families and equally powerful trading interests.

With the fortunes of the city as a whole, the Rialto grew and flourished during the thirteenth and fourteenth centuries. Slowly, the rich, complex and often rather conflicting mixtures of activities developed: international banking, commerce and trade at the highest level competed and jostled with the raucous activities of the city's retail food markets, which by law were now all concentrated here. Indeed, by the end of the fifteenth century, these market activities had become so extensive and concentrated that the shops and warehouses had driven out most of the resident population, rather as can be seen in the City of London in recent decades. By 1509, the census recorded that the two Rialto parishes of San Giovanni and San Matteo numbered barely 450 residents between them, although the *sestiere* (district) in which they stood, that of San Polo, contained as many as 8,500 people in all.[3]

CANALETTO, *San Giacomo di Rialto*, c.1756

San Giacometto is said to be the oldest foundation in the city; on the right is the Rialto Bridge, and on the far right Scarpagnino's Fabbriche Vecchie, built after the 1514 fire. (National Gallery of Ottawa, Canada.)

The urban form of the large rectangular island of Rialto itself developed in a highly distinctive manner. Its principal axis was the Ruga Vecchia di San Giovanni, from which numerous long, narrow, parallel *calli* extended as far as the quay on the Grand Canal, the Riva del Vin. The easternmost of these parallel streets was the Ruga dei Oresi (*orefici* or goldsmiths), the main hub of the markets themselves, and a direct extension of the axis formed by the Rialto Bridge. This pattern is still extremely clear today, and may be closely compared with the street pattern of such important early island-parishes as San Lio and San Barnaba.

By the end of the fifteenth century, the essential form and structure of the whole district was well established. The Rialto served many functions, not all of them as immediately famous as the banks, spice-dealers and markets. Since early times, for example, it has been the location of a number of government departments and magistracies concerned with trade, commerce and taxation, as well as those controlling sea-borne navigation. Here, too, were located the offices for the administration of the city itself, rather than the Republic as a whole, which was governed from the Palazzo Ducale. The regular sailings of convoys of trading galleys, the *viazij*, were organized and auctioned from the square at the Rialto,[4] and bodies such as the Dieci Savii alle Decime, the ten magistrates responsible for collecting tithes, also had their headquarters here. The square in front of the little church of San Giacometto (always referred to by Venetians in the diminutive) was the heart of the Rialto, on a smaller scale but in much the same sense that the Piazza of San Marco was the heart of the Republic's government. The Rialto's importance was further emphasized by the location of a *pietra del bando* in the square, a proclamation stone for the pronouncement of government decrees, the only one in the city other than that at San Marco. The little 'pulpit' still stands today opposite the church. The Rialto was thus regarded in many ways as the second heart of the capital, the commercial core to complement the governmental hub at San Marco.[5]

GABRIELE BELLA, *Il Banco Giro di Rialto*, mid-18th century

Private bankers had their stalls under the colonnades around the square of San Giacometto, as did the Banco Giro, established in 1609. (Galleria Querini Stampalia, Venice.)

The Rialto in 1500

Marin Sanudo's encomium, written in 1493, in which he proudly lists the city's myriad wonders, described the Rialto in these words:

> I would venture to call [the island of Rialto] the richest place in the whole world … here business deals are made with a single word 'yes' or 'no' … There are four banks … that hold very great amounts of money, issue credits under different names, and are called authorized bankers; their decisions are binding. Furthermore, throughout the said island of Rialto there are storehouses, both on ground level and above, filled with goods of great value … Every year goods come in from both east and west, where galleys are sent on commission from the Signoria [cabinet] … On the island of Rialto these stores … pay rent for the most part to [the Procurators of] St Mark's; a high rent is paid for every small piece of space … a shop may cost about 100 ducats to rent and be scarcely two paces wide or long … And in this city nothing grows, yet whatever you want can be found in great abundance. And this is because of the great turnover in merchandise; everything comes here, especially things to eat, from every city and every part of the world, and money is made very quickly. This is because everyone is well off for money. Here at Rialto it is like a vegetable garden … such varieties of fruit are on sale, and so cheap that it is marvellous …[6]

The markets of the Rialto were zoned according to specific functions and requirements. The quays to the Grand Canal were of considerable importance since they were the only public ones down the entire length of the Canal. All under the Republic's control, they were developed as state monopolies, each quay with a specialized dedicated function. They functioned as unloading docks for a variety of wholesale and bulk goods, all under close supervision and subject to taxation. On one side of the Canal, that of San Bartolomeo, were those for unloading coal, iron and steel while on the opposite bank was the Riva del Vin, where wine barrels were unloaded directly below the watchful eyes of the Republic's wine tax office. This last quay was also lined with several other government offices above the ground-floor warehouses: those of the Dieci Savii, the Salt Commissioners, and the Piovego, which was responsible for the maintenance of streets and canals and for the issue of building permits. At the southern end of the quay was the state flour warehouse.

The main axis of the district was formed by a direct continuation of the wooden bridge to form the straight street known as the Ruga dei Oresi. On one side it was lined with shops selling not only gold, but jewellery, precious stones and luxury fabrics. At the foot of the bridge stood a loggia, now lost, but which was a meeting place for the nobility (an echo of the similar loggia at San Marco), and adjacent to which were still more governmental offices, notably those of the City Treasurers (Camerlenghi), and the Razon Vecchie and Nove, two public accounts departments. A considerable amount of metropolitan bureaucracy, therefore, was intermingled with the practical creation of the wealth on which the Republic depended.

Under the colonnades of the square in front of San Giacometto were concentrated the international business activities: the banks, the money changers and, in an adjacent alley still called the Calle della Sicurtà (insurance), the shipping insurance offices. In Sanudo's day, the number of private banks (*banche di scritta*) varied, although there were up to ten in business in the period between 1490 and 1530; that of Alvise Pisani was the largest, but all were in the exclusive hands of the nobility. In general, therefore, the most valuable and prestigious activities were concentrated near the church, the loggia and the bridgehead, while the furthermost parts of the Rialto were dedicated to the humblest of retail trades, with their attendant taverns and brothels.[7]

A little beyond the central square was the market for oriental spices, one of the most valuable of the Rialto's trading commodities, centred on the Ruga dei Speziali; also nearby were stalls specializing in leather goods (the Varotari), rope and string (the Cordaria), and dairy produce in the Casaria. The general retail food markets lined the quays of the Grand Canal to the west of the bridge, so that the great quantities of produce could be unloaded directly from barges, just as they are today. Here, too, the concentrations of produce that was sold survive today in the names of sections of the market, with the Naranzeria (selling luxury foodstuffs including oranges) closest to the bridge. A little further west was the Erbaria (the market for fruit and vegetables), then the Beccaria (for meat), and finally the Pescaria, the fish market, on the farthest corner of the island. The Pescaria had formerly been located next to the bridge but was eventually considered too noisome for the refined sensibilities of the nobles and bankers, and so it was moved to its present location in 1459. At the same time, the quay was extended further into the Grand Canal to provide more space for the stallholders.

Most of the rest of the island was occupied by an extraordinarily dense mixture of warehouses, taverns and brothels, the last two regulated by the government but with varying degrees of success over the centuries. The spiritual needs of the several thousand stallholders, bankers and merchants were assuaged by three churches: San Giacometto, the ancient religious focus of the Rialto; San Giovanni Elemosinario, then as now almost buried within the mass of warehouses and workshops; and San Mattio, founded in 1156, but finally closed by Napoleon in 1807.[8]

The Fondaco dei Tedeschi

The Rialto island itself was not the sole location of market-related and commercial activities, however, and across the bridge at San Bartolomeo, the mercers and other trades ensured an almost continuous chain of such activity as far as San Marco. At the foot of the bridge, adjacent to the campo of San Bartolomeo, stood the Fondaco dei Tedeschi, the trading base for the substantial German community in the city. The building fulfilled several functions under one roof: firstly, it was a trading centre, with booths, shops and warehousing for Germans resident in the city; secondly, it provided lodgings and meeting rooms on the upper floors for visiting traders; and

RIALTO IN 1729: PLAN BY LUDOVICO UGHI (below)

The street-pattern remains very clear, with long parallel *calli* leading to the public quays on the Grand Canal.

LA CAMERA DEGLI IMPRESTITI (right)

This detail of a codex from 1391 shows accountants in the government department of public debt, based at Rialto, counting and sorting money, and keeping records in their ledgers. (Archivio Patriarchale, Venice.)

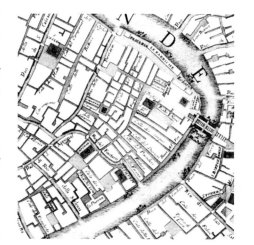

thirdly, naturally enough, it formed a social and cultural focus for the expatriates, who also had their altar at the nearby church of San Bartolomeo.

Founded in the thirteenth century, the Fondaco was extended in around 1300 and survived until 1505, when it was razed in a disastrous fire. The Senate immediately decreed that it should be rebuilt as quickly as possible, and under the proto Giorgio Spavento, the present building was completed within three years, an extraordinary achievement. The importance of German trade to the Venetian economy is directly reflected in the imposing size of the structure, today housing the Central Post Office. The speed of its reconstruction ensured not only that trading losses would be minimized but, since these facilities were all rented from the Republic, the Signoria would quickly be in receipt of rental income once more (the Fondaco did not have embassy status). Spavento was assisted by Antonio Scarpagnino, who may have completed some elements of the Fondaco after the former's death in 1509.

The great block, one of the largest structures in the city, is built around a large square central courtyard, rising to five storeys, including a mezzanine. The whole was planned in a rigorously logical, repetitive manner, with shops and booths around the perimeter of the ground floor. Its principal facade to the Grand Canal echoes something of the early Byzantine palaces in its large, spacious central loggia, and its crowning, rather frivolous crenellation. The present somewhat severe appearance of this and the other facades is a little misleading, however, since at least two of them, that to the Grand Canal and that to the alley at the side (where the main land entrance was originally located) were both decorated with frescos, painted by Titian and Giorgione. A few faded fragments of the latter's work survive today in the Accademia, but the original appearance of the Fondaco must have been a good deal richer and more lively than it appears today.[9]

The great fire and its aftermath

Shortly after the Fondaco was rebuilt, on 10 January 1514 another disaster struck the Rialto, this time across the bridge in the markets themselves. A fire broke out in a shop in the Corderia; fanned by bitterly cold and exceptionally strong winter winds, within six hours the flames had reduced almost all the island of Rialto to piles of smouldering timber and collapsing brickwork. To contemporary chroniclers like Marin Sanudo, standing in the smoking rubble, it was an unparalleled disaster ('like the ruin of Troy' as he put it); to the Venetian Signoria, too, it was an appalling catastrophe. The immediate short-term loss of rental income alone was reckoned at 35,000 ducats a year, while the almost unimaginable losses of merchandise, equipment, fabrics, jewellery and precious metals ran into millions of ducats. The only buildings to survive the fire substantially intact were the Palazzo dei Camerlenghi and the little church of San Giacometto, the very symbol of the Rialto; everything else was ashes. The great capital's entire trading heart had been obliterated, and the Signoria met in emergency session the next morning to formulate plans for its revival. It was immediately decided that the government departments displaced should be rehoused straight away elsewhere in the locality, to attempt to continue their duties while the enormous task of reconstruction was debated and put into effect.[10]

In theory, the disaster gave the Signoria a heaven-sent opportunity for some radical replanning of the entire district, which had long experienced acute problems of congestion and shortage of public space; in addition, the very density of the buildings, and the flammable nature of the stalls, had aided the swift spread of the inferno. An opportunity now arose to replan the Rialto with broader streets, a more spacious Piazza and buildings far more dignified than the earlier accretion of cramped accommodation.[11] In practice, though, other criteria prevailed. One was the desperate urgency of getting the banks and markets functioning again as quickly as possible, to yield the income on which the Republic depended. Any radical reordering of the street pattern would have involved years of legal dispute, the establishment of leases and ownerships, evaluation and

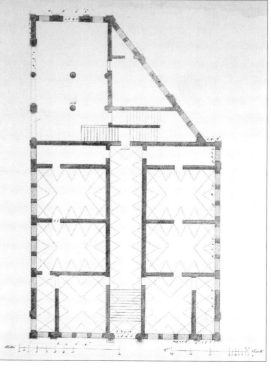

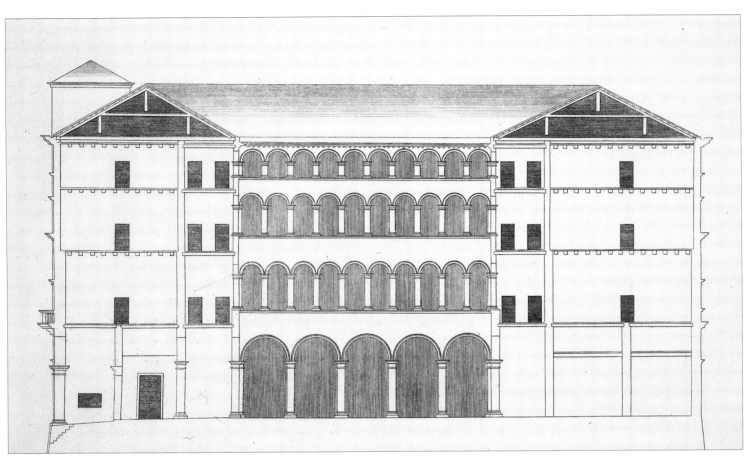

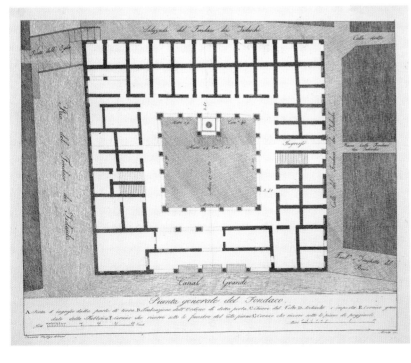

PALAZZO DEI CAMERLENGHI

Facade and plan (far left, below). The palazzo, which survived the 1514 fire, was comprehensively modernized, probably by Guglielmo de'Grigi in the 1520s.

THE FONDACO DEI TEDESCHI

Section (above); plan (left); facade (far left, above). Rebuilt after the fire of 1505, by Antonio Scarpagnino and Giorgio Spavento.

compulsory purchase, endless new legal agreements, to say nothing of the process of commissioning and agreeing a new master plan and its detailed design.

There are few records of the government's debate on these vital issues, although it was immediately decided not to transfer and centralize the many displaced government departments at San Marco, as might have been considered, but eventually to rehouse them all again in new permanent accommodation at the Rialto. Seven preliminary proposals were quickly produced by various architects, of which the scheme by Alessandro Leopardi was initially preferred, since it provided the largest number of new shops and thus maximized the Signoria's income. However, the task was eventually given to Antonio Abbondi, known as Scarpagnino, who was already a government employee in his role as proto of the Salt Commissioners. He prepared two alternative models for consideration, and after some further debate, a course of action was agreed, the eventual result of which was essentially the Rialto that we see today.[12]

Scarpagnino's scheme was an extremely cautious one in its planning, since it retained the original street pattern almost unaltered. Most of the larger new buildings are the work of Scarpagnino himself and, again for reasons of economy, speed and efficiency of erection, are all fairly simple, sober and repetitive in their design. He first completed the long block known today as the Fabbriche Vecchie (the Old Buildings) in 1522; it runs down the whole of the west side of the Ruga dei Oresi, and terminated at the bridgehead in a new building for the Dieci Savii, with a colonnade on to the Riva del Vin; this was also completed in 1522. The Fabbriche Vecchie followed fairly closely the form of the earlier buildings on the site, and their design is a highly repetitive stripped-down classicism, with a continuous ground-floor colonnade and two storeys of accommodation above, the only decorative features being the stone eaves and string courses.

The principles of design established here were then continued in the second phase of the rebuilding works, with new structures around the north and east sides of the square, and again up the northern part of the east side of the Ruga, facing the first block, and forming a coherent, unified whole. All of these buildings were again united by continuous stone colonnades on the ground floor, and by uniform treatment of the upper storeys. The colonnades provided essential shade and protection from the weather for the bankers and money-dealers around the square, much of whose business was conducted at a simple bench in front of their offices. In this way, therefore, the heart of the Rialto re-emerged in a form much like that of its predecessor but with more substantial and dignified enclosing buildings.[13]

Scarpagnino was also responsible for the reconstruction of the market church of San Giovanni Elemosinario in 1527–9. The extreme restriction of the site, with shops and warehouses enveloping it on three sides, led to a highly-centralized plan, a square with a Greek cross (with four equal arms) set into it. The interior is simple but refined, and most of the light had to be contrived from high-level windows and a small central dome.

Apart from San Giacometto, the Palazzo dei Camerlenghi was the only other survivor of the fire. The remaining structure was strengthened, and was extended to incorporate the nobles' loggia, which was now effectively lost within the new building. The resultant combined structure had a rather curious shape but, as befits its importance as the city's Treasury, and as a gesture to the principle of dignified urban renewal that was becoming one of the characteristic features of the city in the sixteenth century, the Palazzo was given a completely new 'skin' of very fine Istrian stone. This was completed in 1523–5, and is almost certainly the work of Guglielmo de'Grigi, an architect from Bergamo who had arrived in Venice at about the time of the great fire. As proto, though, Scarpagnino may also have played a part in its design, and the well-proportioned portico is sometimes attributed to him. The delightfully ornate facades, however, owe much to the tastes and influence of Pietro Lombardo, the master from Carona, on Lake Lugano, whose refined relief

THE FABBRICHE NUOVE

Built by Sansovino in c.1555, this marked the final stage of reconstruction after the great fire of 1514.

THE RIALTO MARKETS IN c.1900

The retail markets continue to feed the city every day, as they have done for a thousand years.

carving influenced a whole generation. The Palazzo's rich decoration, together with its pivotal location on the sharp bend in the Grand Canal at the foot of the Rialto Bridge, makes it one of the most memorable elements of the whole district.[14]

The second, considerably later stage in the reconstruction of the Rialto consisted of the Fabbriche Nuove (New Buildings), designed by Jacopo Sansovino, and begun in 1555, forty years after the fire and after the death of Scarpagnino. This substantial block stands between the square of San Giacometto and the Grand Canal on an extremely long, narrow plot of land. Sansovino's simple, repetitive design is twenty-five bays long, and continues the sober character of the earlier buildings designed by Scarpagnino. Again the ground floor has a stone colonnade, with two upper storeys, all in a simple classical style that is nevertheless a little richer than Scarpagnino's austere blocks. Sansovino varied what would otherwise have been an excessively monotonous facade to the Grand Canal by introducing a change of plane to follow the curve of the Canal, and terminating in a simple three-bay gable facade on to the vegetable market. Since the building was intended purely for market and warehousing functions, there was no need to incorporate any fireplaces or chimneys into its design: hence its pure, unbroken appearance. With the Fabbriche Nuove completed, the physical form of the markets was now largely complete, and remained almost unchanged until the construction of the curiously eclectic Venetian 'gothick' fishmarket in 1907.[15]

The Rialto Bridge

The Ponte di Rialto is one of the universal images of Venice; lined with its little shops, it is the Venetian equivalent of the Ponte Vecchio at Florence, recast in the confident stone of the Renaissance, and with its daring single arch spanning the Grand Canal. Its history, though, is long, tortuous and complex.

We have very little detail of the first 150 years or so of the old timber bridge's successive restorations and rebuildings, although in 1400 the Maggior Consiglio decided on its complete reconstruction.[16] It was thirty-two more years, though, until this decision was put into effect, and the work, still all in timber, cost 2,332 ducats. Later restorations, however, were still frequent; in 1444, a section of the bridge collapsed under the weight of crowds who had gathered to watch the wedding procession of the Marchese of Ferrara, and yet more repairs were necessary in 1458. By now, its form had long been established, with rows of shops down either side and a central drawbridge. The opening, 26 feet wide, was designed to accommodate the ducal state barge, the Bucintoro, as well as the passage of great galleys from the merchant fleet.

The 1472 restoration is that illustrated by Jacopo de'Barbari in 1500 and by Vittore Carpaccio in 1494 in his painting of the *Miracle of the True Cross* (Gallery Accademia, Venice). By 1499, though, it was once again said to be in danger of collapse, its piles rotting, while the combination of heavy usage and of damage to its many supports by passing shipping inflicted a regular toll. Yet more work was necessary under Giorgio Spavento's supervision in 1508 and by Scarpagnino six years later. On 25 June 1524 the doge, Andrea Gritti, was advised not to sail under it in the Bucintoro; prudent advice indeed, since only a few weeks later, on 14 August, the whole of one side collapsed. In the following year, a new magistracy was proposed to develop a more permanent solution to what was now becoming something of a national disgrace in a capital city as great and wealthy as Venice. This magistracy did not come into existence for yet another twenty-one years, when a model was produced of a new proposal. Michele Sanmicheli and Jacopo Sansovino were both asked for their expert opinions, but the scheme progressed no further.[17]

Philosophies of form and structure

In 1551 three new *provveditori* (commissioners) were appointed, and in 1554 designs were called for from all parts of Italy, including Rome, in what has since become one of the most famous (and

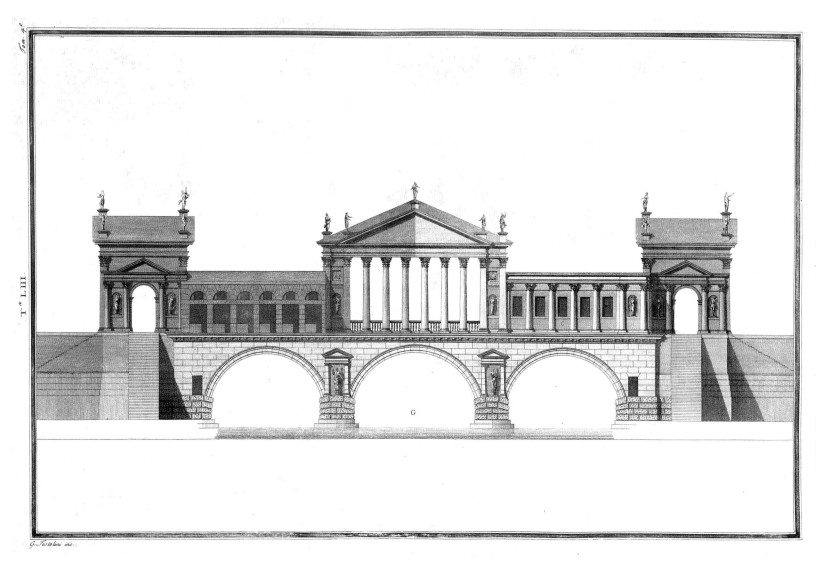

OTTAVIO BERTOTTI SCAMOZZI: PLAN AND
ELEVATION OF PALLADIO'S PROPOSAL FOR
THE NEW RIALTO BRIDGE, from *Le fabbriche e
desegni di Andrea Palladio* (1796)
(above and right)

This is Palladio's most grandiose proposal,
with three large pavilions and no less than
six rows of shops.

ANDREA PALLADIO (far right, above)

Proposal for the new Rialto Bridge c.1554.
An early proposal, with five arches and a
single large central pavilion.(Museo Civico,
Vicenza.)

VINCENZO SCAMOZZI (far right, below)

Proposal for a three-arched bridge, 1587.
Produced during the final stages of the
design process, it was defeated by da Ponte's
single-arch scheme.(RIBA, London.)

RIALTO IN 1500 (extreme right)

Detail of de'Barbari's plan. In the centre is
the old timber bridge, finally replaced in
1589–91 by Antonio da Ponte's stone
bridge. To the left is the little square of San
Giacometto, where the banks were
concentrated.

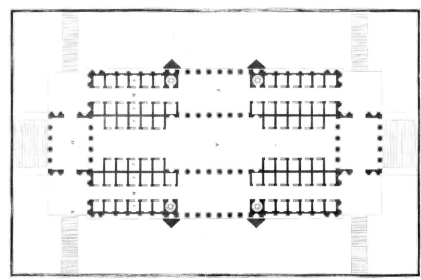

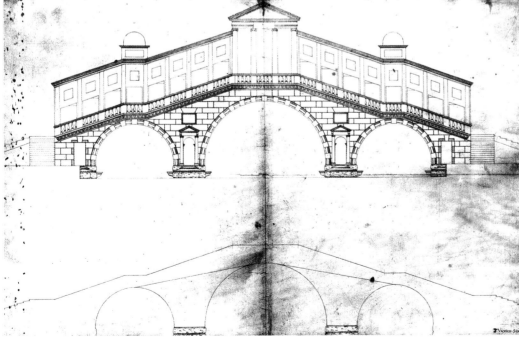

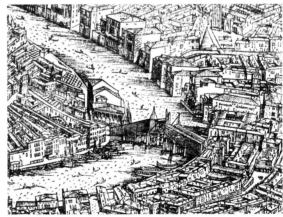

elusive) architectural competitions ever held. The brief was to design a grand new permanent bridge, all in stone, as a vital new element in the city's fabric, and as a monument to the power and wealth of the Republic.

Many schemes were produced, including one proposal from Sansovino, others from Jacopo Vignola and Michelangelo in Rome, from Vincenzo Scamozzi in Vicenza, and two alternative proposals from Andrea Palladio.[18] Palladio was later to have an enormous influence on Venice's architecture, but these early proposals were highly contentious. One of them was designed around a four-columned central portico, with five arches spanning the Grand Canal; his alternative design was even more grandiose and elaborate, and was eventually illustrated in the *I quattro libri dell'architettura* (the Four Books of Architecture), published in 1570. Both schemes were extremely ambitious, extending well beyond the span of the bridge itself to incorporate much of their immediate surroundings. They would have necessitated the destruction of many buildings on both sides of the Grand Canal, with consequent displacement of activities and loss of state revenue. Indeed, Palladio's first scheme was to extend into two great new squares or *fora*, one at each bridgehead, requiring the demolition of much of the recently built Fabbriche Vecchie, the building for the Dieci Savii and the Palazzo dei Camerlenghi. His final scheme was even more grandiose, the proposed bridge now having three nearly equal arches, with pavilions at the centre as well as each end. The bridge was to be very broad, with three aisles of shops, the rents from which would pay for the costly project.[19]

Of all the proposals, Sansovino's was initially preferred. Further progress on it was postponed and then cancelled altogether as a result of the new Turkish wars and Sansovino himself died in 1570, and his scheme with him.[20] The devastating plagues of 1575 and 1577 (which together carried off a quarter of the city's population) cast yet further blight on the project, which was effectively 'frozen' until 1578. In the same period there were also two serious fires at the Palazzo Ducale, in 1574 and 1577, that required more urgent attention and a great deal of the Republic's money. In the meantime, the debate over the final form of the bridge continued, both inside the Palazzo Ducale and outside. In 1580 the building of a new three-arch bridge across the Cannaregio Canal added fuel to the debate over whether the new bridge at the Rialto should also have three spans or whether a single great arch was feasible; technically far more daring, such a structure was potentially far more prestigious.

The 1580s was a period of notable urban renewal in the city, when important works of improvement were undertaken.[21] In 1580, the last stage of completion of the Biblioteca Marciana was under way, and the Procuratie Nuove had also been begun. In 1580–1, the Palazzo dei Prigioni was built, just across the canal from the Palazzo Ducale; and in 1588–9 the Fondamente Nuove were begun, an important engineering operation that extended and reinforced the northern edge of the city.

The new bridge
Finally, in 1587, the concluding stage in the decades-long saga of the new bridge began. Three new commissioners were nominated to commence preliminary procedures for the new bridge. A summary of this last act can be found in D Giustiniano Martinioni's 1663 revision of Francesco Sansovino's classic description of the city, *Venetia, città nobilissima*:

The Senate decided to take down the abovementioned timber bridge, to build a new one all of stone, which would be of great ornament to the city, and a marvel to all who would see it. And so three of the most senior Senators were elected, that is, Marc'Antonio Barbaro, Iacopo Foscarini, Cavaliere and Procurator of San Marco, and Luigi Giorgio (Alvise Zorzi) … they ordered designs and models from the most famous architects … Thus, with great diligence, they accepted,

Plan of the scheme as built, with two rows
of shops, and three pedestrian routes, linking
the Rialto markets with the Merceria and
San Marco.

examined and considered various models made by skilled and famous men, [and] they finally
elected the most beautiful and noble, the design of Antonio known as da Ponte, extremely
experienced in his profession …[22]

Martinioni diplomatically avoids mention of the heated debate still surrounding the final choice of
design. All three Senators were important public figures, all at one time commissioners for the
reconstruction works at the Palazzo Ducale; Barbaro in particular was a notable scholar, a man of
considerable intellect, who years earlier (together with his brother Daniele) had commissioned
Palladio to design his new villa at Maser. Barbaro was deeply involved with architecture, and had
earlier engaged in a debate over the form of the Redentore church; he was also Procurator when
the Procuratie Nuove had been under construction in the 1570s. Barbaro was a strong supporter
of a noble, architectural solution, that is, one of three arches. In December, new
proposals were received, including one from da Ponte with three arches.

The debate recommenced. A single span was not only more daring, but also gave far greater
freedom for shipping, while a three-arch solution was still claimed to be more classical and thus
architecturally 'correct'. Vincenzo Scamozzi then produced a three-arched scheme, although a
majority of the Signoria now favoured a single great span. Da Ponte, too, came to prefer a single
arch and so, finally, on 20 January 1588 the decision was taken to proceed with such a design. The
final scheme is often said to be based closely on the lost proposal by Michelangelo. It involved far
less disruption to the urban fabric than most of the 1554 proposals and it effectively knitted
together the two squares of San Giacometto and San Bartolomeo; the only significant alteration
being the cutting of a short new street (the present Salizzada Pio X) into the square of San
Bartolomeo from the southern bridgehead. The contract for the foundations and piles was let on
28 January 1588, and the entire bridge was completed by early 1591, when leases for the new shops
were put up for auction. The total cost of construction had been 245,537 ducats. After decades of
prevarication, therefore, the work was completed with great rapidity and, as we can see, the
confidence of the Signoria in da Ponte proved to be amply justified.[23]

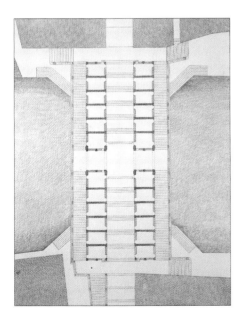

The degree to which da Ponte was indebted to Michelangelo cannot be established with certainty,
but the result was a considerable feat of engineering. In 1663 Martinioni reported that the height
of the arch was 20 Venetian feet and the span 'around 70 feet'. It was supported, he recorded, 'on
12,000 piles of elm, that is, 6,000 on each bank, and each of them ten feet long'.[24] The image of
the bridge today is such a famous, integral part of the city's fabric that the extreme daring of its
construction is rarely appreciated; nor is the powerful impression that it made on da Ponte's
contemporaries, combining architectural dignity with a number of practical, technical functions,
apparently with such ease. Although the detailing is probably less substantial and refined than
Sansovino's or Palladio's might have been, the design is ingenious in several respects: it provides a
broad central route lined with shops, twenty-four in all, in four groups of six, which continue the
commercial network of the city virtually uninterrupted from the Mercerie, across the square of San
Bartolomeo, over the bridge and into the Ruga dei Oresi. The outer flanks of the bridge provide
two further routes, less encumbered by commerce, and which afford generous balconies from
which to observe pageants and other spectacles in the Canal below. The central pavilions, with
their triumphal arches, provide the all-important note of civic grandeur and classical allusion,
while the bas-reliefs in the spandrels record the Republic's patrons, Marco and Todaro, on one side,
and the Annunciation on the other.[25] The bridge's clear span offers the greatest freedom of
movement for shipping, and gave the world a potent symbol of Venetian skill in taming the waters
of their own magnificent Canalazzo.

THE RIALTO BRIDGE

Detail of spandrel (far left) on the Riva del Vin side: the Angel of the Annunciation by Agostino Rubini, c.1589.

Detail of keystone to the central pavilion (above).

View from the south-west (left). One of the universal images of Venice, the bridge was a remarkable feat of engineering.

Part III | the buildings of venice

'It only remains to mention the Ducal Palace, where our most Serene Prince resides. It is ... a most beautiful and worthy building. First of all, [the part of] the Palace where he lives has recently been renovated, the works being finished in 1492, and the Doge has taken up residence there ... The rebuilding took ten years, because the old Palace, dating from the time of Doge Giovanni Mocenigo, was burned down in the night. The present one was then begun, which has cost more than 100,000 ducats up to now. The outside walls are all worked over and inlaid with white marble and with stone from all over the world. Inside, the walls on the ground floor are all gilded and inlaid with panelling, so that it is a very beautiful sight. There are four gilded chambers – I never saw anything more beautiful – which took a great time and elaborate workmanship...'   **Marin Sanudo**, *Laus urbis Venetae*, Venice, 1493.[1]

Palazzo Ducale

The evolution of the Piazza of San Marco as the city's political and spiritual heart was outlined in Chapter 4, together with a summary of the functions of the buildings around the Piazza. In this chapter, these palaces are discussed individually and in greater detail: their practical functions, their architectural styles and their symbolic role in the development of the Republic's institutions. By the fall of the Serenissima in 1797, the entire district of San Marco was devoted almost exclusively to the housing of the institutions of the state. The Palazzo Ducale and the adjacent basilica of San Marco enjoy a symbiotic relationship, despite their strongly contrasting architectural styles and practical functions. The latter is the shrine of the patron saint, the former the palace of the doge, inheritor of the spiritual mantle of the Evangelist, in whose name the Most Serene Republic was governed. The Palazzo is the most outstanding lay medieval building in Venice, but despite its superficial familiarity to so many, the image of its refined Gothic tracery and patterned stonework can easily obscure its many and highly specialized practical functions. Far more than simply the 'palace of the doges', it became a power base, hub of a wealthy and extensive empire, within which were concentrated all the highest organs of the Republic, both administrative and judicial.

The Venetian constitution was complex, but its fundamental guiding principle was the prevention of concentrations of power, and the avoidance of descent into despotism that characterized the history of so many Italian city-states. Its power structure was pyramidal, with the doge as head of state, and three principal chambers to control all aspects of governmental policy.

The Maggior Consiglio, the Great Council, was the foundation stone of the constitution. Since all adult male nobles were eligible to vote, at different times it contained from 1,000 to as many as 2,500 members. The Maggior Consiglio also elected all the other higher officers of state, the Senate, the Collegio and the doge himself. The Senate or 'upper house', was also known as the Pregadi, since, when it was established, senators were 'requested' (*pregadi*) to attend and advise the doge on important matters of policy. The Senate held much executive and legislative power; its nucleus contained sixty men, although a Zonta or *aggiunta* (an additional sixty members) was added later in a further attempt to prevent concentrations of power in the hands of cliques or factions. Later still, the Senate was augmented by the Quarantia al Criminal, forty justices responsible for enforcing criminal law.[2]

The innermost circle or cabinet was the Collegio or Serenissima Signoria, which in later centuries consisted of the doge, his six privy councillors, the Grand Chancellor and the three chiefs of the

THE TORRE DELL'OROLOGIO (above)

Detail of the uppermost storey, with the lion of San Marco and the two 'Moors', who ring the hours on the great bronze bell.

THE PALAZZO DUCALE (right)

Facade to the Piazzetta. The Piazzetta wing was rebuilt after 1424, following the principles of the design of the earlier wing facing the Bacino.

Council of Ten. The doge was elected by an extremely tortuous system of secret balloting of the Maggior Consiglio and, once enthroned, reigned for life. He also chaired all the other governing bodies of the Republic.[3]

The Council of Ten stood just outside this central pyramid of power, but was of considerable importance; it was established in the direct aftermath of the unsuccessful plot of Marco Querini and Baiamonte Tiepolo in 1310 to overthrow the government. The Council's broad remit extended to control all aspects of state security, particularly treason and sedition. It had the power to try and condemn to death any man in the Republic, even the doge himself, if found guilty of treason.[4]

The Palazzo Ducale contained not only accommodation for all these institutions but, as Palace of Justice of the Republic, it also housed the chief appeal court, the Quarantia Civil (the Forty), as well as ancillary facilities such as prisons. Later, as the Republic grew in numbers, extent and complexity, the Quarantia was divided into two bodies, the Quarantie Civil Vecchia and Nuova.[5]

We know very little of Doge Angelo Partecipazio's first *castrum*, begun in the 810s, although by tradition, one of its massive corner towers is said to survive as the present Treasury of San Marco. This castle was damaged, perhaps destroyed, in the fire that also damaged the basilica in 976. Again ruined by fire in 1106, it was rebuilt once more, and was largely complete when the Emperor Henry V was received there ten years later.

The most radical reordering, though, was that undertaken by the indefatigable Doge Sebastiano Ziani in the 1170s. Forming part of his 'grand plan' for the reorganization of the Piazza and its surroundings, Ziani's palace was essentially a Venetian-Byzantine reconstruction, built on two storeys, with open colonnades and logge, supported by rows of characteristic stilted arches; in its general appearance, it probably resembled the rebuilt Fondaco dei Turchi on the Grand Canal, as we see it (much restored) today. The previously rather organic form of the palace, with its varied functions, was now reorganized and rationalized into three component elements, almost certainly identifiable as individual structures: the ducal apartments, the Palace of Justice and the legislature, the last centred on the great hall of the Maggior Consiglio. This group of buildings or wings had towers at the corners, vestiges or reminders of their earlier, more fortified predecessors, and the three wings were built around a large central courtyard, with the flank wall of San Marco enclosing the ensemble on the fourth side. The location of the three wings was of great importance, since their functions were retained in these positions in the Palazzo's successive rebuildings: the Palace of Justice was on the west side, facing the newly-reclaimed Piazzetta; the great council hall stood at right angles to it, facing the Bacino, while the ducal apartments lay on the far side, along the narrow Rio di Palazzo.

The core of the Palazzo was the great hall of the Maggior Consiglio. Although we have no knowledge of the detailed appearance of Ziani's great hall, his reconstruction can be seen as one element in a widespread period of similar activity over much of northern Italy. At this time, most of the Italian city-states were free, independent communes, and based their government on large assemblies of their leading citizens, which were housed in halls of imposing dimensions and appearance. Almost every city in the Veneto still has a Palazzo della Ragione (palace for debate, or for the dispensation of justice) dating from this period; the most imposing is the vast Palazzo at Padua, built in 1218, although Vicenza, (1222), Verona (1193) and Treviso (*c*1217) all built or rebuilt their city halls in this period.

Doge Ziani's refined, elegant Byzantine structures survived for around 150 years, during which time the Republic expanded in numbers and increased in wealth. The numbers of the nobility also increased considerably, as did the government in complexity, such that by the fourteenth century it had become clear that radical new works were now an urgent necessity.

THE PALAZZO DUCALE

Plan at the level of the upper loggia (right),
which contained several departments of
the Republic's administration; the Molo
wing is on the right, the Piazzetta wing at
the bottom, and the rio wing at the top.

Plan at the uppermost floor (below), the
level of the great halls of state. The Maggior
Consiglio occupies most of the Molo wing,
while along the rio wing are the halls of
the Senate, the Consiglio dei Dieci and the
Collegio or Signoria.

The Drunkenness of Noah (far right), on
the south-east corner, next to the Ponte
di Paglia, probably from the very late
14th century.

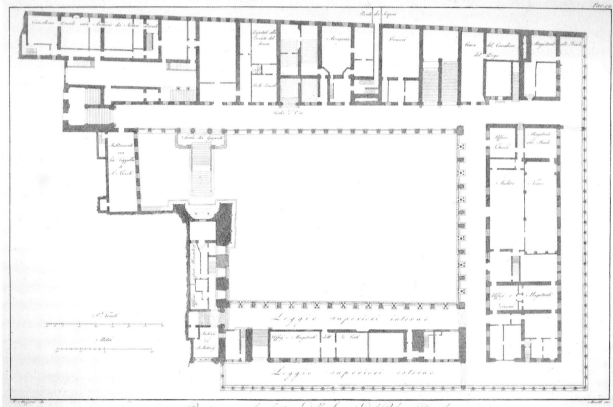

Pianta generale al piano delle Loggie del Palazzo Ducale

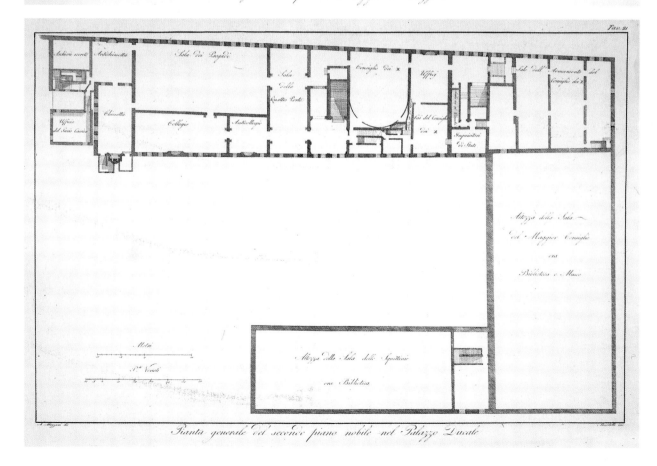

Pianta generale del secondo piano nobile nel Palazzo Ducale

The final definitive rebuilding of the structure of the Palazzo was the result of a government decree in 1340, when it was decided to rebuild the south wing, facing the Bacino, to provide a much larger hall for the Maggior Consiglio.[6] This resulted in the basic form of the Molo wing that has survived today, although it is generally accepted that the structure of the tower at the eastern corner of the Ziani Palazzo was retained and incorporated into the new Molo wing. One of the results of this retention was that the two easternmost windows on this facade are at a lower level than the remainder, corresponding to the earlier floor levels.

Here again, comparison with nearby Padua is instructive; in 1306 Venice's mainland neighbour (and rival) began a comprehensive modernization of its Palazzo della Ragione, which was enhanced by the addition of two storeys of surrounding colonnades, chiefly of brick, and was given a new roof, a great timber vault, today a rare survivor, together with that at Vicenza. It is highly likely, therefore, that when the even wealthier Venetian Republic embarked on its own rebuilding programme it should seek to emulate, and indeed to considerably surpass, its Terraferma rival in grandeur and sophistication.

THE PALAZZO DUCALE

The central part of the Molo facade (below, left), with Pier Paolo delle Masegne's great window of 1400.

The Molo facade (below), with Doge Ziani's column and the lion of San Marco.

The great, imposing mass of the Molo facade remains today the most dominant structure on the whole Bacino waterfront, still the focus of any visitor's approach to the city by water, six centuries after its construction. The Palazzo epitomized the power, wealth and extraordinary stability of the institutions of the Republic. The Molo wing was largely reconstructed between 1340 and the 1370s, when the Paduan artist Guariento decorated the interior with frescos. However, several elements followed later, including the ceilings, which were installed in *c*1400, and the great central window, by the dalle Masegne family, which was carved in 1400–4. Finally, there came the characteristic sheathing of small pieces of pink and white marble which, according to Francesco Sansovino in *Venetia, città nobilissima*, were not added until the reign of Doge Francesco Foscari, that is, after 1423.[7]

The appearance of the Molo wing owes something both to the influence of Terraferma great halls and also to the lingering influence of the earlier Venetian-Byzantine logge and colonnades. Unlike the great hall at Padua, though, and Palladio's later modernization at Vicenza, where the loggia is wrapped around the outside of the hall itself, the great hall of the Maggior Consiglio is raised directly above a double layer of continuous colonnades, which occupy the full length of the facade. Also unlike the brick colonnades of Padua, the arcades here are all of fine Istrian stone, and it is this dramatic inversion of massing, with the hall supported on graceful traceried colonnades, that makes the Palazzo Ducale such an arresting and remarkable structure.[8]

The Molo wing was crowned with a characteristic and refined stone crenellation, silhouetted against the sky, but quite devoid of any defensive purpose; such a feature is Muslim in origin, and similar decoration could be seen adorning mosques at Cairo, Beirut and Baghdad. Its adoption here again reflects Venice's intimate links with the East, and the Palazzo Ducale's prototype was enthusiastically adopted elsewhere in the city in the fifteenth century, notably on the Cà d'Oro.[9]

The two lower colonnades, all of Istrian stone, have come to epitomize the sophisticated character of later Venetian Gothic; although the lower columns had to be of necessity very substantial, their capitals represent some of the finest examples of late Gothic figurative carving. (None of the Molo sculptures can be dated precisely, W Wolters has suggested an early date of *c*1355, in *La sculturo gotica veneziana 1300–1460*, but other dates vary from the 1390s to the 1420s.) The allegorical

THE PALAZZO DUCALE

The south-west corner onto the Piazzetta (below, left), with the sculpted group known as *The Fall* (Adam and Eve).

The first floor loggia (below, centre), which offered the Signoria views of the spectacles in the Piazzetta and in the Bacino.

The Foscari Arch (below, right), begun by doge Francesco Foscari in c.1445 but only completed in the 1460s.

series of the Vices and Virtues, the heads of emperors, great philosophers, the Ages of Man and other themes all evince the lively, indigenous culture, typically Venetian in its broad subject matter and in the quality of the sculptors' skill.

The upper loggia was able to incorporate the refined tracery that structural considerations rendered impractical on the lowest level, as a result of the immense loads that the ground-floor columns had to bear. The alternating trefoil arches and quatrefoils in their circles became a leitmotif for the last stage of Venetian Gothic; like the crenellation, the design of this tracery had a strong influence on a number of fine later fifteenth-century palaces, again including the Cà d'Oro and the house of Doge Francesco Foscari, built in the 1450s.

The great Molo facade effectively forms a screen, with central emphasis provided by the great window. The corners, though, also required some additional visual emphasis and this was provided by two sculpted compositions, both of which had symbolic as well as visual roles. The figures on the upper orders of both corners represented the guiding spirits of the archangels; on the east corner, next to the Ponte di Paglia, was located the Archangel Raphael, protector of pilgrims and travellers, a particularly apposite symbol in this city of international trade and pilgrimage, and directly facing the basin where the ships were moored. On the west corner, the Archangel Michael represented the angel of light and of war against evil, an appropriate expression of the Republic's self-perceived role as the bulwark of militant Christianity.

By way of contrast with these spiritual guides, the lower sculptural groups were intended to emphasize the frailties and weaknesses of man; in this way the aspirations of the nobles within the Palazzo were to be tempered with reminders of human humility. The east corner was therefore marked by the famous *Drunkenness of Noah*, sometimes attributed to Giovanni (Zane) Bon, or to Matteo Raverti. The figure of Noah as a direct representation of human frailty, was balanced by the sculpted group on the west corner, generally known as *The Fall*, depicting Adam, Eve, the serpent and the tree of knowledge. Here, the symbolic representation of the knowledge of good and evil was singularly appropriate for the Palace of the Republic's government.[10]

The final element on the facade to be completed was the great central window, the contract for which has survived. It was carved by the native sculptor Pier Paolo delle Masegne, and was completed in 1404, with allegorical figures in the flanking niches, and the symbolic figure of Justice at the apex, later replaced by the present sixteenth-century work by Alessandro Vittoria. The balcony of the window served a practical and symbolic function, since it gave the doge and Signoria a superb vantage point from which to observe the entire Bacino, a link between the great hall of the Republic and the trading fleets from which its wealth and power derived. Collectively, the architecture and sculpture on the Molo wing represent a fusion of the skills of indigenous masters refining the native tradition, together with the undoubted (although still not clearly attributable) contribution of foreign masters, almost certainly from Milan and Florence, attracted by the city's wealth and opportunities.[11]

The new Molo wing was finally completed in the 1410s, and the Maggior Consiglio met in its new hall for the first time on 30 July 1419. Its internal decoration originally consisted chiefly of frescos; the whole east wall was decorated with Guariento's huge *Paradise* fresco (fragments of which survive), while a series on the other walls was executed by Pisanello, Gentile da Fabriano and others. By 1474, though, many had already seriously deteriorated, and Gentile Bellini began a programme of replacement, assisted by Bartolomeo Vivarini and Vittore Carpaccio, all native painters. The second stage of this programme was begun in 1537, and incorporated works by Titian, Veronese and Tintoretto, again the greatest native masters of the succeeding generations. All of these great works were to be lost in a disastrous fire in 1577.[12]

In 1424, with the new Molo wing now complete and in use, the second stage of this programme of renewal was begun; the old Ziani wing, facing the Piazzetta at right angles to the new wing, still contained the Palace of Justice, but was now well over two hundred years old, and was so badly deteriorated as to threaten collapse. The new Molo wing already had a gable end facing Ziani's two columns, and so it was now decided, after an interval of a couple of decades, to continue the same design along the remainder of the Piazzetta facade, as soon as the Ziani building had been demolished. Today it is not easy to trace where the first phase ends and the second begins, since their appearance is virtually identical, with the same sheathing of small marble 'tiles' and the same stone tracery. Even the design of the column capitals to the ground-floor arcade chiefly repeats the earlier themes; again, too, the centre of the facade was emphasized by another prominent, richly-carved window.

The iconographical theme of this wing, though, was to be clearly articulated in several ways; on the upper loggia a prominent stone tondo represents Venice as Justice, as does the crowning figure to the central window. The latter was considerably modified, in 1536, when four Renaissance statues of classical goddesses were added, and Vittoria carved a new figure of Justice for the pinnacle. The northern end of the new facade was terminated in a similar manner to the two earlier corners, with the last of the three fine groups of late Gothic sculpture; the symbolic themes were also continued, with the Archangel Gabriel on the upper order, and the lower order occupied with the *Judgement of Solomon*. The latter again reflects the purpose of this wing as the Palace of Justice, with representations of historical lawgivers, among them Aristotle and Moses.

The new Palace of Justice wing was complete by around 1438, the two rebuilt wings now presenting an imposing, unified appearance at this most prominent of all Venetian sites. Only a narrow gap remained between the new north-west corner and the south wall of San Marco, but into this gap was inserted the magnificent Porta della Carta, designed and largely executed by the native Bartolomeo Bon between 1438 and 1442. Until now, the Palazzo had had no formal, public entrance, a reflection perhaps of the traditionally introverted, self-perpetuating nature of Venetian government; it seems, therefore, that the Porta della Carta was something of an afterthought, marking a shift in perceptions within the Palazzo Ducale, and reflecting a newly identified need for a formal state entrance, to enhance the Palazzo's dignity. Equally, though, it undoubtedly reflects the strong, forceful character of its patron, the Doge Francesco Foscari, whose effigy, kneeling in front of the winged lion, dominates the Porta just above the portal itself. Rarely, if ever, before had a Republican monument of such prominence been used for such directly personal imagery; individuality of expression of this nature was generally considered impermissible by the carefully constrained oligarchy that formed the Serenissima's government, where collective responsibility was

THE PALAZZO DUCALE

The Judgement of Solomon (above), the last of the three fine sculpted groups on the external corners of the Palazzo; it was probably carved in the 1430s.

Detail of the Porta della Carta (right), Bartolomeo Bon's masterpiece, and the only formal entrance into the palace; it was completed in c.1442.

all. Foscari set a notable precedent here, though, that was to be taken up later by other doges with their minds on posterity, such as Agostin Barbarigo, who employed a very similar device at the nearby Clock Tower a few decades later.

Nevertheless, Doge Foscari was fully aware of the more general symbolic importance of the Porta. Once completed, it remained the only formal, ceremonial approach for the reception of foreign dignitaries and ambassadors, as well as forming a dignified backdrop from which the doge and Signoria could process on feast days. In recognitition of this role it was originally richly decorated and gilded, and incorporated many other symbolic images. The patron saint, for example, was depicted not only as a winged lion, symbol of the Republic itself, but also, in a tondo, as a man, the Evangelist. Foscari also chose the four Virtues, the figures of Temperance, Fortitude, Prudence and Charity that flank the portal (similar figures decorate his own funerary monument in the Frari church), while the whole was once again surmounted by the omnipresent figure of Justice, carved by Bartolomeo Bon. The great central window, again the work of Bon, was to mark the peak of late Venetian Gothic tracery, while the Porta as a whole is probably the finest example of the fusion of such triumphant architectural form with rich, but carefully integrated, symbolic sculpture.[13] The Porta was probably not yet completed before work began on its continuation, a vaulted colonnade that leads from the Porta into the heart of the Palazzo behind. The colonnade, again begun by Doge Foscari, was designed in a rather hybrid style, incorporating some Renaissance elements in the detailing, although it, too, was at least partly the work of Bon. The Foscari loggia, as it is known, was a further attempt to formalize the state entrance by means of an axial progression from the Piazzetta outside; it was originally screened off on the south side and was thus extremely dark, with attention focused on the arch at its far end.

This eastern termination, the Foscari Arch, was once again planned by the same formidable doge, and represents an exercise in ostentatious patronage considerably more elaborate (although significantly less successful) than the Porta della Carta. Surmounted by a complex array of pinnacles and statuary, it took more than twenty years to complete. Initially intended as a triumphal arch to celebrate Foscari's early military successes, it remained incomplete even after his record thirty-four-year reign had ended in 1457. Bartolomeo Bon, who had begun the work, died in about 1464, and it was concluded by the Veronese sculptor Antonio Rizzo, assisted by Antonio Bregno from Lugano; Rizzo's famous figures of Adam and Eve were carved in 1476 for the eastern face of the Arch.[14]

The Arch makes little impression from below, other than as a termination to the loggia; however, its rich pinnacles were intended to be appreciated from the upper levels of the east wing of the Palazzo, where the ducal apartments were located. Its spatial significance is considerable, though, since the Palazzo was now finally provided with a formal axial sequence of spaces for pageants and processions. It graphically illustrates the desire of the Signoria in general, and of Foscari in particular, to enhance the dignity of this civic and political route by imposing a degree of Renaissance order on to the essentially Gothic Palazzo. The next stage in this process, however, was the result of fate, rather than a conscious choice on the part of the Signoria.

Antonio Rizzo, primarily a sculptor, was nevertheless promoted to director of works (proto) at the Palazzo after a disastrous fire on 14 September 1483 had resulted in the loss of most of the remaining Ziani buildings that had survived on the east side of the central courtyard. This wing had contained a range of buildings, at the northernmost end of which were the ducal apartments, abutting San Marco. The reconstruction was to take many years, though, and the first stage probably consisted of the lower facades to the courtyard and the Rio di Palazzo on the other side, the latter perhaps to designs by Mauro Codussi. But the most significant element in this stage was Rizzo's new staircase, which later became known as the Scala dei Giganti, and which was intended

THE PALAZZO DUCALE

Detail of Jacopo Sansovino's figure of Neptune (previous pages), on the top of the Scala dei Giganti, with the east wing behind; the wing was the work of several *proti*, among them Antonio Rizzo, Pietro Lombardo and Scarpagnino.

THE PALAZZO DUCALE

Sansovino's two figures of Mars and
Neptune, dating from 1566, represent the
two components, land and sea, of the
Venetian empire. Newly-elected doges were
proclaimed to the people from the landing at
the top of Antonio Rizzo's stairs.

to complete the axis now formed by the Porta della Carta, the colonnade and the Foscari Arch.

The Scala was built as a direct response to developments in the ritual of the coronation of the doge; after its completion, all newly-elected doges were presented to the people from the large balcony at the top of the stair. As befits this most significant symbolic function, the Scala is richly detailed and lavishly carved. Its martial and heraldic motifs reflected the tastes of the incumbent doge, Agostin Barbarigo, and the turbulent military events of his reign; the chief of these were the defence of Cyprus against the Turks and the grand alliance with Milan and the Holy Roman Emperor against the French, resulting in the victory of Fornovo. The ceremonial axis was thus now complete, and the top of the Scala linked directly to the spacious upper loggia that ran around the courtyard facades of the Palazzo. A few decades after its completion, its dignity was enhanced still further by the addition of Jacopo Sansovino's two giant statues of Mars and Neptune, the figures symbolizing the two elements of the Venetian empire, the Terraferma and sea.[15]

Although the Scala was completed in around 1490, considerable work remained in the new east wing, the reconstruction of the southern part of which had not yet begun. By now, the expansion of the empire and its many governmental institutions had given rise to acute pressures of space on the only available land left at the Palazzo, that along the Rio. A great deal of accommodation had to be ingeniously planned, and the resulting structure was inevitably tall and massive, with four principal storeys and a number of internal staircases. By 1498, great expenses had been incurred (although the wing was still far from complete) and were continuing to increase rapidly. The Signoria, however, had by now identified irregularities in the building accounts: Rizzo was faced with charges of fraud and embezzlement; he immediately fled the Republic to Cesena and then Ferrara where he died shortly afterwards.

Pietro Lombardo was now appointed proto to replace Rizzo, and was assisted by Giorgio Spavento and Antonio Scarpagnino, both of whom continued the work after Pietro's death in 1515. These last stages incorporated the important halls of state on the two uppermost storeys, chiefly the Senate and the Collegio. It was a protracted process and it remains unclear which master was responsible for the design of the various elements of the imposing east wing. Recently, at least some of the design of the canal facade has been attributed to Mauro Codussi. The complex but disciplined facade incorporates rustication on the lowest order, which was still rare in Venice at this time; among the very few earlier examples is Codussi's own revolutionary facade for the monastic church of San Michele. The upper levels, though, were only completed in the 1520s, some time after his death, by Scarpagnino.[16]

The great mass of the east wing can be fully appreciated from the central courtyard; in sharp contrast with the two earlier wings, this last phase is very much richer and entirely clad with fine Istrian stone. Although the two lowest storeys retain the rhythmic discipline of the logge on the other facades, above them are superimposed the vibrant textures and complex rhythms of the upper facades, their rich bas-relief detail the characteristic work of Pietro Lombardo and his immediate followers; there is little of Codussi's influence here. One of the last elements to be completed was the Cortiletto dei Senatori, the small courtyard north of Rizzo's staircase; used as a meeting place for senators, its refined Renaissance facade was added by Spavento and Scarpagnino.

The whole process of reconstruction, ever since the decision to rebuild the Molo wing in 1340, had been piecemeal and organic. Although unity had been achieved in the external facades of the Molo and Piazzetta wings, there had never been an integrated 'master plan' for the Palazzo; instead it had evolved to meet the developing requirements of the government. Stylistically, too, it reflected firstly the maturation of the indigenous Gothic, then the rather complex transitional period between Gothic and early Renaissance. Finally, in the Rio wing, we see the most extensive example of the Lombardesque Venetian Renaissance, the characteristic features of which are rich, refined surface

Parte del Prospetto del Palazzo Ducale sul rio in prossi alle Prigioni

THE PALAZZO DUCALE

The massive east wing (right) is more richly-detailed than any other facade; the uppermost floor housed all the highest institutions of the Republic's government.

Detail of part of the facade (above) to the Rio di Palazzo, the design of which has recently been attributed to Mauro Codussi.

LAZZARO BASTIANI, *Portrait of Doge Francesco Foscari*, c.1450

Foscari's record reign of more than 30 years saw many major building works, including the Porta della Carta and the commencement of the Foscari Arch (Venice, Museo Civico Correr).

decoration, and the selective use of highlighted details in rare marbles, usually in the form of inlaid discs or *paterae*.

The history of the interior of the Palazzo, however, was by no means concluded with the completion of the great new east wing. Decoration continued for some time after the death of Pietro Lombardo, well into the second or third decade of the sixteenth century. One of the last works was the construction and decoration of the Scala d'Oro, the Golden Stair, completed by Sansovino in around 1555. The Scala formed a further link in the spatial sequence between the Porta della Carta, the entrance to the palace itself, and the halls of state on the uppermost floor of the east wing. Once complete, therefore, the processional route begun at the Porta now continued along the Foscari loggia, up the Scala dei Giganti, and then on and up the east wing via the Scala d'Oro to the halls of the Senate and Collegio on the top storey. As befits this important role, the stair was richly decorated, its ceiling a *tour de force* of painted and gilded stucco by Alessandro Vittoria.[17]

Lombardo's new Renaissance interiors were not to survive for very long. Two disastrous fires, in 1574 and in 1577, between them destroyed virtually all the state accommodation on the uppermost storeys of the palace. The first originated in the new east wing, and devastated much of the top floor, including the recently completed chambers of the Senate and Collegio, while the second broke out in the Molo wing on 20 December 1577, and gutted the great hall of the Maggior Consiglio and the halls of justice in the Piazzetta wing.

All the interiors of the Palazzo that survive today, therefore, can be grouped into two: firstly those earlier elements (chiefly on the lower floors) that survived these two fires, and secondly those on the uppermost levels that were rebuilt in the last two or three decades of the sixteenth century. As we have already seen elsewhere, when faced with natural disasters – chiefly fires – the Republic's response was generally cautious and pragmatic. Like the reconstruction of Rialto after the fire of 1514, the rebuilt interiors of the Palazzo Ducale retained most of the essential spatial arrangements of their predecessors, although stylistically they incorporated more recent developments, and naturally had to be decorated by a new generation of masters.

The east wing had always accommodated a rather disparate collection of functions; on the lower levels, for example, were such humdrum functions as stabling for horses, the ducal guardhouse, prisons and armouries. All these activities continued to be housed here both before and after the various fires, firstly that of 1483, and then the later conflagrations in the sixteenth century.

All the halls of state were located on the second and third storeys, above the two logge. The east wing contained two principal staircases, the rich Scala d'Oro and the more functional Scala dei Censori, which together served to define the functions of the upper levels. On the second floor, to the north were the ducal apartments, while in the centre and south were legal departments and halls of justice; on the very top floor, the Senate and Collegio stood directly above the ducal apartments, while the central and southern sections were occupied respectively by the Council of Ten and the group of rooms forming the ducal armoury. All these groupings were retained in the comprehensive restorations after 1574.

The ducal apartments, between the Scala d'Oro and the abutment with San Marco, comprised ten rooms, all of which had already been rebuilt by Rizzo after the fire in 1483; Doge Agostin Barbarigo had moved into his new accommodation in 1492 while the decorations were still being completed. In this location they not only formed a symbolic link between the Palace of the Republic and the national shrine, but they also provided the doge with a means of direct access into the church without leaving the confines of the Palazzo, an arrangement combining convenience with security.

The apartments retain much that is the work of Pietro Lombardo, including fine stone fireplaces. They were planned in a similar manner to the traditional Venetian private palace, with a long central hall or gallery, known in Venice as a *portego*, flanked on both sides by smaller rooms. On one side, towards the narrow canal, were the doge's private apartments, while on the side towards the courtyard were the much more elaborate halls for the reception of visitors. The comparatively modest nature of the doge's private apartments reflects the Republican perception of his role: he was a servant of the state, and although the state's own halls are indeed magnificent, the doge himself was simply one noble among hundreds, whose personal accommodation here was no more imposing than that of his own house. The rooms in which he received visitors, however, the Sala dei Scarlatti, the Sala dello Scudo and the Grimani and Erizzo rooms, are appropriately much more richly decorated.[18]

The remaining accommodation on this floor consisted of the justice departments and halls that served as antechambers for the Maggior Consiglio. The Quarantia Civil Vecchia (the 'Old' group of Forty) was the nucleus of the Appeal Court, which was divided by Doge Francesco Foscari into two branches; the 'Old Forty' remained here and administered civil justice in the city and the Dogado, while the 'New Forty', the Quarantia Civil Nova, were housed across the other side of the courtyard.

The uppermost storey of the east wing contained all the highest institutions of the Republic's government. Although in the Maggior Consiglio we can still identify links with the great communal halls of the other Italian city-states of the Middle Ages, the uniquely complex and sophisticated Venetian constitution incorporated bodies such as the Senate and the Council of Ten, which had no precise equivalents elsewhere. By the sixteenth century, most Italian states were no longer communes, but had become hereditary family princedoms, whose own lavish expenditure on palaces for their own rule forms the only approximate equivalent to the halls of state of the Most Serene Republic.

Within a compact well-defined area on the top floor of the east wing are concentrated the splendid halls of the Senate and the Collegio, and the sombrely impressive hall of the Council of Ten. On 11 May 1574 much of the uppermost part of this wing was destroyed by fire, only a few weeks before the celebrated state visit of King Henri III of France. The disaster resulted in the comprehensive rebuilding of the interiors, with the result that they exhibit a stylistic unity and programmatic integrity that is not found elsewhere in the Palazzo. Most of the earlier interiors of Lombardo and Scarpagnino were lost, but the restoration was planned by GianAntonio Rusconi, with contributions from Andrea Palladio. The work was executed under the overall supervision of the proto Antonio da Ponte, architect of the new Rialto Bridge, which was shortly to be commenced.

Although the halls were gutted, the external walls remained reasonably intact, and were retained as Lombardo had built them, the only significant alteration being the raising of the roof to provide more generous ceiling heights. The internal planning, though, was partly reordered. An opportunity also now arose to introduce comprehensive new thematic programmes in the decoration, and the predominant theme of all the interiors was the celebration of the Republic, its justice and stability, its wealth, its political and military triumphs.

It remains difficult to identify the precise contributions of Palladio, Rusconi and da Ponte, however, and the architectural framework was to be largely subsumed by the rich decoration and the painting cycles. In these decorations this group of rooms epitomizes the power and self-image of the Republic better than any other work of art or architecture in the city. It was clear that only the finest masters would be employed on the project, and equally essential that they all had to be

THE PALAZZO DUCALE

Detail of clock in the hall of the Senate (below, left), which formed part of the restoration works in the 1570s and 1580s.

Interior of the Senate or Pregadi (below); the interior was completely rebuilt after the fire of 1574, with contributions from Palladio, Rusconi and da Ponte. The rich ceiling is the work of Cristofolo Sorte, 1581.

Venetian subjects: no foreign master would be considered for such a commission. Equally clearly, too, the decorative programmes were required to reflect all the attributes – symbolic, religious, metaphorical, military and cultural – of the Republic. Many drew on the flourishing native tradition of narrative painting cycles; this tradition was particularly strong in the Scuole Grandi, most of which had already commissioned such cycles over a period of several decades, executed by such experienced masters as Vittore Carpaccio and Giovanni and Gentile Bellini.[19] The Republic was fortunate in that it could now call upon the services of an unparalleled group of painters from the succeeding generations for this new task, the chief among them Titian, Tintoretto and Veronese.

The reordered planning of this floor was now centred on the Sala delle Quattro Porte, the hall of the four doors. This imposing room was approached by a small lobby at the top of the Scala d'Oro, and formed the hub of circulation to all the halls of state. The Sala delle Quattro Porte had housed the Collegio prior to the fire, but the Collegio was now relocated further north, and the Sala thus became a space for ceremonial occasions and receptions. Its new decorative programme was closely identifiable with the Republic's self-image in this period as 'the new Rome', and its Roman Renaissance ceiling was decorated with frescos of Venice's subject cities. The imperial imagery was enhanced by wall paintings of notable events in the Republic's history, and the whole was completed by Palladio's four richly-carved classical doorways, with their luxuriant Corinthian marble columns.[20]

From the Sala delle Quattro Porte, the two portals on the north wall gave access to the two supreme organs of the Republic, the Senate and the Collegio. The spatial needs of the latter (also known as the Serenissima Signoria) were fairly modest, since only ten men formed its innermost core,

sometimes augmented by a further sixteen ministers to form what was known as the Pien Collegio or 'full cabinet'. Nevertheless, in this hall all major policy decisions of the Republic were formulated, and foreign embassies formally given audience. Its decorative programme thus had to represent the highest attributes of the Republic, with allegorical but profoundly patriotic themes; here were concentrated the finest works of art and the most sumptuous decoration.

The rich, coffered ceiling, probably designed by Palladio, was enhanced by Veronese's paintings, among them Venice's Virtues: Faithfulness and Prosperity in the slightly less convincing company of Meekness and Simplicity. Veronese's *Battle of Lepanto* (1571) depicted not only the famous Christian victory over the Turks, but brings together in one work images of war, faith, patriotism and the triumph of the righteous.

The Senate was the last room to be restored following the 1574 fire. Exceptionally noble and impressive, it had to accommodate the much larger numbers of the Senate itself and the Zonta, around 200 noblemen in all. Second only to the Maggior Consiglio in its grandeur, the hall was to be dominated by the powerful ceiling, designed by Cristofolo Sorte, and completed in 1581. Sorte was the outstanding master woodcarver of the era, and the ceiling heralds the Baroque in its bold scrolls and volutes, strongly contrasting with the rich but more geometrical ceiling of the Collegio.

The only senior department of state not accommodated within this suite of halls was the Consiglio dei Dieci, the Council of Ten. This reflects its position outside the 'pyramid of power', and its different function as a court of justice, rather than part of the legislature. The Council was the supreme judicial body, the permanent court of national security; it was housed immediately south

The Scala d'Oro (above), remodelled by Sansovino in the 1550s, with elaborate stucco decoration by Alessandro Vittoria. The stair gives access to all the halls of state on the top floor.

The hall of the Senate (left). Above the ducal throne is Tintoretto's imposing *The Dead Christ Supported by Angels, with Doges Pietro Lando and Marcantonio Trevisan.*

of the Scala d'Oro, in a spacious but appropriately gloomy hall, which retains its original semicircular plan around which the council sat. The decorative themes are said to have been established by Daniele Barbaro, the notable Renaissance intellectual and humanist, and reflected his own classical interests with depictions of Roman gods and allegorical themes. Annexed to the hall of the Ten were specialized support facilities, among them the Sala della Bussola, the antechamber in which secret denunciations could be placed for investigation by the Ten. Also adjacent were rooms for the state inquisitors. After the new Prisons were built across the Rio di Palazzo, a secure route was provided to them from the inquisitors' room by means of a bridge, the so-called Ponte dei Sospiri, or Bridge of Sighs.

At the southern end of the wing, Doge Andrea Gritti had established a ducal armoury in 1532; it was intended both to contain a practical supply of arms for the guards of the Ten and to house a display collection to show to illustrious visitors. In 1580 Francesco Sansovino had described it as consisting of: 'four ample and spacious rooms, filled with beautiful breastplates decorated with gilding, coats of mail, lances of various shapes … arrows, fine arquebuses, and every other type of equipment to arm a great number of men'.[21] It is a description that remains as accurate today as when it was written.

On 20 December 1577, three and a half years after the fire in the Rio wing, the Maggior Consiglio, too, was destroyed by fire. Coming so soon afterwards, it caused immense disruption to the government of the Republic, since the Maggior Consiglio was the foundation of the entire hierarchy; the only spaces large enough to contain the numbers of assembled patricians were some of the industrial structures in the Arsenale, the oar-making halls and ropeworks, where the nobles now had to assemble, somewhat ignobly, until the hall was restored.

After the fire, the Signoria commissioned reports and recommendations from many of the most notable architects of the day, requesting their proposed course of action: broadly, whether the surviving Gothic shell could be saved and restored, or whether complete reconstruction was the more practical alternative. Among twelve architects approached were Andrea da Valle, Paolo da Ponte, Palladio, GianAntoni Rusconi and Cristofolo Sorte (the last three already involved with the Rio wing reconstruction). This dozen was then reduced to a more manageable six experts, the five noted above together with Guglielmo de'Grandi. Reconstruction was to be supervised by a group of three noble *provveditori* (commissioners). Palladio's view was that the Gothic structure was inherently and fundamentally unstable because of its 'inverted' form, with the great mass of the Maggior Consiglio supported on open colonnades: 'the defects and shortcomings of this structure', he wrote, 'offend all natural principles'. He strongly advised that demolition was the best course, providing an opportunity to build a fine new wing all in a noble Roman style, for which he contributed an initial design of his own.[22] Nevertheless, the perennially cautious Republic, faced with the great cost of restorations barely begun in the Rio wing, was again persuaded that prudence was a wiser counsellor: the Gothic shell was to be retained and reroofed, although the fire had claimed not only the great timber roof and the internal decorations, but also the tracery of the Molo windows, which has never been replaced. The former vaulted timber roof, which must have resembled that still surviving today in the great Palazzo della Ragione in Padua, was replaced with a flat, coffered ceiling, vast and ornate, in a heavy early Baroque style. It is again the work of Cristofolo Sorte, and represents a reworking of his design for the Senate ceiling, here on a prodigious scale.

Once again the ceiling was to form the framework for an extensive series of painting cycles, all of them centred on Veronese's *Apotheosis of Venice* of *c*1583, one of his finest works. Its location directly above the ducal dais reflects the quasi-religious iconography of the hall, with the dais as an 'altar', and the Apotheosis representing Venice as supreme arbiter of peace and justice. Tintoretto's enormous *Paradiso* of 1588–90 was to occupy the whole of the east wall, in place of Guariento's lost fresco. Here, too, a basically religious concept was harnessed to the Republican myth; however, the great scale necessary to dominate the hall seems to have proved too daunting even for Tintoretto, who replaced the deceased Veronese, and it is by no means his finest work. The walls of the hall were redecorated with still more new narrative cycles, that quintessentially Venetian form of painting, ideally suited for the recording of past victories and pageants; most were the work of the Bassano workshop, of Palma the Younger and of Domenico Tintoretto, Jacopo's son.

Contemporary prints suggest that the Piazzetta wing was damaged almost as badly by the fire as the Maggior Consiglio. Its restoration, though, involved a considerable reorganization of the interior. Other than the Quarantia Civil Nova, the whole wing was now transformed into a second great hall, the Sala dello Scrutinio, to be used for the counting of votes in the Maggior Consiglio, and for meetings for the election of new doges and other senior officials. Its decoration continued the themes of the Maggior Consiglio, and the work was supervised by Antonio da Ponte, in his role as proto of the Palazzo. Here again, the disaster gave the opportunity to create an interior with a unified decorative programme, representing Venice's eastern empire and its acquisition, among which were the great naval victories of Lepanto, Cattaro and the Dardanelles. With this restoration, the Palazzo was finally completed in the form that has survived today.

The prisons of the Republic

The Palazzo Ducale, however, had always been tightly circumscribed on its rectangular site; even with the Rizzo and Lombardo rebuildings of the late fifteenth century, it had been feasible only to expand upwards. Allocating space for prisons had long been difficult, although essential, and as early as the fifteenth century the Council of Ten had had to annexe a house across the Rio di Palazzo to ease the pressure on space. But this was clearly far from satisfactory as a long-term solution, and in 1563 proposals and models were invited from architects for a new Palazzo dei Prigioni on the other side of the Rio. GianAntonio Rusconi's proposal was successful, and the first element built was the block to the north, in which he arranged groups of cells in the centre with a perimeter corridor, the whole massively constructed of great blocks of Istrian stone. Not only did this relieve pressure inside the Palazzo, but it removed from it some of the less pleasant and civilized activities of the Republic's government. In 1567 a second stage was begun, but it was only after 1574 that a further proposal was made to considerably enlarge and unify the whole complex. This last stage is almost always attributed to Antonio da Ponte, and his design included the front wing that stands today facing the Bacino, as well as the square internal courtyard.

This prominent site clearly required a facade of some presence, and da Ponte's two-storey screen has a slightly coarse but imposing classical facade, all of Istrian stone. It can be seen as a powerful evocation of the strength of Venetian justice, and is read from the Bacino as a literal and metaphorical extension of the functions of the adjacent Palazzo Ducale. This new wing contained quarters for the Signori di Notte, the nocturnal security police, and the development also incorporated a separate wing for women, as well as prisons for the Inquisition.

After da Ponte's death in 1597, he was succeeded as proto to the Palazzo Ducale by Antonio Contini, a member of a family of masons and architects, who completed the project. The final element was Contini's famous 'Bridge of Sighs', constructed in 1602, and which linked the prisons of the Council of Ten with their own courtroom within the Palazzo Ducale. Its rather fanciful Baroque appearance, clearly differentiated from da Ponte's robust classical facade, appears to deny its somewhat grim function, although again it forms a symbolic link between the seat of government and its penitential annexe.

THE PALAZZO DUCALE

The vast hall of the Maggior Consiglio (above, top) is dominated by Tintoretto's *Last Judgement*, replacing a fresco by Guariento. The hall was gutted by fire in 1577; the redecoration was chiefly the work of Tintoretto, Veronese, Pordenone and Palma the Younger.

The Collegio (above) formed the inner 'cabinet' of government, and its hall contains exceptionally rich decoration and the finest paintings. Rebuilt after the 1574 fire, the ceiling is by Cristofolo Sorte, and most of the paintings are by Veronese.

The Apotheosis of Venice by Veronese (right), in the ceiling of the hall of the Maggior Consiglio is symbolically located directly above the ducal throne.

Despite the rather excessively lurid notoriety of the Prisons in the minds of later writers, they have a significantly wider historical role, since they were among the earliest purpose-built prisons in Europe, with comparatively spacious cells, and other integrated facilities such as an infirmary and a chapel. They remained in use until 1919.[23]

The buildings on the Piazza: The Procurators of San Marco as patrons

The Palazzo Ducale formed one of the two cornerstones of the Republic; the other was that of its faith, and the administration of the shrine of the patron saint. Although closely connected to the Republic's government, the shrine and the properties that belonged to it were nevertheless administered by their own distinctly separate institution, that of the Procurators of San Marco.

Since the Piazza and the land immediately surrounding it was the property of the Procurators, it was they, rather than the Signoria, who were responsible for commissioning the first stage of Renaissance renewal on the Piazza. Both the Clock Tower and the Procuratie Vecchie represent a significant stage in transforming the essentially medieval Piazza into the most noble, dignified setting for the national shrine.

The Procurators occupied a unique position within the Venetian state. The office had been established in 1043 (according to Sansovino), to administer the basilica, its estates and revenues. Procurators were elected by the Maggior Consiglio, but held office for life, a privilege unique to them and to the doge himself, since all other senior public posts were held only for a short, fixed term. In protocol, too, they were second only to the Serene Prince himself. Over the centuries many procurators were elected to the ducal throne, for which the procuracy was seen by many as a natural 'stepping stone'. Three groups of procurators eventually evolved, one of which continued to administer the works at San Marco, while the other two groups were responsible for administering state properties and many other bequests and legacies *de citra* and *de ultra*, that is, on 'this' and on 'that' side of the Grand Canal in relation to San Marco.[24]

The Torre dell'Orologio

The building of the Torre dell'Orologio, the Clock Tower, in the 1490s, marks the first element of the two-part programme of urban renewal. It is a revealing reflection of the way in which civic perceptions were still maturing in this period, that the original intention of the Procurators was not to build a new tower at all but simply to commission a new clock to replace an old, unreliable one that was fixed to the facade of the basilica.

With this original aim, in 1493 Zuan Paolo Rainieri, together with his son Zuan Carlo, both clockmakers of high reputation from Reggio Emilia, were commissioned to construct a new clock. The work was clearly intended to be a triumph of technical skill and ingenuity, a work of enlightened patronage. A couple of years later, in November 1495, their masterpiece was almost complete; only then was it decided by the Procurators, in close consultation with the Senate, to build a new tower in which to house it in more dignified style. Once again, if we glance across the lagoon towards Padua, we find a possible motive for this decision. Padua's ancient astrological clock had been made as early as 1344, and was the oldest in Europe; it was modernized in 1427, though, when it was rehoused in the brick tower of the castle in the Piazza della Signoria, an action that seems to have sparked this act of constructive *campanilismo* on the part of the capital of the Republic.

Venice's Tower was begun in 1496, following the demolition of several bays of the ancient Byzantine procuracy building, and was rapidly completed by December 1497; just over a year later, the whole ensemble was inaugurated, with great festivities, by Doge Agostin Barbarigo. Barely a year later again, though, it was decided to add the two flanking wings, perhaps to strengthen the Tower's structure, although in so doing also giving it a stronger presence onto the Piazza. There is

PONTE DEI SOSPIRI (left)

The famous Ponte dei Sospiri links the
Palazzo Ducale on the left with the Palazzo
dei Prigioni on the other side of the
rio; designed by Antonio Contini, it was
built in 1602.

THE TORRE DELL'OROLOGIO (below)

Completed in 1499, it formed a gateway
into the Piazza from the Merceria. The first
fully Renaissance building at San Marco, its
mechanism is a triumph of engineering.

no firm documentation as to the origin of the Tower's design, although it is usually ascribed to Mauro Codussi, and shows some of his characteristic features, such as the decorative roundels and the refined classical pilasters; the side wings are often attributed to Lombardo, although again without conclusive documentation.[25]

The role of the Tower in the context of the Piazza is extremely significant. Not only was it the first attempt to raise the architectural dignity of the square by the unequivocal use of the Renaissance style, but it plays a key role in the spatial organization of its urban context. It was located directly over the point where the Merceria, the chief commercial street of the city, enters the square, thus providing a new ceremonial approach to San Marco and at the same time directly linking the hub of government with the route to the Rialto, Venice's commercial nucleus. Its strong verticality made a notable contrast with the long, essentially horizontal Procuracy building (which at the time still had only two storeys), while its rich decoration, particularly the gilding and ultramarine, both imperial colours, echoed that on the nearby basilica.

The Tower's rich facade incorporated a number of both practical and symbolic features. On the top, the two bronze 'Moors' (originally known simply as 'giants') strike the hours with hammers on to a bell, their mechanism linked to the clock below. They were cast by Ambrogio delle Ancore, a master founder at the Arsenale, in 1494. On the storey below the Moors, the prominent winged lion represents the Republic and its contribution to the commissioning of the work; the lion was originally accompanied by a kneeling Doge Barbarigo, a composition that repeated the iconography first employed by Francesco Foscari at the Porta della Carta half a century earlier. (The figures of both doges were destroyed by Napoleon, although that of Foscari has now been replaced by a replica.)

Below the ducal group, the storey containing the figure of the Virgin and Child represents the faith of the Republic, and was the focus of an ingenious spectacle during Ascension week, when three figures of the Magi appeared from a doorway, passed in front of the Virgin, genuflected, and returned by a door on the other side. Again this rare feat was controlled by the mechanisms of Rainieri's clock. The festival of the Ascension was, of course, one of the most important in the Venetian calendar, laden with ceremonial and Republican ritual; the new Tower thus made an important contribution to these events, fusing the practical, spiritual and patriotic as did the festival as a whole.

The largest order on the Tower contains the clock itself, with its highly complex mechanism, and its face decorated with the phases of the moon and the signs of the zodiac. It was a celebration of human ingenuity, of science, astronomy and mathematics; but it equally represented the Procurators' enlightened patronage of these skills.[26] Finally, below these four rich layers, the arch performs a ceremonial function, joining the Piazza with the dense, complex texture of the city beyond. Its form, too, represents an early manifestation of the idea of Venice as 'the new Rome', a civic focus echoing the surviving arches in the classical Roman Forum.

The Old Procuracy, or Procuratie Vecchie

Having established their credentials early in the sixteenth century as patrons of both the fine arts and the mechanical crafts, the Procurators faced a rather more daunting difficulty a little later. The whole of the remainder of the north side of the Piazza was still occupied by the ancient Byzantine procuracy buildings of Doge Ziani. They contained a single storey of apartments above a ground-floor colonnade, but were now three hundred years old; they were also by now so notoriously draughty and dilapidated that, despite their entitlement, few Procurators wished to make use of their accommodation. Several bays had been demolished for the Clock Tower, and after a serious fire in 1512, the Procurators decided to take down the entire block and rebuild it. Demolition began in February 1513, and a model was made in the following year. The initial design of the new

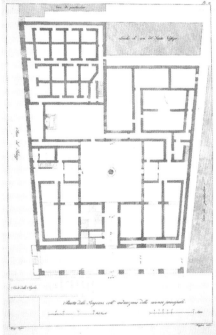

THE PROCURATIE VECCHIE (left)

Detail of the facade to the Piazza. The
Procuratie were rebuilt in the years after
1513, perhaps to an original design
by Mauro Codussi; like their predecessors,
they occupied almost all the north side
of the Piazza.

THE PALAZZO DEI PRIGIONI (above)

Plan and facade to the Bacino. The final
stage in building the prisons was begun
in 1574 by Antonio da Ponte, with a central
courtyard and accommodation in the front
block for the Signori di Notte,
the nocturnal security police.

Procuracy is frequently attributed to Codussi, although he had died in 1504, and its construction was supervised firstly by Bartolomeo Bon, the Bergamasco, who was proto to the Procurators, and then, after 1517, by Guglielmo de'Grigi.

Here, in sharp contrast with the Clock Tower, tradition and caution prevailed over any attempts at startling modernity. The Procuratie, fifty bays long, follows very closely indeed the overall form and appearance of its Byzantine predecessor, although this time it was designed in a rational, highly refined early Renaissance style, which itself strongly suggests Codussi's hand in the process. The facade has an almost hypnotic, repetitive rhythmic progression, again closely following that of its predecessor, although its two upper storeys gave it considerably more presence in the Piazza, and effectively doubled the accommodation available to the Procurators. Again, there is a continuous ground-floor colonnade, behind which were commercial tenancies that provided the Procurators with much-needed revenue, as indeed they still do today. The fenestration to the two upper levels is most refined, the narrow Corinthian columns still decidedly modern in 1512; the only rather more audacious gesture in this sober, restrained composition is the distinctly fanciful crenellation on the skyline, which was perhaps de'Grigi's contribution, and recalling that of the Palazzo Ducale.

The design of the Procuracy can be seen as a characteristic balance between the need to retain the basic form and function of the earlier building, while at the same time rationalizing its planning, and responding to the stylistic developments of the period. The apartments and offices themselves were planned around a row of small, square internal courtyards while water access was provided by a narrow canal at the back. In their highly logical plan and elevational treatment, the Procuratie can be said to represent a very early example of a new building type, one built purely for administration. The building was a forerunner of such later examples at the Uffizi in Florence, which were built by Giorgio Vasari for Cosimo de'Medici after 1560 to bring together various departments of his own government's administration; there, too, the building's form is essentially rational, linear and repetitive. From such practical bureacratic structures the modern office building eventually developed.

The Procuratie were only finally complete in 1532, after Jacopo Sansovino had continued their design around the end of the Piazza to the abutment with the church of San Gemignano.[27] By then the whole north side of the Piazza had been recast in the new Renaissance style, evincing a characteristic Venetian mixture of conservatism, in the retention of the overall form of the Procuratie, together with modernity of architectural language, and considerably enhanced urban richness with the new Torre dell'Orologio.

The work of Jacopo Sansovino at San Marco: Library, Loggetta and Mint.

The august patronage of the Procurators around the Piazza was to continue throughout the middle decades of the sixteenth century. In 1527, Jacopo Sansovino had fled to Venice to escape the depredations of the Sack of Rome. He was to spend the remaining forty-three years of his life here, much of it in the service of the institutions of the Republic, and particularly under the powerful and often enlightened patronage of the Procurators. Two years after his arrival in the city, Sansovino had impressed them so much with his ability that he was appointed their new proto, a post that he retained until his death. In this role he was largely responsible for the most significant transformations at San Marco since Doge Ziani, further developing the city's heart into the 'new Rome', surrounded by dignified, classical palaces.

In 1537, the Procurators decided in principle to redevelop the west side of the Piazzetta, opposite the Palazzo Ducale. The land was occupied by a miscellaneous collection of buildings, including several inns or hostels, but they were to be cleared to provide a site for a new Library of San Marco. Sansovino was asked to prepare preliminary proposals, an important element of which was the relocation of the inns, which generated considerable rental income for the Procuracy. His

THE BIBLIOTECA MARCIANA

The Biblioteca Marciana from the Porta della Carta (above); Sansovino's finest work in Venice, the Library has attracted praise ever since Palladio for its rich, refined detailing and noble proportions.

Ground and first floor plans (right). The library itself occupies the right side of the first floor, with an imposing staircase from the ground floor colonnade.

Interior of the library (far right, above), which still houses Cardinal Bessarion's collection of manuscripts and codexes. The ceiling contains early works by Veronese.

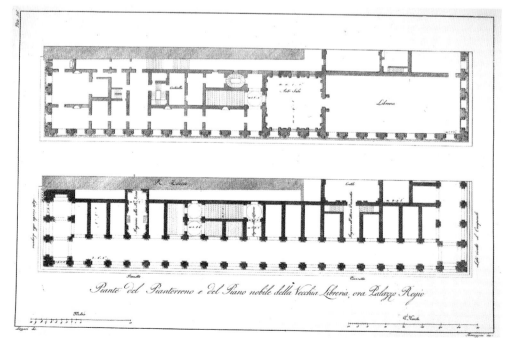

Piante del Pianterreno e del Piano nobile della Vecchia Libreria, ora Palazzo Regio

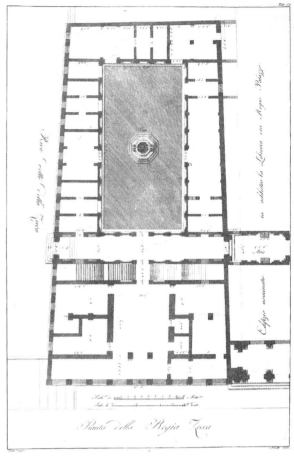

THE ZECCA (MINT)

Sansovino's plan (above) is highly rational, with the production of gold and silver coinage ranged around the large courtyard. The foundries for the two metals were in the front block facing the Bacino.

Facade onto the Bacino (left), with the end facade of the Biblioteca Marciana to the right. The contrast in styles between the two buildings is clear, their external image reflecting their widely different internal function.

successful, phased relocation of these hostelries was a vital aspect of the successful progress of the Library, which perforce also had to proceed in stages.

The Library, formally known as the Libreria or Biblioteca Marciana, was designed to accommodate the famous literary collection of Cardinal Bessarion, which had been bequeathed to the Republic in 1468 on condition that it was suitably housed at San Marco. The Signoria, disgracefully neglecting its obligations, left this priceless collection of Greek manuscripts and incunabula in an obscure corner of the Palazzo Ducale for decades, while obfuscating over their future. Only now, seventy years later, did the Procurators begin to execute their duty, largely as a result of pressure from the great humanist scholar Cardinal Pietro Bembo, and the Procurator Vettor Grimani. The recent commission given to Michelangelo for the Medici Library in Florence in 1524 may also have spurred the classical scholars of the Republic into action.

Sansovino's proposal incorporated the seminal decision to set out the north end of the Library some yards away from the base of the great Campanile, rather than butting up to it, as the earlier buildings had done. The effect of this decision was to free the tower to become an architectonic element in its own right, and to create direct spatial links between the central part of the Piazza and the Piazzetta. His Library, too, was to have a spacious ground-floor colonnade wrapping around this northern end, providing a second, covered link between Piazza and Piazzetta. It was begun at the northern end, nearest the Bell Tower, although work proceeded slowly, and was halted abruptly on 19 December 1545, when a section of vaulting collapsed overnight. Sansovino was immediately thrown into prison pending the results of an investigation; he was later reinstated in his post, but only after strong representations from such influential friends as Titian, the writer Pietro Aretino and Cardinal Bembo himself. He nevertheless had to make good the damage (valued at 1,000 ducats) out of his own funds. Sansovino's original ambitious great vault was now replaced by a timber-coffered ceiling, a much more prudent form of construction in Venice; the first sixteen bays were completed by 1556. After Sansovino's death, the Library was completed by Scamozzi, by the addition of a further five bays at the southern end, following Sansovino's original intention. This final extension was made possible by the removal of the remaining inn and the stalls of the meat market that was still located here, and allowed the Library a short but rich facade onto the Molo.[28]

THE LOGGETTA OF SAN MARCO

Detail of the bronze gates (above, top), by Antonio Gai, 1735.

The central bay (above). The Loggetta was begun by Sansovino in 1537, its rich materials appropriate to the pivotal location adjacent to the basilica.

The figures in the niches of the lower order (right) are bronzes by Sansovino himself, while the upper bas relief panels are the work of Danese Cattaneo and others; the central panel depicts Venice as Justice.

The Library is considered by many to be Sansovino's finest work. Richly decorated, yet disciplined, its stately rhythm of two superimposed orders, Doric below, Ionic above, is strongly modelled and finely proportioned, the result of his profound knowledge of the buildings of classical Rome. It was specifically intended to impress the visitor by its powerful form and its many learned classical references, which were influenced by Bembo. Primarily designed as a Renaissance seat of learning, the Library was at the same time to be open and accessible, in accordance with the wishes of its original benefactor.

Since the time of its completion, the Library has been highly regarded. Palladio praised the building as 'the richest and most ornate work since Antiquity', while Sansovino's close friend, Aretino, called him simply 'the man who knows how to be Vitruvius'. Jacopo's own son Francesco, in his guide to the city written in 1580, was, not surprisingly, equally flattering – 'said by the knowledgeable to be the finest work that one can see in Italy' – although understandably he omitted details of the collapse of the vault.

The Library incorporated several features never seen in Venice before, the most prominent among them the crowning parapet with its statues of mythical gods and goddesses, which the architectural historian, Deborah Howard, recognizes as a classical interpretation of the traditional Venetian crenellation; equally new were the rich swags on the entablature and Sansovino's ingenious method of wrapping the frieze around the corner of the facade; this last was said to have been the reason

why Sansovino was awarded the commission.[29] The rich, deep modelling, too, is shown to fine effect when the principal facade catches the morning sunlight, a bold composition of powerful horizontals (particularly the first floor cornice) and the strong rhythm of the colonnade.

The ground-floor entrance, flanked by two great caryatids, was designed by the sculptor Alessandro Vittoria; the imposing stair is also Vittoria's work, and terminates in a square vestibule, from which the Library itself is reached. The spatial arrangement contrasts with Michelangelo's contemporary Biblioteca Laurentiana for the Medici in Florence, where the stair unites the two elements, rising within the double-height vestibule itself. However, this arrangement reflects the slightly different roles of the two libraries. The decoration of the upper vestibule of the Biblioteca Marciana, for example, has Titian's painting of Wisdom in the centre of the ceiling. This is a reflection of the room's original function, since it was to house a school, sponsored by the Republic, in which young nobles were to be educated in Greek and Latin. The library itself, an impressive, rectangular hall, 26 metres long, still houses an invaluable collection of manuscripts and incunabula, some from the Bessarion bequest. The entrance portal was the first element to be completed, in 1553, followed by the comprehensive thematic programme of the interior decoration of the Library. Sansovino's ornate ceiling, with its shallow, coffered timber 'vaults' was decorated with twenty-one paintings, among them early works by Veronese, and all continuing the pedagogical themes of philosophy, the arts and the classics. Again, the rather over-rich interior forms an instructive contrast with that of Michelangelo, whose simple, muscular classicism, announced in the stair vestibule, is continued throughout the reading room. The Bessarion bequest was finally installed in its new home in the early 1560s, almost a century after it had been donated to the Republic, and only six years before Sansovino's death.

His isolation of the great shaft of the Campanile also made possible Sansovino's second new structure in the Piazza, the little loggia at the base of the tower. Once again, his patrons were the Procurators of San Marco, who now intended to replace an unimpressive temporary loggia, used as a meeting place for the nobility, but which was now seen as quite inappropriate in the context of the important programme of improvements taking place in the Piazza, particularly the new Library, only yards away. The Loggetta was also begun in around 1537, and was complete within three years or so, although Sansovino's own four bronzes in the niches of the facade (Minerva, Apollo, Mercury and Peace) were not installed until 1545. Logge similar in principle to this one, and serving similar functions, could be found in a number of Italian cities, including Verona and Padua, although the most imposing is undoubtedly the Loggia della Signoria in Florence. The Venetian loggia is far more modest in scale than this, but is particularly rich in detail and materials. It takes the form of a triumphal arch, another slightly self-conscious classical reference to Venice as the new Rome, and plays an important urbanistic role since it stands directly opposite the Porta della Carta. The formal axis from the interior of the Palazzo Ducale, from the top of the Scala dei Giganti, along the Foscari loggia and out through the Porta della Carta, was now given a fitting termination at its western end.

To fulfil this noble function, the Loggetta was constructed with rich materials, framed in red Verona marble, and with *verde antico* (green marble) detailing; the freestanding columns, too, are of oriental marble. In the centre was positioned a high-level relief panel with yet another representation of Justice, mirroring Bartolomeo Bon's figure on the top of the Porta della Carta opposite; she was flanked by allegorical representations of Crete and Cyprus, two of the Republic's most important colonies, symbolizing the wealth and extent of the maritime empire.[30]

Rather like the Arsenale gate, the Loggetta was found to be so convenient in its design and location that it was to be much elaborated in later centuries. The two side arches were turned into doorways in 1663, and a small enclosed terrace was formed at the front (again like that at the Arsenale), to

JACOPO TINTORETTO,
Portrait of Jacopo Sansovino, 1548 (left)
(Private Collection)

THE PROCURATIE NUOVE (below)

Detail of facade to the Piazza. Begun
in 1582 to designs by Vincenzo Scamozzi,
and based on Sansovino's Biblioteca
Marciana, the New Procuracy took several
decades to complete.

which bronze gates were later added. In 1902 the entire Loggetta was buried beneath the collapsed Campanile, but the marbles were largely salvaged and the whole painstakingly reassembled.

All the works of Renaissance urban renewal at San Marco that have been discussed so far were commissioned by the Procurators of the basilica: the new Procuracy itself (now known as the Old Procuracy or Procuratie Vecchie), the Torre dell'Orologio, Sansovino's Library and the Loggetta. The final important building commission, too, was to be the result of their sponsorship. But into this otherwise comprehensive pattern of patronage at San Marco was inserted one exception, again designed by Sansovino, although on this occasion his employer was the government itself. The commission was to design a new Mint (or Zecca), a brief not only redolent with symbolism but highly specific in its requirements. The Mint of the Republic had been located at San Marco since 1277, when it came under the direct control of the Council of Ten, via the Mint Commissioners. By the early 1530s, the rapidly expanding economy was placing the old mint buildings under considerable strain, and in 1535 the Ten decided to rebuild completely, with efficient modern premises. The site was extremely restricted, though, next to the south-west corner of the Piazzetta, and sandwiched between the existing hostelries and a narrow canal, beyond which were the great grain warehouses of the Republic, the Granai di Terranova.

Three proposals were sought by the Mint Commissioners, and that of Sansovino was approved.[31] The Mint's requirements were highly specialized; since it contained furnaces for smelting and refining, the building had to be completely fireproof, with substantial masonry vaults and with no timber anywhere in its construction. It also had to be built extremely rapidly to minimize disruption to the essential production of coinage; since the site was so restricted, however, construction again was to proceed in stages. Sansovino devised an ingenious plan, with the front wing, facing the Bacino, devoted to the gold and silver foundries; behind, the consequent production of coin was centred on a large courtyard in the rear wing. The building was to have two storeys, but in both wings, for reasons of security, silver was processed on the lower level and the much more valuable gold on the upper one.

Construction advanced extremely slowly, however, despite the great inconvenience to production, and chiefly as a result of spiralling costs and of rivalry between the Mint authorities and the Procurators of San Marco, who owned most of the adjacent land. Sansovino's design was completed by 1547, although as a result of the constantly changing brief, a third storey was added as late as 1558–66, which may or may not have followed his own design.

The completed building caused something of a sensation, although for rather different reasons than his rich, complex, 'Roman' design of the Library. The facade on to the basin is impressively severe and monumental, highly expressive of its function, with heavily rusticated Doric columns throughout; all in Istrian stone, it is more reminiscent of the massive military architecture of Sansovino's contemporary Michele Sanmicheli than it is typical of his own richer, more refined classicism. The facade's orientation, facing south across the Bacino, renders its appearance dazzling in sunlight, particularly in the afternoons, when its powerful moulding is best appreciated. Imposing and daunting, the Zecca epitomized the strength and stability of the Most Serene Republic in a more directly literal sense than the seat of learning next to it. The facades to the fine central courtyard are simpler, in a more restrained classical Roman manner, but with the same rustication to the ground floor. The Zecca was given an entrance directly on to the Piazzetta a little later; this was incorporated by Vincenzo Scamozzi in the 1580s, when completing the last stage of Sansovino's Library. It was formed through the Library arcade, and flanked (like the Library entrance) by a pair of stone giants, the work of Girolamo Campagna and Tiziano Aspetti.

The New Procuracy, or Procuratie Nuove

Sansovino's original master plan for the Piazza had envisaged that at some stage the design of his Library would have been continued along the whole of the south side of the Piazza, facing the earlier Procuratie, and around the western end to the abutment with the church of San Gemignano. The church itself had been rebuilt in 1505 by Cristoforo da Legname, in a simple early Renaissance style; its facade was added by Sansovino in 1557. It was all of Istrian stone and consisted of two superimposed orders, to relate to the two storeys of his proposed new building on the south side of the Piazza. However, Sansovino died in 1570, with this great new structure not yet begun.[32]

Until 1582, the ancient Ospizio Orseolo still stood against the western face of the Campanile. It was demolished in that year, when the Procurators began their last (and largest) work of urban renewal on the Piazza, the New Procuracy or Procuratie Nuove. With Sansovino gone, they naturally turned to Scamozzi, who was then in the process of completing Sansovino's Library. Scamozzi's New Procuracy was based very closely on the Library; however, he had already unsuccessfully proposed the addition of a third storey to the Library, and his approach to the design of the Procuracy followed the same course. Here, though, he did indeed add a third floor, providing much more accommodation; the building thereby became considerably more monumental, particularly when compared with Bon's earlier Procuracy opposite, with its much lower storey heights. The wisdom of this increased monumentality (and its conflict with Sansovino's original intention) gave rise to intense debate at the time, and considerably prolonged the period of the New Procuracy's construction.

The first ten bays, adjacent to the Library, were begun in 1583 but were only completed thirteen years later.[33] The conclusion of the entire project, though, took decades. After Scamozzi's own death in 1616, several different proti supervised the later stages of the work, including Francesco de Bernardin, who made considerable modifications to the complex internal planning of the block. The work proceeded slowly, involving countless further alterations, until finally, as late as 1640, fifty-seven years after it had begun, the great Baroque architect Baldassare Longhena saw it to completion, including the seven bays at the west end of the Piazza, abutting San Gemignano, which were later to be destroyed by Napoleon.[34]

The facade of the Procuratie Nuove is undeniably impressive, if somewhat overpowering; Scamozzi's resolution of its junction with the Library is notoriously ill-considered. The lower storey repeats Sansovino's Doric order on the Library, and incorporates the same generous colonnade, behind which, as in the earlier Procuracy, were commercial tenancies to yield the Procurators income. The first-floor Ionic order again follows Sansovino, but, in a correctly classical manner, Scamozzi added a Corinthian order to the uppermost storey. The building as a whole nevertheless represents a significant increase in scale over all the earlier buildings on the Piazza, a rather grandiose monumentality now replacing more measured and considered relationships. The Procurators' nine exceptionally spacious, even luxurious, apartments occupied the two upper storeys, and, like the earlier Procuracy, were again planned around a row of internal courtyards; their impressive public rooms and offices were at the front, facing the Piazza, with stairs and access lobbies in the centre, and private, family quarters facing the canal at the rear.

It was only in the mid seventeenth century, therefore, that the final building works in the Piazza were complete. Other than the state Mint, they had all been promoted and funded by the Procurators of San Marco, who, over a period of 150 years had transformed the whole context of the basilica, and indeed that of the Palazzo Ducale as well, into what even Napoleon conceded, when he took the city in 1797, was now the 'finest drawing room in Europe'. The Procurators' duties required them to enhance the setting of the basilica for the benefit and dignity of the city

THE PUNTA DELLA DOGANA

With Giuseppe Benoni's rebuilt Customs House of 1675 (previous pages). The figure of Fortune on the gilded ball of the earth was a beacon for shipping. Beyond is the Giudecca, with Palladio's modest facade to the nunnery of le Zitelle.

The Customs House with Santa Maria della Salute beyond (below). The Grand Canal opens to the right, with the Giudecca Canal to the left of the Dogana.

THE PUNTA DELLA DOGANA (below)

The Punta della Dogana and the Salute from
the Giardinetti Reali at San Marco.

and the Republic; but they also bore practical responsibilities of financial administration, so that to a significant extent these works were self-funded. Both of the great Procuracy buildings were entirely occupied with commercial tenancies on the ground floor, while the progress on the Library had been largely dependent on Sansovino's adroit handling of the relocation of the inns and other retail functions in the Piazzetta. In the developing styles of the various buildings that they promoted, we can trace the Procurators' perceived image of the capital: from the refined, repetitive early Renaissance style of the Procuratie Vecchie to the mature Roman classicism of the Library, and finally to the imposing scale of the Procuratie Nuove.

The Customs House or Dogana da Mar

As the functions of government expanded to occupy all the immediate surroundings of the basilica, there remained acute shortages of land for certain other government-controlled activities. While the hub of the empire remained at San Marco and most of the other financial agencies were at Rialto, one aspect of the administration of the Republic simply could not be fully accommodated at either of these two nuclei.

This was the Customs House, or Dogana da Mar. Until 1414, all goods brought into the city for the evaluation of customs duties were taken to San Biagio in Castello, near the entrance to the Arsenale and facing the Bacino of San Marco, where there was plenty of room for deep-water anchorage. But the quantities of goods became so great that two customs posts had to be established: one, the Dogana da Terra, evaluted goods from the Italian mainland, and was located on the Riva del Vin at Rialto; the other, the Dogana da Mar, fulfilled the same function for sea-borne trade, and was now relocated at the point on the eastern extremity of the sestiere of Dorsoduro, where again there was ample anchorage within sight of San Marco.[35] This location was not only ideal practically, but it served to further emphasize the role of the Bacino as the aquatic hub of the city, the entrepôt of the Republic's trading wealth. The huge medieval warehouses, triangular in plan, had occupied the whole of this promontory until 1525, when they were rebuilt; they were reconstructed once again in 1675, in the form that has survived today. This last design was the result of a competition organized by the Signoria, and the two finalists of which were Baldassare Longhena and the far less well-known Giuseppe Benoni. Longhena's great Baroque church of the Salute nearby was now approaching completion, but he proposed a comparatively reticent scheme for the Dogana, which would not detract from the visual impact of his masterpiece. However, the decision went in favour of Benoni, by six votes to five. His design is more assertive than Longhena's, its simple but powerful rusticated form culminating in a large colonnaded loggia, crowned by bronze figures of Atlas holding a giant ball of the Earth, on which stands the figure of Fortune. Like the Campanile of San Marco, the gilded statue was to serve as a guiding beacon for incoming shipping, and the composition as a whole gave further emphasis to the entrance to the Grand Canal, which was now more precisely defined, as was the entrance to the broad Giudecca Canal on the other side.

This gesture of further defining the ancient confines of the Bacino was to be the last public work around the Bacino carried out by the Most Serene Republic. It is perhaps appropriate, therefore, that this last work should be a reconstruction of the building that most directly symbolized Venice's own mercantile wealth and indeed its *raison d'etre*.[36]

A grand and dreamy structure, of immense proportions; golden with old mosaics; redolent of perfumes; dim with the smoke of incense; costly in treasures of precious stones and metals; glittering through iron bars; holy with the bodies of deceased saints; rainbow-hued with windows of stained glass; dark with carved woods and coloured marbles; obscure in its vast heights and lengthened distances, shining with silver lamps and winking lights; unreal, fantastic, solemn, inconceivable throughout.   San Marco, from **Charles Dickens**, *Pictures from Italy*, 1846.

Venice and Rome

The earliest history of the Venetian Church is inseparably linked with the city's evolution from a number of scattered littoral settlements into the Venetian Republic. Migration from the Roman towns of the Terraferma towards the lagoons had been accompanied by the staged transfer of ecclesiastical authority from Aquileia and Altino to these emergent towns. In 569, the transfer of the bishopric of Aquileia to Grado on the nearby lido, and ten years later the beginning of a new cathedral there, marked a decisive commitment to this new site. It also embodied the division between the Lombard-conquered Terraferma and the still nominally Byzantine-controlled Adriatic shoreline. The bishopric of Altino, on the edge of the Venetian lagoon, was similarly relocated barely a couple of miles away, to the safety of the islands of Torcello.[1] Later, in the ninth century, the final schism took place between the Venetian Dogado and the Terraferma Church; the Church of the lagoons was now independent of that of the Italian mainland and remained at least theoretically subject to the distant authority of the eastern capital of Constantinople.[2]

The Byzantine origin of the authority of the Venetian Church resulted in a relationship between Venice and the established Catholic Church in Rome that was markedly different from that of any other city or state in Italy. Ultimate ecclesiastical authority in the Republic rested with the Patriarch, whose seat was at Grado until 1131, and thereafter in Venice itself, where the church of San Silvestro was assigned to him. Relations with Rome fluctuated considerably over the centuries. Although by the later medieval period, the Republic claimed faithful allegiance, and three Venetian cardinals were elected popes, Venice nevertheless retained complete control over ecclesiastical appointments and jurisdiction within the lands of the Serenissima. Patriarch, archbishops and bishops (of whom there were thirty-eight) were all direct appointees of the Venetian Signoria. On a local level the parishioners of Venice elected their parish priests themselves, at the direction of the Signoria; all had to be Venetian by birth, and Rome was simply notified of all such appointments. Many times the Republic defied the rulings of Rome, from the violation of the Sabbath laws (the Maggior Consiglio always met on Sundays) to Venice's flourishing trade with the Muslim world.

On the political level, the Republic's relationship with the Papal State was sometimes benign, even cooperative when realpolitik demanded it; sometimes strained by conflicts of interest in the peninsula; sometimes directly hostile. On several occasions the Holy See invoked its ultimate sanctions against the Serenissima; in 1308, for example, the entire Republic was placed under papal interdict as a result of Venice's flagrant attempt to add the papal city of Ferrara to her territories. It was only lifted five years later. The highest sanctions were applied again in 1483 and a third time, with even harsher terms, in 1509, during the crisis of the League of Cambrai.[3]

The last and most serious breach of all was in 1606, arising from Rome's long-held grievances over Venetian ecclesiastical independence. The Venetian Senate appointed the skilful theological philosopher Paolo Sarpi to defend its position; Pope Paul V again replied by interdict. The Signoria in turn forbade publication of the edict throughout the Republic. For a short time, the possibility

GRADO CATHEDRAL

The cathedral church of Sant' Eufemia, consecrated in 579 AD, was the seat of Patriarchs, transferred here from Roman Aquileia. The interior retains mosaics from the 6th century.

arose of a permanent schism with Rome and even the official adoption of Protestantism, but after a year the interdict was lifted and a compromise reached.[4]

These examples illustrate the fiercely nationalistic nature of Venice's relationship with Rome down the centuries; theoretical fealty and spiritual obedience were often contrasted in practice with complete independence. As the Venetian adage puts it, 'First Venetians, then Christians.' This independent course has close parallels in the history of the physical form of the churches of Venice; in its churches, as in its political evolution, Venice was a bridge between East and West, between two cultures and traditions.

The earliest basilicas: Torcello

In the furthest lagoon of the Venetian littoral, the ancient cathedral of Grado, begun in 579, is the oldest surviving church of the Republic. Stylistically it forms a link in the evolution of the Venetian church from the classical Roman basilica to the later cathedral of Torcello and to the underlying structure of Venice's oldest surviving parish churches.

The basilical hall was the most dominant form of the early Christian church. Derived from the assembly halls of the Roman nobility, it had been adapted for Christian worship from an early date, as can be seen in several churches in Rome, among them San Clemente and San Paolo Fuori le Mura. The splendour of Theodoric's rule at Ravenna (493–526) is also evinced by the fine basilica of Sant'Apollinare Nuovo and the slightly later Sant'Apollinare in Classe.

Structurally simple, basilical churches gained their beauty by order, symmetry and the serene, disciplined rhythm of their paired colonnades, above which a continuous clerestory allowed generous, even light into the long nave below. Their roofs were not vaulted but were covered with repetitive open timber trusses, further emphasizing their regular, linear bay structure. The strongly axial plan gave clear prominence to the central apse and the high altar, which was often raised above the level of the nave floor. At the easternmost end, the central apse contained tiers of benches for the celebrants, with the bishop's throne in the centre.

Grado's cathedral of Sant'Eufemia is a modest example of this strong tradition. Its long nave is flanked by lean-to aisles on both sides, from which it is divided by twin rows of columns; at the east end, the characteristic apse contained the bishop's cathedra.[5] The church was originally approached by a square, colonnaded forecourt or atrium. Nearby, the small freestanding brick baptistery, octagonal in plan and contemporary with the cathedral, was another characteristic feature of many early Christian churches; dedicated to John the Baptist, baptisteries usually stood near the west entrance to the main church. This location represented the liturgical requirement to be received into the Church by baptism before one could enter the basilica itself. All these elements identifiable at Grado were archetypal features of the early Christian basilica. Equally notable are the extensive contemporary floor mosaics, closely linked stylistically to the rich Byzantine tradition of Ravenna, and reaching a later peak of achievement at San Marco.

Within the Venetian lagoon the Cathedral at Torcello is a natural successor to the modest church at Grado. Most of the present Cathedral dates from its reconstruction in 1008, and in front of the church there was again a freestanding baptistery, the remains of which can still be seen.[6] Torcello Cathedral's external appearance is simple, austere and forbidding, virtually devoid of decoration; although such austerity conforms to the Byzantine tradition of concentration on the glorification of God inside the church, at Torcello the uncertain political climate of the period is also graphically illustrated by the heavy stone shutters to the aisle windows, which could be locked in times of danger.

The Cathedral, dedicated to Santa Maria Assunta, has a plan similar to that of Grado Cathedral although considerably larger, since not only was Torcello a sizable and a wealthy community, but

TORCELLO

The eastern apses of the cathedral and the campanile. The church's basilical form is clearly identifiable.

TORCELLO

In the hemispherical vault of the central apse of the cathedral is the 12th century mosaic of the Virgin and Child, below which are the Twelve Apostles (above).

Plan of Santa Fosca (right). The church has an open colonnade around five sides; its plan is centralized, with the exception of the projecting chancel.

The facade of the cathedral (far right). In front of the austere exterior are the remains of the circular 7th century baptistery.

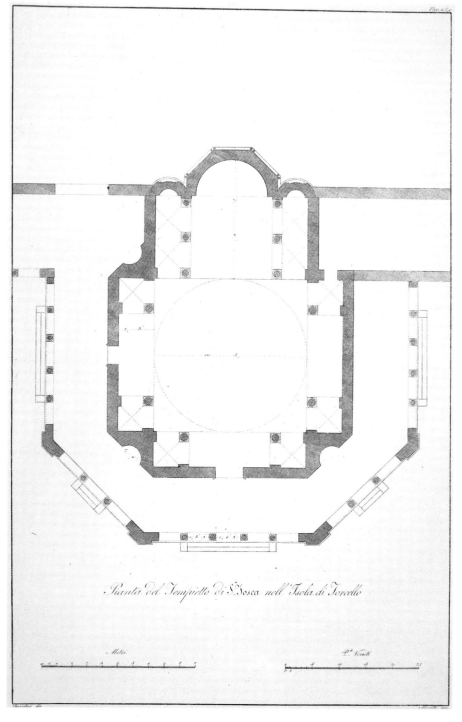

Pianta del Tempietto di S. Fosca nell'Isola di Torcello

Metri

P.^{di} Veneti

the Torcellani made extensive use of the ruins of nearby Roman Altino for the reclamation of building materials. The nave colonnade was formed by monolithic columns of Greek marble, with rich Corinthian capitals, some of which were probably re-used from the earlier, smaller church. This long nave is flanked by aisles, all three spaces terminating with semicircular apses: a typical basilical form in every respect.

The mosaics of the interior were begun some time after the fabric itself was completed, but nevertheless stylistically continued the traditions of both Greece and Ravenna. They played an important role in the symbolic organization of the interior, with the most extensive, on the inner face of the west wall, incorporating the Last Judgement in a series of terrifying images of the fires of Hell, always visible to the celebrant but also to the congregation as they turned to leave the church. At the eastern end, though, the great golden arc of the central vault contains the solitary, purely Byzantine figure of the Madonna, holding the Child, and transfixing the worshipper with a gaze of extraordinary stillness. The image is probably the work of Greek craftsmen from Constantinople and can be linked to the Apostles in the atrium of San Marco. At Torcello, therefore, the Byzantine mosaic tradition was transposed, virtually unaltered, to the lagoon from the Eastern capital.

The basilical plan was to remain widespread throughout much of Italy. In its more developed form, it incorporated a cross-axis, or transept, to become a Latin cross; a number of outstanding Romanesque examples survive, such as the Cathedral of Pisa, which was contemporaneous with San Marco. But Venice was subject to another strong influence in the design of its churches, not from Rome or Ravenna but from Constantinople, the great metropolis to which the peoples of the lagoon still remained, at least notionally, subject. The Eastern Church developed a quite different plan form for its own places of worship, the structure of which was not linear, but was essentially centralized.

The fully centralized plan, the Greek cross of this alternative tradition, was based on a square central bay, surmounted by a dome, and surrounded on all sides by four further square bays, all of the same size, to form a cross with four equal arms, each of them crowned with a dome. Two seminal examples of this more centralized form are the great church of Santa Sofia in the Eastern capital and San Vitale at Ravenna, both churches founded by the Emperor Justinian after 526; the latter reflects the spread of this centralized form into Italy. Neither is a precise Greek cross: Santa Sofia has a great central dome, to the east and west of which are half-domes, all surrounded by subsidiary spaces; San Vitale, by way of contrast, has an octagonal plan, its central space surrounded by a low perimeter ambulatory. Nevertheless, such forms are intrinsically centralized rather than axial, the symbolic global form of the dome reinforcing this centrality.[7]

Ravenna, the Byzantine capital of Italy, provides examples of both of these fundamental forms, basilical and centralized, at Sant'Apollinare and San Vitale. In the Venetian lagoon, too, the two coexist. Immediately next to Torcello Cathedral is the little twelfth-century church of Santa Fosca. It is modest in scale, and although its central space is not domed, but has an open timber roof, the plan is highly centralized, with a square nave, and three short projections forming the arms of the cross; the fourth arm is slightly extended to form the chancel.

The interior has a calm, peaceful simplicity, its harmonious proportions enhanced by the humble, bare brickwork; the only richer elements are the Cycladic marble columns, with their fine Corinthian capitals. Externally, an open colonnade wraps around five of the eight sides, with characteristic Byzantine stilted arches; the decorative brickwork, too, forms part of a strong local tradition, of which there are further examples at San Marco and San Donato at Murano. At Torcello these two basic forms, the linear and the Greek cross, can be seen together; they were to have a profound and effective impact on the history of the Venetian church over the next millennium.

MURANO

Santa Maria e San Donato, c.1125: the church from the adjacent canal. The fine decorative brickwork reflects a strong lagoon tradition.

Santa Maria e San Donato: the nave towards the High Altar. San Donato was completed by 1140, the date on the floor mosaics. The plan is basilical but with cross-transepts added. The ceiling is of the Venetian 'ship's keel' form, although heavily restored.

They reached an early but sophisticated fusion in the fine church of Santi Maria e Donato at Murano, rebuilt in 1140. In several respects, it forms a link between the churches of Torcello and the shrine of San Marco.[8] The underlying form is linear and basilical, but the introduction of transepts makes the plan cruciform, with a focal point at the intersection of the two axes; the spaces have now become more complex and hierarchical. San Donato has extensive surviving floor mosaics, contemporaneous with those at San Marco and are probably by the same masters; it is also constructed of exceptionally fine, rich decorative brickwork, particularly in the eastern apses – another tradition in the lagoon that was to be maintained in the rebuilding of the shrine of the Republic's patron.

San Marco

The basilica of San Marco, the chief religious monument of Venice, epitomizes the history of the Republic of the Evangelist, for centuries representing the heart of its spiritual life and the indissoluble link with its patron. All important Republican ceremonies were held here, from ducal coronations to the celebration of great victories, from the solemn reception of visiting popes to the mourning of national heroes and martyrs.

San Marco's appearance equally symbolizes the city's links between East and West, an essentially Byzantine church set on the edge of a Western, Latin peninsula. The practical, liturgical function of San Marco was as unique as its final appearance, without precedent elsewhere. As the shrine of a patron saint and Evangelist, San Marco was a place of great veneration throughout the Christian West; but its chief function was to serve as the shrine of the Republic and the private chapel of the head of state, the doge. The church thus differs from almost all others in that it was built neither as a cathedral, with a bishop's throne, nor as a monastic foundation, following the rules of an established order; nor yet did it have any parochial functions. Its dean and clergy were all nominated by the ducal Signoria, the supreme organ of government, under no control or influence from Rome or Constantinople. In around 1150, the Patriarchs of Grado (whose title had been bestowed by the Eastern Emperor) had been permitted into the church, although it was not until 1451 that the patriarchate itself was officially and permanently transferred to the city; even today, it remains something of an anachronism, one of only four patriarchates within the Western Catholic church.[9]

The earliest history of San Marco is almost inextricably bound up with legend. A few years after the transfer of the seat of the lagoon's government to Rivo Alto, in 813, two Venetian mariners returned from Egypt with the body of the Evangelist. On their arrival a modest new shrine was begun almost immediately, and Mark joined the Greek Todaro as the new patron. This new chapel stood between that of San Todaro and the *castrum* of the doges; although small, it may have been decorated with marble and other materials salvaged from the ruins of Roman Altino. The church stood until 976 when it was destroyed by the fire that also damaged the ducal castle. It was restored or rebuilt by Doge Pietro Orseolo and survived for a further eighty years, during which time the increasing wealth and population of the city began to render it too small and insignificant for such an august patron. It became clear that a considerably larger replacement was necessary.

Neither the plan of the very first church nor that of Doge Orseolo can be established conclusively, despite centuries of conjecture and some archaeological research. The form of both may have been basilical, broadly similar to the Cathedral of Torcello, although excavation below the present church has suggested that the plan was probably centralized. The final definitive reconstruction, though, was begun in 1063 by Doge Domenico Contarini, and all the essential structure of this church survives today. Most of it, however, was to be clad with later decoration and elaboration, an almost continuous programme of which proceeded over the next four centuries. Construction of this basic fabric took around thirty years, and the church was consecrated in 1094 by Doge

SAN MARCO

Detail of the elaborate late Gothic decoration that was added to the top of the facades in the late 14th and early 15th centuries: San Marco with the Venetian lion (above).

Plan of the church (right). The heart of the plan is a Greek cross, with five bays each surmounted by a dome. A narthex or porch wraps around three sides of the nave.

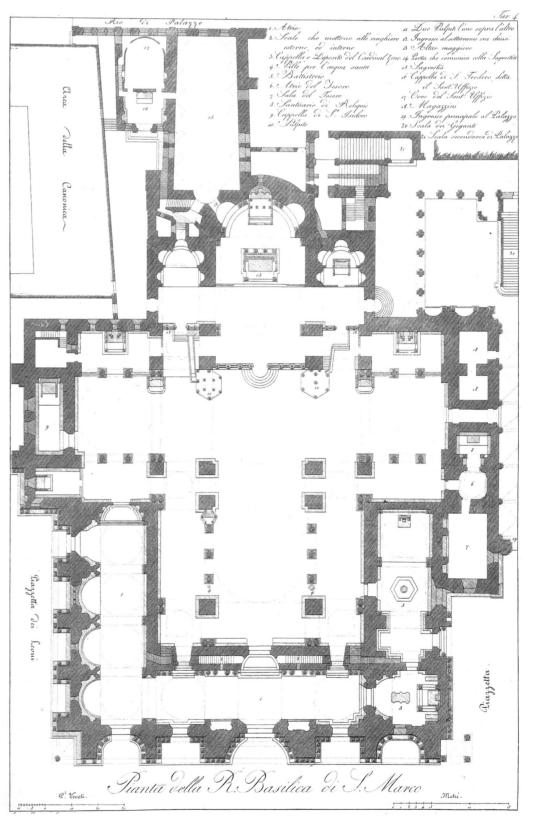

Pianta della R. Basilica di S. Marco

151

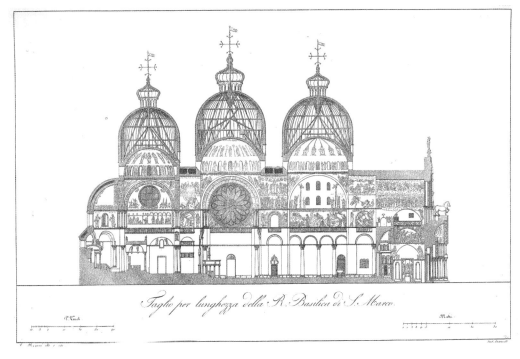

Taglio per lunghezza della R. Basilica di S. Marco.

SAN MARCO

Long section through the church, showing
the tall outer domes supported on a complex
timber framework, and considerably higher
than the inner, masonry domes (left).

The west facade from the Piazza (above); the
shrine achieved its definitive appearance with
the late Gothic decorations on the skyline.
Most of the facade mosaics were replaced in
the 16th and 17th centuries.

Vitale Falier. The relics of the Evangelist had apparently been lost in the fire of 976, but according to tradition they miraculously reappeared, emerging from one of the nave piers during the reconsecration ceremony.

Although of fairly imposing dimensions, the new church was entirely of brick, simple and severe in appearance, and initally, of course, with none of the mosaics that later slowly transformed the interior into a glittering cavern. This original unadorned brickwork can today be seen only on the exterior of the apses and transepts. The kernel of the plan is centralized, with a square, domed central bay, from which project the four square arms of the classic Greek cross; each of these square bays is also roofed by a masonry dome. The chancel, though, is extended slightly and has an apsidal semicircular eastern termination; flanking it are two smaller radial apses, both of these are basilical features, echoing those of Torcello Cathedral. The eastern arm is raised significantly higher than the level of the nave, and below it is the crypt in which the Evangelist's remains were to be housed. The church is approached by a spacious porch or narthex, which was built just after the main fabric, and which itself continues around the two sides of the nave, as far as its abutment with the two projecting transepts. Like the nave, the narthex is roofed with a series of small, shallow domes.

The origin of this celebrated design has been debated for centuries, although one of its antecedents was the Church of the Twelve Apostles in Constantinople, built by the Emperor Justinian in the sixth century. Although destroyed, surviving engravings record that it also had a centralized five-bay plan, with domes roofing each bay, although the nave was again slightly extended. As the second most highly venerated church in the Eastern capital, after Santa Sofia, its influence would undoubtedly have been considerable; many small early Christian churches scattered throughout Turkey and Greece also have a similar form, and it was adopted half a century after San Marco for St Front at Perigueux, in France, where the austere, all-stone interior evokes San Marco itself before the mosaics were begun. In almost all such examples, from Santa Sofia onwards, the means of supporting the dome, which rested on a square bay of piers, was achieved by means of a curved, triangular, sail-like form, the pendentive; the device was not known in the classical Roman era, but it provided a solution that was both structurally sound and aesthetically pleasing, since it formed a transitional surface that could itself be decorated.[10]

SAN MARCO

The chancel, with the iconostasis or rood screen, carved by Jacobello and Piero Paolo delle Masegne in 1394. On the top are figures of the Virgin and the Apostles.

After the basic fabric was complete, the long process of decoration began. Towards the end of the twelfth century the west facade was elaborated with its profusion of marble columns and capitals, many of Eastern origin, while a similar process of sheathing began to the interior. Eventually all the great nave piers and flanking walls were lined with veneers of rare marbles. The process was greatly enhanced by the quantity of booty brought back to the city in 1204, in the aftermath of the seizure of Constantinople during the Fourth Crusade; much of this consisted of rich relief carvings, which were embedded in the facades, but which, because of Venice's close cultural links with the Eastern capital, blended stylistically with the indigenously-produced works. A number of reliquaries and many other surviving objects in the Treasury of the church were also brought back by the conquering Venetians; many elements of the extraordinary altar screen (the Pala d'Oro) again originated in Constantinople. Among the spoils, too, were the four famous bronze horses, which were to be installed on the facade above the main portal.

A unique record of the appearance of this facade shortly after these early thirteenth-century works is given by the surviving mosaic within the northernmost of the five great porches, that of Sant'Alipio. This is the only remaining original mosaic on the facade, and illustrates the story of

The south-west corner (below, left), with characteristic stilted Byzantine arches; the marble columns and capitals came from a variety of sources, some probably re-used from the earlier church. In the foreground is the *pietra del bando*, or proclamation stone, for making public decrees.

Detail of the north-west corner of the facade, by John Ruskin, 1877 (below, right). Ruskin executed a number of exquisite studies of the facade of the church during several long visits to the city.

the taking of San Marco's body against a backdrop of the basilica in around 1250, when the mosaic was made. The facade consisted of two superimposed orders, each of five semicircular arches, and divided by a broad terrace above the narthex. The composition was simpler, considerably more static in appearance than it was to become with later Gothic elaboration. Until the early thirteenth century it was also much lower, since the church lacked the tall outer domes that were later to produce such a distinctive silhouette from the far end of the Piazza. These outer domes were built a good deal higher than the masonry vaults within, and are supported on a complex timber frame, clad with lead. They were added after 1204, but were already in place when the Sant'Alipio mosaic was created.[11]

The five imposing arches of the lower order have retained their original appearance, with a rich collection of sculpted themes, among them the signs of the zodiac, the months of the year and the crafts and trades of the city. The upper order, though, is much altered; not only was it greatly elaborated by the fifteenth-century crowning of pinnacles, statues and wave decoration, but the original mosaics, too, were all replaced in the early seventeenth century. The Gothic elaboration of the upper arches, originally simple semicircular crowns, was to incorporate some fine sculptures (perhaps by Matteo Raverti and the Lamberti family, Nicolo and Pietro), but they transformed the facade from its calm Byzantine profile into a much more complex late medieval work, similar in character to the adjacent Porta della Carta.

The magnificent horses, believed to be Greco-Roman works from the second century AD, became a powerful symbol of Venetian military strength. They had probably once formed an imperial quadriga, and were taken in 1204 from Constantinople, perhaps from the Hippodrome; their relocation in this place of honour on the basilica reflected not only their great intrinsic quality but also the imperial symbolism associated with them. Pietro Doria, the Genoese admiral, was fully aware of this potent image when, in 1378, after taking nearby Chioggia, he vowed to 'bridle those unreined horses of yours', and capture and sack the city. After the Republic's final ignominious fall, Napoleon, equally aware of their symbolic value, removed them to Paris, where for some years they stood on his new triumphal arch, the Arc du Carrousel, before they were returned to Venice in 1815.[12]

The southern facade of the church is today considerably less important than that to the west on to the Piazza. In Republican times, it was of great significance since it faced the approach from the Molo and was the only part of the basilica visible from the lagoon. It was, therefore, particularly richly finished. Much of its decoration, such as the bas-reliefs and marbles, had in fact originated in Constantinople. This approach, though, has been significantly altered over time. In the fourteenth century, two bays of the narthex were partitioned to form the baptistery; later still, in 1504, access from the Piazzetta was removed completely by the construction of the Zen Chapel in the corner bay of the narthex, and the conversion of the portal into a window. Thereafter, the only formal approach to the basilica was the axial route through the central portal on to the Piazza; this 'rationalization' perhaps reflects the increased awareness of formal axial planning in the Renaissance, and the desirability of enhancing the church's dignity in such a manner. Nevertheless, the early importance of the Piazzetta facade is still evinced by the two square stone columns, trophies celebrating the Venetian victory over the Genoese at Acre in 1256, and echoing on a smaller scale Doge Ziani's great columns on the Molo.

SAN MARCO

Above: interior of the nave from the west
gallery. All of the upper surfaces are sheathed
with an almost continuous programme of
mosaics, set against a gold background.

Left: detail of the mosaics to the west or
Pentecost dome, probably the first of the five
to be completed. It depicts the tongues of
fire descending to the Twelve Apostles.

Previous pages: the gilded bronze horses.
These magnificent classical sculptures were
taken by the Venetians, under doge Enrico
Dandolo, from Constantinople in 1204.

Most of the original spatial configuration of the interior has survived unaltered from the late eleventh-century reconstruction. The narthex was vaulted with shallow domes, corresponding to the five great portals of the facade, and resembling atria such as that of Santa Sofia. Its configuration, wrapping around the nave, also provided two subsidiary entrances into the church transepts for processions, while at the same time offering lateral stability to the upper parts of the structure.

The cavernous interior at first appears to be a complex space, difficult to define, but as the eye is led upwards, the richness and extent of the mosaics becomes more clearly apparent. As in the narthex, but on a far greater scale, the predominant colour is gold, reflecting and scattering the natural light from the high-level windows down into the nave below. The spaces, all defined by semicircular arches and domes, are static rather than dynamic, Oriental rather than Western, and there is none of the verticality of the Western Norman and Gothic tradition; nonetheless, the richness of the surfaces is unforgettable.

Spatially, the interior is dominated by the five great domes, one to each arm of the Greek cross and one, slightly larger, in the centre. They were formed of a thin shell of structural brick, supported by massive masonry piers, which were subdivided into groups of four. Despite the powerful mosaic to the eastern apse, drawing the eye towards the altar, the central space is not highly directional, and focuses almost equally on the space below the central dome, where the light is most intense. Although the overall spatial arrangement has survived unaltered since Doge Contarini's rebuilding, two interventions have affected the spaces and the lighting. The side aisles were originally decked over above the colonnades to provide separate galleries for women, *matronei*. The division reflected the influence of the eastern rite, in which women are separated from men, but restoration after a fire in 1145 seems to have involved the loss of these galleries, leaving only the present narrow, high-level walkways. The removal of the galleries allowed considerably more light into the lower parts of the church. Further alterations took place in the fourteenth century, when large circular 'rose' windows were inserted into the south transept and at the west end of the nave; in its original form, therefore, around 1200, the interior was considerably darker, the spaces even more elusive to define.

San Marco's mosaic cycles were probably begun shortly after the basic structure was complete in the late eleventh century. Byzantine mosaic craftsmanship had flourished at both Ravenna and Constantinople, and its application to church interiors had slowly increased in scale and complexity. Initially confined to the vault above the apse, where they generally depicted the Virgin and Child, mosaic decorations were later developed to incorporate narrative biblical cycles on the walls, while the surfaces of vaults and domes were usually reserved for more exalted theological themes. Here the light was stronger, and the curved surfaces scattered this light from the images to the congregation below.

Although the manufacture of glass mosaic in the Venetian lagoon has been traced to the ninth century, the earliest work, at Torcello, was the product of Greek masters. Very little is known of the details of the execution of the great cycles at San Marco, though, which took place over 150 years, and was probably complete by the reign of Doge Pietro Ziani (1205–22). Although there was probably no original 'master programme' for the whole church, it seems clear that these narthex programmes, all narrative and didactic, were intended to form an introduction to the many complex theological programmes in the church itself.[13]

The very earliest were the four saints in their niches flanking the door into the church, but the dominant work in the narthex was to be the richly-coloured and extensive series that covers the domes, spandrels and upper vaults, in a virtually seamless series of images. Begun in the south-west corner in around 1200, work continued for much of the century, in a highly-developed style fusing the Italian Romanesque with characteristic Venetian colour and naturalistic imagery. The themes encompassed many Old Testament stories: the Creation, Adam and Eve and Cain and Abel; the story of Noah and the Flood, the Tower of Babel, Abraham and the histories of Joseph and Moses.

The domes, vaults, arches and pendentives of the church itself were clad with a uniquely comprehensive programme of mosaics, much of which remains intact, although a considerable number of elements have been replaced over the centuries. The principal series was begun in the twelfth century and was probably largely complete by the 1280s, although some work continued into the following century. Their stylistic development still owed much to the Byzantine tradition, although again developing a vigour, a brilliance of colour and a naturalistic quality that is distinctively Venetian.

The themes and programmes of the mosaics mostly fall into three broad categories: some are purely illustrative (such as the depiction of various saints of local significance), others, like those in the narthex, depict narrative, pedagogic stories; others still have iconographic symbolism that embraces the highest spiritual levels of Christian belief. Not surprisingly, these last themes are concentrated within the surface of the five main domes. The first dome, that of the Pentecost, for example, establishes the spiritual basis of Christian belief, with the Holy Spirit descending on the Twelve Apostles, who are ranged around the base of the cupola. The central dome forms the spatial hub of the entire interior, and its depiction of the Ascension is not only perhaps the finest of all of the mosaics, but again represents the spiritual culmination of the Christian creed, appropriately located at the church's heart. The feast of the Ascension was one of the great festivals of the Republic, the culmination of which thus took place directly below its depiction on the dome.

The central axis was concluded with the third dome, directly above the High Altar; its dominant figure of Christ as the Pantocrator is a typically Byzantine image in its traditional location; the dome was damaged by fire in 1419, and the Christ replaced with a copy. According to tradition, Venetian mosaic work was at a very low ebb in this period, and Paolo Uccello was invited from Florence to advise and train new craftsmen, a task in which he seems to have been singularly successful. The main axis of the church is concluded with a half-dome roofing the eastern apse, and containing the solitary figure of Christ in benediction; the Virgin and Child are more frequently found in this location (as at Torcello and Murano), although the Christ Pantocrator is by no means unknown, as he is depicted in the superb mosaics at the Cathedrals of San Pietro, Cefalù and of Santa Maria at Monreale. Indeed, the Venetian example may have been a conscious emulation of the splendid Norman-Byzantine works in Sicily.

If this central axis represents the highest spiritual aspects of Christianity, other mosaic cycles reflected more accessible themes. The two side domes, for example, depict figures of saints, Lunardo in the southern cupola and the life of John the Evangelist in the northern one. The side aisles have different themes again; as in the narthex, these lesser spaces have a didactic function, that on the left illustrating the acts of the Apostles, while the right aisle represents scenes from the life of Christ and the Apostles, among them James and Bartholomew. The remaining mosaics fall into a final group, a long, complex series of narratives of the life and miracles of Christ and the life of the Virgin. These are chiefly located on the soffits of the main arches between the domes, and also on wall surfaces; here, again, their primary function is instructive, rather than spiritual.

In all, therefore, the mosaics form an exhaustive programme of images reflecting almost every aspect of Christian belief. The 150 years of their creation illustrate the maturation of the indigenous style, slowly developing its own character and sense of expressive freedom. After their completion the mosaics required continual repair and restoration, much of which took place in the fifteenth century. However, after around 1500, the influence of the Renaissance resulted in the final abandonment of the Byzantine tradition, and the adoption of the new spirit of the age. Mosaics

SAN MARCO

Detail of the San Alipio porch, the only original surviving mosaic on the façade. It depicts the church itself as it was in the 12th century, before the Gothic decorations were added.

SAN MARCO

Detail of the south portal. The 13th century Moorish arch incorporates earlier 11th century *intarsia* work.

were now replaced rather than repaired, many to designs by Titian, Veronese and Tintoretto; among the additions made in the 1540s was a new Apocalypse mosaic at the west end of the nave.

Within the body of the church, too, several alterations over the centuries have reflected shifting tastes, changing liturgical requirements and the history of the Republic itself. The altar screen, for example, combines both the peak of Byzantine skill in the creation of enamelled icons with the refinement of fifteenth-century Gothic filigree work. It was assembled by Andrea Dandolo, doge from 1343 to 1354, an outstanding patron of the arts, who commissioned this extraordinary work in 1345, unifying the eighty individual icons within a rich, complex framework of gold, containing dozens of rare and semiprecious stones.[14]

Dandolo was the most outstanding medieval contributor to the continuing elaboration of the church. A fine scholar, he was a historian of the Republic and a close friend and patron of Petrarch; fittingly, too, perhaps, he was the last doge to be buried in San Marco. Dandolo spent considerable sums on the creation of the San Isidoro chapel in the north transept, commemorating the saint whose body was brought to Venice from Chios in 1125; his final contribution was the formation of the baptistery, at the end of the south narthex, with its mosaics representing the life of John the Baptist; appropriately, too, his own monument still stands here.

A century later, another outstanding doge, Francesco Foscari, made his own mark on the basilica, in one of many public works instigated during his long reign. Foscari founded the Mascoli Chapel, also in the north transept, and dedicated to the lay religious confraternities of the city. The altar, made in 1430, was largely the work of Bartolomeo Bon, who was to be employed by Foscari again a few years later, when he began work on the Porta della Carta.[15] The final physical alteration to the church was again the result of individual patronage, the bequest of Cardinal Giambattista Zen, who died in 1501, and in whose honour the Zen Chapel was formed in the south-western corner of the narthex.

None of these later works, however, affected the basic configuration of the main body of the church. Although the interior retains a powerful spatial unity, in practice the church had to fulfil several specialized functions, all associated with its unique status. With time, it became necessary to divide the interior into two fundamental elements, that for the congregation and that for the many celebrants; this definition was rendered permanent in the late fourteenth century by the rood screen of red Verona marble, carved by the native masters Jacobello and Pier Paolo delle Masegne, who also carved the great Molo window on the Palazzo Ducale. The screen reflects the increasing scale, elaboration and codification of the ducal rituals in this period and the parallel increase in the number of attendants. Adjacent to it, the right hand or 'Epistle' pulpit played a central role in these rituals. It was assembled in the early fourteenth century from older fragments, and from it the newly-elected doge was presented to the assembled nobility during his coronation rite.

Beyond delle Masegne's screen, and before the High Altar, the broad chancel formed the heart of the basilica's ceremonial functions. The ducal throne stood on the south side, near the pulpit; by tradition, the doges entered the church directly through a doorway in the south transept, from the Palazzo Ducale, so that this was 'their' side of the church. In contrast, the throne of the *primicerio*, the primate of the shrine, was on the north side, and was approached from his own residence immediately north of the church, where the present Palazzo Patriarcale stands. In this way, the Church and State approached the shrine symbolically from left and right, uniting centrally.

All the great festivals of the Republic were focused here. On the day of the vigil before the patronal festival, choral vespers were sung, with a great procession of the doge and Signoria, which began in the Palazzo Ducale and terminated at the High Altar. Much of this ceremony was repeated on

SAN GIACOMO DELL' ORIO (above)

Interior of the nave. A very early
foundation, the church was rebuilt in
1225 on a basilical plan.

SAN MARCO

Left, above: the mosaic in the eastern
apse, with Christ the Pantocrator.

Left, below: detail of mosaic in the
narthex, showing an episode in the story
of Noah and the Flood. The narthex
mosaics depict many Old Testament
stories in a lively, didactic manner.

the feast day itself, attended by the Apostolic Legate, foreign ambassadors, the Scuole Grandi and many others, when a full sung mass was performed, after which traditional gifts were presented to the Serene Prince by the Scuole Grandi. Similar ceremonies took place on several other occasions every year, including the feast of Corpus Domini; at all such festivals the chancel was crowded with dignitaries. Many of these rituals are still celebrated today.[16]

The Venetian parish church

With the unique exception of San Marco, almost all the many churches of Venice performed one of two basic functions: they were either monastic establishments, founded by the religious orders, chiefly the Benedictines, Franciscans and Dominicans, or they were parochial foundations, the spiritual hubs of local, lay communities. Only a very small number formed a third group, votive churches, established either to house a sacred relic or to commemorate a specific event; Santa Maria dei Miracoli and the great church of the Salute respectively represent these two more specialized foundations.

The island-parish, though, was the essential element of daily life in the city, and its church was its spiritual and social focus. Each parish's identity was expressed in the form of its church and its campo, and was located by the landmark of its campanile. The parishes of Venice were large in number but individually very small in area; they rarely served more than perhaps a thousand or 1,500 people. Most parishes also came to rely on two or three wealthy noble families resident on the islet as their chief benefactors for any significant building works. The parish churches themselves were consequently generally modest in size, and none are as large and imposing as the major monastic foundations. The restrictions of land, the irregular shapes of the islets on which they stood, and the extreme density of the urban fabric led to the development of a wide variety of solutions to the design of the parish church, from the survival of a few fairly clear linear basilical forms to the more compact plan of the Greek cross. Still others have less clearly defined or hybrid forms, adapted to their particular context.

The history of the Venetian parish church is a long and complex one, and the fates of many have been extremely varied. In 1493, when Marin Sanudo compiled his guide to the city and its institutions, he recorded sixty parishes in all, twenty-nine on the San Marco side of the Grand Canal and thirty-one on the other.[17] Since the eighteenth century, though, the picture has largely been one of decline; a number were closed or amalgamated by Napoleon, while others have closed in more recent times as a reflection of the drastic decline of the city's resident population.

No parish churches have survived from the very earliest centuries; in most of the ancient foundations the picture is typically one of successive rebuildings over time. Nevertheless, several still retain evidence of their basilical origins. As is perhaps to be expected, such early survivors tend to lie in the poorer, more peripheral parishes, where resources were rarely available for expensive (or expansive) reconstruction projects.

San Zan Degolà (San Giovanni Decollato) is one such survivor, first documented in 1007; like so many of the early parish foundations it was established by a single wealthy family, in this case the noble Venier clan, but was restored by the Pesaro (another patrician dynasty) in the early thirteenth century. The much later eighteenth-century facade masks a basilical interior with Greek marble columns and Byzantine capitals, now surmounted by later Gothic arches. In the far west of the city, too, San Nicolo dei Mendicoli was the parish church of an isolated community of poor fishermen; it also retains its twelfth-century basilical form, notably in the central apse and the rhythmic nave colonnades. It is less clearly defined, however, than San Zan Degolà, since a transept was inserted across the nave at a later date, and it was modernized in 1361. Later still, in the sixteenth century, the simple interior was further compromised by rich high-level paintings and decorations, a fate that befell several of these early churches. The very isolation of the church, though, is probably also the reason for the survival of its transverse portico, a rare survivor of a once more common feature; those of San Giacometto and Torcello cathedral are the only other timber porticos that have survived today.

Clear basilical forms are also recognizable at San Giacomo dell'Orio and at Sant'Agnese. San Giacomo offers another example of noble patronage, since it was rebuilt by the Badoer family in 1225, although modernized in the Gothic style in the later fourteenth century. These churches again lie in the more remote fringes of the city, as does Sant'Eufemia on the Giudecca, another zone traditionally associated with poor boatbuilders and fishermen. Sant'Eufemia has survived without major structural alterations, and the interior is still dominated by the stately eleventh-century nave colonnade, despite the elaborate eighteenth-century stucco decorations. All of these churches retain the clear axiality of the classical basilica. Built almost entirely of brick; their exteriors were generally very simple, sometimes with rows of brick piers or pilasters down the nave walls, still clearly visible, for example, at Sant'Agnese. They were also characterized by open timber roofs, and in some cases the apsidal east end has also survived, again as we find at Sant'Agnese.[18]

The interiors are all dominated by their nave colonnades, and sometimes the arcades retain their original round-arched profile, such as those at San Nicolo and San Zan Degolà. Elsewhere, though, the colonnade was later modernized, and we have the Gothic examples of San Giacomo and of San Polo; the latter is another important early foundation, although much altered (and effectively rebuilt) in the fifteenth century.

During the medieval period, therefore, the basilica remained the dominant plan form for many parish church foundations. Examples of the alternative tradition, that of the centralized Greek cross plan, are much fewer in number, although there is one important survivor in San Giacometto at the Rialto. Reputedly the very first parochial foundation in the city, the present tiny structure was built in the later twelfth century and was consecrated by the great Doge Ziani in 1177. Miraculously it survived the great fire at Rialto in 1514, but was altered in the sixteenth century when the vaults were rebuilt. Despite its diminutive scale, San Giacometto has a surprisingly complex plan, although in essence a compact Greek cross, with a small central dome. Such a plan was particularly appropriate here, in this most congested, central district of the city, where space was extremely restricted; after the 1514 fire, a similar form was to be used by Antonio Scarpagnino when he had a limited site for the rebuilding of the nearby San Giovanni Elemosinario.[19]

SAN GIACOMO (GIACOMETTO) DI RIALTO

Detail of side altar; the tiny church has a centralized Greek cross plan and, although much restored, retains 11th century capitals.

The monastic orders: Benedictines, Franciscans and Dominicans

If the Venetian parish churches were small in size but numerous, fulfilling a local well-defined community role, the requirements of the great monastic orders were quite different. Of the many orders that established houses both in Venice and on numerous islands in the lagoon, the first were the Benedictines. From their famous seventh-century foundation at Pomposa, they spread to the great mainland estates of Praglia and Follina in the ninth century. They also settled in the Venetian lagoon at an early date: on the islet of San Servolo in *c* 800, then at Santo Spirito; at San Giorgio in Alga, San Michele and San Nicolo on the Lido. A little further from the city were their houses at San Secondo, Ammiana (near Torcello) and Malamocco. Most of these monasteries, therefore, remained peripheral to the life of the city itself, forming communities which reflected the founding principles of the order of St Benedict: poverty, chastity and obedience to the scriptures. A typical Benedictine monastery, both in northern Italy and elsewhere, was a sizable, self-sufficient community, which was not only a centre for study and scriptural contemplation, but for practical activity as well: the rules of the order required them to be builders and cultivators of land, both of which activities were sometimes carried out on a very large scale. And naturally, too, the monastery itself required comprehensive facilities for the monks: dormitories, cloisters, chapterhouse, library, refectories, kitchens and barns.

SAN MARCO

The Pala d'Oro, or golden altar-screen
(above). This extraordinary assemblage was
begun in 1105, but was elaborated in 1209
and reached its final form in 1345, under
doge Andrea Dandolo. The Byzantine
enamelled figures of Saints and Apostles are
surrounded by gilded panels with hundreds
of precious and semi-precious stones.

The High Altar (left), with baldacchino
supported by Eastern alabaster columns,
perhaps from the 7th century. Below the
Altar is the sarcophagus of Mark himself,
patron of the Republic.

However, this galaxy of scattered island-monasteries was complemented by equally numerous establishments in Venice itself. San Zaccaria (which became one of the wealthiest and most important of all) was founded in 827, followed by San Gregorio in 850, San Lorenzo, Santa Croce, San Giorgio Maggiore and San Cipriano at Murano. Most of these houses (with the important exception of San Zaccaria) were still in peripheral zones of the city, where their life of contemplation could be followed, and where there was still land to develop and cultivate, although in 900 the Benedictines established a monastery behind San Marco with a church dedicated to Santi Filippo e Giacomo; none of its buildings survive, with the exception of the cloister, the only surviving Romanesque example in the city. Built in the twelfth century, its simple brick arches still provide an oasis of tranquillity only yards from the great Piazza of San Marco.

The orders that made the most profound impression on the city's inner fabric, therefore, were not the numerous Benedictines, but the Dominicans and Franciscans. These two great preaching orders had fundamentally different physical requirements from the Benedictines since, although they both followed the basic precepts of Benedict's founding order, their role was not contemplative but was the practical task of the dissemination of God's word. In the urban context, therefore, they did not isolate themselves from the people but brought the word of God to them. And whereas the Benedictine church was purely designed to take account of their own internal offices and rituals, the churches of the preaching orders were open to the common people, who were welcomed in large numbers. For this fundamental reason, their naves were always large and spacious.

The history of the Dominicans and Franciscans in Venice runs very closely parallel, from their earliest settlement within a few years of each other to the completion of their great mother churches two centuries later. A history of rivalry, it nevertheless produced the two noblest medieval churches in the city, the Dominicans' Santi Giovanni e Paolo and the Franciscans' Santa Maria Gloriosa dei Frari ('the Frari').

The liturgical requirements of the two orders gave rise to the development of a strong, distinctive church typology in Venice, drawing on the general Western Gothic tradition but more specifically on that of northern Italy. Epitomized on the grandest scale at the Frari and Santi Giovanni e Paolo, the style is also evinced on a rather smaller scale elsewhere, from the fine Augustinian Santo Stefano to the more modest San Gregorio. The plan of the Venetian (and indeed the northern Italian) conventual church is basically a Latin cross; the form derived from the basilical-aisled hall but had developed a cruciform plan with the extension of well-defined transepts, while retaining a long nave for large congregations. The Latin cross is widespread throughout Western Europe as a conventual form, although the Venetian and other northern Italian examples are further characterized by exceptionally large bays, greatly simplified colonnades and the omission of an upper gallery or triforium. As elsewhere in northern Italy, the vaulting in Venetian churches remains very simple, with none of the elaborate geometrical forms of the French Gothic. The plans, though, are usually elaborated upon by the protrusion of a prominent facetted central apse, with smaller apsidal chapels on each side. All such churches, Franciscan and Dominican, had two overwhelming practical requirements; the provision of clear, open space for preaching to large congregations, and a further generous space for the monastic choir, with an aisle down the centre for processions.

They are almost entirely built of brick, and in this, too, they form part of a north-east Italian tradition that includes the vast and never completed San Petronio at Bologna, and many other churches in Padua, Ferrara and the Venetian Terraferma. The use of stone is generally confined to the stout nave colonnades, to the ribs of the vaults, and to the framing of doors and windows.

The facade is one of the most distinctive elements of the Venetian conventual tradition. Once again built of brick, its typically three-part form is a direct expression of the nave and aisles that stand

SANT'APOLLONIA (above)

The cloisters, the only surviving 12th century Romanesque examples in the city.

THE FRARI (right)

The nave, towards the choir screen. The great Franciscan church was rebuilt from 1340 to 1445, with a spacious nave for preaching to large congregations. The rich choir screen was completed by Pietro Lombardo in c.1475.

THE FRARI

Above: Detail of the San Marco portal; the fine bas relief sculpture, from the 15th century, is attributed to Bartolomeo Bon or Jacopo della Quercia.

Left: Titian's great painting of *The Assumption* was commissioned in 1516 to stand above the High Altar, and has dominated the church choir ever since.

behind it. The facade is usually embellished with high-level decorative arcading (in brick or stone, or both), sometimes with stone pinnacles on the tops of the buttresses, and also frequently with a central circular window, known as an *ocio*, an eye. The porticos of these churches are often exceptionally fine, with richly-carved door surrounds, and surmounted by statues; within the characteristic lunette there is usually a bas-relief sculptural group incorporating an image of the titular saint. These facades are imposing in their simplicity, only rarely (as at Santi Giovanni e Paolo and the Madonna dell'Orto) incorporating any further elaboration. The few other elements of the exterior that are more elaborately detailed are the facetted forms of the eastern apses. Here the complex, richly-detailed brickwork forms part of the lagoon's long tradition that can be traced back at least as far as the eleventh-century work at San Donato, Murano.

St Francis of Assisi visited Venice in 1220; thirteen years later a monastery was founded on the little islet of San Francesco del Deserto in the northern lagoon. It was the first such monastery after Francis's original establishment at Assisi, and it still flourishes today. In the following year, 1234, a Venetian nobleman, Giovanni Badoer, gave Francis's followers a large, rather marshy tract of land in the western part of the city, between the parishes of San Tomà and San Stin. Two years later again the plot was extended, probably by a further offering from Doge Jacopo Tiepolo, who also gave land to the Dominicans. The first church of the Friars Minor (the 'Frari') was consecrated in 1280, its orientation the reverse of that of the present building. By 1340, though, the order had become so influential that work began on a very much larger structure, towards which offerings were made by many noble clans. This new orientation allowed the retention of the earlier chancel while the long rebuilding process took place. The apses and transepts were begun first, and were complete by 1361, when the great campanile was begun, the tallest in Venice after that of San Marco. The transepts were roofed shortly afterwards, followed by the erection of the massive cylindrical nave columns. The nave proceeded very slowly, though, and only in 1415 was the old church finally demolished; the huge west facade was itself completed in 1440–5.[20]

Despite this century-long building programme the great church retains a strong stylistic unity. The Latin cross plan is exceptionally broad and spacious, with a long six-bay nave to accommodate the assembled congregation. The easternmost bay of the nave is still occupied by the monastic choir, with a central aisle for processions. Within it, the magnificent carved timber choir stalls are the only intact medieval survivors in Venice. Erected in 1468, the 124 stalls were carved by the outstanding Vicentine master, Marco Cozzi. The marble choir screen, which clearly defines the two spaces for worshippers and for the friars, was added in 1475 by the workshop of Pietro Lombardo.

Beyond the great transepts, the chancel was terminated in a polygonal apse, flanked on each side by three narrow side chapels. All the principal spaces have simple cross-vaults, although they are reinforced by stout timber tie beams above the columns. The very last work to be completed inside was the high altar, which was installed in 1516, and behind which still rises Titian's magnificent *Assumption of the Virgin*, commissioned by the friars and completed in 1518.[21]

The importance of the patronage of the order by wealthy Venetian patricians is evinced by the monuments to several doges, perhaps the most remarkable of whom was Francesco Foscari. Even more prominent patronage, though, is shown by the attachment to the church's perimeter of two chapels, both built contemporaneously with the completion of the church itself: the Corner Chapel, dedicated to San Marco, was built in 1417, while the Miani Chapel followed in 1432. The latter was designed as a miniature version of the church itself, abutting the massive campanile; chapels such as these set precedents that were to be followed in many later, Renaissance churches, as the Venetian patriciate realized that their noble patronage could be extended considerably beyond a simple monument to an individual member, to the construction of a substantial chapel as a private place of worship for their family.

Across the city stands the equally imposing Dominican church of Santi Giovanni e Paolo; since both churches were built by rival orders to fulfil basically the same functions, and since they were built contemporaneously, their overall plans are very similar indeed. The Dominicans were also established in Venice in about 1220; the doge, Jacopo Tiepolo, who had given land to the Franciscans, made a similar, remarkably even-handed gift to the Dominicans in around 1230. The site was equally large, in order to accommodate not only the church but the extensive monastic buildings; it was also equally difficult to build on, and was similarly located on the marshy fringes of the city, in this case near the northern shore.

This 'polarity' of the two rival orders on opposite sides of the city was a characteristic medieval arrangement; it can also be seen, for example, in the relative locations of the Dominican and Franciscan houses in Florence, Siena and Bologna. In all cases there is one establishment on each side of the city centre. (In Bologna, too, the churches of both orders were built at the same time as those in Venice.) The Dominicans' Venetian site adjoined the edge of the lagoon, although considerable reclamation was to take place here in stages, so that by the middle of the sixteenth century, the extensive monastic buildings spread almost as far as the Fondamente Nuove, the new quays.

The first church was completed during the thirteenth century, but, as with the Franciscans, the dramatic expansion of the order, coupled with the fact that several doges chose to be buried here, resulted in the urgent need for a larger building. Work began at the east end in the first years of the fourteenth century; by 1368 the apses and transepts had been completed. There then followed a long hiatus due to a shortage of funds; eventually, in 1390 the Maggior Consiglio voted to give the Dominicans 10,000 ducats to continue the work. By 1430 the nave was complete and the church consecrated.

The final element of the fabric was the Chapel of the Name of God, with its elaborate external brickwork, which was added in the 1440s; at the same time work also proceeded on the noble, stately facade, which is similar to that of the Frari, but rather more elaborate, but was never completed. The exceptionally fine main portal, however, was added in 1458 by Bartolomeo Bon, one of the final florid Gothic works in Venice, before the influence of the Renaissance took hold.

Santi Giovanni e Paolo's interior has much in common with the Frari, with similar plain drum-like columns, although the five structural bays are even more spacious than those of the Franciscans, and a cupola was added over the crossing before the end of the fifteenth century. In sharp contrast to the vast, simple nave, the east end is, appropriately, considerably richer and more complex, with a polygonal apse lit by exceptionally tall narrow bays, pierced by traceried lancets, and with two large chapels, similarly detailed, on each side. As at the Frari, the exterior of these eastern apses gave the opportunity to display more finely-detailed decorative brickwork.

The church continued to be chosen as the burial place for many doges, so that over the centuries it became something of a Venetian Pantheon; after the fifteenth century, all ducal state funerals were held here, whether or not the doge himself had chosen to be buried in the church. By the fall of the Republic, Santi Giovanni e Paolo contained the tombs of twenty-five doges, some with exceptionally fine monuments.

The dominant characteristic of both churches is the vast, spacious simplicity of their vaulted naves, reflecting the fundamental moral and spiritual principles of the two orders, but equally reflecting the broader Venetian architectural tradition, in which light and space are abundant. Both have been admired for centuries: Francesco Sansovino praised the Frari's 'memorable construction', while the Dominican church was, 'grand and … noble because of its location … for its construction, albeit in the German (ie Gothic) style of Architecture, for its great size and for the beauty of its paintings, statues and other notable things …'[22]

THE FRARI (below)

Side portal into the nave, a characteristic example of florid late Venetian Gothic, with foliage decoration and the use of contrasting white Istrian stone and red Verona marble.

SANTO STEFANO (right)

The interior contains painted nave colonnades and a very fine 'ship's keel' roof.

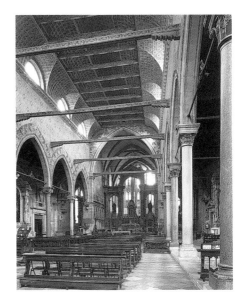

Many of the characteristics of these two great churches are shared, albeit on a reduced scale, by Santo Stefano and the Madonna dell'Orto, the first of which was the chief Augustinian house in Venice. Santo Stefano was built in 1294–1325, although partly reconstructed in the early fifteenth century, when it was extended to the east to bridge over a narrow canal, which thus – uniquely – passes under the chancel. The plan is again a conventual Latin cross, although Santo Stefano's interior has a much narrower bay structure than the Franciscan and Dominican churches, with nave colonnades of alternating shafts of red Verona broccatelle and Greek marble. The appearance of this considerably rich interior is partly the result of the fourteenth-century works, when the decorations were added, and the church was covered by an exceptionally fine 'ship's keel' timber roof, the most complex example that has survived. However, the exterior is very simple, the only more elaborate feature being the vigorously carved portal, in a characteristic late Gothic style, again perhaps produced by the Bon workshop.[23]

The Madonna dell'Orto, which has a rather similar history, is often considered the finest medieval church in Venice, particularly for its unusual but finely-proportioned facade; it is also comparable in size with Santo Stefano. The first church on the site was built by Fra Tiberio from Parma, general of the Umiliati order, and was dedicated to San Cristofolo. However, the dedication was altered after a miracle-working image of the Madonna was found in an adjacent orchard (*orto*); by 1399 the first church had deteriorated so badly that the Maggior Consiglio funded the first stage of its reconstruction. Some elements were retained, including the nave colonnades, with their rather archaic capitals. Although it remained a monastic church, therefore, the Madonna also now incorporated votive functions, with the miraculous image displayed on the high altar.

The protracted rebuilding was only concluded in the 1470s, with the completion of the facade. Its rich portal was itself one of the very last elements to be carved; it is once again the product of the Bon workshop, which was located very nearby at San Marziale, and was completed after Bartolomeo Bon's death, incorporating some Renaissance details in its design. The exceptionally fine facade can be regarded as the final flowering of the Venetian medieval conventual tradition, although it incorporates an unusual feature in the crowning rows of niches, each containing a statue of one of the Apostles. There appear to be no precedents in Venice for such an elaborate arrangement, where facades generally remained simple, although elsewhere in Italy (such as the cathedrals of Pisa, Orvieto and Siena), where there was a tradition of rich sculpted marble facades, the practice was widespread. Perhaps the cathedral facade at Parma exerted some influence, since it, too, was capped by two raking rows of niches.[24]

Four outstanding monastic churches have, therefore, survived in the city; however, the history of the dozens of other medieval monasteries is largely one of loss, decline and mutilation. Only a few have survived broadly intact, although in some cases badly altered. None of them match the scale of the houses of the two great preaching orders, although the Carmelite church of Santa Maria Assunta (the Carmini) and the Lateran Canons' church of Santa Maria della Carità were of some importance. The former remains reasonably preserved; it was founded in 1286, although the church itself was not completed until the mid-fourteenth century. It has a pronounced axial, basilical plan, terminating in three radiused apses, which is particularly extended to accommodate both preaching and choral activities. The striking interior lost its rhythmic basilical clarity in the sixteenth century, though, when extensive, complex decoration was added within the nave. Santa Maria della Carità, however, has suffered a far worse fate; again originally a simple but substantial brick conventual structure, built in the 1440s, and with characteristic apses and facade, it was stripped of most of its external detail in the eighteenth century. It was also deconsecrated and in the early nineteenth century had an intermediate floor inserted when it was converted into accommodation for the Accademia di Belle Arti; today, therefore, little remains of its original appearance.

SANTI GIOVANNI E PAOLO

Above: the richly-carved west portal, one of the very last works of Bartolomeo Bon, begun in 1458.

Right: the crossing and the chancel, with exceptionaly tall traceried windows to the faceted central apse. The original choir stalls are lost, although those at the Frari survive.

171

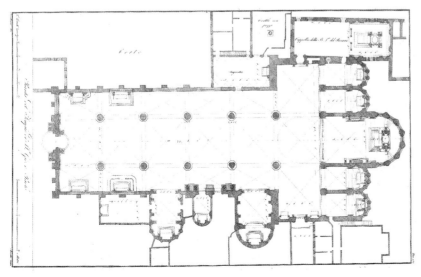

SANTI GIOVANNI E PAOLO

Left: plan. The plans of this church and
the Frari are very similar, both Latin crosses
of remarkable size. The broad spacious naves
provided space for preaching to massed
congregations.

Above: The imposing west facade dominates
the square, with the Scuola Grande di
San Marco on the left. The church facade
was never completed as intended.

Both of these churches represent the 'mainstream' Venetian conventual tradition, and several other surviving facades, for example, those of San Gregorio, Sant'Andrea della Zirada, San Giovanni in Bragora and Sant'Aponal, all fall into this same tradition. Although the last two churches were parochial rather than conventual, the simple three-part brick facade, with its stone portico, square buttresses and characteristic 'eye' window, was just as suitable for cladding a fifteenth-century parish church as it was a monastic one.

One feature common to several of these facades was the device of using a quadrant-shaped panel of brickwork to face the ends of the two side aisles, forming a visual link with the higher central bay of the nave, which itself was finished with a radiused parapet. Such a device can be seen at Sant'Andrea, Sant'Aponal and Bragora, and was to be developed a little later by Mauro Codussi to considerable effect.

For the rest, these remaining Gothic churches are simple structures; four of them (Sant'Andrea, Sant'Elena, Sant'Alvise and Santa Caterina) were Augustinian foundations, and are located in the furthest, most remote corners of the city, where there was still ample room for their cloisters and herb gardens. In most cases the conventual buildings and cloisters also survive; those at Sant'Alvise are particularly attractive, a fusion between late Gothic and the early Renaissance.

These churches can all be regarded as rather distant cousins of the great preaching houses of the Franciscans and Dominicans. Some have a single nave while others also have side aisles, but most of them have a more elaborate eastern apse, concentrating light and attention on the high altar. Stone is used sparingly, and confined to portals and window surrounds. Some of these churches (among them Sant'Andrea and Sant'Alvise) were built for closed orders of Augustinian nuns, and they retain the characteristic choir gallery or *barco* across the west end of the nave interior; this gallery was sometimes reached by a bridge from the adjacent convent so that the nuns could gain direct access without leaving the nunnery or being seen by outsiders. Such bridges also survive in a few cases: Sant'Andrea again, for example, and Santa Maria dei Miracoli.[25]

THE MADONNA DELL'ORTO

Below, left: detail of the west doorway. Like that of Santi Giovanni e Paolo, it is another late work by Bartolomeo Bon, from the 1460s.

Below: facade to the campo; it is often regarded as the finest medieval church facade in the city. The high-level niches with figures of the Apostles are unique.

The early Renaissance: Antonio Rizzo and Pietro Lombardo

In the building of churches the architectural Renaissance in Venice proceeded somewhat tentatively; it is thus perhaps not surprising, given the very strong Gothic traditions of the city, that the first fully Renaissance works were not completely new churches, but instead commissions by enlightened private individuals. A number of wealthy and influential Venetian patricians were highly receptive to new humanist philosophies, far more so than were parochial committees or some of the more entrenched bureaucrats of the Palazzo Ducale.

Renaissance influences can be detected in Bon's porticos for both the Madonna dell'Orto and Santi Giovanni e Paolo, but by the 1450s Bon was no longer young, and it was to be the next generation, notably the sculptor-architect Antonio Rizzo, who made the decisive break with the past. Among the earliest Renaissance works were three privately-commissioned chapels, all attached to existing churches, which illustrate these small-scale beginnings. That of the Martini family at San Giobbe is the earliest, built in 1471–6. The Martini family was from Lucca in Tuscany, and its chapel is a

VITTORE CARPACCIO, *Apparition of the One
Thousand Martyrs* c.1515

The painting celebrates a vision experienced
by the prior of San Antonio di Castello in
1511, and faithfully depicts a Venetian
medieval church interior soon after its
construction. On the left is the choir gallery.
(Gallerie dell' Accademia, Venice.)

Tuscan work transplanted to the lagoons. Its unique dome is covered internally with glazed terracotta tiles, perhaps inspired by Luca della Robbia's work in the Chapel of the Cardinal of Portugal at San Miniato al Monte in Florence during the 1460s; indeed, the tiles themselves were imported across the mountains from Tuscany. Its architect is unknown, however, and it remains an isolated special case; the adjacent Grimani Chapel, built in 1529, exemplifies the stylistic development of such chapels over this period, and is a refined work framed in stone; very much in the style of Mauro Codussi, it offers a strong contrast with the rich glazed tiles of the Martini dome.

Slightly later than the Martini Chapel is that of the Gussoni family at San Lio, built in the 1480s; it is extremely richly detailed, in much the same style as the nearby house built for the same patron, Jacopo Gussoni; although its ornate relief carving has been attributed to Pietro Lombardo, whose most characteristic feature this was, its style is rather too complex and overpowers the architectural form. The third of this trilogy of 'adolescent' works is the Chapel of Zorzi Corner (Giorgio Cornaro) at Santi Apostoli, again from the 1480s, but distinctly more robust and classical in character. Corner was the wealthiest man in Venice and the brother of Caterina, Queen of Cyprus; the small chapel was thus built with little concern for cost. Nevertheless, it is an altogether more architectural work than the Gussoni, its hemispherical dome carried by four finely-carved Corinthian columns, with a coffered ceiling in the apse. The conviction of the detailing is closer

to Mauro Codussi's strong, pure forms than to the ornate style of Lombardo, although we have no documentation. In these last two examples, though, we can already perceive a range of stylistic approaches, which was to be further developed by the three outstanding figures of the early Venetian Renaissance: Mauro Codussi, Pietro Lombardo and Antonio Rizzo. The last was the most purely sculptural of the three, only later broadening his scale to embrace works of architecture.

If private chapels were one location in which the individual taste of the newly-enlightened patron could be expressed, the other was in the funerary monuments that such chapels sometimes housed. Two such monuments by Rizzo, for example, illustrate the increasing strength of the influence of the Florentine Renaissance: the Tron Monument in the Frari (1476–80) and the lost Barbarigo Tombs in the Carità Church. The former is a grandiose development from the Tomb of Vettor Cappello at Sant'Elena (early 1470s, usually attributed to Rizzo), with no trace of the Gothic remaining in its detailing. Designed as a great screen, its five storeys are crowned by a deep semicircular lunette; the dominant features are the superimposed tiers of niches and the bold, box-like form of the sarcophagus. Rizzo's other great monument, now lost, had a horizontal rather than a vertical emphasis, but was equally impressive in scale. The Barbarigo Monument was dedicated to two brothers, Marco and Agostino, doges in succession, and was probably built in the late 1480s, although not complete until after 1499. It was composed of three powerful bays divided by buttresses and integrated into the north wall of the church.[26]

Like Rizzo, Lombardo was trained as a sculptor; again, he was not a native Venetian, but came from Carona on Lake Lugano; once in Venice his family name, Solari, was replaced in favour of his region of origin. He had arrived in around 1467, and developed a flourishing workshop with his two sons, Antonio and Tullio. One of his earliest works was the rich choir screen at the Frari, where he belatedly replaced the deceased Bartolomeo Bon in 1475; the completed screen remains hybrid in style, much of the detail a mixture of florid late Gothic and early Renaissance. Its complex, refined relief carving evinces the characteristic direction in which Pietro's work was to develop.

The first works to be entirely of his own design are three fine monuments, to Doges Pasquale Malipiero, Nicolo Marcello and Pietro Mocenigo, all now in Santi Giovanni e Paolo. Here Lombardo developed his own highly-distinctive style, which was originally Florentine-Lombard in character, but which later became far more clearly Venetian. Ducal monuments such as these were the ideal way in which to project the self-image that the doge wished to leave for posterity, although unless they were commissioned well in advance (which was occasionally the case), the doge himself had no opportunity to appreciate their final form. Nevertheless, his choice of master and subject matter reflected the tastes of the patron more directly than almost any other form of private commission.

The Malipiero Tomb is the earliest work (1470s); it is partly Florentine in character, although it retains the traditional Venetian device of a tent-like canopy over the recumbent figure, much like the earlier monument to Francesco Foscari in the Frari. The frame is purely Tuscan, with a pair of framing pilasters supporting a radiused arch, closely based on earlier monuments in Santa Croce, Florence, such as the Marsuppini Monument by Desiderio da Settignano, executed after 1453. Much of the Tomb is also covered with the precise relief decoration that was such a quintessential part of Lombardo's style. Thus a fusion of two traditions and two eras was created in a single work.

The Mocenigo Tomb, carved in around 1481, has more in common with Rizzo's Tron Monument in its superimposed niches and rows of figures. Mocenigo's brief reign of fourteen months achieved little, but his earlier distinguished career in the Turkish war was to be the basis of the victorious iconography. The strong composition is more of a triumphal arch than a traditional, passive memorial, an impression enhanced by the martial figure of the doge, erect and arrogant on top of his bier. The bier itself is carried by figures of Roman soldiers, the first ever seen in Venice, and the whole has a precision and a worldly confidence unthinkable even a couple of decades earlier.

Lombardo's third memorial, that to Nicolo Marcello, carved in c1481–5, originally stood in Santa Marina, but was reassembled at Santi Giovanni e Paolo after the demolition of the former church in 1820. Simpler in overall composition, it is the richest of all in its detailed carving, its considerable substance seeming to defy the brief, insignificant reign of its patron. The single dominant form is a deep, massive arch, architecturally much bolder than the earlier tombs, with figures of the Virtues guarding the recumbent figure.[27] The three works demonstrate the increasing confidence of his style, as he developed these complex forms of 'interior architecture'.

Pietro's first purely architectural work is at San Giobbe, which was perhaps begun by Antonio Gambello in 1471. The fine west doorway is characteristic of Lombardo's early style, still Florentine, and comparable with the Malipiero Tomb. When he was appointed, the nave was already built, but he completed the richly-detailed chancel and apse after 1472. The chancel's simple dome on pendentives is arguably the first purely Renaissance dome in Venice, although roughly contemporary with Codussi's at San Michele. Its origin appears Florentine (also perhaps due to Martini family influence), as do the pendentive roundels with reliefs of the Evangelists. Lombardo's most distinctive building, and his architectural masterpiece, is the little votive church of Santa Maria dei Miracoli, often described as jewel-like for its rich marble cladding, although in form it also closely resembles a jewellery casket. It was built to house a miracle-working image of the Madonna that had been found in the nearby parish of Santa Marina; as a 'reliquary', therefore, the church had to accommodate no practical parochial functions, although it was to be administered by nuns, Poor Clares of the Franciscan order. By 1480, sufficient offerings had been amassed for a competition to be held to design a suitable chapel; although the details remain rather unclear, Lombardo was appointed and the church was completed in 1488. It shows Pietro's

SAN GREGORIO FROM THE GRAND CANAL

The modest Benedictine monastic buildings were rebuilt in the 14th century, with a rich square portal to the Canal; they are dominated by Baldassare Longhena's massive church of the Salute, built 300 years later.

PIETRO LOMBARDO MONUMENTS

Far right: Monument to doge Pietro Mocenigo, Santi Giovanni e Paolo, early 1480s. A complex composition, it is closer to Antonio Rizzo's Tron monument than to Pietro's other works, with tiers of figures set into niches.

Right, top: monument to doge Pasquale Malipiero in Santi Giovanni e Paolo; this is the first of Pietro's ducal monuments, probably carved in the late 1460s. The intricate relief carving is characteristic of his style.

Right, below: monument to doge Nicolo Marcello, also in Santi Giovanni e Paolo, c.1481–5; it is simpler and more massive in composition than the Malipiero work, but with refined detailed decoration.

SANT'APONAL (above)

Detail of the facade, epitomizing the
evolutionary nature of so many Venetian
churches: the original circular window has
been replaced by a collection of medieval
sculptures, including a late 14th century
Crucifixion.

ANTONIO RIZZO MONUMENT (left)

Monument to doge Nicolo Tron, the
Frari, c.1477–9. The large, complex work
contains two realistic images of the doge,
one recumbent, the other standing.

strengths more clearly than any other of his works; its planning is ingenious, and much of the decorative carving, particularly in the chancel, is exquisite. The extremely restricted site, confined between a narrow street and a canal, resulted in a tall, aisle-less box, with a rich, timber barrel-vaulted ceiling. Its overall volume may have resulted from a study of the Arena Chapel in Padua, which has a similar form and proportions. Here, the whole structure was to be sheathed, both inside and out, with fine marble cladding; the Miracoli was the first church since the shrine of San Marco itself to be so comprehensively decorated in such a manner. Even before its completion, it started to receive lavish praise. Felix Fabri reported in 1484 that the half-completed church had 'such magnificence that to see it is something wonderful'. Even John Ruskin, ardent foe of most Renaissance 'barbarities', considered the Miracoli one of the two 'most refined buildings in this style', that is, of the early Venetian, Lombard-influenced Renaissance.

Externally, the facades all have two superimposed orders, again probably the earliest example of this classical arrangement in the city; the window-less flank walls are framed with pilasters and friezes that evoke the classical Roman tradition, and were designed to be reflected in the waters of the adjacent canal. The same device was used a little later (almost certainly by Lombardo again) at the Scuola Grande di San Marco. The front facade, on to a tiny *campiello*, is terminated with a large semicircular gable, directly reflecting the barrel-vault inside, and is decorated with Pietro's characteristic inlays of marble and porphyry discs. The interior is dominated by the strong axial form, all focused on the chancel, which is raised high above the level of the nave so that the venerated image could be clearly seen by all worshippers. Lombardo took further advantage of this unusual arrangement to tuck the sacristy below the sanctuary and the altar. The rich decorative carving of the chancel, particularly of the balustrading and altar screen, is a *tour de force*, much of it the work of Pietro's son Tullio. The chancel was roofed by a tall dome, directing light down to the altar; this dome is the most purely architectonic element of the whole interior, its clarity of form reminiscent of the stylistic rigour of the third and greatest architect of the early Venetian Renaissance, Mauro Codussi.[28]

Mauro Codussi and his followers

The gleaming white stone facade of San Michele in Isola, standing on the far corner of the cemetery island, is the most memorable feature of any journey from Venice to Murano, and justifiably so since it is one of the seminal buildings of Venetian architecture, the first purely Renaissance church in the city.[29] Like many of the city's outstanding architects, Codussi was not a native but came from Lenna (Lentina), a village near Bergamo. Begun in 1469, when Codussi was in his late twenties, San Michele is a work of youthful but extraordinary achievement, and secured his reputation in the city where he remained for most of the rest of his life. His influence was to be profound.

Codussi first worked for the Camaldolesi order at Ravenna, and was almost certainly familiar with Alberti's great church for the Malatesta at nearby Rimini, much of it built between 1450 and 1454. He was equally influenced by Brunelleschi, though, although we have no firm evidence that he visited Florence. On the strength of his (unknown) work at Ravenna, the monks sent Codussi to Venice to build their new church on the islet of San Michele, between the city's north shore and Murano. Unlike Rizzo and Lombardo, Codussi had been trained as a master mason; he thus had an early understanding of structural form and function, and in this his career more closely resembles that of his great successor, Palladio, than those of his contemporaries. Codussi was a master carver but he was also a practical builder, whose works have a purity, consistency and conviction in which form is rarely compromised by decoration. Like Palladio, Codussi's career was greatly enhanced (and advanced) by his humanist intellectual patrons, men such as Pietro Donà and Pietro Dolfin, abbots at San Michele in succession; Dolfin was elected General of the

Camadolesi order in 1480, and was a man of powerful intellect and considerable influence.

The facade of San Michele was revolutionary in Venice. It was started fifteen years or so before Lombardo's Miracoli, when no church had ever been entirely finished with stone, with the glorious exception of the shrine of San Marco itself. Codussi was building in a city of Gothic, brick churches, where stone was confined to windows, portals and parapets. A closer analysis reveals that his refined composition was both revolutionary and evolutionary, drawing on the traditional Venetian Gothic facade and transforming it in the process. Its three bays reflect the nave and aisles of the church behind, the central one crowned by a semicircular gable, while the side bays are capped with curved, slightly flattened quadrants. Both forms derive from Gothic facades such as those of Sant'Andrea and San Giovanni in Bragora; probably equally influential was Alberti's church at Rimini, the design of which also has a central triumphal arch and flanking quadrants, although the latter were not executed. Codussi thus drew on both local motifs and the powerful new image of the Malatesta facade.

San Michele incorporates, with great precision and confidence, several features never seen in Venice before, among them the radial fluting around the gable, the Latin inscription across the facade and the square rustication that clads the lower order. The only known earlier rustication in Venice is that on the Cà del Duca, the ambitious palace that had been begun by Bartolomeo Bon for the Corner (and later perhaps progressed by Benedetto Ferini for Francesco Sforza), but which was never completed beyond the evocative fragment that we see today. The church's small but richly-carved portal is Florentine in appearance; the three facade windows, by contrast, have Gothic origins but are translated into the new language, the central circular 'eye' following many medieval precedents, while the tall sidelights reinterpret the Gothic lancet. To fully appreciate Codussi's compositional confidence, particularly in the design of the upper order, we need only compare the facade with Lombardo's rich but rather manneristic Miracoli facade, probably completed a few years later, with its curious arrangement of circular windows.

The interior illustrates Codussi's still-developing style. The plan is traditional and basilical, perhaps based on earlier foundations, and with a semicircular apse covered by a hemispherical vault. The nave arcades are light and spacious, again reinterpreting Venetian Gothic traditions, although the capitals are highly inventive, neither classical nor medieval. The chancel has a simple dome on pendentives, and the detailing throughout is restrained and disciplined, characteristics that were to remain the dominant feature of Codussi's church interiors. In the western nave is a freestanding *barco* or monks' choir; built in 1480, its rich eastern face is rather reminiscent of Lombardo. The western face is more simply classical, with distinct overtones of the Roman triumphal arch, and reminiscent of the lower order of the Malatesta temple at Rimini. Spatially the church is uncomplicated, but with maturity Codussi's handling of internal spaces was to become considerably more sophisticated.

His second ecclesiastical work was the new campanile for the Cathedral of San Pietro in Castello. Structurally simple, the tower is, in its way, as startling as San Michele, since it was faced entirely with white Istrian stone. Like church facades, campanili, even that of San Marco, were always built of brick, with stonework confined to the detailing of the bellchamber; even today, San Pietro's tower remains the only tower in Venice faced entirely in stone. Its noble, almost Roman form consists of two orders above a stepped base, the tall recessed panels recalling much older Byzantine

SANT' ELENA (below, left)

Detail of the portal and lunette sculpture. In the later 15th century the monument to naval hero, Vetor Cappello was added to the facade, attributed to Antonio Rizzo.

PIETRO LOMBARDO (below)

Santa Maria dei Miracoli, west facade. The church (1481–89) is Lombardo's architectural masterpiece, ingeniously planned on a very restricted site. It is entirely clad with panels of marble within a refined double-order framework of stone.

SAN GIOBBE (below)

West portal, one of Pietro Lombardo's earliest works in the city, c.1472; it remains strongly Florentine in style.

examples, and the whole representing a simple, classical reinterpretation of an ancient typology.

San Zaccaria, the next church with which Codussi is associated, is one of the most remarkable in Venice, linking Gothic with the Renaissance in a single structure. Founded in the seventh century, it was the burial place of eight early doges, and its wealthy Benedictine nunnery already had a long history when reconstruction was begun by Antonio Gambello in 1458. His task included extensive works to the earlier Gothic church, one aisle of which was now incorporated into the new larger church built immediately alongside. Little is known of Gambello's career, although he died in 1481, and the church was completed by Codussi.

San Zaccaria's plan and structure were established by Gambello. The three very large, spacious nave bays were derived from the local monastic tradition, while the choir, which has an ambulatory and radial chapels beyond, is the only example of this quintessentially French arrangement in Venice; it was perhaps modelled on the famous Benedictine mother-church at Cluny. Gambello completed much of this east end, as well as the great nave piers, with their exceptionally fine and inventive bases and capitals, the last carved by Giovanni Buora. Antonio Gambello remains an elusive figure, however, although he was clearly a master of some originality on the evidence of the two superimposed colonnades to the choir, where we find Gothic and Renaissance arcades one above the other, in a juxtaposition as bizarre as it is surprisingly satisfactory.

SAN GIOBBE (below)

West portal, one of Pietro Lombardo's earliest works in the city, c.1472; it remains strongly Florentine in style.

Gambello also began the facade before he died, and the lowest order is certainly his work, as is probably the second. Codussi was thus faced with a more than half-completed church to bring to a satisfactory conclusion. His most important contribution was the completion of the facade. Its overall dimensions were already established, but the resulting rich, powerfully-formed tiers of superimposed colonnades, once again all of Istrian stone, are uniquely Codussian, a large step beyond the restrained refinement of San Michele. Here again, though, the facade is capped with a great semicircular lunette, with flanking quadrants, all deeply moulded, an imposing culmination to the rising ranks of columns and niches.[30]

If Codussi's development of the church facade culminates with that of San Zaccaria, then his sophisticated ordering of internal spaces reaches its maturity at Santa Maria Formosa. The church had been rebuilt two or three times since its reputed foundation by St Magnus in the seventh century, but by the later fifteenth century it had again become old and unstable. Codussi's new church, begun in 1492, revived the ancient form of the Greek cross, a form that, despite the model of San Marco, had never become as widespread as the basilica or the Latin cross. The church has a centralized plan, but with a nave slightly longer than the other three arms, again closely modelled on the patronal shrine. Three semicircular apses dominate the east end, but there are transepts formed by the cross-axis, and the aisles are also flanked by deep chapels to house the numerous guild altars that were based here. The overall plan is thus almost precisely square, and Codussi's interior is spatially complex, with a finely-modulated hierarchy of volumes, from the peripheral chapels up to the culminating cupola at the crossing. All of the detailing is disciplined and refined. It is executed in only two materials: stonework for the architectural structure (columns, capitals, pilasters and cornices), and simple white stucco for the plain surfaces. Such a refined vocabulary was not to be surpassed in Venice until the more monumental work of Palladio half a century later.

Almost complete by the time of Codussi's death in 1504, the cupola was probably added by his son Domenico, following Mauro's design. The facades, though, remained incomplete. Both of them were eventually funded by the noble Cappello family, that facing the canal in the 1540s and that on to the *campo* as late as 1604. Neither of them match Codussi's tranquil, composed interior, although they both represent early examples of the development of the church facade as a family monument and mausoleum, a practice that was to reach its peak of prominence in the seventeenth and eighteenth centuries.[31]

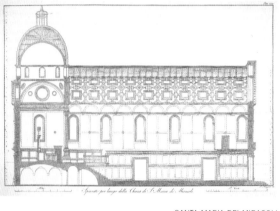

SANTA MARIA DEI MIRACOLI

Above: long section through the church,
showing the richly moulded barrel-vault
ceiling, and the raised level of the chancel,
lit from above by a tall dome.

Right: detail of the High Altar; all of the
detailed carving is the work of Pietro's shop,
chiefly his sons Tullio and Antonio.

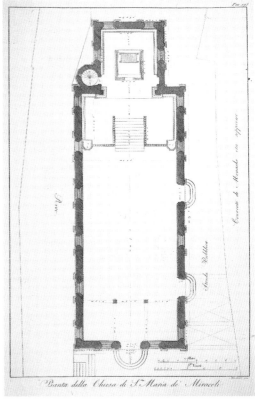

Panta della Chiesa di S.ta Maria de' Miracoli

SANTA MARIA DEI MIRACOLI

Above: plan, a simple aisle-less box, filling the highly restricted site, with a canal down the left side.

Left: detail of the interior of the chancel. Much of the inventive and highly skilful decoration here is the work of Pietro Lombardo's sons, principally Tullio.

San Giovanni Crisostomo is Codussi's last church, although here the context was quite different; in contrast to the large, wealthy parish of Santa Maria Formosa with its noble palaces and spacious campo, San Giovanni was a poor parish, its church occupying an awkward, cramped site. The previous structure was demolished in 1495 and Codussi completed the new one by 1500. Partly enclosed by other buildings, the result is a small, compact form; by no means his most important work, it nevertheless illustrates the clarity of his detailing, and the ingenuity of the plan – its basic form is a perfect square, again a Greek cross with a central dome, and small projecting apses. The facade, too, retains typically Codussian features, including the crowning lunette and flanking quadrants; here, out of economic necessity, the facade is almost entirely of rendered brick, with richer stone detailing confined to the two well-proportioned portals.

In both churches, Codussi's revival of the Greek cross can be seen at least to some extent as the result of the influence of Alberti, particularly of his treatise *De re aedificatoria* (first published in Latin in Florence in 1485), which eulogizes the natural perfection of centralized forms; in the Venetian context, though, the alternative (albeit rather dormant) Eastern tradition of the Greek cross also provided exemplars through such local churches as Santa Fosca at Torcello, San Giacometto and San Marco itself.

Codussi's influence on church design in the early sixteenth century was considerable in several respects: in the revival of the Greek cross plan and the use of the dome on pendentives; in his sensitive organization of internal spaces; and in the spare, refined classical vocabulary of his detailing. Many other attributions to him have been made, although they lack documentation. One is Santa Maria Mater Domini, although since it was only begun in 1503, the year before his death, and completed in *c*1512, his direct involvement must have been minimal. Nevertheless, it is a quintessentially Codussian church, with its Greek cross plan, its cupola, its simple, classical, grey stone piers and its elegant, minimal detailing. San Felice, too, is of Codussian derivation, although only begun in 1531. Formerly enclosed on another restricted site, the church now flanks the broad Strada Nova. The plan is its clearest Codussian feature, although the disciplined vocabulary of the stonework is also characteristic, although it lacks his refinement. Here again, funds were limited, and both facades are detailed sparingly.[32]

Codussi's influence is again clearly apparent in at least some of the work of the much younger Scarpagnino (Antonio Abbondi), who developed similar themes in three churches. San Fantin is usually attributed to him, and was begun in 1506, although only completed decades later, in 1564, under Sansovino's supervision. However, Scarpagnino's more monumental nave already illustrates the tendency towards increased scale and classical richness that is also evident at Giorgio Spavento's San Salvador. Nevertheless, Scarpagnino's detailing is precise and linear, retaining the typically Codussian restraint in materials: refined stonework and plain white stucco. The plan of San Fantin, again on a very limited site, is ingenious, with a domed chancel and two broad nave bays divided by a half bay; the curiously severe west facade, though, is almost devoid of decoration.

San Giovanni Elemosinario, Scarpagnino's second church, had been destroyed in the 1514 Rialto fire and was rebuilt on its extremely restricted site in the form of a simple rectangle, the three-bay nave surmounted by a tall cupola. The strongly Codussian detailing is spare and simple; almost entirely surrounded by shops and warehouses, the church has no facade, but is approached by an archway between two shops.

Scarpagnino's last church, San Sebastiano, was originally a hospital; it was rebuilt in 1455 and again, in its present form, from 1506 to 1548. He reorientated the plan so that the facade (now facing east) terminated the vista from the Calle Lunga of San Barnaba, across a bridge. The tall, elegant, all-stone facade was the last element to be built, and resembles that of San Giorgio dei

SAN MICHELE IN ISOLA (above, top)

Facade of San Michele in Isola, c.1469–75. Mauro Codussi's dramatic all-stone composition, although revolutionary in many ways, also draws on the Venetian Gothic tradition.

SAN PIETRO IN CASTELLO (above)

Rebuilt by Codussi after 1482, the belltower is clad entirely with Istrian stone, the only example in Venice. The facade of the church was designed by Francesco Smeraldi in 1596, based on a scheme by Palladio.

SAN ZACCARIA (right)

Right: plan. Antonio Gambello's plan has three spacious bays to the nave, and an ambulatory with radiating chapels, in the French manner, the only example of this form in Venice. The earlier Gothic church stands on one side.

Right, top: the facade; the lowermost order, and probably the second, are the work of Gambello; all of the upper orders were built by Codussi in the 1480s.

Right below: long section. The nave bays are tall and spacious, quite different from the two orders of the chancel, where the venerated remains of St Zachariah were buried.

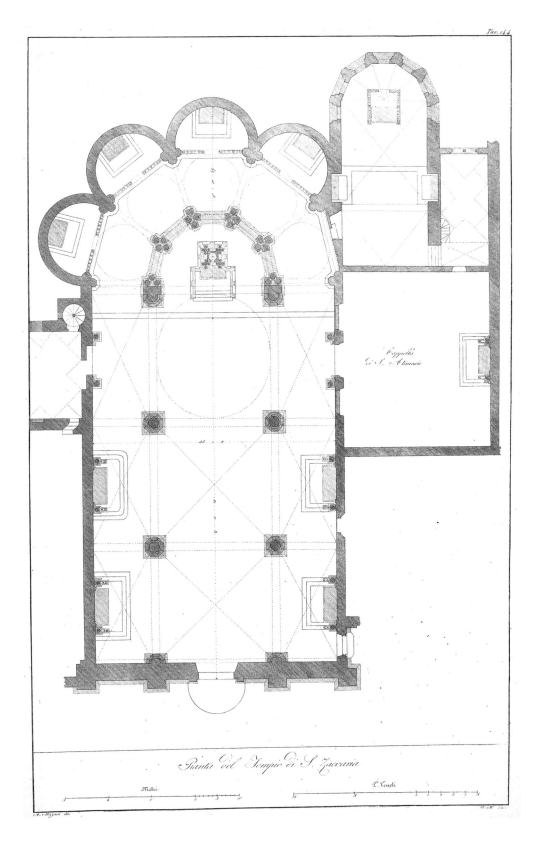

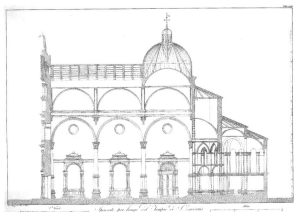

Greci, by Scarpagnino's contemporary, Sante Lombardo, the son of Tullio and grandson of Pietro. Both have two superimposed orders of columns, flanking pairs of piers and central circular 'eye' windows. San Sebastiano's harmonious interior retains its original choir gallery, with an entrance lobby below, but Scarpagnino extended the gallery down both sides of the nave, a highly innovative feature at the time; such an arrangement was later taken up at the Pietà and elsewhere, where it offered an ideal opportunity for the placement of divided choirs.

Scarpagnino's approach to church design, like those of his predecessor Codussi and his successor Jacopo Sansovino, was flexible, his response dependent on the context of the site and on the available funds. He found, as had Codussi, that plans, volumes and the means of lighting the interior all had to be considered individually, and the design carefully tailored to its location in the dense, complex matrix of the medieval city. In many cases, particularly on highly restricted sites, the compact Greek cross was clearly a more suitable, practical solution than more linear, basilical plans.

The High Renaissance: Giorgio Spavento and Jacopo Sansovino

Giorgio Spavento was also younger than Codussi, a native of Como already established in Venice in 1486, when he had worked under Rizzo at the Palazzo Ducale. Closely associated with the rebuilding of the Fondaco dei Tedeschi and other government projects, he was *proto* to the Procurators of San Marco; but his greatest work is San Salvador, the most imposing Renaissance church yet seen in Venice.

It was begun in 1505 or 1506, although Spavento died only three years later, by which time the grandiose plan had been established and the sacristy completed. It followed a model approved by the church, and Spavento's monumental conception was supervised after his death by Pietro and Tullio Lombardo. Most of the main structure should thus be seen as a Lombardo development to the completion of Spavento's approved model, although Tullio's precise contribution to the spatial organization is unclear; the church was completed shortly after 1523, when the great vaults were erected, although the carving of altars and other works continued into the 1530s.

San Salvador marks the arrival in Venice of the mature, monumental Renaissance, as notable for the confidence of its execution as for its imposing scale. The noble interior has a complex rhythm, square bays alternating with narrower half bays, all based on geometrical proportions and modular dimensions; the entire work is thus a carefully-orchestrated composition of elements. Spavento (and Tullio) may have been familiar with Alberti's monumental Sant'Andrea at Mantua (designed 1470), where such alternating bays are also found, although Codussi's San Giovanni Crisostomo is a closer source, albeit on a much smaller scale; Tullio may also have visited Bramante's influential rebuilding of Santa Maria presso San Satiro in Milan (1485). The architectural vocabulary of San Salvador is now muscular and monumental, much of the detailing surely the work of Tullio; its scale is far greater than any work of Codussi, although his legacy remains clearly apparent in the attic and vaults, and perhaps in the inventive capitals which adorn the imposing colonnades below.

Tullio's own early career remains elusive, although he had assisted his father at the Miracoli and the Scuola Grande di San Marco. His later work, though, developed a stronger, more robust style than that of Pietro, as evinced by the Andrea Vendramin Monument in Santi Giovanni e Paolo (late 1480s), which combined the minutely-refined relief carving so typical of his father with the bold overall concept of the triumphal arch. His later Monument to Giovanni Mocenigo (after 1495), in the same church, is more massive, but the composition is again strong and architectonic; by now his father's decorative influence is gone and instead it was Codussi (whose Palazzo Loredan he may have completed), who now asserted his own dignified influence.

SEBASTIANO SERLIO

Plan for a centralized church with Greek cross plan, from the *Five Books*, Book 5, Ch.14, (1547). Serlio's treatise was highly influential, although in Venice the form had already been revived by Mauro Codussi at San Giovanni Crisostomo and Santa Maria Formosa.

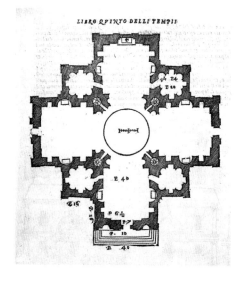

SANTA MARIA MATER DOMINI (below)

Interior, c.1500–1510. The debt to Codussi
is clearly apparent in the internal spaces and
the crisp, refined detailing.

SANTA MARIA FORMOSA (below, right)

The apses from the campo. One of Codussi's
last works, begun in 1492, it demonstrates
his mastery of spatial organization.

Santa Maria Maggiore may also be Tullio's work, a spacious church that had been reduced to almost complete dereliction until very recent times. Long stripped of its internal fittings, the fabric is now restored. It was built very quickly (and cheaply) in 1503–5, a simple Franciscan monastic church, with minimal detailing. The interior is more Tuscan than Venetian, with two stately, refined colonnades, although the influence of the ancient basilicas of Torcello and Ravenna is also prominent.[33]

By the 1520s, therefore, there had already developed in the city a varied tradition of Renaissance interpretations, notably in the organization of internal spaces. Codussi's revived Greek cross had now been rejoined by other forms, such as the monumental Latin cross of San Salvador and Scarpagnino's flexible solutions at San Giovanni and San Fantin; all of them provided a range of possibilities from which to draw, depending on the size, shape and location of the site, and on the resources and intellectual philosophies of the patron. Pragmatism had always to remain a significant determinant in this great, crowded city.

The churches of Sansovino, too, exemplify this flexible approach. His works for the government, and especially for the Procurators of San Marco, are considerably more important than his churches, although his solutions to the particular difficulties of church-building in Venice are also

varied, if less spatially ingenious than those of Spavento or Scarpagnino. Sansovino built six churches here, of which only three survive. The first, San Francesco della Vigna was begun in 1534 on the north shore of the city, to replace an older Gothic church. His patrons were Observant friars, established after a schism with those of the Frari in 1517, and pledged to return to more authentic Franciscan ideals of poverty and humility. Although the fifteenth-century cloisters remained, the church itself was rebuilt on an impressive scale, its eventual form something of a compromise between Sansovino's model and the Renaissance theories of proportion of Francesco Zorzi, one of the friars, and which he published in 1535. Zorzi's theories, like those at San Salvador, were based on harmonic proportions, and he believed that the simple Doric order was the most appropriate for the humble Observant Franciscans.[34]

The spacious column-free nave was designed specifically for preaching to large lay congregations, just as the Frari had been. It was flanked by two rows of deep side chapels, instead of aisles; the construction of the church itself was funded by selling these chapels to the Venetian nobility. The nave has a simple, plaster barrel vault, and equally simple arches define the chancel and transepts, although the planned dome was never built. Behind the high altar, a continuation of the chancel forms the monks' choir, a unique arrangement not seen in Venice before, but which was later to be adopted by Andrea Palladio. The church's plan derives from Sansovino's own earlier San Marcello al Corso in Rome (1519), and from Cronaca's San Salvatore al Monte in Florence (1499). The church was complete by 1554, although Palladio's facade was not added until fifteen years later.

Sansovino's two surviving parish churches are quite different from San Francesco in size, plan and liturgical requirements. San Martino, begun in 1540, was in a poor, remote parish, chiefly inhabited by fishermen and the Arsenalotti, shipyard workers; resources were meagre, and Sansovino's restrained facade is all of exposed brick, with minimal use of stonework. The interior

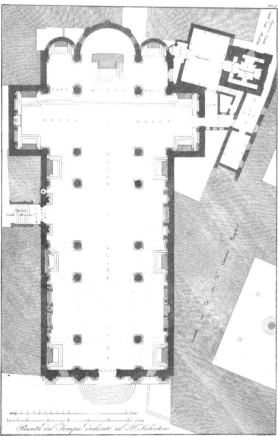

SAN SALVADOR

Above, top: plan, showing Spavento's ambitious design, following precise geometrical proportions, evidence of a rational approach.

Above: long section through the church, showing three major domed bays and smaller half-bays in between.

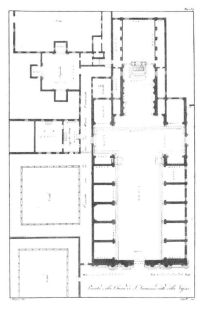

SAN SALVADOR

Opposite page: interior of the nave. The monumental Renaissance church was begun in c.1505 and completed in the 1520s by Tullio (and probably Pietro) Lombardo.

Far left: detail of the Neoclassical facade, added by Giuseppe Sardi in 1663 to Spavento's great church.

SAN FRANCESCO DELLA VIGNA

Above: interior of church, by Jacopo Sansovino, begun 1534. The choir is situated behind the High Altar.

Left: plan. The deep choir is placed behind the High Altar, while the broad nave is unbroken by columns.

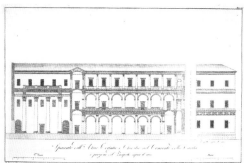

SAN MARTINO (above, top)

Facade of the church by Sansovino, begun 1540. The exterior is chiefly of unadorned brickwork, with only a few key elements detailed in stone.

SANTA MARIA DELLA CARITA (above)

Section through the monastic cloisters; the three orders of brick colonnades are the only surviving element of Palladio's design for a great new monastery in the Roman manner.

MOCENIGO MONUMENT (right)

Monument to doge Giovanni Mocenigo in Santi Giovanni e Paolo, c.1495 by Tullio Lombardo. Tullio's style here represents the more mature Renaissance, with none of his father's intricate relief carving.

FRANCESCO ZUCCHI,
Portrait of Andrea Palladio, early 18th century
(above)

There are no known contemporary portraits
of Palladio; this engraving is based on
a lost painting by Giambattista Maganza
(Ashmolean Museum, Oxford).

has a simple, flat ceiling, and the present rich frescos were only added considerably later, in the eighteenth century, by Jacopo Guarana. The site, too, was restricted, so the adopted plan is a compact Greek cross, with a small chapel in each corner. Some of the detail recalls San Francesco, although adopted here as the result of financial necessity rather than liturgical and spiritual principle.

The parish of San Zulian faced similar difficulties of siting and funding. Situated in the most crowded part of the city centre, only yards from San Marco, the parish campo was little more than a courtyard off the busy Merceria. Rebuilding was begun in 1566, after thirteen years spent accumulating funds, but space was as limited as resources and the resulting church is a simple cube, with three small projecting apses, the central one forming the chancel and divided from the nave by a giant stone arch. Sansovino died in 1570, before the church was completed, and Alessandro Vittoria, the sculptor, supervised its conclusion, including the strongly modelled, rather manneristic proto-Baroque facade. It is adorned with a prominent figure of Tommaso Rangone, a wealthy physician and the church's somewhat egotistical benefactor, above the portal.

All three churches illustrate responses to particular circumstances, not least those of funding and available space. Sansovino's lost San Gemignano, too, was designed with careful regard to context. In 1557 he added the facade to Cristofolo da Legname's earlier nave, together with a central dome. Funding was generous, since this was such a vital site, facing San Marco at the far end of the Piazza, and the facade was a balanced composition of two orders, all in Istrian stone, and with flanking aedicules to enliven the skyline. His lost facade for Santo Spirito was similar, with two superimposed orders, although, unusually, the whole facade was rusticated.

The churches of Andrea Palladio

Palladio's Venetian churches, like his villas, have had a profound influence on the history of architecture.[35] He came late to church building, however, and his reputation in the design of villas and palazzi for the Vicentine nobility was well established before he came to Venice. Between 1540 and 1560 he had built some of his most famous villas, among them the Barbaro at Maser and the Foscari (or Malcontenta) near the lagoon; only in 1558 did he begin his first ecclesiastical work in Venice, a design for the facade of San Pietro in Castello. Palladio did not obtain commissions from the established Roman Church hierarchy, though, and his executed Venetian projects are either monastic foundations or were commissioned directly by the Republic's government. Palladio's seminal contributions to church design lay in two fields: firstly, in the development of internal spaces that fused the complex and rather contradictory liturgical requirements of the age; and secondly, in the expression of these internal spaces on the facade, which he developed in a revolutionary manner, with a design based on the facade of the classical temple.

His fundamental spatial achievement was to resolve a conflict: on one hand, there was a modern humanistic desire for great centralized spaces, themselves epitomized by the symbolic form of the dome, and one of the inspirations for which was the Dome of the Rock in Jerusalem. Codussi's recent revival of the ancient Greek cross had also rekindled local interest in centralized forms, backed by the theories and writings of Alberti. But on the other hand, there remained the widespread traditional need for an axial arrangement of nave and chancel, with the liturgical progression – and procession – from the west doorway to the high altar, and often (in monastic churches) with the further requirement of space for a choir.

The fact that Palladio's churches are all in Venice is significant. Venice's strongly independent ecclesiastical organization was far less influenced by Rome than were any other Italian states; in theory, therefore, Palladio was freer to develop Alberti's spatial concepts and, in particular, his humanist view that a fully centralized space was the ideal form because of its geometrical perfection. It is no coincidence that the closest Palladio came to achieving such an ideal centralized form was in the *tempietto* in the grounds of Marc-Antonio Barbaro's villa at Maser, a small private chapel for one of the most notable Venetian Renaissance patrons and humanist scholars; here, as in the case of the earlier private chapels in the city's churches (but unlike his institutional commissions), the patron's taste was effectively unfettered. Matters were not so simple, however, in the commissioning of Palladio's city churches, where considerable debate still surrounded the fundamental question of ideal form.

Palladio's first Venetian project was the intended reconstruction of San Pietro in Castello, but the death of his patron, the Patriarch Antonio Diedo, led to almost immediate postponement. The facade was eventually executed by Francesco Smeraldi in 1594–6, and departs somewhat from Palladio's specification. Although 'Palladian' in appearance, it cannot be said to be his work. The nave was rebuilt, by GianGirolamo Grapiglia, again in the Palladian manner, after 1619.

SAN ZULIAN (below, left)

Detail of the facade of the church, by Jacopo Sansovino, 1566. The ornate facade was funded by Tommaso Rangone, a wealthy physician, whose image surveys the tiny parish campo.

SAN FRANCESCO DELLA VIGNA (below)

Facade by Andrea Palladio, c.1562. It was added after the completion of Sansovino's church, and was the first of Palladio's three essays in the development of the 'temple front' for the facade of a church.

His next proposal was the planned remodelling of the Monastery of Santa Maria della Carità, one wing of which survives today, with a three-storey cloister facade, all in fine brickwork; its three carefully detailed colonnades, Doric, Ionic and Corinthian, had not yet been seen in Venice used in this 'correct' classical manner. This wing was to have formed part of a grandiose recreation of Palladio's conception of a great Roman city palace, rather reminiscent of Antonio da Sangallo's recent Palazzo Farnese in Rome (begun 1559); Palladio's complete proposal was later to be illustrated in his famous *I quattro libri dell'architettura* (the Four Books of Architecture), published in 1570. However, only a fragment was completed, and he did not repeat this rather over-literally Roman transposition again in Venice; his executed churches have much greater invention, subtlety and allusion.[36]

His commissions at San Giorgio Maggiore were important stages in this development. Founded in the tenth century, this Benedictine monastery was one of the wealthiest and most famous in the city, with the unique advantage of its magnificent site on its own island, facing San Marco across the Bacino. The monastery had been rebuilt after an earthquake in 1223, while the church itself was reconstructed in the late Gothic style after 1461. The extremely long dormitory block was begun in 1450, but only completed by Giovanni Buora as late as 1510, its attractive early Renaissance style influenced by Codussi. Palladio's first work here was the refectory, begun in 1560, a simple but imposing tall, rectangular hall, originally lit by high-level windows, and with its plain barrel-vaulted interior focused on Veronese's great painting of *The Marriage Feast at Cana* (1562), now in the Louvre, which occupied the wall opposite the entrance.

After its construction, Palladio was commissioned in 1562 by the Patriarch Giovanni Grimani to complete Sansovino's San Francesco della Vigna, which still lacked a facade. Sansovino's own proposal, drawn up in 1534, was now considered rather dated, and so Palladio designed a new scheme, all in Istrian stone, to a formula that was to become universally famous. He devised a screen that successfully united the taller central nave with the much lower side aisles, the solution being an ingenious adaptation of the classical temple front, with a grandiose Corinthian portico in the centre, and two smaller, lower, half facades on each side. The powerful central portico, with its four great piers and noble crowning pediment, was to have an almost incalculable influence over the next three centuries: the device came to be employed on virtually every form of building

SAN GIORGIO MAGGIORE

Facade and view across lagoon. The church, by Andrea Palladio, was rebuilt after 1565, although the facade was completed after his death by Simon Sorella. The most theatrical of the three 'temple fronts', with the richest three-dimensional moulding, making a powerful impact on the Bacino.

imaginable, from churches to town halls, from banks to parliament buildings, and from country villas to museums.[37]

Palladio returned to San Giorgio Maggiore in 1565, since the Benedictines now intended to embark on a comprehensive programme of reconstruction, including a completely new church. Unlike its predecessor, this was to be built with a spacious piazza in front, and rising directly across the Bacino from the Palazzo Ducale. The church's facade was justifiably to become one of the most memorable sights in the city, stately and balanced, a perfect backdrop to the activity and pageants in the Bacino.

This facade, once again all of Istrian stone, employs the same basic device as that of San Francesco, although now the central portico and the flanking ones are more balanced. The four great Corinthian columns are raised on tall plinths, and this giant order appears superimposed, breaking forward from the much broader, lower portico, in a highly theatrical manner. The composition can

be appreciated axially from some distance, a rare opportunity in Venice, its finely-balanced stone facade contrasting with the plain red brick transepts rising behind, and the tall campanile, reflecting that of San Marco, providing a vertical focus. The facade itself already incorporated one or two Baroque touches, such as the swags below the pediment, and was completed after Palladio's death by Simon Sorella, although deviating a little from his intentions. In 1609, structures that still stood in front of the church were finally demolished, and the Bacino finally gained an architectural presence on the far side worthy of the civic splendour of the Piazza and the Molo.[38]

The interior is grandiose and light, cool and monumental. Only two constructional materials are visible, stonework and gleaming white stucco, the same minimal palette as that of Codussi, but here employed on a noble, Roman scale. Imposing clusters of Corinthian columns give way at the level of the cornice to simple, soaring domes and barrel-vaults, with only narrow arches to define the spaces. The plan is an ingenious fusion of Latin and Greek crosses, with the three-bay nave opening into a large central crossing, and with transepts terminating in semicircular apses; a degree of centralization is thus adapted to meet the specific requirements of Benedictine liturgy. On certain festivals, these apses were occupied by divided choirs. Beyond the crossing is one further bay and a square chancel; here Palladio adopted the solution that Sansovino had introduced at San Francesco, and built the monks' choir behind the high altar. This arrangement allowed an uninterrupted view of the altar by all of the participants, a requirement of Benedictine liturgy since the 1540s. Above the altar, too, Campagna's bronze of the four Evangelists is visible from both the nave and the choir.

His work at San Giorgio Maggiore continued with the construction of the second great cloister, that of the Cypresses. The first cloister, that of the Laurels, had been designed by Giovanni Buora, and was completed in 1516–40, a refined, restrained Renaissance work with tall colonnades; Palladio's second cloister, begun in 1579, lies beyond it, the simple ground floor arcades surmounted by paired windows, the white stonework and rendered walls relieved by the dramatic form of the cypresses.

Palladio's last important Venetian church is the Redentore (the Redeemer), begun in 1577 as a votive offering by the Signoria, in thanks for the termination of the disastrous plague that had

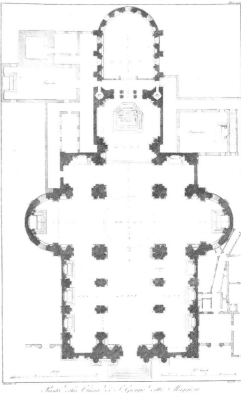

Pianta della Chiesa di S. Giorgio detto Maggiore

SAN GIORGIO MAGGIORE

Far left: the choir. The 48 richly-carved stalls are the work of Albrecht van der Brulle, 1594–8, and illustrate the life of St Benedict.

Left: interior of the nave. Powerful and dignified, the great rich colonnade gives way above the cornice to the clean, sweeping surfaces of the vaults.

Above: the refined plan fuses an axial nave (with side aisles) together with a strong cross-axis, formed with transepts terminating in semicircular apses. The monks' choir is behind the High Altar.

killed thousands in the previous two years. Serious outbreaks of the plague acted as catalysts for major building projects on a number of occasions in the city, when the Republic reacted to their eventual passing by acts of thanksgiving such as this. The Redentore's site has considerable urban significance, since it was decided by the Senate to draw the city's attention to this hitherto rather peripheral island, the Giudecca, and to impose on it something of the spirit of dignified urban renewal that was such a notable feature of late sixteenth-century Venice. The site again faces a broad stretch of water, in this case the Giudecca Canal, and here again the facade was to be visible in its entirety from some distance. An axial solution was essential here, too, since the doge was to visit the church every year, in procession, by means of a temporary bridge of boats spanning the canal. (The festival still takes place today.) The Redentore's facade develops still further the interlocking portico principle of the two earlier churches, but is more rigorously designed, with less small-scale detail, a restrained, disciplined variant of San Giorgio Maggiore. The Redentore summarizes Palladio's development of the temple facade.[39]

The publication of his *I quattri libri* a few years earlier allowed direct comparison between these facades and the classical temples from which they were derived. At the Redentore, two designs were originally requested, one centralized and one axially planned; there followed a rigorous debate as to the relative merits of the two schemes; although Palladio himself apparently preferred a centralized plan (and was supported in this by Marc-Antonio Barbaro), a more axial plan was chosen, which was more appropriate for the liturgy of the order of Capuchins who were to administer the shrine; Palladio then developed the present, more complex arrangement. The interior was designed to take account of three functions: a spacious nave for the large congregation; a central space beyond for the assembly of the many dignitaries at the annual services of thanksgiving; and a monastic choir for the Capuchins. Although the materials are the same as those at San Giorgio Maggiore, the spaces here are more clearly articulated. The nave is enclosed by projecting Corinthian columns, but the colonnade is capped by a strong, continuous entablature; it is also flanked by chapels instead of aisles, while the central space is roofed by a large dome on a drum, flanked by radiused apses; beyond the high altar an inventive open, semicircular colonnade screens the choir, again a detail never seen in the city before.

The last surviving Venetian work attributed to Palladio is the rather anticlimactic monastery of Le Zitelle, also on the Giudecca. Built with very limited funds, its facade is a faint echo of these earlier splendid screens; in one respect, though, it was to be influential, since the church is placed in the centre of the site, flanked on both sides by the enclosing wings of the monastic buildings. Such an arrangement produced a compact plan on a restricted plot, as well as a reasonably dignified, balanced facade, and was later to be adopted by Scamozzi and others.

Vincenzo Scamozzi represents the generation after Palladio, a link between him and the mature Venetian Baroque. Scamozzi made many visits to Rome to study classical architecture, and his chief lay work is the Procuratie Nuove. In 1581 he was appointed architect to the Cistercian nunnery of the Celestia; his original scheme had a centralized plan based on proposals by Palladio, and Scamozzi continued the project until he was dismissed after a dispute with the nunnery. In 1606 his work was demolished and replaced with a more traditional design.

He experienced similar difficulties at his other church, San Nicolo da Tolentino, begun for the Theatine order in 1591. Here, too, differences developed between Scamozzi's own post-Palladian spatial ideas and the requirements of the monks; at one stage, legal proceedings were instigated and Scamozzi abandoned the project, which was completed by the monks themselves. The church has a single broad nave, with a drum over the crossing (the dome was demolished following structural difficulties) and a long, deep choir that derived directly from Palladio. Scamozzi's difficult church-building experiences offer a singular example of the conflicts that frequently arose in the

SAN GIORGIO MAGGIORE (below)

Detail of the crossing and transept.

THE REDENTORE (right)

Facade from the Canale della Giudecca. The third of Palladio's 'temple fronts', it was begun in 1576. The composition is tighter and more disciplined than that of San Giorgio, although it was again designed to be appreciated axially from some distance.

seventeenth century between architects' spatial ideas on one hand, and the increasingly codified liturgical requirements of the Counter-Reformation on the other.

Baldassare Longhena and the Salute

If Scamozzi is a transitional figure, then Baldassare Longhena is undoubtedly the outstanding architect of the Venetian Baroque, active in many spheres over the course of his long, prolific career. Born in 1598, he was one of the few notable native architects of the city; Longhena was a pupil of Scamozzi, and his many works span more than half a century, from Sorella's completion of Palladio's San Giorgio Maggiore to that of his own masterpiece, Santa Maria della Salute.

At twenty-six he received his first important commission, the new cathedral at Chioggia, to replace that destroyed by fire in 1623. His inspiration was San Giorgio Maggiore, and its interior is noble, rhythmic and strongly composed. A little later, in 1630, Venice was struck by yet another devastating plague, which lasted for sixteen months, and carried off more than 46,000 people, one third of the city's population. Longhena's greatest work was a direct result of this disaster; on 22 October 1630, the Senate decreed that since the city had now been spared:

> the doge shall … make a solemn vow to God to build a church in this city and to dedicate it to the most holy Virgin, calling it Santa Maria della Salute [meaning both 'health' and 'salvation']; and every year, on the day that this city shall be proclaimed free of the present sickness, the doge and his successors shall pay a ceremonious visit to that church, with the Senate, in perpetual memory of the gratitude of the commonwealth for this great benefit. Be it further resolved that a sum of up to 50,000 ducats from the public coffers shall be spent on the building of this church…

Like Palladio's Redentore, therefore, Longhena's Salute was a votive church. Like the Redentore, too, it marked an important example of the direct influence of the Senate in developing the form and image of the city. It was intended from the outset to be a triumphant set piece, a demonstration of the Republic's resilience (and wealth) in transcending a dreadful natural disaster. Longhena was then only thirty-two, and won a competition against ten others, thus beginning the immense work that was to take the rest of his life to complete. The Salute remains one of the most outstanding images of Venice, all built of gleaming white Istrian stone, innovative and even revolutionary in more than one respect.

The site is a magnificent one, guarding the entrance to the Grand Canal, and Longhena's masterpiece forms a great Baroque chord defining the transition between the Bacino and the city's chief artery. Structurally daring, the complex form of the church is surmounted by a tall octagonal drum, capped by its great dome, the largest ever attempted in the city; the entire massive structure is supported on more than a million timber piles. The drum of the dome is pierced by large windows, allowing light to flood into the great central space below, while the transition from the drum to the body of the church is ingeniously achieved by great, scroll-like buttresses, a statue crowning each one.

The design of the church is based on its ceremonial function. The central volume has an octagonal plan, with the Grand Canal facade forming one of the eight sides, and taking the form of an imposing triumphal arch, based on a grandiose four-columned portico. The approach to the church is rendered even more imposing by the monumental flight of steps up from the quay; this was the processional route taken by the doge and Signoria, who were to approach the church, just as at the Redentore, by means of a temporary bridge of boats across the Grand Canal. The organization of the interior again reflects the spatial requirements of this august annual pilgrimage. The central octagon dominates the church, and is surrounded by a lower colonnade or ambulatory, beyond which are two groups of three chapels. This arrangement was devised so that the ducal procession entered through the great central doorway and processed directly through the octagon,

THE REDENTORE

Above: interior of the nave. The central
body of the church is defined by a heavy
continuous cornice above the nave
colonnade, with the axial vista closed by a
unique semicircular screen of columns
behind the altar.

Right: plan; and far right, below: long
section. The plan clearly articulates the three
elements: nave, central space and choir. The
section illustrates how the concentration of
light enters from the tall drum of the dome
to illuminate the central crossing.

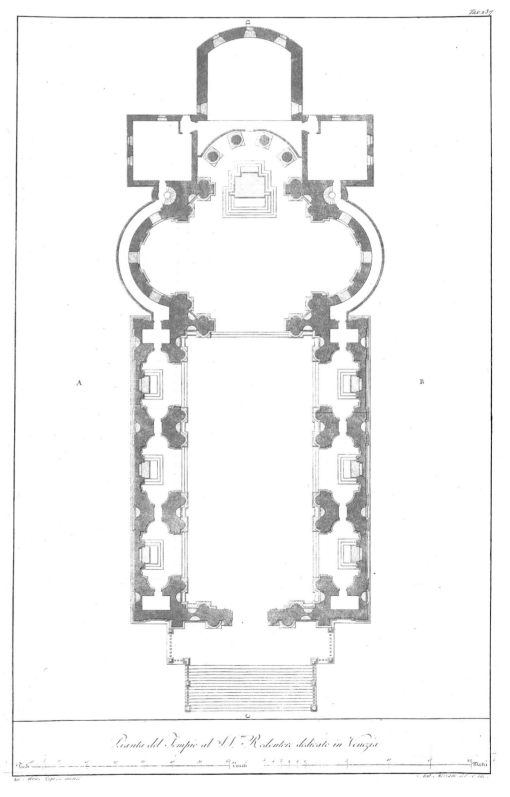

Pianta del Tempio al SS. Redentore dedicato in Venezia

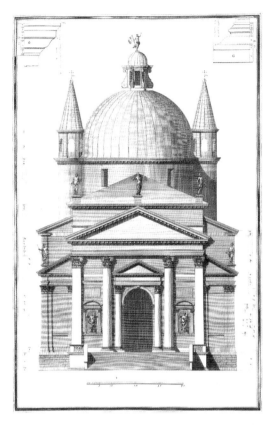

COMPARISON OF PALLADIO'S THREE 'TEMPLE FRONT'
CHURCH FACADES (above)

Left to right: San Giorgio Maggiore, the Redentore and
San Francesco della Vigna, all from Ottavio Bertotti
Scamozzi, *Le fabbriche e disegni di Palladio.*

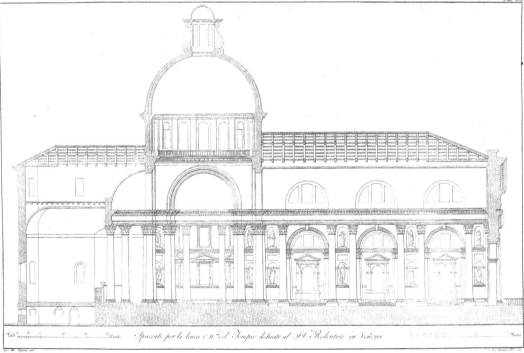

Spaccato per la linea C.D. del Tempio dedicato al SS.mo Redentore in Venezia

while the lay congregation entered the church by the two side doors and then processed around these two perimeter colonnades. Directly opposite the main entrance is the chancel, a broad space with a cross-axis and apsidal ends (like a rather compact transept), where the doge and his many attendant dignitaries gathered for the service. Although much more centralized, these spaces were developed from Palladio's forms at the Redentore and San Giorgio. The huge freestanding high altar is also the work of Longhena; beyond is the choir, like that at San Giorgio, out of sight but not lost to the hearing of the assembled congregation.[40]

Longhena's liturgical and architectural language is a fusion of two approaches; the exterior of the Salute is a grandiose Baroque urban gesture, a richly self-confident *tour de force* of plastic architectonic form; the monumental interior, though, is cool and disciplined, part of a tradition that derives directly from Palladio but which can be traced back further to the dignified restraint of Codussi. Once again, the only constructional materials visible are grey stone and white plaster, with the giant order of columns drawing the eye up to the brilliantly-lit cupola.

While construction of the Salute continued slowly, Longhena also designed a number of other church-related works. In the early 1640s, he built a new library at San Giorgio Maggiore to replace the earlier building by the Florentine Michelozzi Michelozzo, which had been damaged by fire in 1614. Longhena effectively became a rather belated replacement for Palladio at San Giorgio; the Cloister of the Cypresses was only completed after his death, and Palladio himself intended the imposing stair of honour, which was later executed by Longhena. This grandiose composition joins the cloisters to the first-floor audience chamber, a highly-theatrical work and probably the most imposing staircase yet seen in the city. By contrast, Longhena's library is simple and austere, a neutral space in which to place the richly-carved wooden bookcases.

Longhena's later churches are more uncompromisingly Baroque, as he developed beyond Palladian discipline and order towards a more plastic, illusionistic use of space. His early facade for Santa Giustina, for example (*c*1640), is a powerful but ponderous screen, formerly somewhat enlivened by statuary, while Longhena's last phase is exemplified by Santa Maria di Nazareth, known as the Scalzi, and Santa Maria dei Derelitti, most often called the Ospedaletto, both highly ornate works. The former (1660–89), the church of the Barefoot Carmelites, has a slightly later facade by Giuseppe Sardi, one of the most remarkable Baroque works in Venice, but Longhena's own interior (1656–73) matches the facade with its sumptously decorated nave, richly clad with rare marbles and an altar canopy of great complexity; it was formerly even further enriched with frescos by Giambattista Tiepolo, largely destroyed in 1915. By now Palladio's restraining influence had quite disappeared.

The Ospedaletto church forms part of an extensive orphanage, and is one of Longhena's last works, the facade erected in 1670–2. He had begun the modernization of the orphanage in 1666, succeeding Sardi, and had completed the grand oval staircase before turning to the church. Its facade faces a busy, narrow *calle*, and can only be appreciated from an acute angle; to compensate for these difficulties, and to maximize its effect, we see the most dramatically Mannerist of all of Longhena's works, massively articulated and highly theatrical. Some of its component parts can be traced back to the vast, slightly earlier Pesaro Monument in the Frari, built in 1669 in the form of a great triumphal arch; its lower order has giant caryatids instead of columns, features that Longhena developed further at the Ospedaletto's facade. The Pesaro Monument is a triumph of sculptural dexterity over balanced composition, and much the same can be said of the Ospedaletto. The powerful mouldings and violent chiaroscuro of the full-blooded Venetian Baroque are nowhere as rich and complex as they are here.[41]

SANTA MARIA DELLA SALUTE

Baldassare Longhena's imposing composition, crowned by the great dome, is rendered more impressive by the great flights of steps. The church took 47 years to construct, and was consecrated in 1687. Although it appears largely centralized, the form is subtly articulated inside, to take account of specific liturgical functions.

201

Baroque variations

Few of Longhena's many followers could match his conviction in the bold manipulation of architectural form and sculpted modelling. Giuseppe Sardi was his most important pupil, and the most skillful representative of the next generation, although very little is known of his life. According to the writer and historian Tommaso Temanza, Sardi designed the lost facade of San Tomà, built in 1652, but taken down a century later because of its dangerous condition. More important, though, is his impressive facade for the great church of San Salvador, which had been built by Tullio Lombardo a century earlier. This imposing work is comparatively restrained for its date, the lower parts almost Neoclassical in their refinement, although the whole is liberally endowed with statuary. The facade was funded from a bequest from Jacopo Gallo or Gallino, who left the generous sum of 80,000 ducats in his will, 60,000 for the new church facade, and the remainder for the adjacent Scuola di San Todaro, which was also given a new facade by Sardi. That of San Salvador was completed in 1663; it is far larger and more expansive than that of the Scuola, although the overall compositions are similar. Both have two superimposed orders, capped by triangular pediments, and with the skyline enlivened with statues.

At the Scalzi church, Sardi was considerably less restrained, and his facade, much smaller than that of San Salvador (but which still cost 75,000 ducats), matches Longhena's opulent interior. It, too, was funded by a legacy, from the estate of Girolamo Cavazza, whose funerary monument in the Madonna dell'Orto Sardi had already made. Despite some over elaboration, the strong composition is well balanced, with paired Corinthian columns to both upper and lower orders, alternating with niches to contain statues; in all, a remarkable example of Venetian Baroque at its richest, albeit with strong Roman influences. Sardi also completed the facade of San Lazzaro, which had been built by Scamozzi; here he returned to simpler, more restrained monumentality, and his facade of 1673 suppresses Baroque fluidity in favour of an imposing neo-Palladian temple front, only the crowning statues and split pediment hinting at his more lavish tastes.

Sardi's last church, though, Santa Maria del Giglio or Zobenigo (1680–3) marks a return to the full-blooded Baroque, and is a close relative of the Scalzi; again a rich two-storey screen, and again with paired columns and niches. The facade was funded by a donation of 30,000 ducats from Antonio Barbaro, and is a homage to the military triumphs of his own family. As an example of seventeenth-century public ostentation it is almost unrivalled, and is notorious for the almost complete absence of sacred imagery; even the column plinths have fortresses carved on them, while the upper order terminates in a rich assembly of martial figures of the Barbaro, pediments both full and broken, and a token pair of trumpeting angels. The facade's upper profile recalls Renaissance works such as San Zaccaria, as well as Longhena's more recent Santa Giustina, although here the requirements of the Barbaro take clear precedence over the architectural structure. Not surprisingly, Ruskin deplored its 'insolent atheism'.[42]

Sardi's contemporary, Alessandro Tremignon, is known for just one work, which marks a peak in this process of the development of the rich Baroque screen: the extraordinary facade of San Moisè. Funded by the great fortunes of the Fini family, it is again contemporaneous with Sardi's Scalzi facade and Longhena's Ospedaletto, with which it may be compared, although with little else. The rich, overwrought screen is festooned with swags, statuary and busts of various members of the Fini clan; much of the sculpture is the work of Enrico Meyring, a follower of Bernini, and shows great technical ability, although transcends, by a considerable extent, most later critics' limits of acceptable taste. The altarpiece, perhaps also by Tremignon, is almost as arresting as the facade, a great pile of marble depicting Moses, the tablets and Mount Sinai. Not one to temper his language, Ruskin regarded the church as 'one of the basest examples of the basest schools of the Renaissance'.[43]

Spaccato per lungo del Tempio di S. Maria Della Salute

SANTA MARIA DELLA SALUTE

Above: section; and right: plan. The great
central octagon is the dominant volume,
but beyond it is the transverse axis
of the presbytery, itself roofed with a
secondary dome.

Far right: interior of the octagon and dome;
the dome is the largest in Venice. Although
the church exterior is Baroque, Longhena's
internal vocabulary is restrained and still
essentially Palladian.

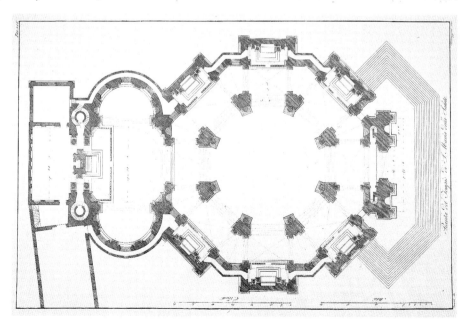

All of these churches share common features: they are rich, ornate Baroque screens on which their sculptural qualities were exploited to the full in the clear light of the lagoon. But they are also intimations of attempted immortality, grandiose gestures of patrician wealth that effectively form family mausolea, monuments to conspicuous consumption now placed outside the church for the whole world to see, rather than in their more discreet, traditional location within the church, in a private chapel. Although the practice of funding facades to incorporate the patron's memorial was established back in the sixteenth century, with the bequests of the Cappello at Santa Maria Formosa and Tommaso Rangone at San Zulian, these antecedents appear bashfully reticent when compared to the Baroque ostentation of both the old patriciate, such as the Barbaro, and 'new men' such as the Fini.

Sardi's long career overlapped with those of a group of younger architects, the chief of them Antonio Gaspari and Domenico Rossi, the latter Sardi's own nephew. Both of them developed a lively Baroque style, though that of Gaspari was rather more Roman in taste. He designed two churches in Venice, San Vidal and Santa Maria della Fava, although his most characteristic (and Berninian) work is the cathedral at Este (begun in 1687), the elliptical plan of which is based on Bernini's Santa Maria di Montesanto in Rome, begun by Carlo Rainaldi and completed by Bernini in 1679. Santa Maria della Fava is more notable than San Vidal, with the heavy Palladian facade which was added later by Andrea Tirali. Gaspari produced several alternative schemes for the Fava, all in a distinctly Roman Baroque manner, and although his facade was never built, the impressive interior (1705–15) has a skilful fluidity of form, albeit not quite as confidently sinuous as Bernini's work in Rome. Although Bernini was much admired in Venice, his followers left no fully Berninian work here.[44]

Rossi (1657–1737) was greatly influenced both by his uncle, Giuseppe Sardi, and by the powerful legacy of Longhena, from both of whom he developed his strong modelling and exuberant plastic forms. San Stae was built in 1710 following a competition that attracted proposals (some of them quite extraordinary) from almost all the leading figures in Venice, including Gaspari and Tirali, and was funded from the legacy of Doge Alvise Mocenigo who lived in the parish. Rossi's facade evinces the almost inescapable influence of Palladio, but is much enlivened by sculptures by Giuseppe Torretto and Antonio Corradini. His Church of the Gesuiti, though, was a rather special case, since it had to incorporate the specific liturgical requirements of the Jesuit order, most of whose churches were modelled on Giacomo da Vignola's great mother church in Rome (begun in 1568). In form the Gesuiti also derived from Alberti's Sant'Andrea in Mantua, with a Latin cross plan and a broad, barrel-vaulted nave flanked by chapels. The interior was completed in 1728, its remarkable richness reflecting the Jesuit principle of dedication to the glory of God, and with lavish decorative detail covering every available surface. The rich, imposing facade, contrasting sharply with the austere flanking monastic buildings, is attributed to the little-known Giambattista Fattoretto, probably to Rossi's design; like so many Venetian Baroque churches, its powerful composition is crowned by a flamboyant collection of figures, in this case all twelve Apostles, together with the Assumption.[45]

Neoclassicism

The career of Andrea Tirali, Rossi's contemporary, offers an instructive contrast, both stylistically and in his professional development, with those of Rossi and Gaspari. Tirali's was a long career of public service, as for many years he was proto or chief surveyor to the Magistrato alle Acque, the agency responsible for maintenance of the lagoon, lidi and sea-defences; in this post he built the well-known Ponte dei Tre Archi (Three Arch Bridge) across the Cannaregio Canal. Later, as proto of the Procurators of San Marco (after 1721), Tirali restored the basilica and designed the present paving of the Piazza and Piazzetta. He came late to architecture, and his early career as a surveyor resulted in a more disciplined, restrained style than Rossi's; his innate reticence made him an early

THE SCALZI CHURCH

Above: detail of one of the side chapels; the rich interior is principally the work of Longhena, and is encrusted with rich polychrome decoration on almost every surface.

Right: facade by Giuseppe Sardi (1672–80), one of the finest Baroque church facades in Venice. Like many such Baroque reconstructions, it was built from a substantial private legacy.

SANTA MARIA DEL GIGLIO OR ZOBENIGO

The Baroque facade by Giuseppe Sardi,
1678–83. Like that of the Scalzi, the facade
has two superimposed orders, with paired
columns alternating with niches of sculpture.
The entire facade is a monument to the
Barbaro family, and is decorated with many
figures of members of the clan.

SAN MOISÈ

The facade, by Alessandro Tremignon,
1668. Arguably the most complex
Baroque facade in Venice, it is once again
effectively a family monument, here
to the Fini clan. The detail shows the
memorial plaque to Vincenzo Fini.

SAN STAE (SANT'EUSTACHIO)

Left: detail of the exuberant Baroque facade, with figure sculptures by Giuseppe Torretto and Antonio Corradini, after 1710.

Above, top: the facade, by Domenico Rossi, begun 1710. Rossi won a competition in which most of the city's leading Baroque architects took part; the facade was funded by doge Alvise Mocenigo, who lived in the parish.

SAN NICOLO DEI TOLENTINI (above)

Portico by Andrea Tirali, 1706, a fine example of the Neoclassical reaction against the perceived excesses of the Baroque.

THE GESUITI (SANTA MARIA ASSUNTA) (overleaf)

Interior of the nave, by Domenico Rossi, completed in 1729. The sumptuous decoration is characteristic of Jesuit churches; ceiling stuccos and extensive *intarsio* panelling by Abbondio Stazio.

precursor of the Neoclassical movement, for which advanced taste he was highly praised by Tommaso Temanza, who analysed the contributions of various architects of the era in an unpublished essay of 1738. Tirali had close connections with the university at Padua, with its chairs of mathematics, hydraulics and physics, and where the rational spirit of the age of the Enlightenment flourished.

Exemplifying this intellectual reaction against the excesses of the Baroque is his completion of the facade of Scamozzi's Tolentini, with a very fine six-bay portico of great fluted Corinthian columns, built in 1706. His Palazzo Diedo exhibits even more pronounced restraint, while among many lesser, and less austere works, Tirali designed the two elegant campanili of Santi Apostoli and San Martino at Burano. In much the same spirit of objective Vitruvian research is Giovanni Scalfarotto's early Neoclassical San Simon Piccolo, which makes a notable impression on the Grand Canal opposite the railway station. The church, begun in 1718, is modelled on the Parthenon, and was intended to form a termination to the Grand Canal, a counterpoint to Longhena's great Salute at the other end, but an even more pointed contrast to Sardi's rich Baroque Scalzi facade on the opposite bank. Although Scalfarotto failed to match Longhena's monumentality, San Simon is distinctive indeed, raised high above a tall flight of steps, and with its distinctive copper dome preceded by a Corinthian portico which is singularly advanced for its date.

The spirit of rational enquiry that was such a distinctive feature of the age is further exemplified in the career of Temanza, who was also related to both Scalfarotto and to Tirali. Temanza studied mathematics and hydraulics, and gained considerable importance as an historian; his built works are few, all of them disciplined and neo-Palladian in character, and the chief of which is the rebuilt Maddalena church. It was constructed after 1760 in a spare, Neoclassical manner, with influences both from the Pantheon and from Palladio's Tempietto at Maser.[46]

The later Venetian Baroque and the more recent Neoclassical movement are both brought together in the long prolific career of Giorgio Massari, the last important native architect in the city. Massari's extensive output was not confined to Venice, though, and he was active over much of the Terraferma as well. His chief lay work is Palazzo Grassi, but he was also a prolific church architect; an early companion and follower of Tirali, his stylistic range was broad, and Massari collaborated on several occasions with Giambattista Tiepolo, with whose scenographic programmes his own architecture was carefully integrated.

The Dominican foundation of the Gesuati (Santa Maria del Rosario) was his first important church, built after 1726 with a distinctively Palladian facade. The plan, too, reverts to a sixteenth-century arrangement, with the choir behind the high altar; other Palladian touches include the two little belltowers and the cupola. Massari's monumentally imposing interior evinces an early collaboration with Tiepolo, whose fine frescos of the life of St Dominic are integrated into Massari's structural form.

In the same period Massari designed the 'hospital' of the Catecumeni, where he placed the accommodation in two side wings, with the church in the centre, following Palladio's precedent at the Zitelle. Later, too, in 1735, when he won a competition to design the new church and orphanage of Santa Maria della Pietà, the same planning principle was adopted. The site was a prominent one, on the Riva degli Schiavoni, but the church's refined interior was designed almost exclusively according to musical criteria, to house the famous choir of the orphanage. The new church was brought into use in 1755, shortly after the death of the hospital's chapel-master, Antonio Vivaldi, although its heavy, rather coarse Palladian facade was barely begun in Massari's own lifetime, and only completed as late as 1906. Massari's work can best be summarized as a rather restrained late Baroque, with a strong tendency towards Neoclassicism, although in a city

where Palladio's strong influence had never really faded, he, like Tirali, espoused something of the powerful, long-lasting impact of San Giorgio Maggiore.[47]

A number of other churches were rebuilt during the eighteenth century, many once again through substantial private donations; a good number, too, replaced much older structures by then in very poor repair. The result, though, was the loss of several medieval churches and their replacement by mostly fairly undistinguished new ones. One of the few worthy of note is San Geremia, rebuilt by Carlo Corbellini on a grandiose, highly optimistic scale after 1753; its chief interest lies in the revival (once again) of the Greek cross plan, with each arm terminating in a radiused apse; the detailing, however, is somewhat cold and pedantic. The church was still not complete half a century later, its scale far too ambitious for an unexceptional and not very central parish; the two facades, to the campo and to the Grand Canal, were only finished in 1871, both in a heavy neo-Baroque manner.

The last significant Venetian church architect was GianAntonio Selva, a pupil of Temanza and, like him, a writer and architectural historian; Selva became the principal Neoclassical architect of the Veneto, but is perhaps best known as the designer of the Fenice Theatre. He also rebuilt San Maurizio in 1806; by this very late date, the Neoclassical movement was well established, and Selva, together with Antonio Diedo, produced an exterior of extreme, mannered severity. The church was consecrated in 1828, its plan once more reverting to the Greek cross form, with a central cupola surrounded by four hemispherical half-domes. The interior is less dramatically stark, and is strongly reminiscent of the refined simplicity of Mauro Codussi. It offers an appropriate final example of the cyclical nature of church design in Venice, its plan an echo of centuries-old exemplars, while its interior recalls the seminal master of the early Renaissance.[48]

SAN SIMON PICCOLO (above, top)

Facade to the Grand Canal, by Giovanni Scalfarotto, 1718. Another example of Venetian Neoclassicism, contrasting with the Baroque Scalzi on the opposite bank.

LA MADDALENA (above)
Drawing of the facade by the architect, Tommaso Temanza, c.1760. (Museo Civico Correr, Venice.)

THE GESUATI (SANTA MARIA DEL ROSARIO) (right)

Interior of the rich, imposing nave by Giorgio Massari, 1668; Massari collaborated on several occasions with Giambattista Tiepolo, whose frescos decorate the ceiling.

After the Churches, Monasteries, Oratories and Hospitals … there are found among the most honoured and devout congregations of the City, six fraternities, commonly known as the Scuole Grandi de i Battuti … In [them] are religious activities, much like those of an Academy or in public schools, where one learns and practises Christian deeds, to the benefit of the souls of the brethren, both alive and departed, [and] they are of great benefit to the poor, and to the glory of God. **Francesco Sansovino**, *Venetia, città nobilissima*, Venice, 1580.[1]

The Scuole Grandi: a history of typology

The Venetian confraternities, known as the Scuole Grandi, originated in the thirteenth century growing out of the pious flagellant movement that was originally centred on Perugia; they became a collective expression of piety and brotherhood, their members gathering regularly for prayer. With time, though, the flagellant element became purely ritual, and instead they evolved as more practical philanthropic bodies, raising funds and disbursing them to those in physical need. Over the centuries, the scuole received countless legacies and donations, dispensing food and aid to their own poorer members; charitable almshouses were also built and hospices established. Membership was very broad; no clerics were allowed, but all classes of lay society could join, nobles, citizens and the common people, although members of the patriciate were not permitted to hold office or to serve on the boards of governors. Although numbers varied from time to time, the Scuole Grandi could enrol up to five to six hundred members each; originally numbering only three, by the fall of the Venetian Republic there was a total of seven, with two later establishments and two having been 'promoted' from Scuole Piccole.[2]

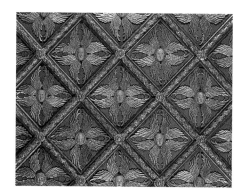

THE SCUOLA GRANDE DELLA CARITÀ

Detail of the ceiling of the Chapter Hall, by Marco Cozzi, 1484. The hall now forms the first principal gallery of the Gallerie dell' Accademia.

By the late fifteenth century they had become important civic institutions, a vital element in the city's social structure. The Scuole Grandi also instigated considerable building activity and commissioned many fine works of art, often produced by their own members. Together, the Scuole Grandi enrolled all the city's finest architects and artists during the fifteenth and sixteenth centuries, among them Pietro Lombardo, Mauro Codussi, Antonio Rizzo, Jacopo Sansovino, Vettor Carpaccio and the Bellini.

The Scuole Grandi were supervised by the Consiglio dei Dieci, and their constitutions were consciously modelled on that of the Republic itself. As Francesco Sansovino put it, each one was 'quasi una propria Repubblica', almost a Republic of its own. Their own 'doge' was the governor or *vardian grande*, who held his elected post for one year; the other officers included a chaplain, a secretary and a governing board or *banca* of sixteen members. Slowly the Scuole Grandi became something of an intermediate institution between the Republic and the individual, both in social terms and in their philanthropic role; they were organizations in which the otherwise disenfranchised common people could participate directly in their own 'government'.

All of the Scuole Grandi built their definitive homes on land adjacent to, and originally owned by, the city's monastic houses, a reflection of their close affinity with the religious orders: that of Santa Maria della Carità was established at the Lateran monastery of the same name; the Scuola of San Marco stood next to the great Dominican house of Santi Giovanni e Paolo; San Giovanni Evangelista was at the ancient Ospizio Badoer, itself an offshoot of the Frari; San Rocco was also near the Frari; the Scuola of the Misericordia stood next to the abbey of Santa Maria in Val Verde; and San Todaro was affiliated to the Augustinian San Salvador.

As they became established, the practical requirements of the scuole became more clearly defined; the plans of the original Scuole Grandi have much in common, although site restrictions (particularly acute at San Giovanni Evangelista) sometimes required considerable ingenuity of planning. The heart of the scuola was a small hall, always on the first floor, and known as the *albergo*, in which the governing board met, and where the gifts, treasures and other relics of the scuola were kept; its name derives from a hostel or place of shelter. The larger bodies of accommodation consisted of two very spacious halls, one on the ground floor and one directly above it. The lower hall, or *androne,* was usually colonnaded to support the heavy floor of the upper hall; it was imposing but usually fairly simple in appearance, with a traditional Venetian open timber ceiling. The first-floor hall, the *sala capitolare* or chapter hall, was used for all general assemblies of the membership, was where votes were taken over important issues, and where masses were conducted. It was always richly decorated, modelled on the example of the great hall of the Maggior Consiglio in the Palazzo Ducale. There was an altar at one end, where the scuola's relics were displayed on feast days.

As patrons of architecture, the Scuole Grandi concentrated their efforts on the main facades of their own buildings, while internally the staircase, and particularly the albergo, usually received the most lavish initial attention, since the latter was the heart of their philanthropic activities. The lower hall remained relatively austere, and only later, as funds permitted, did resources turn to the daunting task of decorating the imposing chapter halls above.[3]

The great building programmes undertaken by the Scuole Grandi in the fifteenth and sixteenth centuries produced a series of masterpieces, both artistic and architectural. They were funded from a variety of sources: from individual bequests; from interest on investments; from donations for specific elements of work; and, from time to time, from requests to the Consiglio dei Dieci to enlarge their membership – each new member paid an enrolment fee. On occasion, too, charitable distribution was reduced or even suspended entirely to fund building operations. This last course of action was harshly criticized by some observers, particularly during the great building programmes of the sixteenth century. Alessandro Caravia, for example, strongly condemned not only the lavish expenditure on new halls and works of art, but condemned equally the blatant rivalry between the scuole that was one of the principal motivations behind these costly programmes. In a long, richly phrased diatribe, *Il Sogno di Caravia* (Caravia's Dream), written in 1541, he wrote of the:

> Four-score thousand ducats they happily spend
> When no more than six would achieve the same end.

and a little later:

> What's due to the poor is splashed out in vast Oceans
> On building, but certainly not on devotions.[4]

The Scuola Grande della Carità was probably the first to be founded, in 1260, and established the basic principles of accommodation for the others; it originally met at the parish church of San Lunardo, but in 1294 the scuola obtained its own hall above the portico of the Monastery of Santa Maria della Carità. In 1345 it acquired some adjacent land on which to build a larger chapter hall, the entrance portal of which still survives. A further agreement with the monastery in 1384 led to the building of their smaller hall, the albergo above the cloister entrance, with a colonnade below. In this way the two main functional requirements were established, the albergo for board meetings and the larger hall for general assemblies and masses. The L-shaped plan was to be followed a little later at both the Scuola Grande di San Marco and at the Misericordia.

The rebuilding of the Carità Church (1442–52) provided the opportunity to replace the adjacent Scuola with a new one on a more impressive scale; the present albergo dates from 1443–4, while the main chapter hall, built over an aisled lower hall, was extended and given a new facade onto the *campo* in 1461.[5] In this way, we see the first example of what was to become the typical

THE SCUOLA GRANDE DI SAN MARCO

Facade to the Campo Santi Giovanni e Paolo. The facade was begun by Pietro Lombardo in c.1489 but completed by Mauro Codussi in 1490–5.

216

THE SCUOLA GRANDE DI SAN MARCO

Above: western part of the facade. Behind this wing are the ground floor androne and the great Chapter Hall above.

Right: detail of the main portal, by Pietro Lombardo and his workshop; some of the detailed carving is probably by his sons, Tullio and Antonio. The figure of Charity was salvaged from the earlier Scuola and re-used.

THE SCUOLA GRANDE DI SAN GIOVANNI
EVANGELISTA

The staircase, by Mauro Codussi, begun
in 1498, based on his earlier one for
the Scuola Grande di San Marco, is more
richly-detailed.

relationship between the Scuola Grande and the monastic house to which it was annexed; the facades of the two buildings stand at right angles to each other on their common open space. The albergo of the Scuola della Carità survives today as room 24 of the Accademia picture galleries; its fine ceiling was carved in 1496, and Titian's great painting of the *Presentation of the Virgin* (painted in *c*1534) can still be seen in its original location. The much larger and imposing chapter hall now forms the first gallery of the Accademia, and it, too, retains a fine gilded, coffered ceiling carved by the Marco Cozzi workshop in 1484. The scuola's original facade on to the campo was of brick and stone, very similar in appearance to the adjacent, contemporary church facade, but it was replaced in the eighteenth century by the present rather ponderous Neoclassical stone screen by Bernardo Maccaruzzi, after a design by Massari.

The Scuola Grande di San Marco

The Scuola Grande della Carità was joined almost immediately by the establishment of the second scuola, dedicated to the national patron, San Marco. This dedication immediately gave the new foundation great prestige, and its members attempted to ensure that justice was done in enhancing this reputation by its outstanding (and ostentatious) patronage of the arts.[6] Although founded at Santa Croce, in the far west of the city, the scuola moved to its present site in 1437, where there was more space for expansion. It was also a far more prestigious location, standing on a spacious campo immediately adjacent and at right angles to the vast and newly-completed Dominican church of Santi Giovanni e Paolo, some of whose land was leased to the scuola. Having obtained the consent of the Consiglio dei Dieci for their new hall, work began immediately. The main wing ran northwards from the campo along the adjacent Rio dei Mendicanti, with the smaller albergo wing on the right, abutting the facade of the church. The relationship between scuola and church thus echoed that at the Carità.

This first hall was built extraordinarily rapidly, and remained until its destruction by fire in 1485, only a few sculptures from the facade surviving. The Republic immediately voted 4,000 ducats to rebuild it, while the Consiglio dei Dieci also allowed a further hundred members to raise entry fees. The original plan and foundations of the earlier structure were retained, and the result is the scuola that we see today, only slightly altered to form the entrance to the city's hospital.

Its facade is undoubtedly the most outstanding surviving feature, and was begun by Pietro Lombardo and Giovanni Buora in 1489; however, Lombardo was abruptly dismissed in 1490, and was replaced by Mauro Codussi, who completed the facade, including the upper lunettes, by 1494. The simple, refined elevation to the canal at the side was almost certainly also executed to Lombardo's design, and is strongly reminiscent of the canal flank of the Miracoli church. The principal facade itself comprises two chief elements, which reflect the larger chapter hall wing on the left and the smaller albergo wing to the right. Its elaborate bas-relief decorations indicate that much is the work of the Lombardo shop, and it is unlikely that Codussi's role included significant alterations to the agreed overall design. Lombardo's contract, though, excluded the statuary, and the figure of Charity above the portal, carved by Bartolomeo Bon, had been salvaged from the fire for re-use. The ground storey, including the prominent porch and the curious illusionistic relief sculptures, is the work of Lombardo's shop, and the latter were probably carved by his son Tullio; the marble sheathing, too, is closely reminiscent of the Miracoli church. Some elements of the upper storey, though, are more clearly Codussian, notably the chapter hall windows and the semicircular crowning gables, which recall San Zaccaria and San Michele, although they equally, and almost certainly intentionally, echo the facade of San Marco itself.

The scuola was extremely proud of this rich, eclectic facade from the time of its completion; it set a standard for the other scuole to attempt to emulate and was highly regarded by visitors down the centuries. Canon Casola wrote on its completion that it was, 'a beautiful sight, so richly decorated is it, ornamented with marbles and gold'; in 1493, Marin Sanudo also commended it, 'newly built

THE SCUOLA GRANDE DI SAN GIOVANNI
EVANGELISTA

Above: the entrance screen, generally
attributed to Pietro Lombardo, and erected
in 1484. The Scuola itself stands beyond the
screen to the right.

Right: detail of angel at the top of the
entrance screen; the figure carving may be
the work of Tullio Lombardo, while the
finely-carved frieze is typical of the work of
his father Pietro.

and very beautiful'; Francesco Sansovino admired its 'encrustation with the finest marbles'; and even John Ruskin conceded its merits as, 'one of the two most refined buildings' of its style, the other being Lombardo's Miracoli church.[7]

Codussi's contribution was not confined to the completion of the facade; he also designed the unusual double internal staircase, an ingenious arrangement which rises in two flights, one from each end of the lower great hall, and meeting in the middle at the top to provide a grand portal into the centre of the chapter hall. The stair is simple, refined and classical, typical of Codussi's maturity, and in strong contrast with the rich, elaborate facade. A monumental stair of this type had not been seen in the city before, and it was much admired, particularly by the rival Scuola of San Giovanni Evangelista, where Codussi was also employed some years later. Largely demolished in 1815, the stair has recently been rebuilt in replica, using some surviving material.

The lower great hall has a simple but imposing basilical plan, with two rows of stone columns, a form later used at San Rocco. But the completion of the interior was to be a protracted process; the albergo was the first priority and has a fine ceiling, with the walls originally decorated by Gentile Bellini and Giovanni Mansueti. Many prominent artists were members of the scuola, not only the Bellini family, but also Bartolomeo Vivarini, and the architects Antonio Scarpagnino and Giorgio Spavento. The chapter hall ceiling was not completed until 1535, while in 1548 Tintoretto was commissioned to paint a great cycle of paintings for the same hall, depicting the life of the patron; they are now dispersed, although three remain in the Accademia galleries.

The Scuola Grande di San Giovanni Evangelista: rivalries

The acute rivalry that developed between the scuole is exemplified by the relationship between those of San Marco and San Giovanni Evangelista, dedicated to two of the four Evangelists. San Giovanni had been founded in c1261, within months of the former scuola, and became equally remarkable as a patron of the arts. In 1301, it moved from the parish church of Sant'Aponal to a site next to San Giovanni Evangelista, and then into a nearby hospice, whose patrons were the Badoer or Partecipazio family, notable patricians who had provided the state with no less than seven early doges. In 1340 the Badoer donated some land, although the site was comparatively small and awkwardly shaped, bounded on three sides by other ownerships. The rebuilding process took place after 1414 when the hospice was relocated.[8] The long, narrow ground-floor hall was completed in 1421, with the chapter hall above it; the configuration of the site, however, meant that the smaller wing, containing the albergo, had to be placed at the end of the larger wing rather than at right angles to it. The albergo was of particular importance since it contained a priceless relic of the True Cross, an object of great veneration and pilgrimage.

By the last decades of the fifteenth century, the scuola had become acutely aware of the shortcomings of its immediate surroundings, with no spacious campo in front for processions, nor was there a prominent approach by water as there was at the Carità. In 1481 the scuola decided to make the best of its location by constructing a screen wall across the courtyard that separated it from the church of San Giovanni. This rich, beautiful screen, the scuola's most striking feature, is almost always attributed to Pietro Lombardo, and it transformed the square by providing both a triumphal arch through which to approach the building in procession, and a semi-private courtyard inside the screen that could be identified as their own. The scuola's domination over the outer atrium thus created was also enhanced by a refined framework of pilasters, cornices and plinths applied to the wall surfaces on either side.

The screen itself is extremely richly detailed, the surfaces clad with sheets of marble very much in the manner of the Miracoli church, and the slightly later facade of the scuola's rival, that of San Marco. Its classical detailing is rich and precise, with extensive bas-reliefs, some probably the work of Pietro's sons. The segmental pediment that crowns the fine portal was formerly completed with

THE SCUOLA GRANDE DELLA MISERICORDIA

Begun by Jacopo Sansovino in c.1535, the huge structure was never completed.

SANTA MARIA IN VALVERDE (right)

The Baroque facade is adjacent to the earlier Scuola Vecchia della Misericordia, built in the mid quattrocento. All the Scuole Grandi were originally built next to monastic foundations.

a characteristic relief panel depicting San Giovanni blessing the members of the scuola, a widely-used motif in these institutions.

If their employment of Pietro Lombardo was to be eclipsed, at least in terms of scale, by the Scuola of San Marco when it commissioned him to execute its own principal facade some years later, this 'poaching' of architectural skill was to be reversed a few years later again in the case of Mauro Codussi, the other outstanding master of the period. In 1498 the Scuola of San Giovanni approached Codussi with the specific intention of creating a formal staircase to surpass that which he had designed for the Scuola of San Marco. Its only possible location was at the rear of the site, on a long sliver of land acquired from the adjacent owners, and here rose Codussi's second double-flight staircase. It is indeed grandiose and monumental, much more imposing and richly detailed than that at the Scuola of San Marco; the basic plan is the same, with two flights rising to meet in the centre, but Codussi took advantage of the difficult shape of the plot to increase the width of the stair as it rises, creating a particularly effective spatial progression. The stair is all vaulted, with small domes over the lower, intermediate landings and a central dome over the top landing. Codussi may perhaps have also designed the Scuola's main entrance on to the square, although it is not entirely typical of his style and may even have been a direct collaboration with Lombardo,unlikely though this may appear.[9] The Scuola's interior is much altered; in 1727 it was comprehensively modernized by Massari, and the famous cycle of paintings formerly in the albergo, illustrating the Miracles of the Cross (by Gentile Bellini, Carpaccio, Giovanni Mansueti and Lazzaro Bastiani), were all removed to the Accademia in 1820.[10]

The Scuole of the Misericordia and San Rocco

If the histories of the Scuole of San Marco and San Giovanni run closely parallel in their rivalries and in their competing choice of architects, the story of the Scuola della Misericordia is a little different, epitomizing the even more grandiose building projects that characterized the mid sixteenth century, the period of the mature Renaissance. The Misericordia had fairly humble origins; it was founded a little later than the first three, in 1303, and was attached to the Abbey of Santa Maria in Val Verde, in a quiet, rather remote corner of the city, then chiefly occupied by gardens and orchards. The scuola grew during the fourteenth century and was enlarged in 1411, when further land was acquired; in 1430 a more radical enlargement was begun, and the present building, known as the Scuola Vecchia, was completed by around 1460. Its appearance and its relationship with the monastery was very similar indeed to that of the Carità, with the facade on to the campo once again at right angles to that of the monastic church. The Scuola Vecchia is entirely typical of the era; its one outstanding distinguishing feature was the great sculpted tympanum that stood above the entrance, carved by Bartolomeo Bon, but now in the Victoria and Albert Museum in London.

By 1492, this first scuola had already fallen into disrepair. It was never as wealthy or influential as the others, and had a long history of financial difficulties and ineffective management, which was later to degenerate almost to the level of farce. The Consiglio dei Dicci allowed a hundred new members to raise funds for restoration, but in 1498 the board made the extraordinary decision that the scuola was too small and that a new, much larger one should be built.[11]

Progress was predictably slow and erratic. In 1507 several models had been called for, and that by Alessandro Leopardi had apparently been preferred. Two years later, though, Pietro and Tullio Lombardo were appointed proti but the new project was then abandoned for twenty years, the result of political crises and tax levies. In 1531, by which time Leopardi's design was apparently considered out of date, four new models were requested, among them proposals from Giovanni-Maria Falconetto and Jacopo Sansovino. The latter's proposal was accepted, but the project was grotesquely overambitious for the available resources, and Sansovino embarked on a long, deeply unhappy relationship with the scuola. Construction began in 1535, but this great *folie de grandeur* was still nowhere near completion thirty years later, by which time there were no funds at all for the scuola's charitable activities, all available income being poured into the new building. By the time of Sansovino's death in 1570, it was still unfinished; although the interior was largely complete, it still lacked a permanent roof and staircase. The lower hall was, and remains, grandiose and imposing, with two rows of paired columns on tall plinths, supporting great continuous stone beams, forming a three-aisled basilica. Only in 1582 were the roof beams installed, and the chapter hall was decorated with frescos in time for the doge's ceremonial inauguration visit in 1588. The exterior, though, remained quite unadorned. In 1570 Palladio had produced a design for the facade, perhaps after Scamozzi, but it was never begun; ten years later Sansovino's son Francesco remarked, prophetically, that in his opinion it might never be completed, and it remains a massive pile of bare brickwork to this day.[12]

The Scuola Grande della Misericordia is one of the two most prominent examples of the overweening ambitions of the Scuole Grandi to surpass each other in size and richness during the sixteenth century; the other is the Scuola Grande di San Rocco, the fifth and last of the original Scuole Grandi to be founded. To a large extent its history reflects its time and context as a new foundation, by contrast with the more organic growth of the older scuole. It also reflects, to the highest degree, both the most positive aspects of the scuole in the sixteenth century – their generous patronage of the fine arts – and their most vehemently criticized: their ostentatious rivalries and lavish expenditure; both of them, of course, were sides of the same coin.

The scuola was founded in 1478, almost two centuries later than the others, and as a direct result of the increasing importance of the cult of San Rocco (Saint Roch), the patron of plague sufferers. Despite this late start, within a century it was by far the wealthiest of them all, since it was the recipient of generous donations, particularly when there were new outbreaks of the plague. In this it represents another thread in the story of the city's response to this terrifying disease, both at an institutional and a personal level; the Redentore and the Salute churches, of course, were both votive offerings, exemplifying the Republic's own response, both devotional and practical.[13]

The scuola met at the Frari Church until 1485, the year in which the body of their patron was stolen by the Venetians from Montpellier and brought to the city. Only four years later the Consiglio dei Dieci granted it the status of a Scuola Grande, and in 1491 their first modest hall was built, across the campo from the present imposing building. It still survives today, although it rapidly became too small and, by 1517, some land had been acquired from the nearby parish of San Pantaleone, on which to commence a far more ambitious home. In this case, unlike that of the Misericordia, there was initially no shortage of funds.

In 1517 Bartolomeo Bon, the Bergamasco, was appointed proto and remained in the post until 1524, by which time the ground floor was complete, as were the albergo walls and perhaps those of the chapter hall. The plan was based closely on that of the Scuola di San Marco, with a lower hall of the basilical type, and two rows of columns on tall pedestals supporting a traditional Venetian timber ceiling. The magnificent chapter hall stands directly above this hall, while the smaller wing contains the all-important albergo, the two elements thus forming the typical L-shaped plan.

However, the later stages of the construction reveal a catalogue of disputes, difficulties and changes of direction on the part of the Scuola's governing board. In 1524 Bon was abruptly dismissed from his post, ostensibly for refusing to follow the approved dimensions of the main staircase; he was replaced by Sante Lombardo, then only around twenty, but with his father Tullio as consultant. Between them, though, they seem to have achieved comparatively little, although Sante did design the upper part of the facade on to the canal at the far end. In 1527 Sante, too, was dismissed with

CANALETTO, *The doge visiting the Scuola of San Rocco*, c.1735 (above)

The Scuola's facade dominates the painting; it was completed by Scarpagnino in the 1540s. The doge made an annual pilgrimage to the Scuola on the saint's day every year. (National Gallery, London.)

THE SCUOLA GRANDE DI SAN ROCCO: THE CHAPTER HALL (right)

This magnificent hall, modelled on that of the Maggior Consiglio in the Palazzo Ducale, was entirely decorated with a great cycle of paintings by Tintoretto.

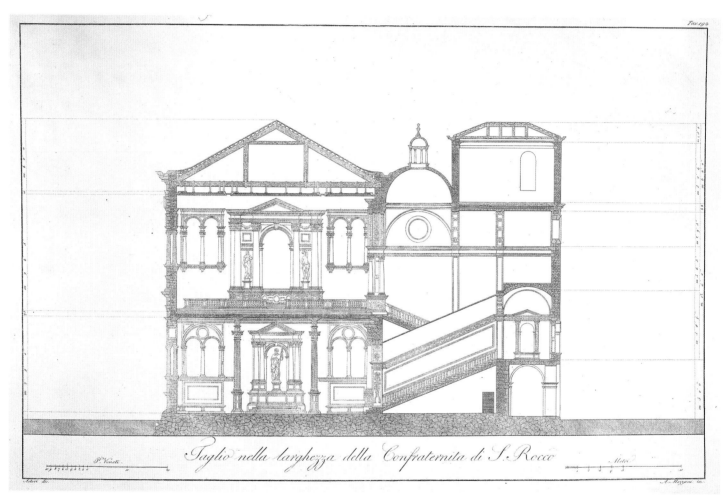

Taglio nella larghezza della Confraternita di S. Rocco

THE SCUOLA GRANDE DI SAN ROCCO

Above: section through the Chapter Hall and staircase. As in all of the Scuole Grandi the Chapter Hall stands directly over the lower hall or androne.

Right: plan. One facade of the Scuola gives onto the parish campo, while the other has a loggia onto a canal. The impressive staircase is attached to one side, while the albergo wing stands at the front, to one side of the androne.

THE SCUOLA GRANDE DI SAN MARCO
(second right)

Lower hall or androne, by Pietro Lombardo and Giovanni Buora; the androne is generally far less elaborate than the Chapter Hall.

THE SCUOLA GRANDE DI SAN ROCCO (far right)

The great staircase. The present stair, by Scarpagnino (1544–6), replaced an earlier one designed by Sante Lombardo. A small part of Tintoretto's ceiling for the Chapter Hall can be seen beyond.

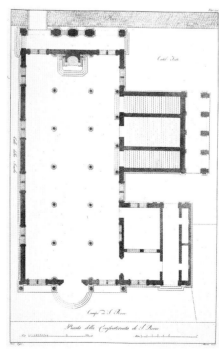

the building still not complete. Finally, his successor Scarpagnino saw the project to its conclusion, including the rest of the first floor and the decorative screen of columns that were belatedly applied to the campo facade.

The design of the staircase was perhaps the most contentious aspect of the scuola's eventful construction history. In 1521, the board had been unable to reach a decision on its form, and in 1524 (the records reveal) they had instructed Bon, their first architect, to implement a design that was not his own, but was the work of another, the elusive Tuscan architect, Zuan (Giovanni) Celestro. When Bon refused, he had been promptly sacked, and acrimonious legal proceedings were then instigated between the two parties. Sante Lombardo, however, began Celestro's approved scheme, in the years 1524–7, and this stair was then completed by his own successor, Scarpagnino. The board then had a further change of mind, and on 21 June 1545 the entire stair was torn down in preparation for an even more imposing successor; Scarpagnino then began building the monumental staircase that we see today. The scuola was fortunate in possessing sufficient land at the side of the great hall to make this newest design feasible, and it took what was then a most unusual form, with two parallel lower flights meeting at a large intermediate landing, from which a third broad flight rose in the centre to the great chapter hall above. Familiar enough today, such a stair had almost certainly never been seen in Venice at the time, and the principles of its design were followed later at the Scuole of the Carmini and of San Todaro.[14]

The protracted history of the building of the lavishly detailed scuola, and in particular the saga of the staircase, gave rise to much critical comment at the time. Not only was the board indecisive and unprofessional in its treatment of its architects, as was widely believed, but the scuole, and the others, were seen by many to be neglecting their charitable duties at the expense of these monuments to their own pride. Once again, Caravia's criticism was trenchant and unequivocal:

> To tell you the truth, each new board's intention's
> To show itself ever so full of inventions:
> by moving the stairs and changing dimensions,
> They make doors useless, and so interventions
> Breed more interventions …

A little later, Caravia's bitterness becomes even more direct:

> On trivial projects they've money to burn,
> When their care and affection to Christ they should turn,
> And for love of Him use all their badly spent money
> On clothes for the naked, on bread for the hungry…

Caravia's claims of the sums expended were undoubtedly somewhat exaggerated, although San Rocco had spent no less than 47,000 ducats on their new home up to 1564, a sum equivalent to twenty-one years' disbursement on charitable activities. There is little evidence on the ground, though, that much heed was paid to Caravia's words, certainly not by the successive boards of the Scuola Grande di San Rocco, which proceeded to surpass all the others, particularly in its magnificent internal decorations.

The scuola's exterior rather belies the tortuous, controversial manner of its construction. Much of it today remains the work of Bon, who established the imposing but perforce asymmetrical facade dominating the small campo. In its rhythm, loosely based on that of the Scuola of San Marco, it has three bays to denote the chapter hall, while the two bays on the right represent the smaller albergo wing. However, the facade is considerably more powerful and disciplined than that of the earlier Scuola, and the two wings are united by a common plinth, by cornices and by their regular, classical rhythm. The windows were modelled on those designed by Codussi three or four decades

THE SCUOLA DI SAN TODARO (above)

The facade, begun in 1655, is by Giuseppe Sardi, as is the adjacent church of San Salvador.

THE SCUOLA DI SAN GIROLAMO AND SAN FANTIN (right)

The early Baroque facade to Campo San Fantin, 1592–1600, by Antonio Contini, probably with Alessandro Vittoria.

earlier, and indeed the lower order remains strongly Codussian in character; the upper part, though, is the work of Scarpagnino, whose proposal for its completion was approved in 1535. This stage included the rather curiously applied classical screen of Corinthian columns on the left wing, intended to further enhance an already imposing facade.

The fabric was only finally completed in the later 1550s, shortage of funds protracting the conclusion of the grand staircase for more than a decade. A few years later, the scuola turned to the decoration of the interior, and their appointment of Tintoretto as their chief master led to the magnificent cycle of paintings produced over more than twenty years, and which have assured the scuola's international fame ever since.

The interior thus represents the apogee of this particular and uniquely Venetian building type. In conformity with the traditional priorities of the scuole the albergo was the first hall to be decorated, and in a sumptuous manner. In 1564 a competition was held, which was won by Tintoretto in what has been chronicled as a less than fair manner: he produced for the board's evaluation not the preparatory 'concept' sketch that had been stipulated, but instead presented a finished canvas. He then offered it as a gift to the scuola, which they were not empowered to refuse, and despite the protestations of his rivals (among whom was Veronese), he was duly appointed to paint the albergo's decorations. The incident reflects the great prestige attached to such a commission, which resulted, in this first stage, in Tintoretto's magnificent *Crucifixion*, which still occupies the whole wall opposite the doorway.[15]

Although the lower hall again conforms to the Scuola Grande tradition in its comparatively restrained decoration, it incorporates a cycle of eight paintings, again by Tintoretto, in a characteristically dramatic style. It is in the chapter hall, though, that the scuola surpasses all others in its rich, imposing grandeur. Modelled closely on the hall of the Maggior Consiglio in the Palazzo Ducale, even its proportions are very similar, while the altar at one end echoes the ducal dais; the ceiling, too, is decorated with a great thematic cycle of paintings set into elaborately-gilded frames. Unlike the Maggior Consiglio, which was decorated with representations of the apotheosis of the Venetian Republic in allegory and metaphor, here the even greater (and more genuinely spiritual) themes represent stories from the Old and New Testaments and episodes in the life of the scuola's patron. Nowhere but here can we see so clearly the full range of Tintoretto's style, his dramatic lighting and the free manipulation of both technique and perspective. These painting cycles, all perfectly integrated into the fabric, represent the culmination of the great Venetian tradition of such works, which had originated a century earlier in the cycles of Carpaccio and Gentile Bellini for the other Scuole Grandi.

The Scuola Grande di San Rocco remained the wealthiest of the confraternities, despite the enormous expense of its own building programme. The saint's special significance to plague sufferers resulted in considerable funds being left to the scuola on a regular basis, while later disastrous outbreaks, particularly that of 1630, gave rise to notable increases both in piety and in practical donations; the doge and Signoria made a solemn pilgrimage to the scuola on the saint's day, 16 August, every year. The confraternity acquired a great deal of land, particularly in its own part of the city, where it developed a number of housing projects, some of them for occupation as *amor dei* (rent-free) almshouses for the poor, others as commercial schemes to provide rental income. Threatened with demolition by Napoleon, the scuola was spared in 1806, although its priceless treasury was dispersed; it still functions today as a charitable foundation.[16]

The minor confraternities: the Scuole Piccole

The numerous minor religious confraternities were voluntary groups of laymen who met together at regular intervals to do pious and charitable works in honour of a patron saint; their activities thus closely resembled those of the Scuole Grandi in principle, although generally on a much more modest level. The monastic orders, particularly the Franciscans and Dominicans, strongly encouraged these brotherhoods to feed the hungry and to engage in practical good works; most of their efforts were directed at the crippled and orphaned, and they were thus also linked with the work of the monastic hospitals.

Modelled on the Scuole Grandi, the Scuole Piccole also echoed their organizational principles, and to some extent their practical spatial requirements. The minor scuole were regulated by the Provveditori di Comun (City Commissioners) and their statutes, like those of the Scuole Grandi, were subject to approval by the Consiglio dei Dieci. Their extraordinary proliferation, though, directly reflects the strong Venetian desire for group rather than individual activity that permeated every level of Republican society; after all, from the very highest level downwards, the structure of the Serenissima itself was built on the foundation of collective responsibility.[17]

The Scuole Piccole averaged perhaps sixty to seventy members each during the fifteenth century, far fewer than the Scuole Grandi; membership was again broadly based, and included traders, building craftsmen, Arsenalotti, mercers and merchants. However, unlike the Scuole Grandi, no nobles were permitted to join. The scuole were scattered all over the city, although comparatively few had the resources to build their own halls; according to the diarist Marin Sanudo, no less than 210 Scuole Piccole participated in the state funeral of Cardinal Zen in 1501.

The wide spectrum in their size, wealth and resources is reflected in the fact that two of them, that of San Todaro and that of the Carmini, were eventually elevated to the status of Scuole Grandi, an indication of their importance and membership; many, though, at the other end of the scale, simply maintained their own altar in a parish church as the focus of their activities.

The buildings of a handful of the more important Scuole Piccole still survive, and illustrate the developing architectural styles of this building type. That of San Girolamo and San Fantin is perhaps the earliest survivor; it was rebuilt after a fire in 1562, and was completed by Antonio Contini, assisted by the sculptor Alessandro Vittoria, in around 1600. The heavy proto-Baroque facade dominates the little parish campo, and is more imposing than the church; the generous patronage of the scuola also resulted in the lower hall's ceiling by Palma the Younger, and the fine first-floor chapter hall originally decorated by Palma and Tintoretto. Some of the Scuole Piccole, therefore, applied significant resources to building works, which were sometimes richly finished.

That of San Todaro, dedicated to the Republic's original patron, was a little unusual in that it grew out of the important trade guild of the mercers; this guild itself was an 'umbrella' organization for many allied crafts, among them makers of gloves, hats, mirrors, stationery and luxury goods. Not surprisingly, the mercers were the most numerous and the wealthiest of the many trade guilds. They originally met in rooms above the portico of San Salvador, thus continuing the traditional close physical relationship with the monastic houses that is so characteristic of the Scuola Grande; they began their own hall in 1530, though, and twenty-two years later were promoted to the status of a Scuola Grande by the Consiglio dei Dieci.

The present building retains this close relationship with its monastic 'sponsor', its facade once again at right angles to that of the church, only a narrow street separating the two. It was rebuilt in 1655–63, the new facade being the work of Sardi, who also designed the imposing facade of San Salvador, a century after the fabric itself was complete. The common authorship of both facades gives an impressive unity to the small, crowded campo.[18]

Santa Maria del Carmine is the third significant Scuola Piccola, founded in 1594, although the present building was begun in 1625 by Francesco Cantello; the powerful stone facades were added by Longhena in the 1660s. A rich staircase decorated with complex stucco decoration leads to the splendid upper hall, whose ceiling has a notable cycle of nine paintings by Giambattista Tiepolo;

THE SCUOLA DEI BATTJORO (GOLDBEATERS) AT SAN STAE (above)

The attractive little Rococo facade was built in 1711, but is dwarfed by the adjacent church.

THE SCUOLA DEI CARMINI (right)

The small first floor hall, known as the Sala dell'Archivio, has rich dado carvings attributed to Francesco Pianta.

they were considered so successful that he was immediately made an honorary member of the scuola on their completion in 1744. The Carmini was 'promoted' to a Scuola Grande in 1767, only thirty years before the fall of the Republic.[19]

These three prominent examples demonstrate that the demarcation between Scuole Grandi and Piccole was not always precisely defined, at least in terms of their own buildings and resources, and in all three cases the confraternity was able to construct imposing accommodation similar to that of their 'superiors'. More typical of the Scuole Piccole, though, were the many much more modest confraternities, a few of whose buildings still survive. One of the earliest is that of the Spirito Santo on the Zattere, founded in 1506; the Scuola della Passione, in the Campo dei Frari, was built in 1593; the Scuola del Cristo at San Marcuola in 1644; and one of the last and largest, the Scuola del Angelo Custode (Guardian Angel), originally founded in 1557, but rebuilt in its present restrained, Neoclassical form by Andrea Tirali in 1713. The hall later became the church for the German community in Venice, which had always been concentrated nearby at the Fondaco dei Tedeschi. With the exception of the last example, they are all fairly modest, usually consisting of a single meeting room above an entrance hall, and in this they closely resemble the numerous halls built by the trade guilds.

The trade guilds

Firstly, it is desired and ordered that in this *Arte* there are and will be three supervisors, good and honest men, to be replaced every year, who will hold for this sacred Arte the duty of ruling and governing according to the form of the *Capitolare* [Charter] … The said supervisors must diligently inspect every workshop where stone is kept and the said stone is worked … and declare that the shop is being run in good faith…Extract from the *Mariegola* or statute of the Guild of Stonemasons, 15 September 1307.

Like those of all great medieval cities, Venice's working population embraced an extraordinarily wide range of specialized skills and crafts. As elsewhere, too, they had been organized into formal guilds from an early date, all of them under the supervision of one of the government's agencies, the Giustizia Vecchia. The registration of these guilds, which were always known in Venice as *arti*, took place after 1200, when they began to submit their statutes (*mariegole*) to the Giustizia Vecchia for approval and registration; they then became statutory obligations on all their members. There were over a hundred of these guilds, together comprising the large majority of the city's working male population. Although similiar in many respects to such trade guilds in other European cities, they differed in certain respects: for example, their members could not engage in foreign trade of any kind, nor could they take direct part in the government of the Republic, which remained the sole right (and duty) of the patriciate.

The range of crafts was great, but most of the arti fell into a few broad categories: domestic crafts such as the building trades; makers of goods and artefacts in wood or metal; the cloth, fabric and textile industry; the highly specialized Arsenalotti; and finally, the large numbers engaged in the food and drink trades. Some of the Arsenalotti were registered as early as 1233 (ropemakers) and 1262 (sawyers); the guilds of carpenters and builders in 1271 and the stonemasons in 1307.[20]

The guilds had two broad functions. One was their universal role, based on the fact that all their members worked in the same craft and were trained in the same skills; these functions were concerned with standards, quality of produce and the training of apprentices. But the Venetian arte was also a lay religious confraternity, whose members had charitable obligations towards each other, and to members' families; they distributed alms to the needy, looked after widows, paid for funerals, and conducted services. They thus combined the traditional role of the trade association with the functions of the Scuole Piccole, similarly joined together by the Christian spirit of *caritas* (charity).

THE SCUOLA DEI CALEGHERI (SHOEMAKERS) AT SAN TOMÀ

Detail of the 15th century lunette above the entrance, depicting St Mark healing the cobbler, Anianus, generally attributed to Antonio Rizzo.

THE SCUOLA DI SAN GIORGIO DEGLI SCHIAVONI (right)

Dating from 1551, the Scuola was the spiritual and social focus for the Slav or Dalmatian community.

Each guild had its own administration, with a warden (*gastaldo*) elected annually by the members, and a board, responsible for keeping accounts, inspecting workshops and levying fines for breaches of the statutes. No man could work at his own craft unless he joined the appropriate guild; the oath of allegiance to the Republic was also a condition of membership, and at times the guilds had to provide members to man the fleet in times of war.

Many of the larger guilds built their own scuola, the building that formed the focus of all their activities: social, professional, philanthropic and devotional. Some were concentrated in certain parts of the city, particularly in the dense tangle of streets between Rialto and San Marco, which were the home of mercers, cabinet-makers and others. Production of silk was chiefly in the hands of expatriates from Lucca, centred on Santi Apostoli, while goldsmiths and spice-dealers were naturally concentrated at the Rialto. Many guilds, though, had members scattered all over the city, particularly the building trades, boatbuilders, vintners and bakers. Some held weekly services in a convenient church, their identity established, like that of the other Scuole Piccole, by paying for an altar and commissioning an altarpiece, often by the finest painters of the day.

Several guild halls survive today. The Scuola dei Calzolai (*calegheri* or shoemakers) is probably the oldest, a characteristic late Gothic structure opposite San Tomà, built in 1478, and with a fine bas-relief above the doorway sometimes attributed to Lombardo or to Antonio Rizzo. Rather later is the Renaissance Scuola dei Mercanti (merchants), built in 1570, reputedly to a design by Palladio, next to the Madonna dell'Orto church. Later again is the plain, functional Scuola dei Varotari (tanners), in the campo at Santa Margherita, the present structure rebuilt in 1725. Of a similar date but quite different appearance is the Scuola of the Goldbeaters (*battjoro*), its delightful little Rococo facade (1711) overwhelmed by that of the adjacent church of San Stae. Still others include the halls of the woolworkers at Santo Stefano, builders at San Samuele and painters at Santa Sofia.

Despite their varying styles, most are modest structures; the chief element of accommodation was an upper-floor hall for meetings of the membership and for services, annexed to which was sometimes a smaller room for meetings of the board, and where the guild's funds, banners and other possessions were kept. They are thus virtually indistinguishable from the lay Scuole Piccole, although they were usually identified on the facade by a plaque representing their craft.

Among the guilds with altars or chapels in churches, the most prominent were those of two important foreign communities, the Florentines and the Milanesi. Both had chapels at the Frari; the Milanesi's altarpiece, depicting their patron Sant'Ambrogio, was painted by Alvise Vivarini and Marco Basaiti and completed in 1503; while the Florentines' altar is decorated with Donatello's haunting wooden sculpture of St John the Baptist, carved in 1451, his only work in Venice.

Different faiths, different forms: synagogues and the Greek rite

As a great city whose wealth depended on international trade, Venice was a cosmopolitan capital. Although Philippe de Commynes exaggerated when he remarked at the end of the fifteenth century that, 'most of their people are foreigners', nevertheless, his impression illustrates the reactions of one from a monocultural background when faced with the diversity of races and religions that crowded the alleys of the Rialto and the quays of San Marco. Much of this mixture represented transient mercantile activity although Venice's resident population, too, was more heterogeneous than that of most Western cities. Several important foreign communities were permanently resident in the city; the largest was the Ghetto of the Jews.[21]

As discussed in Chapter 6, the establishment of the Ghetto in 1516 had led to a clear reordering of the Jewish groups in the city; by 1534 they already formed three distinct sub-communities, the Levantine, Ponentine and Tedeschi groups, representing respectively Jews whose origins were in the Middle East, in the far west of Europe (Spain and Portugal), and Italy and north of the Alps.

The most important physical legacies are the five synagogues, three in the Ghetto Nuovo and two in the Ghetto Vecchio, survivors of the nine that originally stood here. In design and appearance these synagogues (or schole) epitomize both the integration and segregation of Jewish groups in the city: integration in that the architecture of their interiors reflects stylistic development in Venice as a whole, but segregation in that they had to reflect aspects of the Jewish rite that have no equivalent either in the surrounding parish churches or in the lay scuole of devotion. Spatially, their interiors have something of the quality of some of the smaller monastic churches, since they all incorporated *matronei*, or separate galleries for women, to reflect the requirements of the Jewish rite that women should not be visible to men during the services.

The prototype of the surviving synagogues is the tiny Schola Luzzatto, originally housed in one of the apartment blocks on the great square in the centre of the Ghetto Nuovo, but reassembled in 1836 on the ground floor of the Schola Levantina. The Schola Luzzatto is modest in the extreme, with simple early sixteenth-century panelling, and in scale more of a *yeshiva*, a room for the study of the scriptures, rather than a focus for important festivals. Nevertheless, it represents the first generation of the Ghetto's synagogues, and reflects the modest means and numbers of some of the earliest settlers.

Three of the larger schole are within the original nucleus of the Ghetto: the Schola Tedesca, the Canton and the Italiana. All are absorbed into an upper storey within the fabric of the towering apartment blocks; indeed, the Canton is virtually indistinguishable from the exterior, while the presence of the Tedesca is indicated solely by a simple five-light window. The Republic forbade the direct expression of non-Christian places of worship, for example, by a prominent facade, although this discreet location also gave the synagogues the additional security that was felt necessary at the time. The Tedesca was the first to be founded, in 1528, although all their interiors were extensively remodelled later as these groups gained in wealth and increased security, and most that survives today dates from the seventeenth and eighteenth centuries. Although small, these interiors are without exception rich, ornate and elaborate, a reflection of their function in the glorification of God. The focal points of their interiors, as in all synagogues, were the eastern wall with the *aron*, the cupboard containing the scrolls of the Law, and the pulpit or *bimah*. These were the elements always singled out for particularly rich decoration; since they were usually located at opposite ends of the hall, however, the synagogue interiors typically express a duality of focus that contrasts strongly with the simpler, mono-directional quality of the Christian scuole.[22]

The Schola Canton was built in 1553 to a simple rectangular plan, with the aron at one end and the pulpit at the other, the entrance being a doorway in the centre of one of the long sides; the women's gallery runs around the perimeter. Although much of the interior has fairly restrained timber panelling, the two foci were richly carved, with bold relief work typical of the later seventeenth century.

The Schola Tedesca has undergone successive rebuildings and restorations; founded by Ashkenazi Jews, its plan is a slightly irregular trapezoid, rendered less prominent by the elegant ellipse of the women's gallery. The refined interior panelling was carved in the later sixteenth century, but here again the ark is much richer, a three-part early Baroque composition, with superbly rich gilding, broken pediments and Corinthian columns.

From the early Baroque of the Schola Tedesca there is a natural progression to the even more elaborate Rococo interior of the Schola Levantina; this synagogue, and the Spagnola (or Ponentina), the last of the five, were both built in the second part of the Ghetto, and have a significantly stronger external architectural presence. They face each other across a small square, although the Levantina has the more powerful, dignified exterior, with tall stone windows, a particularly fine doorway and a prominent projection for the ark. This clearer identity partly

THE SCHOLA TEDESCA

Details of the interior (above and right). The synagogue was first built in 1528 but much elaborated in the 17th century. The elegant oval women's gallery masks the slightly asymmetrical plan.

reflects the increasing confidence and security of the Jewish community as a whole within the city and the Republic; by now, too, the Republic's legal requirement for self-effacement of the Jewish places of worship had been significantly relaxed. Longhena's name is often associated with both of these last Schole; the facades of the Levantina have much in common with his Collegio Flangini, for example, while the Spagnola was modernized by Longhena in the 1630s.

Both of these were richly decorated internally. The hall of the Spagnola, modernized by Longhena in 1635, retains a certain rhythmic dignity, while its carved timber ceiling, characteristic of his manner, recalls some of his ceilings at Cà Pesaro. Its spacious rectangular hall is the largest synagogue in Venice, and retains the elliptical women's gallery of the earlier Schola Tedesca. The ark is typical of Longhena, with its paired Corinthian columns, and is stylistically very close to his Vendramin Chapel at San Pietro in Castello. We have no documented details, though, and Gaspari may have made a contribution; it is known that he had Jewish patrons elsewhere.

The Levantina's interior was to be the most sumptuous of all, again broadly in Longhena's manner, but with the least Venetian detailing. The hall itself was located on the *piano nobile* of the building, its interior dominated by a pulpit of extraordinary richness, reached by a pair of curved stairs. The speaker's position was designed to be theatrically lit by high-level windows from behind, while the heavy, ornate canopy to the dais, supported by its twisted columns, recalls Bernini's great baldacchino at St Peter's. In this context, however, the columns are a traditional Hebrew representation of the Temple of Solomon in Jerusalem. They provide a foretaste of Longhena's High Altar at the Scalzi church, and their craftsmanship is almost certainly the work of Andrea Brustolon, the finest woodcarver of the seventeenth century in Venice. The ark, at the other end of the hall, itself elaborate, is less overpowering than the pulpit; its form closely resembles contemporary church altars, with paired Corinthian columns and a balustrade of red Verona marble. In these rich Baroque synagogue interiors, therefore, the characteristic ecclesiastical features of the era – canopies, altars, ceilings and balustrades – which were commonly applied to altars and chapels, were adapted and modified, with no great difficulty, to provide the chief fittings of these rather different interiors.

The Jewish Ghetto was by no means the only substantial ethnic city within the city. The architectural legacy of the important Greek community is also one of the richest of the city's ethnic enclaves. Greeks have lived here since earliest times, and as a result of the ignoble Fourth Crusade, Crete, most of the islands in the Aegean Sea and Negroponte (Euboea) had been Venetian colonies since 1204; Corfu, too, became a Venetian island in 1386. In addition to these close imperial and trading links, there was a notable influx of Greeks into Venice after the Fall of Constantinople to the Turks in 1453; thereafter they were permitted to celebrate their rite at altars in several city churches. In 1470 San Biagio became their religious home, and in 1498 a scuola of devotion was established, dedicated to San Nicolo. Finally, in 1526 a new permanent site was allocated to the Greeks in the parish of Sant'Antonin.[23] Around their new church there was developed housing for expatriate residents, a hospital, the scuola, a 'university' and a burial ground. The Greek district lies between two parallel canals, the Rio dei Greci and the Rio della Pietà, a compact, well-defined 'ghetto', although the Greeks did not suffer the constraints imposed on the Jews. They were far better integrated into Venetian society in general; a number of prominent Greek families from Venice's overseas empire were admitted to the nobility, among them the Flangini from Cyprus. At its largest, the Greek community probably numbered as many as 4,000 people.

Their church, San Giorgio, was begun in 1539 to a design by Sante Lombardo; it was consecrated in 1561, although the cupola was added ten years later. Its form is defined by the narrow, restricted site, and the tall, elegant stone facade shows some of the characteristics of Sante's father, Tullio, as well as the influence of Sansovino. Although the external appearance of the church gives little

THE SCUOLA DI SAN NICOLO

The Greek community in Venice: from left to right are the Collegio Flangini, the Scuola di San Nicolo (both by Longhena), the church of San Giorgio dei Greci and its campanile.

evidence of its different rite, the interior was built with a separate women's gallery at the west end, and the aisle-less axial interior is focused on the rich traditional Orthodox altar screen. In such features we can see links with a number of other Venetian churches, such as San Sebastiano, whose facade resembles that of San Giorgio, and which also has an internal gallery. The latter thus represents a compromise between a different liturgy and strong local traditions.

In the 1670s, Baldassare Longhena was appointed proto to the Greek community to unify the architecture of the enclave. The stone screen wall along the canal at the front, with its strong rustication, was erected to define the complex, and the Scuola di San Nicolo was rebuilt just north of the church, again in Longhena's characteristically robust manner, and reminiscent of the Scuola dei Carmini. Immediately adjacent again is the imposing Collegio Flangini, once again designed by Longhena in his role as proto, and built from the legacy of Tommaso Flangini, a wealthy Greek merchant whose family had been enrolled in the Venetian patriciate in 1664; Longhena imposed a strong sense of unity onto this heterogeneous group of buildings.[24] Like their church, the Greeks' construction of the Scuola di San Nicolo (built by expatriates from Crete) exemplifies their absorption of the strong Venetian tradition of these scuole and their adoption by foreign groups as well as by natives. They were a natural means of expressing national identity, where patron saints could be honoured and their own religious rites followed.

An equally strong Venetian tradition was the commissioning of narrative cycles of paintings to decorate the walls of the scuole, which was again adopted by at least two further foreign minorities in the city, the Albanians and Dalmatians. Although by no means as numerous as the Jews or Greeks, both groups had a particular significance to the city since many towns on the eastern Adriatic coastline were, like the Greek islands, Venetian possessions; in 1420, much of the Dalmatian seaboard had been established as a Venetian colony. The Albanians' first Venetian nucleus had been at San Severo; they moved to San Maurizio at the end of the fifteenth century, where they remained until 1780, with a small scuola attached to the parish church. It was originally decorated with a famous cycle of paintings by Vittore Carpaccio, *The Life of the Virgin*, begun in *c* 1502, now scattered among different museums.[25]

The Dalmatians, always known in Venice as Schiavoni (Slavs), were based near the Greek enclave; by 1451 they had already established a scuola of devotion, the hub of this small community of sailors and traders, on land belonging to the Knights Templars. Their own scuola is very similar to those of the Venetians themselves, with an upper main hall built directly over a simpler, ground-floor androne. Its prestige increased greatly in 1502, when a relic of St George was acquired; as a result the scuola commissioned its own cycle of paintings from Carpaccio; originally in the upper hall, they were relocated in the ground-floor hall in the 1550s, where they remain today. The facade of the hall, built in 1551 by Giovanni de Zan, proto of the Arsenale, is a substantial work in the manner of Sansovino.[26]

The last of these foreign communities to establish a stable base in Venice were the Armenians. Once again, their numbers in the city increased sharply as they, like the Greeks, fled the Turkish conquests in the East, and particularly when Constantinople fell. The Armenian community was small but comparatively wealthy and influential; they were based at San Zulian since the thirteenth century, where they owned several houses, a hospice and a small oratory for the Armenian rite. At the end of the seventeenth century the tiny chapel was enlarged, to become the church of the Holy Cross, reconsecrated in 1688, and attributed to Sardi. There was another small Armenian community in Ruga Giuffa at Santa Maria Formosa, the name derived from a town in Armenia. In the lagoon, too, the island that had once housed the lazzaretto, the leper colony, was given by the Republic to Armenian monks in 1717, after it had been relocated in the city. They were a branch of the Benedictines, the Mechitaristi, and the island became a rich centre of Armenian culture.

The poor people of Venice who are driven by want, and who cannot live by their own industry or manual labour on account of infirmity, shall be placed in and distributed among the hospitals or wherever it seems they can best get support. This measure shall be applied to those persons of either sex who have no fixed abode.   **Decree of the Venetian Senate**, 3 April 1529.[1]

Hospitals and the poor

Of the three orders of Venetian society, the nobility typically comprised only around 4–5 per cent of the city's population, the citizenry perhaps 8–10 per cent, while the common people (the *minuto popolo*) formed the remainder. Many were members of trade guilds, which, as we have seen, offered them some degree of social security and protection. But, as in all large urban societies, there was always a stratum of the very poor who could not support themselves: the blind, orphans and those with serious infectious diseases. As always, poverty often merged almost imperceptibly with malnutrition and disease. Venice, though, was a very wealthy city, far better placed than most to offer a safety-net to such people; in the 1563 census, for example, beggars and foundlings accounted for only one per cent of the city's population, perhaps 1,500 people.[2]

They were aided in many ways. As well as the numerous trade guilds, the Scuole Grandi looked after their own impoverished members. The majority of assistance, though, came from the religious orders, which were often given considerable financial help through private bequests and donations. In the medieval period, this charitable network was still rather random and ill-coordinated, although it was extensive, with many small hospitals, hospices and the like. In 1500 one visitor put their number at forty, although in the same period Marin Sanudo listed only twenty-one of the larger institutions.

Two of the oldest of these many foundations were the Ospizio Orseolo and the Ospizio Badoer, both founded by wealthy doges; the former stood on Piazza San Marco, the latter behind the Frari church. The Cà di Dio, too, on the Riva degli Schiavoni (and which survives today), is an ancient foundation, established in 1272 as a hospice and an oratory for pilgrims; the Crociferi was also founded in the thirteenth century by another doge, Renier Zeno.

San Lazzaro, the leper colony, was established on an island in the lagoon in 1261, the island that was much later to become the Armenians' monastery. Towards the end of the sixteenth century, a wealthy group of nobles offered a large site on the northern edge of the city that had been reclaimed when the Fondamente Nuove were built. The new foundation, San Lazzaro dei Mendicanti, offered succour not only to lepers (of whom there were now far fewer) but also to poor children, orphans and others, who were educated and taught a craft. From this re-foundation, the Mendicanti developed to become one of the four 'musical orphanages'. Finally, in this earliest group there was San Giovanni di Malta with its adjacent hospital of St Catherine, originally the house of the Knights Templars, and then, after their dissolution in 1312, the home of the Knights of Rhodes and Malta.

A little later, these earliest foundations were joined by Santa Maria della Visitazione, the Pietà, founded in 1346 by Fra Petruccio, a Franciscan from Assisi, and which became one of the most richly endowed of all, patronized by popes, and visited every Palm Sunday by the doge – who was also its patron – in procession.[3]

There was then something of a hiatus in the lives of such foundations until the notable philanthropic activity of the sixteenth century. This activity took two directions: one was a comprehensive reorganization by the Republic to rationalize and improve these facilities, as indicated by the Senate decree of 1529 cited above; the other was a remarkable increase in

THE PIETÀ CHURCH

Interior, by Giorgio Massari, consecrated in 1760. The Pietà (properly known as Santa Maria della Consolazione) was the most famous of the 'musical hospitals', and was designed almost exclusively for the performance of concerts. The choir galleries can be seen at each side.

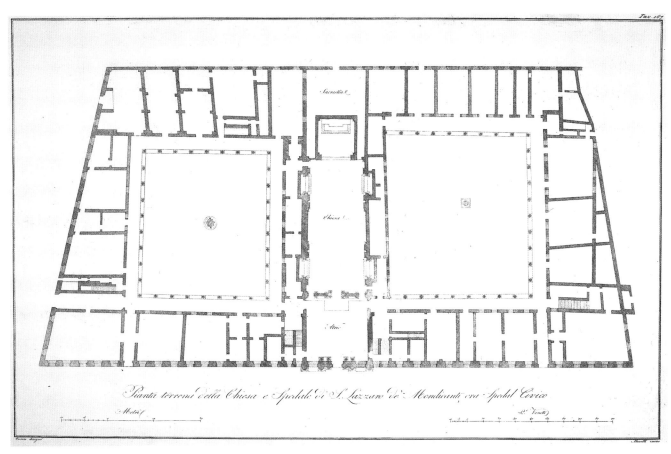

Pianta terreni della Chiesa e Spedale di S. Lazzaro de' Mendicanti ora Spedal Civico

SAN LAZZARO DEI MENDICANTI

Above: plan of the church and hospital. The church has a simple aisleless nave but is separated from the canalside by a spacious atrium

Left: facade onto the canal of the same name; the heavy Palladian facade is by Giovanni Sardi (1649), flanked on both sides by the austere hospital buildings.

provision as a result of that great wave of religious fervour, the Counter-Reformation. This phenomenon was also spurred on by the devastating recurrences of the plague in the sixteenth century, which generated waves of charitable activity. One of the first of this new group of foundations was the Incurabili Orphanage, on the Zattere, established by San Gaetano of Thiene in 1522, and funded by two noblewomen, Maria Malipiero and Marina Grimani. It was followed, a few years later, by Santa Maria dei Derelitti, known as the Ospedaletto. The Catecumeni, too, established a base in Venice in 1571, in the immediate aftermath of the Battle of Lepanto, their special role being the introduction of Christianity to former slaves and 'infidel' prisoners of war. Later in the century they were joined by the Soccorso, founded by the intellectual poetess and courtesan of legendary beauty, Veronica Franco, its own purpose, appropriately enough, being a home for 'fallen women'.[4]

THE CÀ DI DIO

Exterior to the Riva degli Schiavoni, by Jacopo Sansovino, begun in 1545. The residential accommodation is in a three-storey wing at the side.

Many of these foundations combined some or even all of the functions of almshouse, hospital, oratory, hospice and teaching establishment. Their physical forms varied considerably, not only for this reason but also with their financial status and the level of their endowments. A number have left substantial surviving buildings today, one or two of them impressive in size although austere in appearance; the Cà di Dio, for example, on the Riva degli Schiavoni, still functions as a home for the poor. Its present buildings, simple and utilitarian, were designed by Jacopo Sansovino and begun in 1545, with a three-storey wing of accommodation along the canal at the side and a chapel at the front.[5] Perhaps the most significant, though, were the four 'musical orphanages'.

Several Venetian institutions played a pivotal role in the history of sacred music and in so doing also made an important contribution to architecture, more particularly in the design of spaces almost exclusively dedicated to music. After the ducal chapel, San Marco itself, the four chief foundling hospitals were the most notable patrons of music in the city. They were the Mendicanti, Ospedaletto, Pietà and Incurabili; all became centres for the development of both instrumental music and the oratorio, which in turn were to lead the way in the evolution of the symphony and the modern concerto.[6] The standards of music at all four were extremely high, and the training given to the young girls in their charge was of an exceptional standard. They became famous throughout Europe for their concerts, and their choirmasters were among the most notable composers of the era: Antonio Vivaldi at the Pietà, Benedetto Marcello, Tommaso Albinoni and Baldassare Galuppi, the last of whom was master at the Incurabili. The celebrated views of the French visitor, Charles de Brosses, in 1739, were widely held by Venetians and foreigners alike:

They sing like angels, play the violin, flute, organ, oboe, cello, bassoon – in short, no instrument is large enough to frighten them … nothing is so charming than to see a young and pretty nun, dressed in white, a sprig of pomegranate blossom behind one ear, leading the orchestra, and beating time with all the grace and precision imaginable.[7]

The first of the four to be founded had been the Incurabili, established to house syphilis victims; its buildings were designed in the form of a very large rectangle, with the church, attributed to Sansovino, in the centre of the courtyard. The church is lost, although the main quadrangular building survives, completed after Sansovino's death by Antonio da Ponte; imposing in scale, it is simple and rather daunting in appearance and contained large open dormitories for the residents. The design of the church was most unusual, its elliptical plan based on acoustic and musical principles. Such a form had never been seen in Venice before, although Sansovino (if it was he) was perhaps influenced by Giacomo da Vignola's Sant'Andrea in Rome (1554); Sebastiano Serlio, too, had published a plan for an elliptical church in 1547, in developing some of the precepts of Alberti. The Incurabili became famous for its oratorios, the concerts free and open to all. Although demolished in 1831, the church's design was to be an influential model for the 'concert churches' of the other three ospedali.[8]

The church of San Lazzaro dei Mendicanti was built by Vincenzo Scamozzi in 1601–31, and remained in use until the fall of the Republic. The planning of the complex was derived from Andrea Palladio's Zitelle convent, with the church (itself of clearly Palladian derivation) in the centre of a large site, facing the Rio dei Mendicanti; the accommodation was in two substantial flanking wings, each built around a large courtyard. The accommodation is, like the Incurabili, severely rational in plan and appearance, but again the church plan is unusual, with a large vestibule at the front to form a lobby and a 'buffer' between the concerts inside and the noisy activities on the busy canal outside; the same solution was adopted later at the Pietà.

The third foundation, the Ospedaletto, had been established in 1527, but shortages of funds precluded the completion of its buildings until the late seventeenth century, when a new start was made by Giuseppe Sardi in 1662. He built the refectory and the dormitory before a dispute led to his dismissal in 1666 and his replacement by Baldassare Longhena, who designed the unusual oval staircase (modelled on Palladio's at the Carità) and reordered the church. Unlike the others, the site was extremely restricted, with no room for a spacious courtyard; the plan is long and narrow, with an equally restricted frontage to the main street. Longhena was also responsible for the extraordinary facade of the church (1670–2), whose encrustations of Baroque monumentality loom over the narrow street, the Barbaria delle Tole. It was funded by Bartolomeo Carnioni, whose will stipulated that the facade was to be so notable that never again would the Ospedaletto be referred to in the diminutive, but would henceforth be known simply as the 'Ospedale'; in this last aim, though, he was only partially successful.[9]

The best known of the four hospitals is the Pietà, which again cared for female orphans. Much of its fame was the result of the prodigious musical activities of Antonio Vivaldi, chapel-master for thirty years. The present church was designed by Giorgio Massari, who won a competition in 1735; it was not begun until after Vivaldi's death in 1741, though, and was consecrated in 1760. The refined interior is again designed almost exclusively around the choir and the principles of acoustics; its nave has a rectangular plan, but with quadrants at the corners, intended to promote the even diffusion of sound. The choir itself was positioned in two larger balconies down the sides of the nave, with smaller galleries in the quadrants; all were faced with complex lattice grilles so that the young members of the choir could not be seen from below; here, too, as at the Mendicanti, a transverse entrance lobby ensured that noise from the busy quay outside would be kept at bay. Regular concerts maintain Vivaldi's association with the church today.

Housing the poor and the 'common people' of Venice

Although Venice contains a prodigious number of fine churches and great palaces, the general matrix of this densely packed city consists, as do most others, of very many less noble buildings: the houses, cottages and apartments of the ordinary Venetians. All of the many institutions discussed above offered aid to the truly poor, sick and indigent, but Venetian society in general contained representatives of every level, including many who were of very modest means. The surviving examples of these simpler houses cover as long a time span as that represented by the noble palaces, and there are at least a few representative samples of more humble houses and cottages from every era from the Byzantine period onwards. These earliest examples are rare, though, most having been long swept aside by later and larger developments. However, smaller houses from the Gothic era onwards can be found in almost all parts of the city.[10]

Housing for the 'minuto popolo' in Venice can be identified by two very broad categories, houses built individually, in an 'organic' manner, and those constructed on a larger scale, generally by a philanthropic institution, as part of a terrace or some other form of rationalized, repetitive development. Individual houses begin at the very bottom of the scale – and the social ladder – with tiny cellular cottages, some of the simplest forms of habitation to be found in otherwise advanced

BURANO

A typical group of cottages, mostly from the 17th and 18th centuries. Almost all such houses are small and simple in appearance.

Western societies. These little cottages were formerly numerous in the city, but now survive chiefly in outlying satellites, particularly at Burano, where many hundreds of examples can still be seen, mostly dating from the seventeenth and eighteenth centuries. They also survive in some numbers at Murano and on the littoral of Pellestrina.

Within Venice, a few can still be found in the poorer peripheral districts such as Mendigola, historically an isolated zone of impoverished fishermen. All these cottages share common features: they are extremely simple, built of rendered brick, and with a tiled timber roof. The simplest of all consists of a single 'cell', or perhaps two, on only one storey, although more typical are the two-storey examples both in the city and (in large numbers) at Burano. In these cottages, family life, highly congested as it was, focused on the open fire or range, which can always be identified on the exterior by a prominent chimney. Naturally enough, these humble dwellings are devoid of any decoration. They are asymmetrical in appearance, with a staircase on one side, and were generally built by and for their owners; they were then extended, when and where possible, in an organic manner, so that collectively they form a complex mass of basically cubical forms. The use of expensive stonework is confined to the facades, where it is limited to the simplest of rectangular frames for door and window openings. Such cottages are virtually timeless (and extremely difficult to date), those from the sixteenth century being almost identical to those of the eighteenth, although there are probably few, if any, survivors from before the early part of the sixteenth century.[11]

A handful of the earliest smaller houses evince their Byzantine origins in the form of their windows; they are rare, but two close together in Salizzada San Lio, and both of the thirteenth century, give an indication of the typical appearance of these rather narrow Byzantine houses. Both have characteristic tall, stilted two-light windows on the first floor, although they are much altered in every other respect.

From the later, Gothic era there are rather more surviving examples. By now they were usually built on two or sometimes three storeys, to maximize development on fairly confined sites; this is a reflection of increased population and land shortages, particularly in the period immediately prior to the great plague, the 'Black Death' of the 1340s.[12] Once again they are identifiable chiefly by the form of their windows and doorways, which have typical Gothic profiles. A number of such houses can be found around the Arsenale, a traditional quarter for large numbers of fairly poor Arsenalotti, and in many parts of northern Cannaregio and Dorsoduro. They were, therefore, chiefly built for the artisan classes, those with a marketable trade or craft, and hence with a degree of financial security.

A little higher up the social scale again, one can identify rather more substantial houses, that mark a significant step forward in their design beyond these first, smallest examples. Such houses do not represent the city's poor, since they are not only significantly larger, but they are also essentially symmetrical in both plan and in their appearance; they are the distant cousins of the great palaces on the Grand Canal, and their own stylistic development mirrors that of their much wealthier neighbours, which will be discussed in Chapter 12. Indeed, their symmetrical form is itself a scaled-down version of the planning of these great houses. They were built for the moderately prosperous craftsman class or for the citizenry, and the survivors date from the mid fourteenth century onwards, although many have been lost as the result of later redevelopment; in de'Barbari's time, around 1500, they were a good deal more numerous, a direct reflection of the important role of this class in the economy. Generally built on two storeys, they were planned around a central hallway, which echoed the great hall of the patrician palace; their builders were also usually prosperous enough to apply at least some carved stonework to the portal and the windows on the principal facade. The characteristic external feature of these houses is thus a symmetrical facade,

THE OSPEDALETTO (SANTA MARIA DEI DERELITTI)

Above: interior of the music room, decorated with *trompe l'oeil* and stucco work by Jacopo Guarana, 1776.

Right: detail of the facade of the church to Barbaria delle Tole, by Baldassare Longhena, begun in 1670: one of Longhena's most highly mannered and powerfully-modelled later works.

usually with a prominent window or a group of windows to mark this first-floor hall, again an echo of their more illustrious contemporaries.[13]

Examples of such houses remain fairly widespread, although today they are concentrated in the less central districts; there is a prominent group, for example, on Campo Santa Margherita, and others in Cannaregio, although in some cases additional storeys were added later. They can be defined broadly (if rather imprecisely) as *palazzetti*, since their builders adopted not only the basic plan but also the aesthetic spirit of their wealthier contemporaries. They survived into the Renaissance, although naturally their stylistic vocabulary was transformed, and instead of florid Gothic arches we now find a fairly simple, minimal classicism in the detailing of windows, doorways and cornices.[14]

To identify examples from the sixteenth and seventeenth centuries in any numbers one must go to the lagoon villages such as Murano and Pellestrina. On the latter island a number of such houses survive, mostly from the seventeenth and early eighteenth centuries; they were built not by the urban citizenry but as farmhouses by a group of reasonably prosperous local farmers. Their planning, however, and indeed their appearance, again resembles the surviving palazzetti in the city itself.[15]

All these housing forms were built individually, usually for one-family occupation, whether it was by small artisans, by modestly well-off citizens or by farmers in the lagoon islands. However, there is a second, fundamentally different type of housing development in the city (and indeed in the lagoon villages, too), and that is the larger-scale repetitive development. It is a remarkable feature of Venice's urban history that, as a result of acute restrictions of space and the early rise of the city as one of the largest and most populous in Europe, commercial property development for rent developed here at an early date; there are still examples of repetitive terrace housing from the thirteenth and fourteenth centuries onwards. Terraces were sometimes developed by noble landowners as investments, and they often incorporated workshops on the ground floor, with living accommodation in one or two storeys directly above. If the land was available, or could be acquired, there were clear economies of scale in building rows of identical houses (*case a schiera*), in which almost all features could be standardized. The characteristic Calle del Paradiso at San Lio is one of the most remarkable of these early terraces, perhaps built in the thirteenth century (although much altered later); its typical first-floor jetties indicate the desire to maximize floor area in this very central location, and it still retains some workshops on the ground floor, as it did when first built.[16]

A number of other medieval terraces survive, mostly a little later in date, but all of them evidence of a type that has always been widespread in the city; Calle Zotti at Santa Sofia is another example, with others again at San Lio, Santa Giustina and elsewhere. Most of them have simple, repetitive plans, with a regular arrangement of doors and windows, and with stonework confined to the bare necessities: door and window frames and cornices.

But another, quite different purpose in building simple, repetitive accommodation was to provide shelter for the poor and needy; the chief developers in these cases were the monastic houses and other philanthropic organizations, notably the Scuole Grandi. The Procurators of San Marco, too, in their role as administrators of estates and bequests, built and maintained a number of such developments, all of them either administered as charitable almshouses or else rented at highly subsidized levels. All of these bodies were particularly active in the sixteenth century, from which period date a number of such surviving developments. They often take the form of two parallel terraces facing each other across a comparatively spacious, central, semi-private street, in which the

PALAZZETTO CORNER ON CAMPO SANTA MARGHERITA (below, left)

A fine example of a medium-sized 'palazzetto' from the 14th century, with the principal accommodation (like that in the much larger palaces) on the first floor.

CASTELFORTE SAN ROCCO (below)

Exterior from the Rio di San Pantalon. This imposing apartment block was built in the 16th century by Scarpagnino, for the Scuola di San Rocco, which stands next door. It is an early but refined example of high-density development for rent to fairly wealthy citizens.

HOUSING ON FONDAMENTA RIZZI, IN THE
TERENI NUOVI (below)

The district was developed in stages during
the 16th–18th centuries, with a mixture of
developments, mostly in the form of terraces
or blocks of apartments.

HOUSING IN CASTELLO (below, right)

Such housing was occupied by most of the
craftsmen class. The houses retain their
characteristic Venetian chimneys.

communal well was located. They are usually collectively known as *corti*, and several such groups still known today as Corte Nova attest to these sixteenth-century philanthropic activities. Examples of the double terrace, 'Corte Nova' type of development can still be seen at Via Garibaldi in Castello, at San Lorenzo, San Cassan and the Misericordia. Other terraces were built by monastic houses; the long group known as Borgoloco San Lorenzo was built by the adjacent monastery of the same name in 1539, while Corte dei Preti in Castello was built in the same period by the hospital of Santi Pietro e Paolo. In some cases, the precise use of the terrace changed over time; houses originally built as *amor dei* (rent-free) almshouses, for example, were later turned into apartments for rent on the open market, to raise income for other purposes, charitable or otherwise.

There were other, more complex and sophisticated examples of larger-scale development, again from a fairly early date. Once again the sixteenth century offers a number of examples of more ambitious schemes. In the 1540s, the Scuola Grande di San Rocco developed a site next to its own premises, the imposing block of apartments known as the Castelforte San Rocco, designed by Antonio Scarpagnino. It offers a fine example of the rationalization and maximization of real estate

development, in this case for rent to fairly wealthy families. The Castelforte represents high-density housing of an extremely sophisticated type; its internal planning is ingenious, with its five storeys carefully designed to provide a broad range of facilities. The ground floor is occupied by stores and service accommodation, while the upper floors, each reached by its own private entrance, contain four very large, spacious maisonettes, each with its own *piano nobile*, secondary accommodation and attic space. The rents charged were correspondingly high; at up to 80 ducats per year, they were ten times the rent of a modest apartment. These were apartments tailor-made for wealthy citizens or patricians, and this was a development purely intended to provide the maximum income for the scuola's other activities.[17]

In practice, though, there was little physical difference between such charity-funded development (for rent on the open market) and purely commercial projects, such as the Pasqualigo family's development of two substantial blocks on Campo Santo Stefano in the 1520s. These, too, are sizable buildings, on four or five storeys (although later slightly altered), containing shops on the ground floor, with a range of apartments of different sizes above. Again, like those at San Rocco, some were spacious and elegant, closely resembling the principal apartments of a private palace.

The lower orders, too, were provided for by numerous other commercial developments of terraces, again many examples from the sixteenth and seventeenth century have survived. The street known as Riello at San Geremia is one; originally built as a charitable development by the Scuola Grande della Carità, it was bought from them by the Muti family, and thereafter was a purely commercial investment in the form of a single long terrace of seventeen houses.[18]

The large-scale reclamations at Santa Maria Maggiore, the Tereni Nuovi discussed in Chapter 2, represent two centuries of piecemeal but rational development, in a variety of types and styles. By the end of the sixteenth century this extensive newly-reclaimed zone still contained a mixture of gardens and orchards, as well as the monastic buildings of Santa Maria Maggiore and some early charitable developments in the form of two-storey cottages. Among them was the surviving Corte San Marco, built by the Scuola Grande of the same name, in the form of an irregular rectangle around a central courtyard. A little later, more substantial apartment blocks were begun in this zone, built by the nobility for income and investment, all to an efficient, rational, repetitive plan.

Two adjacent developments, both in the Tereni Nuovi, illustrate the range of this accommodation. On Fondamenta Rizzi a long 'slab block' of apartments was developed by the Rizzi family in the 1680s; they are four storeys high, and have the appearance of five contiguous palazzi, all with two principal piani nobili and with service accommodation above and below. Like the sixteenth-century examples, these were generously planned, with ingenious interlocking stairs to provide the highly sought-after private access to the apartments. As an attempt at 'gentrification' of this district, though, the project was not entirely successful and, since the nineteenth century at least, it has remained largely a backwater of poor fishermen and workers in the more recent factories and docks. And to illustrate the range of houses built here, at the other end of the social scale, on the next block is the much more modest terrace of fourteen cottages on Rio delle Burchielle, developed by the nobleman Antonio Bernardo in the 1650s. They are extremely small, each cottage has only two rooms on each of its two storeys. The entire fabric is simple and repetitive.[19]

By the end of the seventeenth century, the encroaching urbanization in the Tereni Nuovi was well advanced. However, it still retained the ancient Venetian tradition of a dense social mix, from cottages to spacious apartments, all closely intermingled. There was little such development in the eighteenth century, simply because the city's urbanization was now virtually complete; one of the characteristic features of the nineteenth century, though, is the reconstruction of a number of earlier terraces to even higher densities, sometimes, for example, on four storeys instead of the previous two or three; in some cases, too, the original fabric (some of which was by now two or three hundred years old) needed complete replacement, although the foundations were frequently re-used. It is clear, therefore, that the tradition of high-density apartment dwelling in Venice has a history as long as the much more famous history of the great patrician palaces.

Entertainment: from football to the Fenice

The Venetian Republic employed the 'bread and circuses' maxim with great skill down the centuries, ensuring that, as far as possible, the common people were reasonably well fed and gainfully employed. As we have seen, ritual and pageant played a vital role in the governance of the Most Serene Republic, and a regular and frequent diet of diversions was provided, in which, on many occasions, the people themselves could take part. Some were purely religious festivals, some were both patriotic and religious; still others, such as the Carnival, were nominally religious but in practice were, like the Ascension Day Fairs, skilfully exploited by the Republic for social and commercial advantage.

In addition to these festivals decreed 'from above', there were many others largely organized from below, and none of which required much by way of permanent constructions; indeed, most of them took full advantage of the 'natural' fabric of the city itself. There was football and baiting of both bears and bulls in the larger squares, for example, notably those of San Polo and Santa Maria Formosa; there were also large-scale, barely organized fist fights on the bridges between two rival factions of the city's working classes, the Castellani and Nicolotti. The former were chiefly Arsenal workers, the latter fishermen from the poor western end of the city; their ritualized brawls often involved thousands, and at the end many of the participants ended up in the canals (the chief aim of the combatants), while quite a few required medical attention. Such raucous 'wars' undoubtedly served an important function as a social safety valve, and more serious violent disturbances in the city were remarkably rare.[20]

Needless to say, forms of entertainment for the patriciate were not only considerably more genteel, but certain activities developed specific building types of their own. An early example was the development of cultural academies of various forms, although for most Venetian nobles the fundamental source of a higher education was the famous and ancient university of Padua which, after the annexation of Padua in 1405, was effectively the university of the Republic as well. And

PROCURATIE NUOVE: HALL INTERIOR (above)

One of the halls remodelled by Napoleon in the early 1800s to form part of the Palazzo Reale for his Italian Viceroy.

FRANCESCO GUARDI, *Concerto di Dame nella Sala dei Filarmonici*, c.1782 (right, above)

In the 18th century, Venice was the musical capital of Europe; this concert was given in 1782 to honour the state visit of the Grand Duke of Russia. The all-female choir and orchestra were drawn from the four 'musical hospitals'. (Alte Pinakothek, Munich.)

FRANCESCO or GIANANTONIO GUARDI, *Il Ridotto*, c.1775–80 (right, below)

Gambling-houses proliferated in 18th century Venice, and were owned and patronized by the nobility. (Museo del Settecento, Venice.)

since, at maturity, all male nobles were required to participate in the Republic's government, the Palazzo Ducale itself was their other, more practical centre of learning, or 'university'.

One of the first academies in Venice was the school of grammar and rhetoric established by the Republic at San Marco in 1450, to train the sons of the nobility for the ducal chancery. This school was later rehoused in Sansovino's new Library. Shortly after its foundation in 1464, Ermolao and Francesco Barbaro formed the Accademia dei Filosofi on the Giudecca; it was later re-established by Giambattista Nani as the Accademia dei Filareti.

The pattern continued into the sixteenth century, as Renaissance philosophy gained an ever wider currency among the patriciate: the Accademia della Fama was founded in 1557, and the second of the same name in 1593. Finally, the famous Accademia dei Nobili was established in 1619, again on the Giudecca near Sant'Eufemia. It is the only one to have left us its surviving premises, an unassuming Gothic villa on the canal waterfront, later modernized, but originally with the further attraction of one of the extensive gardens for which the Giudecca was so famous. The purpose of all of these academies was essentially the same: for the nobility to gather away from matters of state and politics and to engage in philosophical debate and discussion.[21]

GABRIELE BELLA, *Bull race at San Giobbe*, mid-18th century

Bella recorded many aspects of contemporary city life in a long series of views. The larger squares were often used for raucous activities such as bull-running and football. (Galleria Querini Stampalia, Venice.)

In the eighteenth century two less rarefied diversions of the Venetian patriciate developed new building types. The first was the coffee house, which proliferated as a cultural and social phenomenon. Of the many dozens that flourished in the city two early survivors remain on the Piazza: Florian was established by Floriano Francesconi in 1720 and the Quadri a little later. The interior of Florian was remodelled by Ludovico Cadorin in 1858 in the form that has survived today. Both cafés became foci for Venice's cultural establishment in the eighteenth and nineteenth centuries. During the Austrian occupation in the early nineteenth century, Florian became a hub of patriotic activity by the citizens themselves, while the Quadri, by contrast, was patronized by officers of the occupying forces and their sympathizers.

The other entirely new building type that was developed exclusively for the patriciate arose from the proliferation of an old-established Venetian vice, gambling, which became a great passion among the nobility. The Republic first attempted to regulate gambling by the establishment of an official gaming house, the Ridotto, as early as 1638; it became immensely popular and provided useful revenue for the Republic by taxation on winnings, but the habit was not so easily monopolized, and it spread, as did the establishment of private *ridotti*, to all parts of the city. They were owned and managed by the nobility for the nobility, and the earlier establishments combined the attractions of gambling with learned discourse and music, thus to some extent overlapping with the functions of the earlier academies. Slowly, though, the gambling aspect seems to have overshadowed, indeed overwhelmed, these more uplifting activities. Finally, the Republic closed the state Ridotto in 1774, partly because some of the patriciate were losing considerable sums, which they could ill afford, and thus brought the nobility itself into disrepute. The private ridotti continued to function, however, although only one has itself survived until our own day, the Ridotto Venier at San Zulian. Elegantly decorated with rich stucco work, it contains several rooms where various games of chance could be played, planned around a central saloon. It was owned by one of the Procurators of San Marco, Federico Venier, and managed by his wife Elena. Comprehensively restored in the 1970s, its delightful decorations are notable for their refinement and delicacy, chiefly datable to the decade after 1750; some of the decoration may be the work of Jacopo Guarana. The equally refined stucco has been attributed to Giuseppe Ferrari, who was also responsible for decorating some of the most extravagant and opulent palaces of the era, among them Palazzo Zenobio and the great Pisani house at Santo Stefano.[22]

THE CAFFE FLORIAN (below)

Is the oldest surviving coffee-house in Venice, founded in 1720, although its present appearance is largely of the later 19th century.

THE GRAN TEATRO LA FENICE (overleaf)

The interior of the auditorium as remodelled by Tommaso and Giambattista Meduna after the 1836 fire; the theatre was destroyed by fire again in 1996.

There were two other spheres of cultural activity, though, both of them closely linked, in which Venice played a central role in the development of a European tradition: the theatre and lay musical development. The first theatre in the city is said to have been a temporary structure erected by Andrea Palladio in 1565 in the courtyard of the Monastery of Santa Maria della Carità, but the first purpose-built permanent theatres were established soon afterwards. Several were built in the early seventeenth century, all constructed privately by wealthy landowning members of the nobility. The theatre at San Luca was erected by the Vendramin family in 1622 and two were constructed at San Cassan. That at San Moisè was built by the Zane family, while the famous theatre at San Samuele was built by the extremely wealthy Grimani in 1655–6; the same clan also built the theatre at San Giovanni Crisostomo in 1677, then the largest in the city. Martinioni, writing in 1663, also records theatres at Santi Giovanni e Paolo (once again owned by the Grimani) and at San Salvador.[23]

As the century progressed, a degree of specialization seems to have become more clearly defined. San Samuele, for example, specialized in comedies, many of them written by that quintessentially Venetian playwright, Carlo Goldoni; others, though, were built specifically for a revolutionary new musical form: lyric opera.

In the early development of opera, Venice led the world. Claudio Monteverdi, the progenitor of this new form, had seen his first operas (*Orfeo* and *Arianna*) performed at Mantua, but in 1613 he was appointed chapel-master at San Marco to replace the deceased Giovanni Gabrielli. In 1637 the first public opera house in the world had been built at San Cassan, with both seats and private boxes available to all, a revolutionary concept in itself. Monteverdi's long residence in Venice was crowned in 1642 when, at the age of seventy-five, his *Incoronazione di Poppaea* was first performed at the theatre of Santi Giovanni e Paolo. By the end of the century there were seventeen theatres and opera houses in the city, and the tradition established by Monteverdi was continued by the prolific Domenico Cavalli, by Baldassare Cimarosa and Galuppi, some of whose libretti were written by Goldoni. This strong tradition was maintained in the following century, too, with Gioacchino Rossini, who arrived in Venice in 1810 and three of whose works were premiered here in the next couple of years: *L'Inganno Felice* in 1812 was quickly followed by *Tancredi* and then by *L'Italiana in Algeri*, in 1813.[24]

These new theatres, both for drama and lyric opera, developed their own distinct form, usually with a proscenium-arch stage, a flat auditorium floor, and with galleries of boxes around the upper levels. In this they resembled many contemporary theatres elsewhere in Italy, although few, if any, other cities could boast so many, and such a flourishing theatre culture. There was a clear hierarchical division between the 'stalls', that is, the flat auditorium floor, intended for the common people, and the tiers of boxes for the wealthy. The lost theatre at Santi Giovanni e Paolo, for example, had a horseshoe-shaped auditorium with five tiers of boxes, no less than 140 in all; that at San Samuele was also built with five galleries while San Benedetto had four encircling rows of boxes.

Sadly, none of these earlier theatres has survived today. The oldest extant theatre in Venice, at least until the disastrous fire in January 1996, was the remarkable Teatro alla Fenice (Phoenix), one of the finest opera houses in Italy. Begun in 1791, it was also to be the last significant public building constructed before the fall of the Republic six years later. The Fenice was opened on Ascension Day 1792, to designs by GianAntonio Selva, one of the chief Neoclassical architects of the era. The theatre was ingeniously planned on an extremely difficult site in one of the most densely built-up and most central parts of the city, very close to San Marco. It effectively consisted of two parts, the

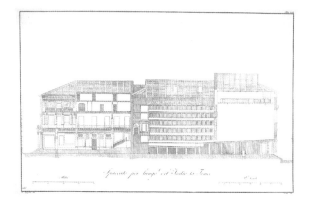

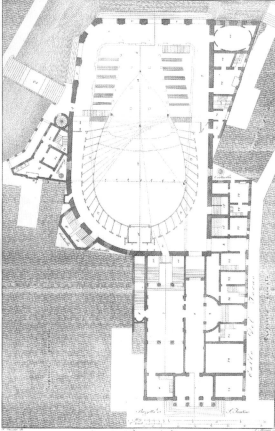

THE GRAN TEATRO LA FENICE

Far left, above: section. Far left, below: plan.
The theatre, the largest in Venice, was
planned with great ingenuity on a very
restricted site.

Left: the stage was home to many first
performances of the world's most famous
operas, including Verdi's *La Traviata* and
Rigoletto.

Above: Gian-Antonio Selva's restrained
Neoclassical facade was the only element to
survive both the fires of 1836 and 1996.

entrance, foyer, stairs and vestibules forming the smaller one, and connected to the larger volume comprising the auditorium itself and the stage. Its facade on to the little *campo* of San Fantin is a model of Neoclassical restraint, although the interior has had a rather more eventful history.

On its completion, the Fenice was not only by far the largest and best equipped, but it rapidly became the chief theatre of the city. On 13 December 1836, however, most of the interior was destroyed by fire. True to its name, the theatre was restored with extraordinary rapidity by Giambattista and Tommaso Meduna, partners of Selva, and it reopened only one year later; the Meduna effected further restorations in 1854, when the interior finally achieved its definitive appearance. Sadly, history repeated itself when the interior was totally destroyed by the fire of 29 January 1996. Nevertheless, the authorities, taking the reconstruction of the collapsed Campanile of San Marco in 1902 as their inspiration, have vowed to rebuild the theatre 'com'era e dov'era', 'as it was and where it was'.[25]

The Fenice was also the first theatre to have a strong architectural presence in the city; with its massive fly-tower it became one of the most prominent buildings in the city centre. The interior, in its final form, was considerably more ornate than Selva's reticent facade, the horseshoe-shaped auditorium dominated by Meduna's five richly-detailed, superimposed tiers of galleries, which continued the traditional Venetian theatre arrangement. The Fenice acquired considerable political significance during the periods of French and Austrian occupation in the early nineteenth century, when it became a symbol of native cultural life; it was also the focus of Daniele Manin's rebellion in 1848. In the same period, the theatre had a very close association with Giuseppe Verdi; in 1844 *Ernani* was premiered here, followed by a (highly censored) first performance of *Rigoletto* in 1851. After a disastrous first night, *La Traviata* became one of Verdi's most acclaimed works, and *Simon Boccanegra*, too, was first performed here in 1859. A few decades later Richard Wagner conducted his own works here, while in our own century Igor Stravinsky was closely associated with the theatre, and died and was buried in Venice. The Fenice thus represented in the last century, as it has continued to do so in our own time, one of the most outstanding elements in Venetian cultural life. Its reconstruction will enable this role to be fulfilled once again.[26]

As the gondola brought us back along the Grand Canal, we watched the double line of palaces between which we passed reflect the light and angle of the sun upon their pink planks, and alter with them, seeming not so much private habitations and historic buildings as a chain of marble cliffs at the foot of which one goes out in the evening in a boat to watch the sunset.

Marcel Proust, *A la recherche du temps perdu*, 1925.

The Venetian palace, that most evocative and universally recognized symbol of the wealth and longevity of the Most Serene Republic, has misty origins; it developed slowly from a building type more widely identifiable with the Muslim Middle East than with Western Europe. Several features characterized the early development of this unique building type; the chief of these was the fact that, as it developed, the Venetian palace came to serve two quite distinct though complementary functions under a common roof. One was the family residence of the merchant-noble, and the other was his trading headquarters or *fondaco*. The etymology of the latter term is particularly revealing, since it derives from the Arabic *funduk*, a warehouse, and reflects Venice's intricately close connections, cultural, financial and even linguistic, with the Muslim world. The requirements of the fondaco (or sometimes *fontego*) had a profound influence on the design of the Venetian palace, since direct access by water was essential for the unloading of goods. Much of the lowest storey, therefore, was devoted to commercial activities and to the storage of the commodities in which the owner dealt. These commodities embraced an extremely wide variety of goods, among the most important being textiles of many kinds, and 'spices', a term which, when used in the medieval sense, included almost all traded goods of high value but comparatively small bulk, from peppers to rare dyes, from perfumes to medicinal ingredients.

The second unique feature of the Venetian merchant's palace derived from the city's site, safely harboured within the broad natural moat of the lagoon. The extraordinarily high degree of security that the lagoon offered resulted in the early abandonment of almost all features of design that might have provided some protection against external aggressors: there are no massive walls, no narrow defensive windows and no stout battlements. Even from earliest times, therefore, certainly from the twelfth century, Venetian palaces were richly caparisoned with colonnades and logge, light, airy arcades surrounding the accommodation within. Such colonnades, like those of the Muslim palaces of Granada and Seville, offered shade from the sun, protection from inclement weather, and a close proximity to the element of water, which was such a central feature, albeit an artificial one, of many Muslim palaces; here, of course, the Venetians had no need of such artifice. The only concessions to security in the Venetian palace were the stout iron bars to the ground-floor windows; these, though, were intended to deter the native *malavita* (criminal classes) of the city rather than offering serious defence against an external aggressor.

In this, the Venetian palace from the twelfth century onwards remains unique in the Western experience. Contemporary noble houses elsewhere, particularly in Florence and Genoa (arguably the two cities most similar to Venice in their banking and trading activities) remained massive stone-built fortresses, designed as much for defence against internal insurrection and bloody family feuds as against the real threat of external aggression. Not only was Venice never attacked by an external aggressor until the Genoese threat of 1379, but, after the brief rebellion following the institution of the Maggior Consiglio in 1172, there were only two significant civil disturbances in nearly two centuries; such internal, factional feuding as the Guelf-Ghibelline struggles in Florence found no equivalent in Venice.

THE FONDACO DEI TURCHI

Facade to the Grand Canal. Although almost entirely rebuilt in the 19th century, the spacious colonnades still evoke the finest of the Venetian Byzantine palaces of the 12th and 13th centuries.

The third remarkable feature of these many palaces is their homogeneity, the broad 'family resemblance' of so many dozens of examples; even Renaissance palaces from the sixteenth century have a clearly identifiable relationship with their earlier, Gothic predecessors. In this consistency, the palaces collectively represent the ruling social order, the patriciate, united by their nobility, their shared responsibility in governing the Republic, and their shared commercial activity; united, as well, of course, by an extremely close common cultural heritage. The real core of the patriciate was said to have been the twenty-four clans or *casade*, the 'long families', who claimed to be the only true original nobility, and among whom were such august names as the Contarini, Giustiniani and Dandolo. The 'short' families, some of whom were probably as ancient and many at least as distinguished, were larger in number, and included the Foscari, Grimani and Loredan, among several dozen others. Still newer were those thirty clans ennobled after the 1380 war with Genoa, the real *nouveaux riches* of the late fourteenth century. Despite wide variations in wealth and in numbers (the Contarini clan had a dozen different branches), their common bonds were considerably stronger than these fluctuating differences, and even the smallest clans managed at some time to build at least one substantial palace as their combined family headquarters and trading base. Each palace, of course, served patriotically to enhance the image and beauty of the city, their city, as much as it did the reputation of their own clan. Here, too, though, as at the Scuole Grandi, rivalry and self-glorification undoubtedly played an important role, as we can see particularly in the florid Gothic palaces of Venice's first 'golden era', the late fifteenth century. The most important of these family headquarters were frequently referred to as 'Cà', rather than palazzo, a Venetian abbreviation for *casa da stazio*, or principal family seat.

Byzantine survivors

CÀ DA MOSTO

Facade to the Grand Canal. Only the two lowest orders evince this palace's Byzantine origins; it was later a famous inn, and has been much altered and extended.

A handful of the earliest Venetian-Byzantine palaces survive today substantially intact, with a further dozen or so recognizable in more fragmented form, and most of them much altered in later centuries. They were almost always built originally on only two equally spacious storeys, with a simple two-part division of function: warehouse and trading activities below and family apartments above. They often retained small towers or *torreselle* on each corner, faint echoes of earlier, more troubled times, when a higher degree of fortification had been necessary. Today almost all of these Venetian-Byzantine houses have had additional storeys added, thus radically disturbing their original spacious, harmonious and essentially horizontal proportions.

The largest and best known of these palaces is also sadly the least authentic, the most drastically altered; the building now known as the Fondaco dei Turchi is said to have been built during the later twelfth or early thirteenth century by a wealthy merchant, Giacomo Palmieri from Pesaro, who was admitted into the Venetian nobility and whose clan was from then on known as the Cà da Pesaro. Despite the fact that the Fondaco was in such a ruinous condition by the nineteenth century that it had to be virtually rebuilt, it remains a highly distinctive reminder of the appearance of the grandest of such houses. Its layout is very broad, with two storeys and distinctive corner 'turrets'. The architectural language throughout is essentially a Venetian interpretation of the Byzantine; its most characteristic feature being the tall, stilted semicircular arch. Much of its width is occupied by an exceptionally spacious ground-floor colonnade or loggia, terminating at each end in large square rooms representing the bases of the vestigial towers. Above the loggia, on the first floor, is an equally generous transverse hall or gallery. The facade is remarkable for the extent of its openings; there is far more void than solid, and the only substantial areas of masonry are at the two ends. The building also has a very deep plan, with a large rectangular central courtyard around which, on both storeys, were ranged the principal rooms. Remarkable even by the standards of the day, the palace was acquired by the Republic in 1381, which initially donated it to the Marquis of Ferrara; it was later confiscated and thereafter was used by the Republic for housing or entertaining eminent foreign visitors, among them Emperor Frederick III of Germany in 1452 and the Queen

CÀ LOREDAN (Far left) AND CÀ FARSETTI (left)

On the Riva del Carbon at Rialto. Both have
been altered by the addition of the second
and third storeys, although they remain
important survivors of the Byzantine palace,
with their characteristic stilted arches, and
broad, refined colonnades and logge.

PALAZZO DONÀ (above right) AND PALAZZO
DONÀ DELLA MADONETTA (above left)

Both are Byzantine in style, but the larger
Palazzo Donà already shows the division of
the facade into three component elements,
one of the most distinctive aspects of
Venetian palace design.

of Hungary in 1502. Only in 1621 did it become the Fondaco dei Turchi, the city's Turkish trading base, although thereafter its decline and deterioration was rapid, and was virtually rebuilt in 1860.[1]

The most significant grouping of the other remaining substantial Venetian-Byzantine palaces is centred around the Rialto, a direct reflection of the early rise to pre-eminence of this district of mercantile and banking activities. On the Riva del Carbon are two adjacent houses, Cà Loredan and Cà Farsetti, which have a strong family resemblance, although differing in certain significant details. Both were again originally two storeys high, and although also much restored, retain something of the refined grace and balance of such palaces. The Farsetti was probably built by the Dandolo clan, and was owned by Doge Andrea Dandolo in the 1340s, a notable scholar and historian of the Republic. The house suffered a serious fire in 1524 when still owned by the Dandolo; it passed to the Farsetti, a wealthy Florentine family in 1669.

PALAZZO MOROSINI SAGREDO AT SANTA SOFIA (below left)

Several stylistic phases can be identified, from the Byzantine stilted arches on the first floor to the 15th century quatrefoils above the central windows.

PALAZZO AGNUSDIO AT SAN STAE (below)

Detail of the characteristic 14th century water-gate.

The adjacent Loredan house has had an equally complex history; in the fourteenth century it was owned by Federico Corner, then the wealthiest man in Venice. Later it passed to the Loredan by marriage, and both houses now form the City Hall. Although very similar, they have somewhat different plans expressed by subtly different facades. The Farsetti house has a continuous first-floor colonnade, fifteen bays wide, occupying the full width of the palace, and reflecting the full-width gallery inside. Cà Loredan, though, has a slightly different arrangement, since here the first-floor loggia stops short of the full width of the facade, and there are square rooms in each corner, reminiscent of the lost torreselle, rather like the Fondaco dei Turchi. On the ground floor, too, there are rather more substantial flanking bays.

In both houses, though, behind the front loggia there is a long, deep hallway running back into the house, producing a plan in the form of a 'T', a characteristic feature of most Venetian-Byzantine houses. In detail, too, both houses, although heavily restored, evince the characteristic stilted arch, often supported on narrow paired columns, and with the outer surface of the arch decorated with dogtooth carving. Many such facades were further decorated with thin sheets of marble facing, and with inserts of paterae or shallow relief panels set into the surface. It is likely that at least some were brought back to Venice as booty after the infamous Fourth Crusade, although many others may be of local origin; cultural traffic between the city and Constantinople, in both directions, was extremely close.[2]

These two palaces probably represent the most impressive of the Venetian-Byzantine era, other than the Fondaco dei Turchi, and their overall scale and dimensions were to be broadly followed in the many generations of palaces, in many different styles, that were to come in the succeeding centuries. However, the group of four houses facing these two on the opposite bank of the Grand Canal together give us a clearer impression of the original range and variety of such palaces; they are Palazzo Donà, Palazzo Donà della Madonetta, and the Businello and Barzizza houses, all of roughly similar date. Palazzo Donà della Madonetta is the smallest of the four, so called from the small Madonna and Child on the facade. Built on a particularly narrow site, it is dominated by a continous loggia across the first floor, eight bays wide. Here, though, there was no room for the arrangement seen at Cà Loredan and Cà Farsetti, although at the other three neighbouring, more spacious houses, the loggia is restricted to the central part of the facade, with separate rooms on either side, each of them lit by two single windows. Palazzo Donà is the largest and most handsome of the group, although, like the others, altered by later additions above. Its broad facade clearly exhibits the two more solid bays that now flank the five-bay central loggia, and thus divide the

PALAZZO SORANZO ON CAMPO SAN POLO

Two contiguous palaces, both built by
the Soranzo clan, but the left one (mid 14th
century) is slightly earlier than the other.

facade into three elements of equal width. While at the Businello house the basic plan is still a 'T', albeit with much shorter 'arms', at Palazzo Donà these two arms have gone entirely. The central loggia is now a simple expression on the facade of the long hallway or *portego* that lay behind it, and which was to form the central axis of all important Venetian houses for the next five hundred years. The Venetian palace had undergone a notable transformation, and the principles seen here at Palazzo Donà were to be developed and refined over many more decades. The facade is rational and symmetrical, with three equal bays, the well-lit central bay balanced both visually and structurally by the two more substantial flanks, in which tall individual windows replace the open loggia.[3]

The internal planning of the Donà house is now as fully rational as the facade; there is a long central hall, flanked on both sides by square rooms, and with a courtyard behind. However, since Palazzo Donà is something of a precursor of this new stage of rational planning, its architectural vocabulary remains Venetian-Byzantine, with stilted stone arches, and the facade further enlivened with paterae and discs or inserts of rare marbles.

These are the only substantial surviving Byzantine palaces in the city; other contemporary houses survive only as evocative fragments, albeit significant ones. The thirteenth-century Cà da Mosto, for example, stands beyond the Rialto Bridge opposite the markets, a faded remnant of a once remarkable house. Formerly the home of Alvise da Mosto, the noted explorer of West Africa in the 1450s, it later became a famous inn, the Leon Bianco or White Lion. Part of the ground-floor loggia remains, as does the fine six-light window to the first floor, with an exceptional collection of contemporaneous relief carvings. Nearby, and better preserved, is the slightly later Cà Falier at Santi Apostoli, home of the ill-fated Doge Marin Falier, who was executed for treason in 1355. Here the facade is very broad, and clearly divided into three parts as at Cà Dona, although the ground-floor colonnade is now a public quay. A number of solitary, but richly-carved portals survive elsewhere in the city; most of them are water gates, whose bold sculpted moulding contrasts with the simple dogtooth detailing on almost all of the palaces discussed above; they include the so-called house of Marco Polo in Corte del Milion and another on Rio di Cà Foscari. The robust naturalistic carving of these portals is influenced to some extent by the Romanesque from the Italian mainland, although they were perhaps also inspired by the great portals of San Marco.

Venetian-Byzantine palaces exhibit a refined poise and equilibrium, rational but elegant. While there are undoubtedly close connections with the Middle East in the surface decoration and other features, they can also be related to certain Romanesque works in mainland Italy, such as the colonnades of the cathedral complex at Pisa. However, the Venetian palaces are never as muscular as almost all other contemporary Romanesque examples on the Italian Terraferma, or those of the Normans in Sicily, their refinement being both a reflection of the Venetians' unique security and of their own cultural rapport with Byzantium. The Venetian palace of the twelfth and thirteenth centuries is the lay equivalent of San Marco in the architectural evolution of the city, a building type unique to Venice, and which was to reach its maturation in the indigenous Gothic style.[4]

During the thirteenth century, Venetian palace design developed further in its own particular stylistic direction. Although still influenced to a degree by the East, its specific function was now well established, and its plan essentially defined. Slowly an architectural language evolved, rather as the native dialect evolved, recognizably related to the mainland Italian experience, but with many nuances of vocabulary that remained clearly of the lagoons. Stylistically this development is seen most clearly in the forms of window and door openings, famously analysed by Ruskin 150 years ago in his extremely influential *The Stones of Venice*, and whose analysis is still of value today, although his chronology has undergone significant revision.

From Byzantine to Gothic

The first development from the simple stilted semicircular arch was the alteration of the profile of the *extrados*, the outer face, to form a pointed crown or cusp. Comparatively few surviving houses illustrate this essentially transitional form, although it can be seen already at Cà da Mosto and the Falier house, both from the late twelfth or thirteenth century. Shortly afterwards, the inner profile of the arch also became inflected, examples of which (Ruskin's 'third order') can be seen at the fine Palazzo Moro at San Bartolomeo and the equally notable Vitturi house on Campo Santa Maria Formosa. These examples vary a good deal in refinement but can be dated to around 1250–1300.

This stage in stylistic evolution still retains a strong Islamic influence since this arch is an Eastern form, but in the fourteenth century Venice became increasingly receptive to Western mainland influences, particularly from Lombardy, where the trilobate or three-lobed arch evolved. It was first used in the city in the early fourteenth century, and is distinctly different from the earlier forms, with its rich, complex profile. Examples survive in all parts of the city, although there are more in the smaller and middle-ranking houses than in the large palaces. Few can be accurately dated, although the little Palazzetto Foscolo Corner at Santa Margherita, for example, was built in the 1380s, and this type of window survived until the last great era of Gothic palace building in the mid fifteenth century.

In the longer term this fourteenth-century form can be seen as representative of an era of transition, when the strong Byzantine derivations were superseded by a more definitive Venetian style. Nevertheless, styles by no means developed in a continuous linear path, one succeeding another: anachronisms abound. We often find very late examples of 'archaic' forms, just as we often see two or even three different orders on a single facade. In many cases dating remains extremely difficult to determine with any precision. Facades frequently indicate a long process of adaptation and modernization, although in most cases the basic structure and foundations of an original, probably Byzantine house, were retained. Palazzo Sagredo, near the Cà d'Oro, for example, shows very clearly the organic nature of this modernization process over a period of more than two centuries; its earliest windows are stilted, Byzantine; others have the trilobate fourteenth-century form, while still others are 'florid' Gothic of the fifteenth century.[5]

However, the later fourteenth century was characterized by a stronger desire for order and balance, by the elimination of a good deal of the randomness and caprice that typified some earlier palaces, and by the suppression of archaic details; above all, and particularly after 1380, a new era of confidence witnessed the final maturation of the truly native style of Venetian Gothic.

A fine example of this maturational process is the *palazzata* or double palace of the Soranzo on Campo San Polo, still today owned by the same clan after six centuries. The left-hand palace is probably from the mid fourteenth century, while that on the right is three or four decades later. The great first-floor window on the latter house, for example, is considerably more disciplined than that to the left. Palazzo Priuli at San Provolo is also from the same period, although elaborated in the early fifteenth century, as is the fine Palazzo Marcello on Rio di San Luca. Characteristic of such houses is the continuation of the grouping of windows, usually of refined proportions, in the centre of the facade, although a few anomalies also survive, unique examples that defy categorization, such as the *tour de force* tracery of Palazzetto Cicogna Arian, of a complexity never seen before or since.[6]

In general, the plans of the fourteenth-century palaces retain the three-part arrangement that had evolved in the later Byzantine houses. This discipline resulted equally in the rationalization of the facade and of the structural form behind it. The central axial hall, flanked by two wings of equal width, produced a plan consisting in essence of four parallel structural walls, on which all the internal floors and much of the roof were supported. This rationalization had considerable

RIO DEI CARMINI (above)

On the right is Palazzo Cicogna Arian, built in the later 14th century, with its unique *tour de force* geometrical tracery.

FACADES AND BALCONIES (right)

On the Grand Canal near San Moisè, embracing every period from the 15th century to the 19th.

advantages, both structurally and in the process of construction itself. With three bays of equal width, virtually every floor beam in the house could be of the same size and length, leading to considerable simplification of ordering and procuring materials; the spans of the beams were such that large quantities of timber were available of the appropriate dimensions. Structurally, the loads on all four walls were distributed as evenly as possible, and since the beams all spanned 'left to right', or parallel to the main facade, this facade had to carry no load other than its own weight and a small part of the roof. This in turn allowed the freedom with which the great central windows could be expanded and developed with ever greater refinement of tracery, seen most clearly in the imposing palaces of the mature fifteenth century.[7]

The mature Gothic: the Cà d'Oro and its contemporaries

The Venetian Republic experienced three profound changes in the late fourteenth and early fifteenth centuries, two of which had an equally fundamental effect on the development of the city's noble palaces. Firstly, in the 1340s, Venice suffered the devastating effects of the Black Death, from which its population took several decades to fully recover. Secondly, while this recovery was still taking place, in 1380 the Republic survived its fourth and last great struggle with Genoa, the ancient sea rival, in the momentous battle to regain Chioggia from Venice's traditional enemy.

THE CÀ D'ORO

Below left: the courtyard with Bartolomeo Bon's well-head of 1427, and typical Gothic open staircase.

Below: detail of the facade; the two richly-carved upper logge were the work of Matteo Raverti in the 1420s.

Although the war brought the Republic to the brink of defeat, Genoa's repulsion finally gave Venice undisputed mastery of the eastern Mediterranean sea trade. And thirdly, after 1400, Venice began to acquire an important empire on mainland Italy for the first time in its history. With the new century, therefore, there began a long period of growth and consolidation, such that already by the 1420s the Republic had become the wealthiest state in Europe, unrivalled at sea and with a populous and highly developed Terraferma empire, which embraced such important cities as Padua, Verona, Vicenza and Bergamo.

The Venetian patriciate expressed its own confidence in this golden era by an extraordinary phase of building activity, on a scale never witnessed before. Palaces were modernized, enlarged, adapted and in many cases built completely anew; the result was to transform the banks of the Grand Canal and every large campo within two or three generations with a magnificent new assemblage of palaces, many of which have survived today, from Cà Giustinian to Palazzo Bernardo, from Palazzo Pesaro to the almost legendary Cà d'Oro.

Although established structural forms were generally retained, numerical growth and prosperity led to palaces becoming larger, more imposing and often with rigorously symmetrical, disciplined facades. These facades clearly expressed the hierarchy of spaces within the house; there was a single portal giving water access to the *androne*, the ground-floor main hall, flanked by simple windows to the adjacent storerooms. Here, as in earlier centuries, goods were received and visitors greeted. There is often a mezzanine floor on each side of the androne, which offered additional storage space where there was greater safety from flooding and from possible robbery, as well as accommodation for servants and the merchant's own office.

Above this tall 'basement' was the piano nobile, although almost as frequent in this period were two superimposed piani nobili, such as those at Palazzo Barbaro and the Cà d'Oro. This arrangement partly reflected a rising population and acute land shortage in the city centre; the population rose from around 100,000 in 1400 to perhaps 140,000 by 1500. However, it also reflected the desire to maximize investment in these very expensive new houses; and thirdly, such palaces sometimes accommodated two branches of a noble clan within the same walls. They were often brothers or cousins who frequently formed trading partnerships, and who could thus share

THE CÀ D'ORO (below)

Facade to the Grand Canal. Recently restored, Marin Contarini's masterpiece remains the richest medieval facade in Venice. Begun in c.1420, it was completed in the mid 1430s, by Matteo Raverti and the Bon workshop.

CÀ FOSCARI AND THE TWO GIUSTINIANI PALACES, (below, right)

The finest Gothic group on the Grand Canal. Cà Foscari (on the right), begun in 1452, dominates the length of the Canal as far as the Rialto Bridge.

the warehouse accommodation below their two apartments; Cà Bernardo still shows this arrangement particularly clearly.[8]

The heart of the palace remained the great hall on the first floor; this imposing gallery typically measured 4 or 5 metres (13–16 feet) in height, 5–6 metres (16–19 feet) in width, and around 20 or 25 metres (65–80 feet) in length. It was occasionally used for banquets and receptions, although on a day-to-day basis it simply formed a grand access corridor to the smaller habitable rooms on either side. It was as much a traditional status symbol as a practical space, and some of these halls became very impressive indeed. The two front rooms on either side of the hall facing the canal were the chief living rooms, and behind them were bedrooms, up to three or four down either or both sides. Kitchens were sometimes located in one corner of the piano nobile, or more frequently on the top storey, with storage in the attic. Sanitary facilities were located in the mezzanines or attached to the flanking bedrooms where a drain connected to an adjacent canal. The top storey was almost always given over to stores, pantries and servants' rooms.

The piano nobile of the fifteenth-century palace was always more carefully designed than any other element, with a tall, refined multi-light window, all in stone, facing the canal, and usually with a richly-carved stone balcony; the window was intended to provide as much light as possible into the

long portego. The two flanking rooms were lit by the now familiar pairs of tall single windows, usually variants of those in the great hall. All the rooms were spanned by exposed floors of closely spaced beams, often richly painted and decorated; the universal floor finish was polished terrazzo.

The courtyard (*cortile*) was a vital feature of these palaces; sometimes it remained at the back of the house and was screened from the street by a high brick wall, into which an imposing stone portal was set bearing the owner's coat of arms. More frequently in the fifteenth century it was in the centre of the house, which was wrapped around it, producing a plan roughly in the form of a 'C'. Within the courtyard rose the principal external staircase, giving direct access to the first floor, and supported on a row of brick and stone arches. Sometimes the courtyard was divided into two, each with its own staircase, and each serving one of two superimposed piani nobili; Palazzo Soranzo-Van Axel, built in the 1470s, is an ingenious example of such an arrangement. In all cases, though, the courtyard contained the cistern, which collected rainwater from the roof and from the brick-paved courtyard itself to store for the use of the household. In dozens of such palaces the traditional wellhead (*vera da pozzo*) remains in place today.

Steadily increasing pressure on land to rebuild at higher densities not only gave rise to taller houses, by now usually on four or even five storeys, but on occasion new palaces were joined together to produce a continuous frontage to the all-important Grand Canal. The remarkable development at Cà Foscari is the most prominent of these *palazzate*, with the two contiguous Giustiniani houses immediately adjacent. Such continuing shortages of land, most acutely on the Grand Canal, later gave rise to the row of no less than five contiguous Mocenigo houses on the opposite bank.

The chief glory of these great Gothic houses is their facades, particularly since so many have been drastically altered internally over the centuries. Noble and majestic, these fifteenth-century facades epitomize the power, stability and order of the patriciate and their own Serene Republic. They are all constructed of brick although there is extensive use of finely-carved stonework for all their decorative features: quoins, balconies and cornices are all of Istrian stone, as are the portals and windows. These last offer the most characteristic features, and their tracery was developed in several sophisticated forms in the period from around 1420 to the 1470s. The Palazzo Ducale was the initial spur or catalyst for this development, particularly after the completion of the new Molo wing in the 1380s or 1390s. Its own tracery was first adopted (and further refined) at the Cà d'Oro in the 1420s, and later again in many other palaces, where these elegantly proportioned windows became a leitmotif for the mature, refined style uniquely recognizable as Venetian Gothic.[9]

Marin Contarini's 'House of Gold', the Cà d'Oro, was built in 1421–36, and is the finest example of the fifteenth-century native style in brick, stone and marble; the date of its construction marks the beginning of this last great era of indigenous Gothic palaces. Although many aspects of its design are not untypical of the mature Gothic palace, and its facade masks a fairly conventional (although asymmetrical) plan, it is this magnificent and once dazzling facade that has given the house its fame down the centuries. This sumptuous screen, impressive enough today, originally incorporated no less than 23,000 sheets of gold leaf with which its principal features were adorned; the palace remains unique as one man's conspicuous expression of wealth and confidence in his own trading skills, in his ancient noble clan and in his apparently eternal Republic.[10]

The facade was chiefly the work of two teams of master masons, one led by the highly skilled Milanese Matteo Raverti, and consisting chiefly of immigrants from Milan and Como; the other was the native workshop of Zane (Giovanni) and Bartolomeo Bon, father and son, who between them, but particularly Bartolomeo, mark the peak of skilful creativity of the last stages of the truly indigenous Gothic style. The two superb screens to the upper logge are the work of Raverti, who refined considerably the design of the tracery of the Palazzo Ducale, setting a new standard for the last Gothic palaces, several of which are directly inspired by his example. Raverti also carved the richly ostentatious land gate and the refined (although highly traditional) courtyard staircase. The Bon workshop, on the other hand, carved almost all of the rest of the facade, including the distinctive crenellation (derived from Byzantine examples via the Palazzo Ducale), and the intricately detailed smaller windows, with their delicate pendant tracery, a difficult form rarely seen in Venice. Once complete, the remaining surfaces of the facade were clad with marble, yet another gesture of unparalleled extravagance, since no other private palace in the city, as far as we know, was entirely finished in such a manner. The final touches to this opulent screen were given by the decoration, by the gilding, the ultramarine and other colours, a truly regal gesture and one which was only matched a decade later when the same Bartolomeo Bon carved the Porta della Carta, the new state entrance to the Palazzo Ducale.

Contarini's 'House of Gold' was followed by many other very fine palaces, although no other patrician attempted to emulate his extravagant facade. Palazzo Bernardo, on the Grand Canal at San Polo, is one of the most imposing of them, probably built in the 1430s, and an example of a 'double palace', with two superimposed apartments, each with their own water gate on to the Grand Canal. The facade epitomizes the style today known as *gotico fiorito*, or florid Gothic, its fine upper windows modelled on Bon's at the Cà d'Oro. Florid Gothic is characterized by tall windows surmounted by a prominent stylized flower or *fiore*, and by the surrounding of the windows by a narrow rectangular outer frame of stone, in the upper part of which are often incorporated decorative discs of fine marble; these last features represent the survival of an ancient Venetian-Byzantine tradition, now highly rationalized and formalized. Balconies, too, were widespread, often supported on lion's head corbels, while the facade as a whole was also framed with stone, with a cornice-gutter along the top and miniature columns down the outer corners.

The group at Cà Foscari is the most imposing of these late florid Gothic palaces, partly for their sheer size and highly prominent site; partly for the massing and rhythmical order of their three contiguous facades. Cà Foscari itself has one of the noblest, most highly-disciplined of all medieval facades, and was begun by Doge Francesco Foscari in about 1452, although only completed after

CASA GOLDONI (PALAZZO CENTANI) COURTYARD

The typical 15th century courtyard is very restricted in size, but retains its well-head and open stair.

CÀ FOSCARI: DETAIL OF THE FACADE (right)

The largest and most rigorously disciplined of all medieval facades, it was completed after Doge Foscari's death, in the later 1450s.

his fall from grace and ignominious death five years later. The palace dominates the *volta dil Canal*, the great bend in the Grand Canal, and even Francesco Sansovino, that forthright apologist for the Renaissance new order, conceded its continuing importance 130 years later. The detailing of both Cà Foscari and the two adjacent Giustiniani houses is very similar and consistent, their window design derived from that at the Ca d'Oro; Foscari's palace also has one or two small Renaissance touches already discernible in the bas-relief screen, notably the *putti* who hold the Foscari family arms.[11]

Several later palaces also exhibit this new sense of order, symmetry and discipline, together with further variants of the all-important tracery to the windows of the great hall. Palazzo Loredan degli Ambasciatori (after 1450) has much in common with Palazzo Contarini degli Scrigni, for example, both of their dignified facades with an elaborate piano nobile, centred on a four-light window with quatrefoils, again based on the tracery of the Palazzo Ducale.

Three final examples form a coherent group with features in common: the Giovanelli, Cavalli-Franchetti and Pisani-Moretta houses, all built between 1450 and about 1470. Like so many of these palaces, neither the precise dates of their construction nor their builders are known, but the three share some remarkable tracery to the piano nobile windows, of which that of Palazzo Giovanelli is the most impressive, despite the fact that it stands not on the Grand Canal but on a minor *rio*, and despite its heavy later restoration. Palazzo Cavalli, too, was 'restored' by Baron Franchetti at the end of the nineteenth century, but still retains a serene harmony rarely achieved even in these mature, refined late Gothic houses. Collectively, though, they epitomize the sophisticated variations on a stylistic theme that are so characteristic of the era, almost fugue-like in their harmonic order and patterned rhythms.

In many cases, however, it was not possible to achieve these heights of symmetry, for a number of different reasons. Often funds did not permit a completely new start, and the nobleman had to re-use earlier foundations (which were extremely expensive to replace), or incorporate elements of an earlier asymmetrical structure. It is significant that Doge Foscari did indeed raze all of the earlier structures on his site to the ground before he began building his own symmetrical, grandiose palace. In strong contrast is the vast, rambling but imposing Palazzo Pesaro at San Beneto (*c*1470), the largest medieval palace in the city, covering an entire city block, with one facade onto the parish square and the other on to a narrow canal. The two facades are connected by a great hall no less than 45 metres (150 feet) long, but the palace's plan is complex, ranged around two internal courtyards, and this complexity is reflected in its rich but quirkily asymmetrical facades. As Arslan remarked, here we are a long way from the stylistic rigours of houses such as the Cavalli or Giovanelli, and Palazzo Pesaro is florid in every sense. Its ownership was equally eventful; it became a theatre in the sixteenth century, and a concert hall in the eighteenth; in the nineteenth century it was bought by Mario Fortuny, photographer, inventor, painter and creator of exotic fabrics and textiles, and whose memorial museum it has now become.[12]

Yet other great Gothic palaces remain unique as a result of exigencies of their sites; the fine Palazzo Soranzo (later Van Axel) has a most unusual form on a highly irregular site at the junction of two narrow canals. It was built in 1473–9, with two courtyards each with an open stair; the whole design is a triumph of ingenuity, with an upper-floor hall in the form of an 'L', with one arm facing each of the two canals.

Other palaces are rendered unique in still other ways. Palazzo Bembo at Rialto, from 1460, has a most unusual form, being effectively two houses fused into one, with two parallel halls lit by two groups of adjacent multi-light windows. Again, it was built for two branches of the same clan, one of which was later headed by Petro Bembo, the classical scholar and intellectual who was elected a cardinal in 1539. Bembo was the patron of Aldo Manuzio, the publisher, whose workshop and

PALAZZETTO CONTARINI FASAN (above)

Facade to the Grand Canal; the exquisite detailing to the balconies is a masterpiece of late quattrocento carving.

PALAZZO VENIER CONTARINI AT SANTA MARIA DEL GIGLIO (right)

Smaller than the greatest medieval palaces, it nevertheless retains a serene order and perfect symmetry.

CÀ BERNARDO (left)

The two water-gates indicate that the house contained two separate apartments on the upper floors.

PALAZZO GIOVANELLI: FACADE TO RIO DI NOALE (above)

Although heavily restored in the 19th century, the house retains its noble proportions and unusual window-tracery.

PALAZZO CORNER CONTARINI DEI
CAVALLI (left)

Built in 1445, it takes its name from the
two relief sculptures on the facade. Next to
it is the tiny Palazzetto Tron, also of the
15th century.

THE LAND-GATE TO PALAZZO SORANZO
VAN AXEL (above)

Contains the only surviving timber
medieval door in the city, probably carved
in the 1460s.

publishing house was at nearby San Paternian; Bembo's fine palace became an important focus of Venetian Renaissance culture.[13]

Wherever possible, though, the principles of balance, harmony and symmetry were imposed on these many dozens of new palaces. Even those of 'secondary' rank, such as the refined Palazzo Venier-Contarini at San Moisè, evince this disciplined harmony, despite its much more modest scale. It may be instructively compared with its neighbour, the tiny Palazzetto Contarini-Fasan, which stands at the very opposite end of the scale from the great houses of Francesco Foscari and Marin Contarini. The palazzetto is barely one third the size of a more typical fifteenth-century palace, but it directly reflects the riches and the sensibilities of the era in its exquisitely carved balconies, masterpieces of elegance and refinement of carving.

Although few such houses can be dated with accuracy, the period of their construction begins with the Cà d'Oro of the 1420s, and effectively ends with houses such as the Soranzo and the Giustinian house at San Moisè, another rare documented example, constructed in 1474. This extraordinary proliferation of great medieval houses forms part of a complex, extended architectural family, collectively reflecting the Venetian patriciate itself in this era of great wealth and stability. These houses, though, remained *fonteghi* as well as palaces, that is, they were still hubs of commerce as well as noble residences, their ground-floor halls crowded with goods unloaded from the ships moored outside, and their secure stores crammed with a great variety of goods from bolts of silk to sacks of pepper. Although wealthier than most, Marin Contarini was typical of many in his extensive trading interests; the contents of the Cà d'Oro's stores, full of luxury fabrics and spices, were equally typical of a hundred other palaces.[14]

This era of florid Gothic marks the last phase of this truly indigenous style, painstakingly evolved over four centuries or more. The century culminated in the artistic achievements of Giovanni Bellini and his contemporaries, but it was also, of course, the era of the Renaissance. No longer a cultural island with its own architectural language, Venice embraced but adapted these new philosophies to make the Venetian Renaissance palace once again a contribution uniquely appropriate to the glittering waters of the lagoon.

The early Renaissance: Mauro Codussi's contribution

With the remarkable exception of the work of Mauro Codussi, the early application of Renaissance principles to the design of the Venetian palace is, like that in ecclesiastical architecture, a rather fragmented, hesitant story; many great clans, after all, had only recently built fine new houses as the family headquarters in the florid Gothic style. One of the earliest, and potentially the most magnificent of all Renaissance palaces was begun by Bartolomeo Bon for Andrea Corner in *c*1453; the site was then bought by Francesco Sforza, Duke of Milan, for his Venetian home, and it is probable that the evocative fragment that remains today – a few courses of great rusticated stone blocks and a massive but truncated corner column – is the work of Sforza's 'go between' Benedetto Ferrini, influenced perhaps by Antonio Averlino (Filarete), and even by Bon himself. Relations between Sforza and his host city thereafter deteriorated so badly that the Republic confiscated the site and the project was abandoned; the fragment is still known as the Cà del Duca.[15]

Several houses bridged the rather uneasy gap between the two styles, some more Gothic than Renaissance, others in which the new style is clearly easing away the old. There remain a few simple, early Renaissance buildings of unknown authorship, such as the elegant Capitaneria del Porto (begun 1492), and a few unorthodox houses that are effectively *sui generis*, such as the famous Cà Dario and Palazzetto Gussoni.

Both have often been attributed to Pietro Lombardo, chiefly for their marble cladding and rich, small-scale relief decoration. Cà Dario is truly unique; built by Giovanni Dario in around 1487,

VETTOR CARPACCIO, *The Leavetaking of the Betrothed Pair*, from the St Ursula cycle, 1495 (above)

On the right is a group of new Renaissance palaces, veneered in marble in the style of Pietro Lombardo. (Gallerie dell' Accademia, Venice.)

VETTOR CARPACCIO, *Departure of the Ambassadors* c.1496–8

Again from the St Ursula cycle, it displays the Venetians' love of rich, sumptuous colours and textures. The wall finishes are reminiscent of Lombardo's work at the Miracoli church, then newly-completed. (Gallerie dell' Accademia, Venice.)

VETTOR CARPACCIO, *St Augustine in his study*, c.1502 (far left)

A typically fairly sparsely furnished late medieval interior, although the niche at the rear is a 'new' Renaissance element. (Gallerie dell' Accademia, Venice.)

like the Cà d'Oro it seems to be a direct reflection of the colourful character of its builder, one time Venetian consul in Constantinople, with its wilful surface decoration of marble, its pronounced asymmetry and its picturesque (although not original) chimneys. It does have features in common with Lombardo's Miracoli church, and with the exotic creations in Vittore Carpaccio's paintings, a rather fanciful Venetian image of the rich, mysterious Orient. But Cà Dario finds no niche in the mainstream development of the Venetian Renaissance palace, and remains a delightful special case. Palazzetto Gussoni, smaller and less well-known, stands on a narrow canal at San Lio, but is equally asymmetrical, its Istrian stone stone surfaces richly carved with bas-reliefs. The lopsided facade is again reminiscent of Lombardo, but seems more arbitrary and undisciplined than his attributed works are.[16]

As with the Venetian church, Renaissance palace design often incorporated elements of the new rubbing shoulders with the traditional; Palazzo Contarini del Bovolo, for example, is a typical late Gothic house, but was augmented in 1499 with its unique helical stairs, rising in the rear courtyard. (*Bovolo* is the Venetian word for a snail.) The stair rises through five levels and is connected to the body of the house by a small wing containing five superimposed logge, all in brick and stone. It was built by Giovanni Candio, a builder sometimes engaged at the Scuola Grande di San Marco, and exhibits the enthusiastic skills of a master builder rather than those of a trained architect. Although the architectural language is that of the early Renaissance, the scale is rather awkward and the junctions between the component elements not all fully resolved. That a more coherent development of the lighter, more decorative Lombardo style did indeed develop becomes apparent a little later, but these first tentative examples represent the adolescence of the Renaissance palazzo. It was Mauro Codussi who perfected the new style as a means of clothing the palace.

Codussi's seminal contribution towards the development of a refined classical church architecture, with its subtle spatial hierarchies, has already been attested. His contribution to the evolution of the Venetian palace was equally important, although in this case he reinterpreted a long-established typology. Although documentary sources are few, three houses are today accepted as his work: Palazzo Zorzi at San Severo, Palazzo Lando-Corner Spinelli and the impressive Palazzo Loredan, later Vendramin-Calergi. None can be precisely dated, although the first two predate the last by some years. All are characterized by highly inventive facades entirely of Istrian stone, in a city where stone was still traditionally confined to the detailing of windows, portals and other elements, but rarely to an entire facade.

CÀ DARIO: FACADE TO THE GRAND CANAL (below, left)

The rich eclectic facade derives from Pietro Lombardo, although the architect is unknown. It dates from c.1487.

MAURO CODUSSI: PALAZZO LANDO CORNER SPINELLI (below)

The house incorporated some revolutionary features, including rustication to the ground floor and the large paired lights to the piani nobili.

Palazzo Zorzi is most unusual in its plan, and probably dates from the 1470s or 1480s. The form is L-shaped, following the shape of the site, and with an exceptionally long facade to the Rio di San Severo. Codussi's design was ingenious, with a spacious inner courtyard flanked on one side by a refined colonnade of classical arches with inventive Corinthian capitals. The facade has a complex rhythm, with an extremely long central balcony to the nine-light window of the great hall. Codussi's architectural vocabulary is restrained but fully developed, the strong horizontal emphasis further accentuated by cornices and string courses.[17]

His other two palaces have more conventional plans, but their facades are more highly creative, significant developments from the local tradition. Palazzo Corner-Spinelli was built for Pietro Lando (cousin of the Pietro who was elected doge in 1539), passing to Zane Corner in 1542 and to the Spinelli in 1740. It was probably built in the 1480s, and the facade remains intact, although the interior was remodelled for the Corner by Michele Sanmicheli.

PALAZZO CONTARINI DEL BOVOLO: STAIRCASE

The unique stair is attached to a Gothic palace, and is in a still tentative early Renaissance style.

The facade is almost precisely square, the tall ground storey and the mezzanine both clad with the flat rustication that Codussi had first used at San Michele, and still almost unknown in the city. This lower facade, with its unusual contrapuntal arrangement of windows, is framed by classical pilasters, typically Codussian in themselves, but the first time that such a detail had replaced the narrow, traditional Gothic colonnettes. The two upper storeys, both treated almost identically as piani nobili, are divided into three bays, but the result is not the traditional equal tripartite pattern, since the two side wings each have a single large window, while the great hall is emphasized by a pair of such lights. The form of these windows, with two round-arched lights within a larger semicircular arch, and with a circular light or 'eye' above them, is a uniquely Codussian arrangement, and was to become almost a trademark of his work; they can also be seen at San Zaccaria, and were last used, in his most self-assured manner, at Palazzo Loredan.

The facade of Palazzo Corner-Spinelli is also enlivened by inset discs of marble (porphyry and verde antico), reflecting the continuation of this strong Venetian-Byzantine decorative tradition into the new style, although they are now incorporated in a more disciplined, rigorous manner. The house is traditional in its plan, but it was probably the first Venetian palace in which the staircase is brought inside the body of the house instead of rising in the courtyard, a reflection of the increasing importance of convenience, and even luxury, in the evolution of palace design. It was located on one side of the great hall, the most usual location for the stair in palaces thereafter.[18]

Palazzo Vendramin-Calergi, formerly Loredan, is Codussi's third, last and most monumental Venetian palace. It was built for Andrea Loredan, who had known Codussi since his work at San Michele in the 1470s, where Loredan had paid for the building of the church's chancel. He was an enlightened patron of the arts, and after his assassination at Creazzo in 1513, was buried in San Michele. The great facade of the palace at San Marcuola marks a notable development from the

Corner-Spinelli house, and has attracted the highest praise ever since its completion for its monumental size and grandeur. Francesco Sansovino cited the house as one of the four most important in Venice, 'a very noble work … the front all sheathed in Greek marble, with great windows colonnaded in the Corinthian style'.

Little is known of its construction, and it had not yet been begun in 1500; Codussi himself died in 1504, and so it was almost certainly completed by others, perhaps by his son Domenico. It was completed by the time of the Cambrai crisis of 1509, though, and perhaps a little earlier; the diarist Girolamo Priuli, writing in that year, called the palace, 'a very honourable and worthy house … with a facade which is the most beautiful to be found in Venice at this time'.

The palace remained in Loredan ownership until 1566; after Andrea's death it was rented for a time, and then bought by the Calergi at auction in 1589 for 36,000 ducats. Vettor Calergi's daughter married into the Grimani clan and in 1614 Vincenzo Scamozzi added a new wing at the side, rebuilt again in 1660. In 1739 the house passed to the Vendramin, wealthy patrons of the arts, and then to the Duchesse de Berry, who remodelled most of the interior in extravagant nineteenth-century taste. Richard Wagner lived in the house, and died there in 1883.[19]

The plan is unusual in that it reverted to the ancient Byzantine 'T' shape, with a broad loggia onto the canal and a narrower great hall behind it, although in other respects the palace was fairly traditional. But the magnificent facade remains the house's most outstanding feature. Of truly Roman grandeur and self-confidence, it has three extremely spacious storeys (with no mezzanines), each one defined by a powerful horizontal: a balcony to the first floor, a large entablature to the

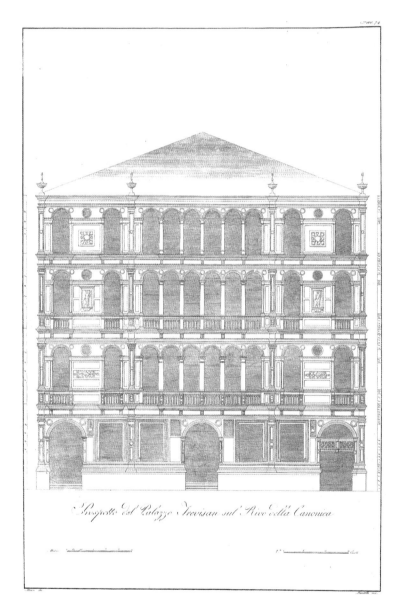

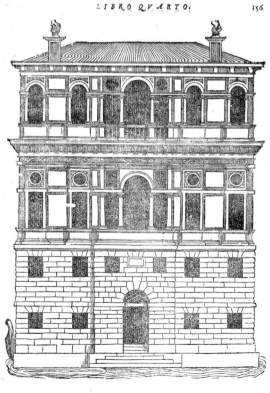

**PALAZZO TREVISAN IN CANONICA:
FACADE (above)**

A very rich early Renaissance facade, with an
unusual arrangement of three superimposed
piani nobili.

**SEBASTIANO SERLIO: proposals for palace
facades in Venice from *The Five Books of
Architecture*, 1537 (above right and right)**

Serlio acknowledges the tripartite Venetian
tradition of facade design, but also advocates
non-Venetian features such as rustication
and a great central window, the 'Serliana'.

**MAURO CODUSSI: PALAZZO LOREDAN
(far right)**

Monumental and imposing, the facade was
probably completed just after Codussi's
death in 1504. The great paired windows
derive from Palazzo Lando, but the scale
here is far nobler and self-confident.

second, and a massive cornice to the roof, the last strongly reminiscent of Alberti's designs, and in particular of Palazzo Rucellai in Florence. A cornice of such imposing classical dimensions had never been seen in Venice before, but was a natural progression from Codussi's powerful forms at San Zaccaria, and was to influence both Jacopo Sansovino and Michele Sanmicheli. The other dominant features of this great screen are the large, confident, rhythmic Codussian windows, now fully matured, and with five bays on each storey, the central three grouped together to light the loggia and the outer ones defining the corner rooms. The entire composition is grandiose and richly modelled, the only slightly weaker element being the first-floor balcony, which was perhaps added by another; it has a delicacy rather at odds with the nobility of the remainder. Codussi's inventive Corinthian order is applied throughout, with the piano nobile given further emphasis by the fluted columns. The powerful classical form probably owes much to the intellectual rigour of Codussi's patron, but in Codussi he found a master more than able to meet the challenge, and despite the motto of the Loredan clan, 'Non nobis, Domine', which is inscribed on the facade, it remains one of the noblest palaces in the city.

Mauro Codussi's legacy and Pietro Lombardo

In the period from 1480 to the 1520s or 1530s, the two fundamental influences on Venetian architecture were those of Codussi on the one hand, with his strong, refined, clearly articulated classical forms, and on the other the much lighter, more decorative work of Pietro Lombardo; the latter's approach was continued to some extent by his own son, Tullio, while the work of Guglielmo de'Grigi has much of the same quality. Giovanni Buora's style is less easy to identify, although he was a sculptor of skill and originality. The known work of Antonio Scarpagnino, inventive though it sometimes is, also owes much to Codussi, although in his busy capacity as government proto Scarpagnino had little time for private palace commissions; none have been confirmed by documentation. During this rather extended lacuna, before the emergence of the mature, monumental Renaissance, a number of palaces were built, most unattributable with certainty, and often exhibiting a mixture of influences. Several, though, were rather more of the Lombardo 'school' than that of Codussi.

One is Palazzo Cappello or Trevisan 'in Canonica', so called because it was built on land owned by the canons of San Marco. Built by the Trevisan, it was strongly influenced by Lombardo, if not in fact by his hand. In the 1490s, when the house was being built, Lombardo was working just across the canal at the Palazzo Ducale, and the decorative inlays of marble and surface decoration are typical of his work. Certainly it is too intricate to be the work of Codussi, with its very extensive glazing, its six-light central windows, and its four storeys of almost equal height. Francesco Sansovino regarded the house highly, noting that it was, 'all encrusted with the finest marbles, magnificently and beautifully formed'; comprehensive cleaning would undoubtedly reveal much fine detail at present undiscernible.[20]

Two palaces owned by the numerous Contarini clan again display a similar lightness of style, although differing somewhat in their degree of indebtedness to Lombardo and to Codussi. Palazzo Contarini dal Zaffo is probably from the 1490s, and has been attributed to both masters, as well as to Pietro Lombardo's son Tullio. Elegant and well proportioned, its facade contains Lombardesque influences in the decorative paterae, but also reveals a stronger, more Codussian discipline in its architectural form. The other Contarini house, known as that 'delle Figure', for the caryatids that support the balcony, is a little later; begun in 1504, the year of Codussi's death, its cartouches recall Palazzo Loredan, and is sometimes attributed to Scarpagnino. In the 1570s the palace was owned by the Procurator Jacopo Contarini, patron of Andrea Palladio, who stayed in the house during his many visits to Venice.[21]

Two or three further significant houses are derived from both Codussi and the Lombardo school, taking their proportions and self-assured architectural vocabulary from the former, while their fine decorative detailing is reminiscent of the latter. One is the small but beautifully proportioned Grimani house at San Polo, an exceptional example of the poise and refined detailing of the best of these houses; entirely traditional in its composition, with a balanced three-part facade, it again incorporates the familiar marble inlays within its sparing classical framework.

Rather more substantial is the Bembo house (later Malipiero and Trevisan) at Santa Maria Formosa, which is more strongly modelled, with substantial balconies and prominent arches to the main windows. It is often atributed to Sante Lombardo, son of Tullio, but if this is the case it must have been a very youthful work since Sante was barely an adult when it was built in the 1520s. Nearby, the imposing Palazzo Grimani, a grandiose but most unusually planned house, once housed the priceless art collection of Cardinal Giovanni Grimani, patriarch of Venice. Built very early in the sixteenth century, it was extended in 1540, and this later phase is attributed to Sanmicheli, chiefly on the basis of the strongly rusticated portals to both the land and water gates.[22]

These palaces can all be read as a series of exercises in the transformation of the Venetian palace into the new stylistic language, but which retained both the traditional plan and the overall arrangement of fenestration of the traditional Gothic models.

By the 1520s, the influence of Pietro Lombardo had largely evaporated, and even that of Codussi was now beginning to wane; there were already newer forces at work to determine the direction of palace design in the city. Although Codussi's work had proposed a future line of development, two figures, who arrived in Venice in the same year, 1527, took the process an important stage further. Both came as a direct result of the disaster of the Sack of Rome by the Imperial army; the first was Sebastiano Serlio, author of a highly-influential treatise on architecture, the first part of which was published in Venice in 1537. The other was Jacopo Sansovino, who made Venice his home for the rest of his life, and many of whose contributions to the city's urban development over half a century have already been discussed.[23]

Serlio, a friend and contemporary of both Titian and the writer Aretino, influenced not only Sansovino; many of his ideas were also taken up and developed by Palladio in his own treatise, published in 1570. Serlio's proposals for palace facades 'for a marshy site' and 'in the Venetians' manner' have many echoes in the work of Sansovino, Sanmicheli, their contemporaries and successors. Two proposals illustrated in Serlio's 'Fourth Book' specifically recommend the rusticated lower storeys already introduced into Venice by Codussi, while developing further the great central window in the form later to be identified as a 'Serliana'. This was a tripartite window consisting of a larger central light with an arched head, flanked by two smaller lights, each with square heads. The more complex version developed in Venice also incorporated small square lights above the side windows, but in its simpler three-part form the window became known in the English-speaking world as a 'Palladian' window, chiefly as a result of the enormous influence of his own writings.

The period from the 1520s to the publication of Palladio's *I quattro libri dell'architettura* (The Four Books of Architecture) in 1570 saw important developments in the way in which the Venetian nobility both regarded and used their city palaces. Many patrician clans had bought Terraferma estates after the Venetian annexation of the Padovano, Vicentino and Veronese during the fifteenth century; by the end of the century many of these estates were well established and were often of considerable extent. Great wealth now derived from the land, and the Terraferma estate was accompanied by the rise and refinement of the country villa, partly for the pleasures of the *villeggiatura*, the annual escape from the city in summer to the cooler countryside, but also as bases from which to administer these estates.[24]

At least some of the city palaces, therefore, slowly became less important as trading warehouses, but in all cases, including those palaces that remained commercial hubs, their comfort and

PALAZZO CONTARINI DAL ZAFFO (above)

The palace, with characteristic inlays of marble, derives from both Codussi and Lombardo, and has been attributed to Giovanni Buora, c.1500–1510.

PALAZZO CONTARINI DELLE FIGURE
(left, above)

It was comprehensively modernized in 1545; Palladio stayed here when in Venice, although its architect is unknown.

PALAZZO CONTARINI AT SAN BENEDETTO:
FACADE (left, below)

Probably completed in the 1560s, and attributed to Sante Lombardo, the facade incorporates a large 'Serliana'.

decoration were regarded as ever higher priorities. The precedent of the fine, richly-carved facade, all of stone, had been established by Codussi in the 1480s and 1490s; by the middle decades of the sixteenth century, stone facades were virtually a prerequisite of any large new house, even though there were still few who could afford the huge cost of a facade such as that for Andrea Loredan.

Staircases were now always located within the house for greater convenience, while the courtyard and the ground floor hall, the androne, became more imposing and more 'Roman', setting the scene for the sumptuous banquets and other delights and entertainments in the great hall on the first floor.

Nevertheless, there remained (in theory) practical limits to the internal decoration of the Renaissance palace. The Republic had passed a sumptuary law in 1476 that, among other clauses, restricted the use of rich wall hangings and bed curtains (of silk, brocade and satin), limiting them to more modest fabrics, such as taffeta and ormesin, although contemporary paintings suggest that it was frequently ignored. There were many later regulations, particularly in 1530, 1562 and 1644, which controlled numerous aspects of the domestic interior, but it remains difficult to estimate their effectiveness; then, as now, fashions constantly changed. Many Renaissance interiors remained fairly simply furnished, in principle not dissimilar to their gothic predecessors, and it must have only been the exceptionally wealthy to whose lavish tastes the sumptuary laws were specifically addressed. However, after the later sixteenth century, the popularity among the very wealthy of interior fresco decoration reflects not only a strong local and regional tradition, but was also perhaps one way of enriching the wall surface without attracting too much attention from the Provedadori sora le Pompe, the sumptuary magistrates.

PALAZZO GRIMANI ON THE GRAND CANAL NEAR SAN POLO (above, left)

The detailing of the palace, c.1510, is in a highly refined Renaissance style but the pattern of fenestration remains entirely traditional.

PALAZZO DOLFIN MANIN AT RIALTO (above)

The first of Jacopo Sansovino's three Venetian palaces, begun in 1538, it is the simplest and most 'Roman' in style.

Jacopo Sansovino and Michele Sanmicheli

Jacopo Sansovino's son Francesco provides an insight into what were considered the most important features of a noble palace in the sixteenth century:

… the window openings are regularly arranged, and the doors likewise, in such a way that every opening is in proportion; and besides being offered a beautiful view, the eye is free to range unimpeded and the rooms are light and full of sunshine … all the windows are covered not with waxed cloth or paper, but with fine white glass mounted in wooden frames … not only in palaces and houses but in all places, however humble, to the amazement of foreigners… In composing the structure, the windows of the great hall are placed in the centre of the facade so that all can clearly see the location of the hall.[25]

The contribution of Jacopo Sansovino to the development of the Venetian palace consisted, like that of Codussi, of three substantial works. The first was a house built for the merchant Zuane Dolfin, who had a notable diplomatic career culminating in the post of Governor of Verona. Zuane inherited a house on the Riva del Carbon, opposite the Rialto, but on an awkward site just across a canal from the imposing Gothic Palazzo Bembo. In 1538 permission was obtained for its reconstruction, although a colonnade had to be built to maintain the important public right of way along the quay. Dolfin later acquired the site next door so the new palace was built in stages; he died in 1547, the new house not yet complete, and work was concluded by his sons. According to Giorgio Vasari, in his *Lives of the Artists* (1550), the house cost 30,000 ducats to build, a considerable sum. The facade block that we see today is the only original part surviving, however, since the remainder was remodelled by Ludovico Manin, the last doge, in the 1790s. This facade, though, is highly distinctive, restrained and disciplined, one of the most literal, severe Roman works in Venice. The ground-floor colonnade, with its six equal bays, has bold Doric arches covering a generous quay for goods to be unloaded into the six long, narrow warehouses that occupied the ground floor. The two upper storeys, though, respect the Venetian tradition, with a four-light window in the centre, flanked by pairs of single windows. Sansovino equally respected the classic precepts of Vitruvius in his use of the orders: Doric below, Ionic to the first floor and then Corinthian above. Despite the strong contrasts in style and materials, the overall volume relates sympathetically to the Bembo house, and its bold, clear modelling is reflected by the waters of the Grand Canal.[26]

PALAZZO TREVISAN AT MURANO

Sometimes attributed to Palladio, and dating from 1555–8, its rather severe facade was originally adorned with frescos, and the interior was decorated by Veronese.

Sansovino's second Venetian palace was built for the ancient Corner family, whose requirements were a little different. In 1527 Procurator Zorzi Corner had died, leaving a considerable fortune as well as extensive estates in Cyprus. (He was the brother of Caterina, Queen of Cyprus.) He left four sons and a house at San Maurizio, reputedly one of the finest in the city, together with some adjacent cottages and a boatyard. But the palace was destroyed by a disastrous fire on 16 August 1532; by a dreadful turn of fate, the family's other palace, at San Polo, also burned down three years later. Although very wealthy, the four brothers took the unprecedented step of petitioning Doge Andrea Gritti directly for aid, and half of Caterina's considerable dowry of 61,000 ducats, which had been left to the Republic, was redirected towards the rebuilding of the two palaces.

Sansovino was commissioned in 1537 to design the new house on the Grand Canal at San Maurizio, which was to become known as the Palazzo Corner della Cà Grande, although it was probably only begun in 1545, after Zorzi's complex estate had finally been resolved. By an instructive contrast, the rebuilt house at San Polo was to be the work of Sanmicheli, and was also begun in 1545; it was complete by around 1560, when it was described by Vasari as 'magnificent and very richly decorated'. Sansovino's palace at San Maurizio was probably completed just after 1581, and although there appears to be no basis for the theory that the top floor was designed by Vincenzo Scamozzi, he may have supervised its completion after Sansovino's death in 1570.[27]

Comparison between the two contemporaneous houses is valuable. Both are extremely large, although their sites are quite different; while Sansovino's is very prominent, that of Sanmicheli faces the narrow Rio di San Polo, with one corner looming over the parish square at the back. Sansovino's massive, powerful design has been regarded by some as his masterpiece; in Vasari's view, it, 'surpasses all the others in majesty, grandeur and convenience: nay, it is reputed to be, perhaps, the most splendid residence in Italy', with its three Doric, Ionic and Corinthian orders superimposed. The palace retains a generous ground floor to accommodate the family's extensive trading interests, and the imposing facade is divided by virtually continuous balconies, rather like that at Palazzo Loredan. The powerfully rusticated ground floor recalls Serlio's precepts, while in contrast the two upper storeys, each with seven bays, are divided by paired columns reminiscent of Bramante's House of Raphael in Rome (also known as Palazzo Caprini, begun in c1510, demolished 1661), with which Sansovino was almost certainly familiar. Unlike the traditional Venetian facade, though, the whole is designed as a great screen; with the exception of the three portals there is little central emphasis, and on the upper levels Sansovino established a rich, regular bay-rhythm comparable to that at the Biblioteca Marciana. The monumental structure contains numerous classical allusions and details, again evidence of Sansovino's Roman studies, while also reflecting the Corner family's claim to have descended from Roman nobility themselves. The

JACOPO SANSOVINO: PALAZZO CORNER
DELLA CÀ GRANDE

Facade to the Grande Canal, and elevation.
The imposing facade, begun 1545, has
features in common with the Biblioteca
Marciana, notably the piano nobile windows
but the massive rustication is less typical
of his work.

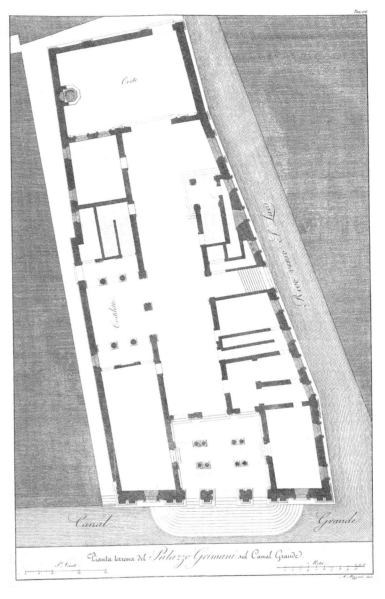

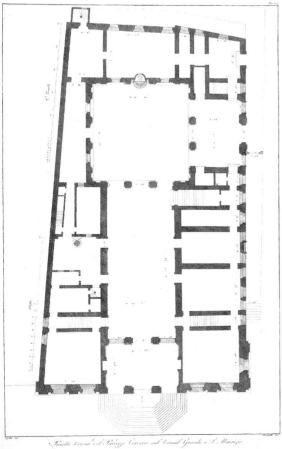

PALAZZO GRIMANI AT SAN LUCA

The imposing facade, with three great
orders, is an essay on the theme of the
triumphal arch by Michele Sanmicheli,
begun in 1556.

COMPARATIVE PLANS

Sansovino's Palazzo Corner (left) and
Sanmicheli's Palazzo Grimani (above) are
both broadly axial, although Sanmicheli had
to resolve a very difficult site with
a trapezoidal loggia, and an off-centre
portego.

formally axial plan again reflects Serlio's influence, with the fine square courtyard placed on axis at the end of the spacious entrance hall; neo-Roman in its ordered, regular severity, it recalls the courtyard at Sansovino's new Mint at San Marco.

Sanmicheli's palace at San Polo, also extremely tall, by contrast was not clad with stone since such extravagance would have been wasted on such an inconspicuous site. Its extreme height derived from the fact that a further piano nobile was built above the first one, for leasing to another family. The facade's great height is broken down by rather complex fenestration, yet again owing a good deal to Serlio, with ground-floor rustication and prominent Serlian windows to the upper great halls.[28] These were the largest new palaces in Venice since Codussi's for the Loredan, and they re-established the scale and monumentality of the houses of the wealthiest patricians.

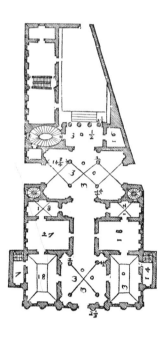

Sanmicheli's own Venetian masterpiece is the slightly later Grimani Palace, begun in 1556, and comparable in its strength and vigour with Sansovino's for the Corner. It was built for the Procurator Girolamo Grimani (father of Marin, who became doge in 1595), and at 'incredible expense', according to Vasari; the house was to remain in Grimani hands until 1806, after the fall of the Republic. The imposing facade once again had three orders, although the uppermost storey was continued by GianGiacomo de'Grigi after Sanmicheli's death in 1559; it was itself only completed in 1575, after de'Grigi's own death. Cà Grimani, like the Corner palace, was regarded by Francesco Sansovino as one of the four finest in the city: it was 'extremely rich in execution … there are also magnificent colonnades around the courtyard and the facade is abundant with exquisite richness, both in its component parts and in its workmanship, the work of Michele di San Michele …' The plan is equally impressive, its axial progression of spaces reminiscent of Palladio's design for a canal-side site in the *Quattro libri*.[29]

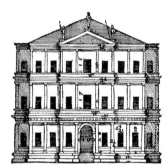

FECI

The two facades of Sansovino's Corner palace and that of Sanmicheli for the Grimani, while both massive and impressive, differ considerably in character. Sansovino's stands on a strongly rusticated base, its already rather Mannerist side windows hinting at the imminent emergence of the Baroque. The three central portals echo much of the work of Sanmicheli, while also evoking triumphal connotations, as was doubtlessly intended. The scale of Sanmicheli's facade is different, with fewer and larger bays, and with massive cornices dividing the three orders, recalling Codussi's superb facade at the Loredan house. More clearly than Sansovino's, the facade can be read as an essay on the theme of the classical triumphal arch; the two tall principal storeys, with their central Serlian windows, again stand above a tall base, which is not rusticated (as is so much of Sanmicheli's work) but instead is enriched with strong fluted Corinthian pilasters. Sanmicheli's allusion to the Venetian tripartite form is fairly subtle, with paired columns defining the central bay, and by his treatment of the entrance portal which is more clearly a triumphal arch than that of Sansovino.

Both imposing works make full use of the strong chiaroscuro resulting from the clear lagoon light and the effect of reflections in the waters. In their rather different ways they further enhanced the image of Venice as the new Rome, not only in the architectural vocabulary but in the influence that these powerful images had on their contemporaries: these were palaces to match those of the dynasts of ancient Rome, noble, rich, powerful, dignified, centres of political power but also of intellectual and aesthetic discourse.

Andrea Palladio, the Four Books and the villeggiatura

A further new influence arrived in Venice with the publication in 1570 of Palladio's *I quattro libri dell'architettura*. With time the *Four Books* were to become the most influential treatise since Vitruvius, their precepts later adopted with equal enthusiasm by Inigo Jones in England, by Claude Ledoux in France and by Thomas Jefferson across the Atlantic. Palladio's influence on Venetian palace design was less pronounced than his extraordinary importance in the development of villas and the facades of churches; indeed, there are no documented palaces in Venice, although one

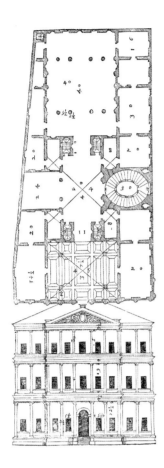

ANDREA PALLADIO

Proposals for palaces in Venice, from the
Quattro Libri of 1570 (Book 2, pp.71 & 72).
In both examples Palladio reconciles a formal,
axial plan with an acknowledgement of
the difficult shapes of many Venetian sites.
However, Palladio never built a palace
in the city.

proposal in the *Four Books* is specifically designed for 'a site in Venice', on the Grand Canal, it is safe to assume. It is particularly notable for its formal axial plan, a succession of spaces progressing from a square entrance vestibule on the canal towards a central atrium and a large rear courtyard.[30] Palladio also acknowledged the difficulties often encountered in Venice in building on awkward shaped sites, where an axial sequence was particularly difficult to arrange; two of his palace plans reflect this practical problem, and one bears a close resemblance to the wedge-shaped site that Sanmicheli had to develop for the Grimani.

This formal axial progression marks a notable feature of the sixteenth-century palace: Sansovino at Palazzo Corner, Sanmicheli at the Grimani house and Palladio (on paper) all attempted to develop spatial sequences that reconciled their own classicizing desires with the practical requirements of the Venetian merchant noblemen. To this end they all devised schemes that began with a spacious loggia onto the canal, followed by the traditional axial hall, the portego, which now opened at the far end (still on axis) into a square central courtyard containing the well, and at one side of which was a grand stair to the piano nobile. In this way local tradition was fused with classical symmetry.

Similar refined manipulations of space can be seen in the fine Palazzo Trevisan at Murano, tragically neglected today, but built in the 1550s perhaps after designs by Palladio, and originally decorated by Veronese. Here the entrance hall terminates in an unusual transverse hall with apsidal ends (reminiscent of Palladio's Palazzo Chiericati at Vicenza), beyond which a colonnaded loggia led on to one of the extensive gardens for which Murano was then so famous.[31] Later still, similar axial plans were to be developed on a grandiose scale by Baldassare Longhena and later again by Giorgio Massari at Palazzo Grassi. However, Palladio found no client in Venice itself who was willing to proceed and commission a palace from him; this loss can be at least partly ascribed to political and economic circumstances, particularly in the uncertain 1570s, with plague and the Turkish wars to deter investment. Palladio's palace proposals were grandiose, but although his plans were no more radical than those of Sansovino, his facades, essentially variations on the temple front theme, were rather more revolutionary. Although adopted with great critical success at San Giorgio Maggiore and the Redentore (and, of course, on many of his Terraferma villas), these temple fronts were never applied to a Venetian palace, even by his successors. Indeed, the Venetian patriciate developed an aversion to the large-scale domestic application of pedimented porticos, except for the individual treatment of doors and windows; this was probably a reaction from their association with public buildings, originally classical temples, now Christian churches. But equally entrenched was the ancient Venetian method of organizing their still almost universal tripartite facades, which had survived the transformation from Gothic to Renaissance, and remained by far the most widespread arrangement, even into the seventeenth century. The prominent tympanum of Palazzo Contarini delle Figure, for example, remains remarkable for its rarity, and Palladio's Venetian legacy is thus confined to his outstanding churches.

Two related typological developments in the sixteenth and early seventeenth century were closely connected with the process of refinement of the great Venetian palaces of this era. One was the development of the Terraferma estates and the evolution of the design of the villas from which they were administered, and the other was the short-lived but significant development of Murano and the Giudecca by the Venetian patriciate as places of short-term resort, to escape from the city centre. Most of the Giudecca waterfront was redeveloped in the middle decades of the sixteenth century, although very little evidence survives today. One fragment that remains is the once elegant Mocenigo house, probably designed by Francesco Contini (son of Tommaso), in the very early 1600s. The house has a broad, two-storey facade, and once had extensive gardens at the rear, running down to the open lagoon. Despite its proximity to San Marco it was a true villa (or perhaps more accurately still, a *casa di delizie*, a house of pleasurable resort), rather than a palazzo, with no commercial functions attached to it; in its present mutilated condition it remains a rare valuable survivor.[32]

A few similarly damaged villas also survive at Murano; the Trevisan house noted above remains quintessentially urban, despite its function. although others have more of the appearance of a villa, such as the two houses once built by the Soranzo family, the two substantial Contarini houses and particularly the Casino Mocenigo. This last was again a casa di delizie, even less substantial than the Giudecca villa, little more than a single-storey pavilion, with a suite of delightfully fresco-decorated rooms for entertainment and philosophical debate.[33]

With the development of the Terraferma villeggiatura on a much larger scale, though, the patrician interest in Murano and the Giudecca declined rapidly. The evolution of the country villa, though, was a slow process, albeit one that gathered great momentum in the later sixteenth century. Many of the earliest villas were simply converted castles or fortified manor houses, gradually 'civilized' with time and effort. The later ones, most notably those of Palladio, represent a fusion of the desire for the most refined context in which to conduct the villeggiatura together with many of the practical necessities for the running of a rural estate: stables, barns, dovecotes and other ancillaries. In the sense that they attempted to fuse the ultimate in urbane sophistication with more humdrum, bucolic matters, the villa replicated something of the traditional dual roles of the city palace, with the hub of courtly culture above and the essential facilities for international trade (or farming) below. Nevertheless, while the villa developed its own distinctive form and appearance, the city palaces of the Venetian nobility were to develop still further the social and cultural requirements of a class that remained an extraordinarily important and influential patron of all the arts: of architecture, painting and, especially in the seventeenth and eighteenth centuries, of music. The basic form and appearance of the palace, though, was such an essential element in the perceptions, indeed in the very existence of the patriciate, that its fundamental form was never seriously reappraised or radically altered. It had already served the nobility well for four or five centuries, and the slowly evolving architectural styles could all be accommodated within its 'shell' with no necessity for dramatic revision.

PAOLO VERONESE, *Portrait of Daniele Barbaro*, 1565

Daniele and his brother MarcAntonio were outstanding patrons of architecture in the later 16th century, employing both Palladio and Veronese to complete their villa at Maser. (Pitti, Florence.)

The early Baroque

As the Renaissance had emerged fragmented and piecemeal, so too did the Baroque evolve slowly, with a cartouche here, a small Mannerist broken pediment there. Several houses of the later sixteenth century display clear Baroque tendencies, and several architects also span this rather elusive transition from a mature, rational classicism to more fluid and imaginative forms.

GianGiacomo de'Grigi, the son of Guglielmo, bridges this divide, and his style owes a good deal to the lighter, Lombardesque touch of his father, although he was a contemporary of both Sansovino and Sanmicheli. His work is best seen at Palazzo Coccina-Tiepolo, built for the Coccina clan in about 1560. The family came from Bergamo, as did de'Grigi himself, although the house is still sometimes (with some justification) attributed to Alessandro Vittoria, and (with far less) to Palladio. The facade shows the strong influence of Serlio; following his dictum that facades should have 'generous fenestration', it has no less than three large, superimposed Serlian windows in the central bay, although hints of Palladio can be detected in the sidelights and of Sansovino in the oval attic windows. The elegant facade is capped by tall obelisks, a typical proto-Baroque feature, as are the bold relief panels on the first floor.

Similar detailing and equally prominent obelisks can be seen at the imposing Palazzo Balbi, on a prominent site on the Grand Canal opposite Cà Foscari. The house is a little later, built after 1582 for Nicolo Balbi, sometime Governor of Mestre, and is generally attributed to Vittoria, much better known as a sculptor. As Bassi has written, Palazzo Balbi for the first time, 'imposed on Venetian culture the pomp of a new century – the *seicento*, the century of the Baroque'. Most

PALAZZO BALBI (left)

Facade to the Grand Canal, 1580s; the imposing early Baroque facade is sometimes attributed to the sculptor Vittoria.

PALAZZO COCCINA TIEPOLO: FACADE (above)

Attributed to GianGiacomo de'Grigi, and completed in 1560, it already heralds the Baroque, with its obelisks and prominent coats of arms.

prominent among the Baroque touches were the many broken pediments, instead of the 'correct' triangular classical pediments of Palazzo Coccina. Here, too, the facade was enlivened with a pair of extremely florid coats of arms, while the ground and mezzanine storeys was rusticated, with three prominent, somewhat theatrical water gates. Perhaps it took a sculptor rather than an architect to more fully appreciate the effects of chiaroscuro and plasticity that the Baroque made possible, although Vittoria was undoubtedly encouraged by the prominent site and the effects of light; he had also already worked closely with architects such as Sansovino, with whom he had collaborated at the Biblioteca Marciana.[34]

PALLADIO'S VILLAS

Below left: the Villa Foscari ('La Malcontenta') on the Brenta, near the edge of the Venetian lagoon, 1559–60.

Below: Villa Barbaro at Maser, 1557–8; built for the brothers MarcAntonio and Daniele Barbaro, the villa's side wings or *barchesse* contain practical farming accommodation.

Vincenzo Scamozzi, too, was prolific in the later sixteenth century, although one of his most prominent houses, Palazzo Contarini dagli Scrigni, despite its later date (*c*1609), still lacked Vittoria's bravura modelling. Here, though, Scamozzi was constrained by an earlier Gothic structure, which he remodelled; the result is rather rigid and formal, with an unusual single light in the centre of the facade. His introduction of a pedimented mansard to enliven the roofline, however, was to prove an enduring feature. As an ingenious solution to a difficult problem, the palace influenced the work of the Contini and of Bartolomeo Manopola; the refacing of older palaces in more modern styles was to be a burgeoning activity in the seventeenth and eighteenth centuries. Manopola was active in the same period as Scamozzi, and his own most prominent work, Palazzo Ruzzini-Priuli (*c*1600–10), with its elegant but markedly asymmetrical facade, dominates

one end of Campo Santa Maria Formosa. Both of these houses, the Ruzzini and the Contarini, have rather austere facades, with little of the plasticity of the Balbi or Coccina, and seem to suggest something of a reaction against such perceived self indulgence.[35]

The great Pisani palace at Santo Stefano, one of the largest and most imposing in the city, is also often ascribed to Manopola. It was built by descendants of the famous fifteenth-century banking family in around 1615, at a reputed cost of an extraordinary 200,000 ducats, although to Martinioni, writing in 1663, it was simply an 'incredible expense'. The palace was greatly enlarged a century later for Almoro, brother of Doge Alvise Pisani, and the two phases display instructive differences of style. Manopola's massive but rhythmic facade has a certain restrained richness, but the additions of Girolamo Frigimelica were more opulent and imaginative, with two wings connected by tiers of superimposed logge; Frigimelica also designed the immense villa at Stra for the same family, probably the largest ever built on the Venetian Terraferma. The palace at Santo Stefano became an important cultural focus, and hosted many illustrious visitors, among them the King of Sweden in 1784.

This last observation highlights an important aspect of the Venetian palace as it evolved after the late sixteenth century; many of these houses were undergoing further significant changes in their *raison d'etre*. Although some, such as Sansovino's palaces for the Corner and Dolfin, retained their traditional commercial functions as hubs of trade, with their ground floors and mezzanines still at least partly devoted to the storage of goods, in other families such concerns became less important. Some of the most prominent patrons of new palaces, for example, were bankers, while others were wealthy prelates. Two of the grandsons of Zorzi Corner, for example (whose palace Sansovino had designed), were neither bankers nor merchants, but went into the Church, and both became cardinals; neither bankers nor cardinals required storage for spices and luxury fabrics in their halls. Still other nobles again owed more and more of their income to Terraferma landed investments. In all the most prominent examples, the function of the city palace was now being regarded more and more clearly in two well-defined senses: firstly as a long-term dynastic investment, and secondly as a nucleus for civilized living on a grand scale.

VILLA BARBARO

Interior of the central salone, with *trompe l'oeil* frescos by Paolo Veronese.

The palaces of Baldassare Longhena

In the long prolific career of Longhena (active from *c*1620 to 1682) we can trace the development of the Venetian Baroque until its last and most confident stage of richness and elaborate decoration. His career can be followed closely in his palaces where his stylistic development of this single building type can be traced over more than half a century. Longhena's earliest works are not surprisingly developed from proto-Baroque models such as Palazzo Balbi, with the now almost obligatory use of stone for the entire facade, and with the prominent display of family arms and cartouches, expressions of family identity that had hitherto been restricted largely to the land gates of palaces, rather than emblazoned on the Grand Canal facade. Such overt displays of identity and patronage have a close parallel in the way in which church facades became more and more prominently used as family 'mausolea', as discussed earlier.

Longhena's many patrons represented a broad cross-section of 'old' and 'new' aristocracy and in this sense his career also reflected the important shift in the balance of these groups in the government of the Republic in this period. It was a blunt fact of life that, for many complex and still not fully understood reasons, the numbers of the Venetian patriciate declined significantly in the later sixteenth century, from around 2,500 adult males in 1550 to less than 2,000 by the end of the century. The devastating plague of 1630 wrought further damage such that only around 1,600 had survived into the later 1630s. Faced with such alarming statistics (and with the same number of government posts to fill) the Signoria decided that the only way to ensure the continuing survival of viable numbers was to 'unlock' the Maggior Consiglio. Between 1647 and 1718 no less than 127 new members were admitted to the aristocracy, and they altered profoundly the character of the nobility. A price was to be paid, however, for this overnight status, in the form of a large 'membership fee', a contribution to the Republic's coffers. Of those newly ennobled, about a quarter were established noble clans from the Terraferma empire, from Verona, Padua and elsewhere, although sixty per cent were 'promoted' from the Venetian citizenry, chiefly merchants and traders. They thus represented a clear subclass of the new rich, and as such were rarely accepted on equal terms by the older noble clans. By definition they were all extremely wealthy, though, and as appears inevitable with such groups, they sought to express their wealth and the status that now accompanied it in the most prominent manner available: by building new palaces, preferably, of course, on the Grand Canal.

While some of Longhena's patrons still represented the most ancient and prominent of the older aristocracy, such as the Contarini and Pesaro, several others were members of these *nouveaux riches* who bought their seats in the Maggior Consiglio, as the Republic attempted not only to reinforce numbers but also to raise urgently needed funds to support the epic struggles with the Turks, and in particular the battles and seiges of Candia (Crete). Among these new families, Longhena could number as patrons the Widmann, Belloni and Rezzonico, the first two ennobled in 1646–7, each as a reward for the payment of 100,000 ducats towards the war effort. In their palace building, we see clearly the instructive expression in stone of this new money, and the image that they wished to project as they joined the ancient facades of the Corner, Foscari and Dandolo. Almost every swag, cartouche and *stemma* (armorial device) on these new facades served to draw attention to their arrival both in the Golden Book, the register of the nobility, and on the Canalazzo.

One of Longhena's first commissions was Palazzo Widmann at San Canciano, built in the 1620s for a family originally from Carinthia, in present-day Austria. It is clearly a youthful work (he was then only in his twenties), although the facade is well ordered, with characteristic rustication and large, deep consoles supporting the central balcony; the palace retains its rich interior decoration by Gaspare Diziani. Palazzo Giustinian-Lolin is another early work, indebted to both Serlio and Scamozzi, particularly in the two large Serlian windows to the principal upper floors. It was under

construction in 1623, and when completed presented a lively facade with two large coats of arms (now lost) and obelisks on the roof.[36]

Longhena was retained as proto ('house architect') to the da Lezze family, which originated from Lecce in Puglia, and he designed their imposing palace at the Misericordia as well as their villa at Callalta. The palace marks a notable increase in scale from the two earlier houses, and was built in 1645–70; its grandiose salons were originally decorated by Giambattista Tiepolo, although the interior was cruelly sacked when the Republic fell in 1797, and the rich decorations were largely destroyed. The plan is unusually broad, as is the monumental facade, which has a complex rhythm of fenestration reflecting the highly atypical interior. Since land was comparatively underdeveloped in this part of the city, there was space for a sizable garden, terminating in a small *casino*, or summerhouse, which still survives.[37]

From the same period the palace at San Stae built for the Belloni clan (today known as Palazzo Belloni-Battagia), showed a marked development in his style towards more powerful three-dimensional forms. It was probably built in the 1650s, and was highly praised by Martinioni in his new edition of Francesco Sansovino's *Venetia citta nobilissima et singolare*, published in 1663. Such characteristic Baroque features as broken pediments are prominent, and again two large stemme adorn the facade. The house thus had affinities with Vittoria's much earlier Balbi palace, and forms a link between it and the truly monumental house that Longhena was shortly to begin for the Pesaro clan. That Longhena's style was still not confined to a single path of ever greater elaboration is evinced by the slightly later Zane house at San Stin; he was also retained as proto by the Zane family, and the restrained rhythmic quality of the facade contrasts strongly with the lively ebullience of the Belloni house.

Two magnificent palaces stand above all these others, though, in their size, richness and in the supreme self-confidence of their execution: Cà Rezzonico and Cà Pesaro are unquestionably the two finest Baroque palaces in Venice. They have much in common, not purely stylistically, but also in the long histories of their construction; neither was to be completed within Longhena's own lifetime.

Cà Rezzonico was begun in 1667 for the Bon family, when Longhena was appointed by Procurator Filippo Bon to redevelop a site formerly occupied by some cottages. By the time of the architect's death in 1682, however, only the ground floor and the first piano nobile were complete, capped by a large temporary roof. After the death of Filippo, his successors lacked the funds to complete the work, and the house remained in this unfinished condition until 1750, when it was bought by Giambattista Rezzonico. The Rezzonico was an extremely wealthy clan, originally from the shores of Lake Como, ennobled in 1687, when Aurelio Rezzonico had donated 100,000 ducats to the Republic. In the 1750s work recommenced to bring the grandiose structure to a conclusion; two years later, Giambattista Rezzonico's son Carlo was elected pope, taking the name of Clement XIII. Many other family honours followed: procuracies from the Republic and cardinalates from Rome, all accompanied by lavish festivities in the still uncompleted palace. The architect belatedly appointed to replace the long deceased Longhena was Giorgio Massari, whose contribution included the second piano nobile, as well as the grandiose formal staircase and the sumptuous ballroom at the rear of the palace.[38]

Despite some differences in the completed second storey, the palace exhibits a powerful unity that does not reflect its protracted two part, seventy-year building history. Longhena's facade is immensely rich and confidently modelled, although he did not employ the traditional tripartite Venetian form. The portal is formed by a triple opening with square architraves, and with the ground floor faced with massive rustication in the spirit and scale of the great works of Sanmicheli. The upper storeys have seven bays, and although the three central bays represent the great hall, the

BALDASSARE LONGHENA: CÀ REZZONICO (above)

Facade to the Grand Canal. Begun in 1667, it was completed by Massari in the 1740s.

CÀ REZZONICO (left)

The imposing ballroom was added to the rear of Longhena's already massive palace by Giorgio Massari in c.1756. Massari also completed the upper storeys of the palace itself.

facade is effectively designed as a continuous screen, with none of the traditional Venetian patterns of fenestration. Each individual bay has a window flanked by small columns and framed in turn by the larger columns of the principal order, a composite arrangement based on Sansovino's Library at San Marco. The plan behind this massive, opulent facade is basically traditional, although imposing in scale; following the principles of Sansovino's palace for the Corner, behind the ground-floor hall is a central axial courtyard, beyond which, still centred on the axis, is the great ballroom added by Massari. The palace is flanked by a canal down one side, and the ballroom is approached by Massari's monumental, rather Neoclassical staircase, perhaps after a proposal by Longhena, which is reached from a small courtyard off the quay.

The decoration of the interior was to be as sumptuous as its external appearance, and the whole epitomizes the Venetian Baroque palace as a hub of cultural activities and entertainment. Four ceilings were decorated with frescos by Giambattista Tiepolo in *c*1758, as were some of the lesser rooms; many of the interiors parallel those of the Baroque churches in the complex integration of architectural form and surface decoration which is so characteristic of the style. It was a skill in which Tiepolo was the outstanding master.

Cà Pesaro is Longhena's other Baroque masterpiece. It is also his last major work, and, as at Cà Rezzonico, the enormous cost and protracted building programme meant that he died before its completion. However, the family history of the palace is rather more straightforward than that of the Bon and the Rezzonico. The Pesaro were an ancient patrician dynasty, and Giovanni Pesaro first bought an existing house at San Stae from the Contarini. In 1559 he also purchased an adjacent plot from the Malipiero, and finally in 1628, a third piece of land was bought from the Trevisan to assemble a large enough site for this great work.

The new palace was begun at the back of the site while the family continued to live in the front section, the former Contarini house, facing the Grand Canal. This rear section was well advanced by 1652. Six years later Giovanni Pesaro, Longhena's patron, was elected doge. However, his reign was extremely brief; after his death in the following year, 1659, Longhena designed his massive funerary monument in the Frari, carved at a cost of some 12,000 ducats, and remarkably at odds with the modest achievements of his short reign. Work on the palace was continued by Giovanni's nephew, Lunardo; in 1673 the facade was begun and in 1676 the piano nobile was commenced. The first floor, but not the second, was completed by 1682, the year of the death of both Longhena and his patron, Lunardo.[39] The second storey was added by Gaspari, after a ten-year hiatus, while the palace's impressive east flank, along the Rio delle Do Torri, was also completed by Gaspari as late as 1741, in a rather restrained Neoclassical manner.

The scale of the palace, like Cà Rezzonico, is imposing, self-confident and assured, although here the square courtyard is at the rear of the house, behind an extremely long great hall. The facade is of seven bays, again like the Rezzonico house, although there are many lesser differences of detail between the two despite their close family resemblance. Here, for example, Cà Rezzonico's tripartite portal is replaced by two grand individual arches, and the ground floor has a mezzanine within its massively rusticated base. A degree of central emphasis is also given to the upper floors by the paired columns flanking the great hall windows.

In all, however, both palaces represent a fairly decisive break with the Venetian facade tradition, and their only true predecessor was the facade of Sansovino's Palazzo Corner. Only in Sansovino's

PALAZZO PISANI AT SANTO STEFANO (below, left)

Detail of the unusual superimposed logge to the inner courtyard.

BALDASSARE LONGHENA: CÀ PESARO (below)

One of Longhena's two Baroque masterpieces, it was begun in 1628 but completed by Gaspari after Longhena's death.

BALDASSARE LONGHENA

Palazzo da Lezze at the Misericordia,
an imposing work of mid-career, begun
in 1645.

rich detailing could Longhena find a worthy antecedent for the strong, powerful modelling that he developed in these two great houses; neither of them were to be surpassed in size or richness in the century that followed.

Baldassare Longhena's contemporaries and successors

As in the design of his churches, Longhena was to influence an entire younger generation of palace architects, among them Giuseppe Sardi, Alessandro Tremignon and Andrea Cominelli, as well as a further generation, younger again, which included Andrea Tirali, Antonio Gaspari, Antonio Visentini and Giorgio Massari. While in the work of some of this last group we can trace the increasing influence of the Neoclassical movement, much of their earlier work remains the result of Longhena's powerful influence. Few, however, were fortunate enough to obtain commissions from patrons as extravagantly wealthy as those of Longhena.

Like Longhena, Sardi was retained as proto by several families, including the Galli and Cavazza. He designed three substantial surviving palaces, all fairly close together in Cannaregio; the location reflects the rather belated development of this more peripheral district, since by now a large, more central site was extremely difficult to obtain, as the Pesaro had discovered. Of the three, Palazzo Flangini at San Geremia is the most strongly modelled and impressive work. The Flangini were again 'new nobles'; originally from Cyprus, they joined the Venetian patriciate in 1664, and a few years later their house at San Moisè was modernized by Tremignon. Girolamo Flangini also began

a palace *ex novo* at San Geremia, although he never acquired the adjacent site, and thus built only two-thirds of the intended impressive tripartite palace. It was built between 1664 and 1682, its style again reflecting Sardi's close links with Longhena, whose nearby Scalzi church he completed in the same period. The bold Corinthian columns, the swags and cartouches, are all strongly reminiscent of his mentor.

Sardi's other palaces, Palazzo Surian and Palazzo Savorgnan, stand on each bank of the Cannaregio Canal. They are both impressive, the latter more lively and reminiscent of Longhena's early work, while the Surian house is rather restrained, evidence of an early reaction against the perceived excesses of the mature Baroque. The Surian house was completed in 1663, while the Savorgnan is first recorded in Martinioni's new edition of Sansovino, published in the same year; in his view, both were 'superb structures, with extensive and delightful gardens'. This was by now one of the few remaining districts of the city where such gardens were feasible, and that of the Savorgnan house became one of the most notable in the city, full of rare plants and trees; later transformed into an English garden, it survives today as a public park.[40]

The final outstanding palace of the mature Baroque is the impressive Palazzo Labia, once again in Cannaregio, but standing on a prominent site near the junction of the Grand Canal and the Cannaregio Canal. This pivotal location produced a palace of considerable dramatic impact. Its history, however, is still far from clear. Andrea Cominelli and Alessandro Tremignon are both associated with the house, which was built by Giovanni-Francesco Labia, an extremely wealthy Catalan noble; he had joined the patriciate in 1646 and immediately began construction of this sumptuous new palace for his clan. Many legends attached to his prodigious wealth, the best known built on the famous punning phrase, 'L'abia o non l'abia, sarò sempre Labia' (whether I have or I have not, I will always be a Labia), supposedly uttered while gold plates were tossed into the adjacent canal after a banquet. Equally apocryphal, no doubt, is the claim that a net had been placed below the water's surface for the prudent recycling of the utensils. Even as a popular anecdote it illustrates the perceived image of extraordinary and ostentatious wealth of the Venetian

PALAZZO ZENOBIO AT THE CARMINI (left)

Ceiling of the ballroom, with frescos by
Louis Dorigny c.1695–1700.

PALAZZO ZENOBIO (above)

Gaspari's reticent exterior gives no hint
of the palace's internal riches: the archway
connects the ballroom with the more
traditional *portego* beyond; above the
archway is a musicians' gallery.

nobility in the seventeenth and eighteenth centuries, and the primary function of the palace in this era; once vital hubs of international trade and banking, now stately pleasure-domes.

Palazzo Labia seems to have been built in two phases and in its final form has three facades, its fourth side abutting a block of apartments. They are by different hands, the long facade to the Cannaregio Canal and the shorter return on to the Grand Canal being more opulent than the massive but more restrained facade on to the campo. The former facades are probably the work of Cominelli although they strongly reflect the confidence of a master such as Longhena, and several details recall Cà Pesaro. By contrast, the campo facade may be the work of Tremignon. It was completed later, in around 1720, and again seems to evince a puritanical reaction against the full-blooded Baroque of Longhena. The palace's interior is remarkable for the superb cycle of Tiepolo's frescos in the ballroom, executed in 1745–50, and depicting the lives of Antony and Cleopatra.[41]

PALAZZO LABIA

The great house was built in several stages. This facade, to the Campo San Geremia, perhaps by Tremignon (1720s), is fairly restrained.

The most notable and prolific architect of the following generation was Gaspari, and the nature of his work represents yet a further development of the desires and self-image of the patriciate. Perhaps the most extraordinary of several palaces is Palazzo Zenobio at the Carmini. It has an extremely broad, but restrained and otherwise unremarkable facade, although the interiors have an outstanding opulence with few peers in the city. The Zenobio were once again 'new aristocrats', who bought their place in the Maggior Consiglio in 1646, and appointed Gaspari to design a palace that was in a sense closer to a villa, with side wings embracing a large rear courtyard, beyond which was the garden. The interior is centred on a grand atrium with colonnades, and the principal first floor accommodation consists of a large ballroom with the traditional axial hall behind it, in the form of a 'T'.[42]

Gaspari also remodelled two other houses, reflecting the significant trend in this period to modernize existing palaces, sometimes with a new facade, sometimes with remodelled interiors, and occasionally with both, such that only the basic structure of the earlier house remained. One is Palazzo Michiel delle Colonne, the other is the impressive Palazzo Giustinian at Murano. The latter was formerly a large Gothic house, the Palazzo Cappello, but its plan was reordered and Gaspari gave the house a new Baroque facade. The palace became the seat of the bishops after the transfer of the see from Torcello to Murano, and was bought by bishop Marco Giustinian in 1707. These transformations often required considerable skill and ingenuity, and Gaspari focused his new facade on a large central window group, with a triangular pediment and a florid coat of arms; the interior was also comprehensively redecorated.

The Baroque and Rococo interior

These palaces of the seventeenth and eighteenth centuries served very different functions from those of their predecessors. Many became a means of self-expression for the new aristocracy. They epitomized their changing use in the importance, for example, of the garden (where space allowed), and the concentration of external expression on the all-important facade, with particular emphasis on the family arms. Their interiors, too, exhibited qualities not seen in any earlier century. Extraordinary effort and expense went into the internal decoration, and on such a scale that few of the many remaining medieval palaces retain much (if any) evidence of their original, simpler interiors.

Two fifteenth-century palaces, among many, that underwent remarkable transformations in this period were Palazzo Pisani-Moretta and the Barbaro palace at San Vidal. The former, a fine Gothic house on the Grand Canal near San Tomà, was reordered in a sumptuous eighteenth-century manner by Chiara, daughter of Procurator Francesco Pisani, in 1739–46. Among the new works was a new three-branch staircase by Andrea Tirali; Chiara also commissioned paintings by Tiepolo (some still in place), while the modernization was continued by her two sons in the 1770s. The

PALAZZO LABIA

Left: the ballroom is entirely decorated with frescos by Giambattista Tiepolo (c.1745–50), and collectively form one of his masterworks.

Above: the facades towards the Grand Canal and the Cannaregio Canal are richly modelled in the manner of Longhena.

decoration of the principal storey, by Jacopo Guarana and others, including wall hangings and Murano chandeliers, has survived virtually intact.

Palazzo Barbaro was similarly transformed in this period. The house consists of two side by side, the original Gothic house, built by Bartolomeo Bon in the 1420s, and the new wing added by Gaspari in 1694. The Barbaro were outstanding patrons of the arts; an earlier member of the clan, Daniele, Patriarch of Aquileia, had commissioned Palladio and Veronese to complete the family's new villa at Maser. The sober exterior gives little indication of the uniquely rich internal decoration; Gaspari's new wing contains a ballroom decorated with paintings by Sebastiano Ricci and Giambattista Piazzetta *c*1695–1705, all in elaborate stucco frames. Indeed, the almost obligatory ballrooms that were attached to so many Baroque palaces reflect their primary function as centres of leisure, culture and (especially) of musical entertainment. The days of halls packed with merchandise were long gone, and the great hall was now chiefly used for concerts, banquets and private theatrical performances.

The interiors of the Zenobio and Albrizzi Palaces mark the apogee of this extravagant interior decoration, and are the most luxurious (and luxuriant) interiors in the city. The Albrizzi house was built for the Bonomo family but was patiently acquired from them, floor by floor, by the Albrizzi, over a period of more than forty years; they then transformed the interiors over almost as long a period. The richest work dates from *c*1700–10, and includes the great hall and the unique stucco 'tent' ceiling to the ballroom, supported by two dozen plaster putti. Stucco decoration had been used for some time as a framing device for wall paintings, but in both of these houses it was extended far beyond this modest role, so that it takes over the complete form of the room, the real dimensions of which are lost beyond these complex, three-dimensional forms. In many places, too, the applied stucco is combined with *trompe l'oeil* painting and fresco, to further dissolve the distinction between the real and the imagined. The love of *trompe l'oeil* is a characteristic feature of the Venetian interior;

earlier popularized in the interiors of Palladio's villas (and elsewhere) in the sixteenth century, it was a form of intellectual amusement developed specifically by the patriciate. It reflected the skills of the master chosen by the patron in creating amusing and fanciful illusions for visitors to admire. Palazzo Zenobio, for example, contains an extensive work of dramatic false perspective in the illusionistic painting on the ballroom ceiling. Although some of its interiors also utilize stucco in a refined early Neoclassical manner, the overwhelming impression remains that of the Baroque. In this case, the great hall is divided from the ballroom by an elegant archway, above which is a sinuously formed gallery for a small orchestra. Facilities for musical performances were now so important a consideration that they formed an integral part of the fabric of the building.[43]

The swan song: Giorgio Massari and the Palazzo Grassi

The last great Venetian palace builder was Giorgio Massari. Although he completed several works begun by others, Massari was responsible for the one house that in many ways can be regarded as the swan song of the genre that had developed over so many centuries: Palazzo Grassi. The family history of its builders epitomizes the progress of the Republic's new nobility; the Grassi clan had originally come from Bologna to Chioggia, where they became the town's most prominent and wealthiest citizen family, and where they also built a substantial palazzo. They moved to Venice, where they were enrolled in the ranks of the nobility in 1718 on payment of the obligatory contribution, in their case, 60,000 ducats.

PALAZZO FLANGINI (below, left)

Situated on the Grand Canal near San Geremia and dating from after 1664, it was never completed. Giuseppe Sardi's rich facade evokes the work of his mentor Longhena.

PALAZZO SURIAN (below)

By Sardi, but in a more restrained monumental style. The banks of the Cannaregio Canal still allowed space for development, often with gardens at the rear.

PALAZZO GRASSI (below)

Begun in 1748 by Giorgio Massari, it was the last great noble palace built in Venice before the fall of the Republic.

PALAZZO CORNER DELLA REGINA
(below, right)

Detail of portal; the chief lay work of Domenico Rossi, begun in 1724 in a fairly restrained Neoclassical manner.

Their new palace, begun by Angelo di Paolo, was on a large prominent site on the Grand Canal at San Samuele, directly opposite Cà Rezzonico. The foundations were laid in 1748, and the palace took twenty years to complete. Its plan is grandiose, formal, axial and symmetrical, with a ground-floor spatial progression derived directly from Sansovino and Palladio. The quayside loggia leads in to a square, colonnaded hall, which in turn opens in to a large, originally uncovered, square courtyard, again surrounded by colonnades; at the far end, still on the same axis, is a grand, three-branch staircase up to the piano nobile. It is not a traditional Venetian arrangement, but a classicized Terraferma design, reminiscent of the plans of some of Palladio's Vicenza palaces, and of Sansovino's 'Roman' plan for Palazzo Corner. At the first floor, the stair gives onto a colonnaded balcony from which two rows of rooms, one down each side, in enfilade, direct the visitor back towards the chief reception room with its splendid views over the Grand Canal. The detailing of the interior throughout is rich but rather restrained, strictly Neoclassical despite the engaging frescos and *trompe l'oeil* decorations around the stairwell.[44] The facade is equally controlled and measured, and again a restrained Neoclassicism is the dominant impression; the complex chiaroscuro of the Baroque was now definitively replaced by a more restrained style.

Palazzo Grassi was the last substantial private noble palace to be built in Venice, and there is a

touch of irony in Massari's return to cool, Neoclassical 'Roman' forms. Back in the sixteenth century, Venice had grandiloquently proclaimed itself as the 'new Rome', and was in many ways a worthy successor of this august mantle, as the palaces of Sansovino, Codussi and Sanmicheli clearly show. Now, though, the historical context was entirely different, and Massari's work was to be a final fanfare for a dying Republic. Soon after the palace's completion, after a millennium of independence, the Most Serene Republic was extinguished by Napoleon, the self-styled 'Attila for the Venetian state'. Thirty years later, the Grassi clan itself was extinct, and was followed into oblivion by many others during the long, declining nineteenth century, among them the Barbarigo, Duodo, Erizzo, da Lezze, Pesaro, Spinelli and Rezzonico. Palazzo Grassi thus marks a worthy final example of this most characteristic of Venetian building types; we are fortunate indeed that, despite two further centuries of vicissitudes, so many of these fine palaces survive today.

On 12 May 1797, with Napoleon's troops gathered on the shores of the lagoon, the Maggior Consiglio assembled in the Palazzo Ducale, and by 512 hands to 20 voted itself out of existence. Doge Ludovico Manin, 120th successor to the throne of San Marco, handed his ducal *corno*, his cap of office, to his aide, with the now legendary words, 'Take this away, I will not be needing it any more.' After a millennium of independence, the Most Serene Republic existed no longer, and four days later, for the first time in the city's history, foreign troops stood, uninvited, on the Piazza.

After Napoleon: urban development in the nineteenth century

Napoleon's contribution to Venice's urban history is in part encapsulated by his dissolution of the monastic houses and by his removal to Paris of an incalculable collection of works of art. But the Napoleonic era also saw important changes to the city's fabric, not immediately, but after 1806 and Venice's incorporation into Napoleon's Italian Kingdom.[1]

Not only had the Dominante's political destiny been radically and permanently altered, but its physical fabric, too, was now to be brought into the modern era by some drastic interventions. These included further land reclamations, among them that of the Sacca Sant'Angelo behind the Mendigola peninsula, to provide a vast new Campo di Marte, or military parade ground. Much of the eastern end of the Giudecca was also cleared, with the intention of laying out a large new public park, while a similar clearance in Castello, involving the demolition of the monastic houses of San Nicolo and San Antonio, led to the establishment of the Giardini Pubblici, the Public Gardens, which survive today. Further opening-up works in the same quarter included the filling in of the Canale di San Pietro to form the present Via Garibaldi, while the Riva degli Schiavoni was also broadened and extended.

Some of the most dramatic interventions were at San Marco, as discussed in Chapter 2, and where the Procuratie Nuove were transformed into a palace for Napoleon's Italian viceroy. To this end the medieval Granai di Terranova were demolished, with the intention of building a new monumental southern facade to the Procuratie; this was never executed, but the Giardinetti Reali were instead set out on the site of the granaries. As part of the same programme, the west end of the Piazza was demolished to build the Ala Napoleonica, the Napoleonic wing, providing a grandiose new entrance and ballroom for the Palazzo Reale.[2]

The motives behind these and many other urban works in the early nineteenth century were several. At the simplest level they represented a statement of newly-imposed foreign control, of the imposition of centralized government from Paris, devolved via Milan, capital of the Italian Kingdom, just as the Palazzo Ducale itself had formerly symbolized the independence of the Most Serene Republic. At the same time they represented a determination to modernize the city, while in the process 'cleansing' it of its now anachronistic Republican past. To achieve these ends, though, much of this nineteenth-century 'rationalization' led to the coarsening of the city's complex organic fabric, particularly through the filling in of a number of canals, the widening of streets and considerable demolition.

Certain works were less destructive than others, and a few had lasting civic value: the Public Gardens; the development of the city's cemetery at San Michele, for example, and the establishment of the hospital at Santi Giovanni e Paolo. Far more dramatic, though, were Napoleon's policies towards the Church; the number of parishes was reduced from seventy-two to

SANTA LUCIA RAILWAY STATION

Planned in the 1930s, the station was not built until the 1950s by the State Railways (Ferrovie dello Stato).

forty and then to only thirty, leaving many churches redundant. Dozens of monastic houses were also either closed or amalgamated, leaving a further extensive patrimony of redundant buildings, some of which later became schools or barracks, while others were left empty and abandoned. The Scuole Grandi, too, were all abolished, although three were later reconstituted.

The Austrian occupation after 1814 provided some alleviation in the city's condition, in that many works of art were returned to Venice from Paris, but the economy remained shorn of its traditional trading network; with the Austrian decision to develop Trieste as a free port and its principal outlet to the Mediterranean, Venice's own shipping and entrepôt functions continued to stagnate.

Nevertheless, the economic situation slowly improved until the unsuccessful Republican revolution of Daniele Manin in 1848. Two years earlier, Venice's ancient physical isolation had at last been ended by the construction of the railway causeway to the Terraferma, followed by construction of the railway station. As always, progress had its price, in this case the immediate demolition of Andrea Palladio's nunnery of Santa Lucia, although the railway itself, together with a degree of political stability prior to 1848, had led to a notable increase in tourism and a consequent improvement in the city's economic condition.[3] The first station was completed in 1861; it was an undistinguished structure, but survived until 1934, when a competition was held to design a new one. Unlike the highly successful contemporary new design for Florence station, however, none of the submitted schemes was accepted, and the outbreak of war in 1939 delayed the project until the present unassuming structure was built by the state railways in 1955.

LIDO DI VENEZIA: THE EXCELSIOR
HOTEL (above)

The hotel, by Giovanni Sardi, c.1908, in an eclectic Moorish style, proved a catalyst in the development of the Lido as a resort.

THE MOLINO STUCKY ON THE GIUDECCA
(above, right)

Built by Ernest Wullekopf in 1894, it represents the brief period of the Giudecca's importance as an industrial zone.

The nineteenth century as a whole was characterized by a striking shift in the balance between the two communications networks of the city, from that of the waterways to that of the streets. Many more canals were filled in (*interrati*), improving pedestrian communications but again simplifying the water network, reducing access by boat, and impeding the natural cleansing effect of the tides. The opening of the station itself led to several further operations to enhance the pedestrian network, including two new bridges across the Grand Canal, the first since the 'new' Rialto bridge of the 1590s. The Carità or Accademia Bridge was built in 1852 and that at the station (the Scalzi Bridge) two years later. Both were originally of iron and steel, and were later rebuilt to different designs, that at the Accademia in 1932 in timber, the other in stone in 1934. A further programme of street widenings and demolitions was specifically intended to improve communications between the city centre (Rialto and San Marco) and the station, culminating in the cutting of the Strada Nova in 1871. The station itself now became an important nucleus in the city's fabric.[4]

Two significant efforts were made in this period to coordinate and produce a development strategy for the city as a whole; one was begun in 1866, the other twenty years later. Both attempted to reconcile the existing historic fabric with the needs of modern forms of transport, and the vital necessity of reviving the city's economy. To this end many further works were undertaken in the historic centre, far more widespread in their effects than is usually appreciated today. Most of the present buildings on the Riva degli Schiavoni, for example, were built in this period to encourage the burgeoning tourist industry, while elsewhere campi were enlarged (such as those of San Luca and San Bartolomeo), yet more canals reclaimed and new bridges built.

These transformations continued after the unification of Italy in 1866; the Via XXII Marzo at San Moisè was cut through in 1875; the Bacino Orseolo, behind the Piazza, was formed in 1869; the Merceria 2 Aprile from San Bartolomeo to San Salvador was enlarged in the same period. In the 1880s, too, the extensive Stazione Marittima was reclaimed to the west of the city, with direct rail connections from the new docks to the causeway and thence to the mainland network; this was the most ambitious effort yet seen to revive the port and attract seaborne trade once again.

The Piano Regolatore (Development Control Plan) of 1886 for the first time recognized the need to improve the housing stock, particularly of the working classes, rendered more urgent by a notable rise in population from 120,000 in 1868 to 160,000 by 1911. Only after 1904, though, was practical progress made, with new housing at San Giobbe, San Lunardo, on the Giudecca and in eastern Castello, where the large new quarter of Sant'Elena was built on reclaimed land. Nearby in the same district was established the Biennale d'Arte, first accommodated in 1887 in a temporary pavilion and then a large new permanent pavilion in 1895; this was followed by a number of individual national pavilions.[5]

Modernization and industrialization affected the city in two ways: by encircling the historic centre with an ever increasing variety of new building types, and by greatly increasing the scale and 'grain' of the environment of the lagoon. New buildings such as the station brought a much larger, nineteenth-century scale to the hitherto small, fragmented, essentially medieval scale of the historic city.

Creation of wealth and the expansion of the local economy continued to preoccupy the city's authorities into our own century. The Arsenale was revived, the Stazione Marittima flourished and much of the Giudecca became industrialized, with new factories, boatyards and the vast Mulino Stucky (flour mills). New glassworks similarly covered much of Murano's backland, formerly the sites of the gardens of sixteenth-century patrician villas. In the city itself, much of the western fringe not already devoted to port activities was developed with cotton and tobacco factories.[6]

The scale of these new activities was again far greater than any historic industrial or commercial operations (with the exception of the Arsenale), and this increased scale was extrapolated in the early part of this century, with development no longer confined within the city's historic limits. The period between 1918 and 1939 was dominated by the establishment and rise of Porto Marghera and by the expansion of the former satellite community of Mestre, which became a major residential and commercial centre. In 1932–3 the ninety-year-old railway bridge was joined by a parallel road causeway, terminating in a large new square, Piazzale Roma, and with the consequent influx of cars accommodated in two new multi-level car parks. This first road link, inevitable though it probably was, has given rise to a series of urban difficulties, as the number of vehicles attempting to reach and park at Piazzale Roma increases every year. More recently still a large new island, Tronchetto, has been reclaimed from the lagoon, solely for parking and for a new wholesale market. But the longer term implications of continuing vehicular growth have not yet been seriously addressed.

The period since 1945 has seen the further continuation of several of the developments of the interwar period. The former fort-village of Mestre has become one of the largest urban centres of north-east Italy, with a population much larger than that of Venice itself, and now a major commercial centre in its own right. Mestre itself is now surrounded by dormitory suburbs that were until recently farming villages, while Marghera continues to employ thousands, although ecological pressures together with economic difficulties have curtailed expansion, and have had some considerable success in reducing industrial pollution.

Post-imperial architecture: eclecticism and modernism

The nineteenth century was an era of great variety and eclecticism in Venetian architectural style, as it was throughout western Europe. Here, though, it was also accompanied by the arrival in the city and its immediate environs of many new building types, some of them universally new, others simply new to Venice. Among the former were the great *fin de siècle* hotels, an entirely new building type representing the emergent 'world industry' of international tourism, and a type difficult to

LIDO DI VENEZIA: VILLA MON PLAISIR

Although altered, the villa, by Guido Sullam, 1906, represents the broad eclectic taste of 20th century buildings on the Lido.

THE BIENNALE GARDENS

The Gardens contain a fine collection of
works by modern masters. Left to right: the
Dutch pavilion by Gerrit Rietveld, 1954; the
Austrian pavilion by Josef Hoffmann, 1934;
and the Electa bookshop by James Stirling
and Michael Wilford, 1991.

accommodate within Venice's fine urban structure. Among the latter building types were the late nineteenth-century industrial developments at Murano and the Giudecca.

Although the Neoclassical movement remained the most prominent stylistic trend in the early part of the century, after the middle of the century the Gothic revival became the most dominant style, although here (naturally enough) it remained specifically Venetian Gothic in character. Its revival was greatly enhanced by the publication of John Ruskin's *The Stones of Venice* in 1851–3. Venetian Gothic or a mixture of Byzantine and Gothic was to be used for a variety of new buildings, from the new fishmarket at Rialto (1907, by Cesare Laurenti and Domenico Rupolo), to several highly eclectic houses and villas, among them the studio designed and built by the artist Mario di Maria for himself, on the Giudecca waterfront, and the Palazzetto Stern (by Giuseppe Berti, 1909–12) on the Grand Canal at Cà Rezzonico.

Giovanni Sardi was probably the most prolific neo-Gothicist, with his Scarpa house on the Zattere, Palazzetto Ravà at San Silvestro and the Hotel Bauer at San Moisè. His own work, though, is generally more literal and academic. Similar neo-Gothicism was used by Meduna in his extensions to the fine medieval Palazzo Cavalli, bought by Baron Franchetti, in 1886, although internally his Mannerist style is more an Anglicized Gothick than Venetian. The native fifteenth-century florid Gothic style was also followed with a dogged lack of imagination at the Palazzo Genovese on the Grand Canal near the Salute (1892, Tricomi-Mattei). Nineteenth-century neo-Gothic thus took two broad paths in the city, a rather literal and uninspired academicism on the one hand, and a highly eclectic, whimsical and wilfully picturesque interpretation on the other.[7]

The rapid development of the Lido as a resort, after the rather tentative beginnings in the 1890s, gave rise not just to a new building type in the lagoons, the great international luxury hotel, but it also allowed further experimentation with different styles to suit these large new structures. The

two largest and earliest examples are also the most opulent, and epitomize this stylistic exploration: the Grand Hotel des Bains and the Excelsior. The former was begun in 1900 by Francesco Marsich and follows a fairly solid, massive Neoclassical form, imposing rather than inviting, while, in sharp contrast, Giovanni Sardi's equally monumental Excelsior (*c*1908) is an extraordinary Veneto-Moorish confection incorporating elements of the Art Nouveau or Liberty style that became particularly popular on the Lido.

Indeed, modern architecture on the Lido has since been little constrained by the unavoidable considerations of taste and concern for the ancient urban fabric that have affected new buildings in the historic centre; later developments, particularly of villas on the Lido, continued to experiment with Art Nouveau and Art Deco; Guido Sullam's villa 'Mon Plaisir' (1906) was, until its later alteration, one of the more delightfully eclectic examples. That Sullam was also able to develop a more powerful and sober style when required is shown by his Cimitero Ebraico, the Jewish Cemetery, a simple, powerful essay in brick and stone.[8]

Large-scale industrial architecture was another of the more revolutionary building types to belatedly reach the lagoons at the end of the nineteenth century. Again, there was little opportunity for such extensive development in the historic city, and many buildings, notably the glassworks of Murano, did not rise above the strictly utilitarian. Nevertheless, some impressive works were produced; one was the severely rational City Slaughterhouse (Macello Comunale), by Giuseppe Salvadori, on the edge of the lagoon near the railway station. It was built in 1842, with a classical simplicity worthy of the powerful functional tradition of the great shipbuilding sheds of the Arsenale. Considerably later, and also considerably more self-conscious, is the great Molino Stucky, the flour mills built by Ernest Wullekopf in 1894 on the Giudecca; these were designed in a towering Hanseatic Gothic style, all in fine brickwork and rising to nine storeys. The Molino marks the high point in the Giudecca's fortunes as an industrial zone, though, and after 1918 most new industrial development took place at Porto Marghera on the mainland shores.

The international art exhibition, the Biennale, has had an important influence both on the city's role in patronizing the development of modern art movements, and on the fabric of a large sector of the eastern part of the city. The Public Gardens in eastern Castello had been laid out in the Napoleonic era in 1808–12 by GianAntonio Selva, and the first National Exhibition of Modern Art was held here in 1887. It was followed by the first International Exhibition in 1895, and the latter has continued to be held here (with one or two omissions in times of war) to the present day. The large central Italian pavilion was designed in 1895 by Mario de Maria as a literally classical temple of culture; but was enlarged on successive occasions, each time changing its appearance to follow stylistic developments: in 1914 it became less classically ornate, with Liberty detailing; in 1932 it was stripped down to produce a fascist 'white modern' facade. Still later, in 1968 it was transformed and humanized by Carlo Scarpa, and most recently of all, in 1995 it has been returned to its prewar appearance for the Biennale's centenary celebrations. The pavilion has thus represented a microcosm of the changing styles of the century.

Gradually, too, it became surrounded by the national pavilions of the chief participating nations, some of which are of considerable quality: Josef Hoffman's Austrian pavilion of 1934; Gerrit Rietveld's Dutch pavilion of 1954; the Venezuelan pavilion by Carlo Scarpa of 1956; Finland's pavilion by Alvar Aalto of 1956; and, most recently James Stirling's bookshop of 1991, which replaces an earlier one by Carlo Scarpa, destroyed by fire. In this way, too, there developed representative examples of each nation's own interpretation of the Modern Movement, from Hoffman's minimal cubist essay to Stirling's striking nautical forms.[9]

The most recent cultural phenomenon to have given rise to a specifically new building type is the cinema. Here again, as in the cases of the much earlier development of lyric opera and the more recent evolution of the Biennale, the city played an important role in nurturing this new medium which was to transcend the local and the regional. The Venice Film Festival is the oldest and one of the most important in the world; first held in 1932, the purpose-built Palazzo del Cinema was constructed shortly afterwards, in 1937 by Luigi Guagliata, again in a fascistic interpretation of the international modern style; It was joined on the same square, and in the same style, by the contemporaneous Palazzo del Casinò (begun 1936). Eugenio Miozzi's striking INA Multistorey Garage at Piazzale Roma is another notable early 'white modern' work, completed in 1934.

Post-war architecture in the city centre has varied considerably in its relationship to the ancient urban fabric and the historic styles by which it is inevitably surrounded; it varies equally in its success in addressing these highly sensitive difficulties. Broadly, two approaches have prevailed: that of the unabashedly mainstream Modern Movement and its derivations on one hand, and more sensitive vernacular-based interpetations on the other. The former, though, are by far the most

THE MACELLO COMUNALE (MUNICIPAL SLAUGHTERHOUSES), CANNAREGIO

By Giuseppe Salvadori, 1824. A fine example of 'the functional tradition', behind a restrained classical facade.

LIDO DI VENEZIA: THE CASINO MUNICIPALE
(below)

An example of a 'white modern' work from
the 1930s, showing fascist influences.

PALAZZO QUERINI STAMPALIA (below right)

Carlo Scarpa's remodelled interior of the
Palazzo, of 1961–3, illustrates his meticulous
attention to detail and his intimate
understanding of the nature of materials.

prevalent. Certain developments have been intrusive by their very scale and nature; one of the most prominent is the still highly controversial Cassa di Risparmio (Savings Bank), by Angelo Scattolin and Pier-Luigi Nervi (1964–71); it occupies an entire block between Campo Manin and Campo San Luca, on the site of Aldo Manuzio's famous sixteenth-century publishing works, the Aldine Press. Even more bulky and repetitive is the ENEL building on the Rio Novo, also by Scattolin, still intrusive but fortunately not on such a sensitive site. A few more carefully considered modern buildings have been successfully inserted into the urban fabric, among them are the offices and flats next to the Papadopoli Gardens by Giuseppe Samona and Egle Renata Trincanato (1955–8).

A different approach entirely is that of a reinterpretation of traditional forms and detailing. This approach has been generally employed for new housing, among which the 'Saffa' scheme by Vittorio Gregotti in Cannaregio (1984–9), and that by Iginio Cappai at Sacca Fisola (1982–9) are among the most interesting and successful. The most striking example of this philosophy is the housing by Giancarlo di Carlo at Mazzorbo in the northern lagoon, in 1979–86. Again

controversial, the complex nevertheless represents an attempt to retain the spirit, scale and traditional materials of the lagoons, coupled with the freer, more sculptural forms of the modern movement. The result has been criticized as excessively self-conscious but it is one of few recent works that attempt to contribute to, rather than detract from, a subtle, traditional vernacular environment.[10]

But the minor though sensitive interventions of the native Carlo Scarpa are the most sympathetic to the materials and the ancient traditions of fine craftsmanship of the city; among them is the evocative remodelling of the Palazzo Querini Stampalia, where the adjacent canal was brought into and around the ground floor of the house itself; the Olivetti showrooms in the Procuratie Vecchie; the remodelled galleries of the Correr Museum in the Procuratie Nuove, as well as those to the Accademia and the Cà d'Oro (Galleria Franchetti) and the entrance to the Istituto Universitario di Architettura at the Tolentini. All are small-scale works which, although modern in style, are clearly differentiated from the original, and respect the slow, organic growth of the city's fabric. In this they echo, on a smaller scale, Scarpa's seminal reinterpretation of the museum at the Castelvecchio in Verona.[11]

The most characteristic features of all of Scarpa's work, other than its spatial subtlety, are his attention to detail and his profound knowledge and understanding of the nature of materials. He cooperated extremely closely with the craftsmen who worked with him, often over many years, and was deeply involved with the physical processes of creating each element of his work. Scarpa always clearly differentiated between the original historic fabric and his new interventions, thus ensuring the honest expression of both components. Although he was a truly modern architect, at the same time, therefore, he reinterpreted the strong Venetian tradition of fine craftsmanship that can be traced back to the Renaissance proto and the medieval maestro.

Postscript

The architects of Venice, both foreign and native, mastered the use of light, of chiaroscuro, and coupled this mastery with the freedom that the city's security made possible to construct buildings that were unique in their response to this context. While many of Venice's greatest painters were natives (the Vivarini, Vittore Carpaccio, the Bellini, Tintoretto and Giambattista Tiepolo), most of its greatest architects were not. Pietro Lombardo came from Lake Lugano; Mauro Codussi was from Bergamo; Jacopo Sansovino came from Rome, although born in Florence; and Andrea Palladio came here from Padua and Vicenza. The city and the institutions of the Republic became the catalyst and patron for these masters enabling them to realize their fullest abilities; they responded to the environment of the lagoon in ways that would not have been possible in their home towns: Palladio's San Giorgio, Codussi's San Michele, Lombardo's Miracoli, are uniquely fitted to their sites and would not have been the same buildings had they been constructed on the Terraferma, without the light of the lagoon and the reflective quality of the water.

Of all of Venice's great architects, only the last, Baldassare Longhena, was a native. On inheriting Palladio's intellectual mantle, he transformed it by producing the Salute with a final Baroque flourish. It is the building in which the possibilities of form and light are developed further and more boldly than any other in the city.

The Republic's final century was an era of considerable achievement, in which the Venetian preoccupation with colour and chiaroscuro reached ever more audacious heights in the paintings of Tiepolo. Nevertheless, we can perhaps identify in these paintings and in the architecture of his contemporaries, Antonio Gaspari, Giorgio Massari and Giuseppe Sardi, the triumph of technique and illusion over intellectual depth and spiritual profundity. In this, of course, with the priceless wisdom of hindsight, we may identify the beginning of the end of Venetian creativity and of the creative will of the Republic itself.

Today, two centuries after the fall of the Republic of the Evangelist, we find an extraordinary mixture in the city's fabric: of violent change coupled with equally widespread continuity. Of the great institutions of the Republic itself, although the doge and Maggior Consiglio are of course long gone, a surprisingly large number remain: the Procuracy of San Marco, still responsible for the basilica and the buildings on the Piazza; the Patriarchate; the Arciconfraternità of the Scuola Grande di San Rocco, and that of the Carmini; religious orders such as the Franciscans, Jesuits, Carmelites and Dominicans; charitable institutions including the Cà di Dio, the Soccorso and the Pietà; and the Magistrato alle Acque, the ancient Republican agency which still today bears responsibility for the maintenance of the canals, lidi and sea defences. Many of the Republican festivals are also still celebrated, with much the same mixture of piety and commercial opportunism as they were in the days of the Serenissima itself: the feast of the patron saint, the festivals of the Redentore, of the Salute and the Carnival.

The fabric of the city, too, functions much as it always has done; the markets at Rialto still feed the city as they have done every working day for the last thousand years, although even here the gold ducats and sacks of pepper and saffron have been replaced by more staple fare and by the trinkets for tourists; and the ferries across the Grand Canal still ply from the same jetties that they did in Marin Sanudo's time.

Today, though, Venice forms part of a complex network of urban forms, no longer confined to the historic centre, or even to the lagoon itself. This network now extends over the Terraferma well beyond Mestre, and embraces the communities of the lagoon from Chioggia to the resorts on the littoral of Iesolo. The city remains the administrative centre of the Region of the Veneto, one of the wealthiest and most highly-developed regions of Italy, with more than four million inhabitants. It is also a significant centre for banking and insurance, and for further education. But the phenomenal rise of mass tourism is, of course, Venice's chief economic activity, and is by far the largest employer, together with many associated cultural activities. The Lido has developed from a littoral of fishing hamlets into an international resort, but it is also an extensive dormitory suburb of the city; large numbers now also commute daily into the city from Mestre and the Terraferma.

To Ruskin, writing 150 years ago, Venice – Torcello's daughter – was already a widow, and although his verdict now seems somewhat premature, the many threats to the city's survival remain, in some ways more serious than ever before. Since the appalling floods of 1966 (and several serious floods since then) extraordinary efforts have been made to restore and conserve this unique cultural legacy; hundreds of buildings have been painstakingly restored. Two fundamental threats, however, remain. One is the continuing damage from flooding, of the slow, steady reclamation of the city by the waters from which it grew; the other is less dramatic (and far less well-known internationally), but even more insidious: the steady loss of the city's real heart, the Venetians themselves. The resident population has halved since 1945 and continues to decline; unless it can be reversed, there can be no genuinely living city, but simply a husk of bricks and stone, occupied by daily commuters who then leave the city deserted. Formidable difficulties remain, therefore, as Venice attempts to find a new equilibrium of numbers, of purpose and, indeed, of identity.

To Italo Calvino, with whose words I began this book, Venice represents the ultimate metaphysical city, a collection of images of the possible, of the extraordinary triumphs which our civilization is capable of achieving. But as a metaphor for all historic but still living cities, Venice is no more frozen in time than any other; rather, it is, like all the others, organic and cyclical. Death and decay are the inevitable corollaries of life and creativity. Many cities have recreated themselves over the centuries, many lives overlaid on one another; Damascus and Rome, for example, have been 'reinvented' and still flourish as great cities today, as does Constantinople, once inheritor of Rome's own mantle, today Istanbul, metropolis of the Near East.

But history is, of course, equally littered with cities that could not rebuild themselves, from which history and cultures have moved on: Babylon, Petra, Thebes. Closer to Venice is Aquileia, once a great Roman city, now a scattering of stones among farms and vineyards; closer still is Torcello, within sight of Venice. Once a powerful bishopric ringed by wealthy monasteries, today it is a hamlet, surrounded by fields of artichokes and muddy creeks, with its solitary bell tower silhouetted over the marshes.

The task remains prodigious. Few cities in the world retain their historic centre so well preserved; few contain so many outstanding buildings, many still in need of urgent restoration. In the meantime, those who cannot directly contribute towards the survival of the city can still observe, record and try to comprehend what we see; that is our pleasure and our unique privilege.

'I will put together, piece by piece, the perfect city, made of fragments mixed with the rest, of instants separated by intervals, of images one sets out, not knowing who receives them ... You must not believe the search for it can stop.' Italo Calvino, *Invisible Cities*.

Notes on the text

CHAPTER 1

1 For Venice's origins, see especially W DORIGO, *Venezia: Origini*, Milan, 1983; G FEDALTO, *Le Origini di Venezia*, Bologna, 1978; G MARZEMIN, *Le Origini romane di Venezia*, Venice, 1937 and G BELLAVITIS and G ROMANELLI, *Venezia, Le città nella storia d'Italia*, Rome and Bari, 1985, esp Ch 1.

2 For the network of Roman roads in the region, see L BOSIO, *Itinerari e strade della Venetian romana*, Padua, 1970.

3 C COSTANTINI, *Aquileia e Grado*, Milan, 1916.

4 The extensive bibliography includes D TALBOT RICE, *Byzantine Art*, London, 1954; A CALASANTI, *L'arte bisantina in Italia*, Milan, 1912; D M NICOL, *Byzantium & Venice: A Study in Diplomatic and Cultural Relations*, Cambridge, 1988, pp1–19.

5 Still fundamental for Venice's constitution is G MARANINI, *La costituzione di Venezia*, 2 vols, Florence, 1927; new pbk edn, 1974, Vol 1, pp21–36.

6 MARANINI, *La costituzione*, Vol 1, Chs 1 and 2.

7 R CESSI AND A ALBERTI, *Rialto: l'isola, il ponte, il mercato*, Bologna, 1934.

8 U MARCATO, *Storia di Chioggia*, Chioggia, 1976, *passim*. See also I TIOZZO, *Chioggia nella storia, nell' arte e nei commerci*, Chioggia, 1920.

9 There is no good general history of Murano, although there are several works on the glass industry; see A GASPARETTO, *Il vetro di Murano dalle origini ad oggi*, Venice, 1958; V ZANETTI, *Guida di Murano e delle celebre fornaci vetrarie*, Venice, 1866 (new facsimile edn, Sala Bolognese, 1984).

10 NICOL, *Byzantium*, pp23–5. See also; J J NORWICH, *Venice:The Rise to Empire*, London, 1977, pp52–3.

11 R CESSI, *Documenti relativi alla storia di Venezia anteriori al Mille*, 2 Vols, Padua, 1942, Vol 1, pp 101–8; NICOL, *Byzantium*, p28. For the Dogado, see BELLAVITIS and ROMANELLI, *Venezia*, p23.

CHAPTER 2

1 For Rialto, see Ch 7. See also S MURATORI, *Studi per una operante storia urbana di Venezia*, Rome, 1959, pp44 & 75–8.

2 MURATORI, *ibid*, pp69–71.

3 For the Benedictine monasteries, see Ch 10 below; see also BELLAVITIS and ROMANELLI, *Venezia*, pp17–20; G PEROCCO and A SALVADORI, *Civiltà di Venezia*, 3 Vols, Venice, 1973–6, Vol 1, pp71–91.

4 MURATORI, *Studi*, pp45,67,70,85 & 94. See also U FRANZOI & D DI STEFANO, *Le Chiese di Venezia*, Venice, 1976, pp19, 123, 146, 175, 359 & 363.

5 MURATORI, *Studi*, pp29–31 and especially the maps on pp40–1.

6 *Ibid*, *passim*. See also P MARETTO, *L'edilizia gotica veneziana*, 2nd edn, Venice, 1978, *passim* but esp the island parish studies on pp59–131.

7 For the wellheads, see P MOLMENTI, *Le vere da pozzo di Venezia*, Venice, 1911.

8 For analyses of the squares see PEROCCO and SALVADORI, *Civiltà*, Vol 1, pp261–70, and MARETTO, *L'edilizia*, *passim*.

9 SHAKESPEARE, *The Merchant of Venice*, II, ii.

10 G PIAMONTE, *Venezia vista dall'acqua*, Venice, 1966, *passim*.

11 MARANINI, *La costituzione*, Vol 2, pp131–269; R CESSI *Storia della Repubblica di Venezia*, 2 Vols, Milan, 1968, Vol 1, pp94–101.

12 For the First Crusade, see *ibid*, CESSI, Ch 5; also S RUNCIMAN, *A History of the Crusades*, 3 Vols, Cambridge, 1951–4, Vol 1, p299 et seq.

13 One of the best general accounts of the Republic, with particular emphasis on foreign trade, commerce and shipping, is F C LANE, *Venice: A Maritime Republic*, Baltimore and London 1973, especially Chs 5, 6 and 7.

14 MARIN SANUDO THE YOUNGER, 'Laus urbis venetae' (In praise of the city of Venice) written in 1493 and published, together with other codices, in A R ARICÒ (ed), *La città di Venetia*, Milan 1980; hereafter referred to as SANUDO, *La città*.

15 For the Maggior Consiglio see MARANINI, *La costituzione*, Vol 1, pp207–40. For voting procedures see also LANE, *Venice*, pp95–100 & 254–62.

16 MARANINI, *La costituzione*, Vol 1, p207–40.

17 For the Fourth Crusade, see NICOL, *Byzantium*, Ch 8; DE QUELLER, *The Fourth Crusade: the Conquest of Constantinople 1201–4*, Philadelphia, 1977; NORWICH, *Venice*, pp146–167. For the Serrata of the Maggior Consiglio in 1297 see MARANINI, *La costituzione*, Vol 1, pp332–364.

18 Paolino's plan is in the Biblioteca Nazionale Marciana, Ms Lat Zan 399. It was first analysed in a paper by Tommaso Temanza, the architect and historian, as *Antica pianta dell' inclita città di Venezia*, Venice, 1781; new facs edn, ed U STEFANUTTI, Sala Bolognese 1977. Temanza also published an engraved transcription of the plan.

19 TEMANZA, *Antica pianta*, pp83–6.

20 *Ibid*, pp73–82; and BELLAVITIS and ROMANELLI, *Venezia*, pp53–6.

21 D CALABI *Il mercato e la città*, Venice, 1993, p54; R MACKENNEY, *Tradesmen and Traders: The World of the Guilds in Venice and Europe 1250–1650*, London, 1987, especially the map on p86.

22 Among several contemporary accounts of the war is that of GALEAZZO GATTARI in *Rerum Italicarum Scriptores*, Vol XVII; RAFAIN CARESINI in *ibid*, Vol XII, Bologna, 1923. See also; LA CASALI, *La guerra di Chioggia e la pace di Torino*, Florence, 1866; LANE, *Venice*, pp190–6.

23 A brief but authoritative and useful summary of the period is that of DS CHAMBERS, *The Imperial Age of Venice 1380–1580*, London, 1970.

24 N RUBINSTEIN, 'Italian reactions to Terraferma expansion in the 15th century' in JR HALE (ed), *Renaissance Venice*, London, 1973.

25 CHAMBERS, *The Imperial Age*, esp Ch 2; LANE, *Venice*, Ch 16; F BRAUDEL, *The Perspective of the World*, Civilization & Capitalism, Vol 3, London, 1985, pp116–137.

26 S RUNCIMAN, *The Fall of Constantinople*, Cambridge, 1965; A PERTUSI, *La caduta di Costantinopoli*, Verona, 1976.

27 A lively account is J MORRIS, *The Venetian Empire: A Sea Voyage*, London, 1980.

28 G ZUCCOLO, *Il restauro statico nell'architettura di Venezia*, Venice, 1975.

29 SANUDO, *La città*, esp pp40–65. For de'Barbari see G CASSINI, *Piante e vedute prospettiche di Venezia 1479–1855*, Venice, 1971, pp32–3;

E A CICOGNA, *Delle iscrizioni veneziani*, Venice, 1824–53, 6 Vols, Vol 4, pp699 and 751.

30 For population studies see L BELTRAMI, *Storia della popolazione di Venezia dalla fine del secolo XVI alla caduta della Repubblica*, Padua, 1954. For comparative European figures see; J DE VRIES, *European Urbanization 1500 to 1800*, London, 1984.

31 G FANELLI, *Firenze, le città nella storia d'Italia*, Rome and Bari, 1980.

32 SANUDO, *La città*, p21.

33 CHAMBERS, *The Imperial Age* pp12–30; W J BOUWSMA, *Venice and the Defense of Republican Liberty*, Berkeley, California, 1968.

34 See below Ch 4; also D HOWARD, *Jacopo Sanovino: Architecture and Patronage in Renaissance Venice*, Yale, 1975, esp Chs 2 and 3.

35 H F BROWN, *The Venetian Printing Press*, London, 1891; M DAVIES, *Aldus Manutius: Printer and Publisher of Renaissance Venice*, London, 1995.

36 Discussed in M TAFURI, *Venice and the Renaissance*, translated by J LEVINE, Cambridge, Mass, 1989, pp139–60.

37 For both of these works, *ibid*, p161–96.

38 For a detailed study of the Tereni Nuovi see G GIANIGHIAN (ed), *Dietro i palazzi: tre secoli di architettura minore a Venezia*, Venice, 1984, pp 45–57, with many drawings and plans.

39 R J GOY, *Venetian Vernacular Architecture: Traditional Housing in the Venetian Lagoon*, Cambridge, 1989, esp p185 et seq, on Murano and pp208–30 on the Giudecca.

40 *Ibid*; see also ZANETTI, *Guida di Murano*. The bibliogra-phy on Palladio's villas is extensive, but see esp P HOLBERTON, *Palladio's Villas: Life in the Renaiss- ance Countryside*, London, 1990; and D COSGROVE, *The Palladian Landscape*, Leicester, 1993.

41 LANE, *Venice*, pp369–74.

42 *Ibid*, pp409–10.

43 B PULLAN (ed), *Crisis and Change in the Venetian Economy in the 16th and 17th centuries*, London, 1968; E BASSI, *L'architettura del sei e settecento a Venezia*, Venice, 1980.

44 GIANIGHIAN, *Dietro i palazzi*, pp45–57 and 122–147. See also E R TRINCANATO, *Venezia Minore*, Milan, 1948; P MARETTO, *La casa veneziana nella storia della città*, Venice, 1986, both of these last with numerous examples.

45 For the fine arts in this period see J MARTINEAU AND A ROBISON (eds), *The Glory of Venice: Art in the 18th century*, New Haven and London, 1994; for architecture see BASSI, *Architettura*, *passim*.

46 See below; Chs 9 and 13.

CHAPTER 3

1 The outstanding recent work on all three practical aspects of Venetian architecture, materials, craftsmen and techniques, is G CANIATO and M DAL BORGO, *Le arti edili a Venezia*, Rome, 1990; ZUCCOLO, *Il Restauro statico*; GOY, *Venetian Verna-cular*, Ch 4, pp21–34 (for a summary in English).

2 CANIATO and DAL BORGO, *Le arti*, pp75–108; G SEBESTA, 'Gli edifici e l'uomo, in *ibid*, pp259–305.

3 For Istrian quarries, see esp S CONNELL, *The*

Employment of Sculptors and Stonemasons in Venice in the 15th Century, London and New York, 1988, *passim*, but esp Ch 8; see also SEBESTA, cit above.

4 GOY, *Venetian Vernacular*, pp25–8; CANIATO and DAL BORGO, *Le arti*, p179 et seq.

5 For all of these materials see CANIATO and DAL BORGO, *ibid*: lime and kilns, pp86–91; 109–16; for sand, pp92–8; for brick kilns, pp 76–86; and Sebesta in *ibid* pp268–73.

6 CANIATO and DAL BORGO, *Le arti*, *passim*; GOY, *Venetian Vernacular*, pp35–90.

7 For this section, see CANIATO and DAL BORGO *Le arti*, *passim*; GOY, *Venetian Vernacular*, pp 35–90; TRINCANATO, *Venezia Minore*, pp83–116.

8 ZUCCOLO, *Il restauro*, pp60–7; GIANIGHIAN and PAVANINI, *Dietro i palazzi*, pp33–7; CANIATO AND DAL BORGO, *Le arti*, pp134–5.

9 CANIATO and DAL BORGO, *Le arti*, pp282–9.

10 *Ibid*, pp141–58.

11 For wells, see MOLMENTI, *Le vere da pozzo*; TRINCANATO, *Venezia Minore*, pp111–14.

12 TRINCANATO, *ibid*, pp98–9; and elsewhere; GOY, *Venetian Vernacular*, pp51–6.

13 TRINCANATO *ibid*, pp94–5; the maximum permitted projection for *barbacani* was set by a stone marker, still visible on a house on Calle della Madonna, San Polo.

14 E ARMANI and M PIANA, 'Le superficie storiche esterne dell'architettura veneziana'; for a conference: *Restauro e conservazione delle facciate dipinte*, Genova, 1984.

15 TRINCANATO, *Venezia Minore*, pp117–20; GOY, *Venetian Vernacular*, pp91–110; GOY, *House of Gold*, pp61–4. See also; *ibid* CANIATO and DAL BORGO, thus: for builders p117 et seq; for stonemasons p159 et seq; for carpenters p179 et seq.

16 For the guild statutes, see the references in CANIATO, note 15 above. The statues were all published in G MONTICOLO, *I capitolari delle arti veneziane*, 2 Vols, Rome, 1905; see also the new edn of the statutes of the *mureri*, in G GIANI-GHIAN (ed), *Ricerche venete*, No 2, Venice, 1993, pp159–211.

17 GOY, 'To the glory of God: building the church of S Maria della Carità, 1441–1454' in *Architectural History*, No 37, 1994, pp1–23.

18 McANDREW, *Venetian Architecture*, pp48, 237 and 371; for Spavento pp391, 396, 400, 416, and 420; See also; PUPPI and PUPPI, *Mauro Codussi*, pp190–95.

CHAPTER 4

1 G SAMONA, et al, *Piazza San Marco*, Padua, 1977; for its spatial development see especially pp43–77.

2 See note 1 above, and PEROCCO and SALVADORI, *Civiltà*, Vol 1, pp138–43.

3 G SAMONA, *Piazza*, esp plans pp56–7.

4 PEROCCO and SALVADORI, *Civiltà*, Vol 1, pp138–43.

5 For the lion of San Marco, see UNESCO, *Venice Restored 1966–1986*, Milan, 1991, pp166–7, with bibliography.

6 The market stalls in the Piazzetta are visible on

a number of views of the city, the earliest is that of Erhard Reuwich (1486).

7 See Ch 9 below; also J McANDREW, *Venetian Architecture of the Early Renaissance*, Cambridge Mass and London, 1980, pp378–97; L PUPPI and L O PUPPI, *Mauro Codussi*, Milan, 1977,pp208–14.

8 HOWARD, *Jacopo Sansovino*, pp8–37; and Ch 9 below.

9 SAMONA, *Piazza*, pp56–7; HOWARD, *Jacopo Sansovino*, pp81–4.

10 SANUDO, *La città*, p24; F SANSOVINO and G MARTINIONI, *Venetia, città nobilissima et singolare*, 2 Vols (1st edn Venice, 1580; revised edn Venice 1663; new facsimile of the 1663 edn, Venice, 1968) Vol 1, pp292–3.

11 SANUDO, *La città*, p25

12 SANSOVINO and MARTINIONI, *Venetia*, Vol 1, pp294–5.

13 SANUDO, *La città*, pp59–60; SAMONA *Piazza*, pp81–91; also E MUIR, *Civic Ritual in Renaissance Venice*, Princeton, 1981.

14 MARANINI, *La costituzione*, Vol 2, pp35–77; also SANUDO, *La città*, pp85–8.

15 For the ducal ceremonies see SANSOVINO and MARTINIONI, *Venetia*, Vol 1, pp476–88; also SANUDO, *La città*, pp88–90; and D S CHAMBERS and B PULLAN, *Venice: A Documentary History 1450–1630*, Oxford, 1992, pp45–50.

16 SANUDO, *La città*, pp90–1; and CHAMBERS and PULLAN, *Venice*, p45.

17 For the many festivals, see SANSOVINO and MARTINONI, *Venetia*, Vol 1, p406 et seq; the 'holy festivals' are also listed by SANUDO, *La città*, p56; for Corpus Domini see SANUDO *ibid*, pp60–2.

18 SANUDO, *ibid*, pp58–61.

19 *Ibid*, pp59–60; and SANSOVINO and MARTINIONI, *Venetia*, Vol 1, pp498–501.

20 SANSOVINO, *ibid*, Vol 1, pp441–9; L PUPPI, *Andrea Palladio*, Milan, 1973, pp248–50.

21 For Tirali, see E BASSI, *Architettura del sei e settecento a Venezia*, Naples, 1962, pp282 and 293.

22 B P TORSELLO, 'Il neoclassico nella Piazza' in SAMONA, *Piazza*, pp187–94.

23 *Ibid*, and PEROCCO and SALVADORI, *Civilta*, Vol 3, pp1211–19.

CHAPTER 5

1 The most important works on the Arsenale are: E CONCINA, *L'Arsenale della Repubblica di Venezia*, Milan, 1984; and G BELLAVITIS, *L'Arsenale di Venezia: storia di una grande struttura urbana*, Venice 1983.

2 BELLAVITIS, *L'Arsenale*, pp24 & 27, et seq.

3 For the twelfth and thirteenth centuries see CONCINA, *L'Arsenale*, p9 et seq. For fourteenth century *ibid*, p25 et seq.

4 P GAZZOLA (ed), *Michele Sanmicheli*, Venice, 1960 pp130–133, with further bibliography.

5 E CONCINA (ed), *Arsenali e città nell' Occidente europeo*, Rome, 1987 with studies of the Arsenals of Toulon, Palermo, Rochefort, Genoa, etc. For Pisa, see F REDI, 'L'arsenale medievale di Pisa' in *ibid*, pp63–8. For Genoa see; E POLEGGI 'L'Arsenale della repubblica di Genova' in *ibid*, pp83–96.

6 LANE, *Venice*, pp163–5; CONCINA, *L'Arsenale*, p25 et seq; BELLAVITIS, *L'Arsenale*, pp46–54.

7 CONCINA, *L'Arsenale*, pp51–73; and McANDREW, *Venetian Architecture*, pp17–23.

8 SANUDO, *La città*, p36.

9 BELLAVITIS, *L'Arsenale*, p78 et seq; LANE, *Venice*, p167; see also F C LANE, *Venetian Ships and Ship-builders of the Renaissance*, Baltimore, 1934; new edn, 1992, pp1–34.

10 For example, the two eastern corner towers bear the date 1526 and the arms of the Pesaro and Priuli families.

11 For the sixteenth-century *renovatio*, see CONCINA, *L'Arsenale*, pp95–110.

12 GAZZOLA, *Sanmicheli*, pp192–3 for the Bucintoro shed; see also BELLAVITIS, *L'Arsenale*, pp102–5 & 110.

13 *Ibid*, BELLAVITIS, p 127–31 (the Corderia), pp116–18 (Canale delle Galeazze).

14 For Lepanto, see, LANE *Venice*, pp369–74.

15 SANSOVINO and MARTINIONI, *Venetia*, Vol 1, pp366–7.

16 T CORYAT, *Coryat's Crudities*, 2 Vols, London, 1905, Vol 1, p358.

17 J EVELYN, *Diary and Correspondence*, 6 Vols, E S DeBEER (ed), Oxford, 1955, Vol 1, p208.

18 P MUNDAY, *The Travels of Peter Munday*, Cambridge, 1907, Vol 1, pp96–7.

19 For social analyses, see; R C DAVIS, *Shipbuilders of the Venetian Arsenal*, Baltimore, 1991, esp Ch 3. See also MURATORI, *Studi*, p 106, et seq.

20 TRINCANATO, *Venezia Minore*, pp158–71; and MARETTO, *La casa*, pp358–60.

21 DAVIS, *Shipbuilders*, esp pp83–117 & 150–82.

22 BELLAVITIS, *L'Arsenale*, pp169–206 & 207–45.

CHAPTER 6

1 Cited in CHAMBERS and PULLAN, *Venice*, pp338–9.

2 Among several useful works on the Ghetto are: R CURIEL and B D COOPERMAN, *The Venetian Ghetto*, New York, 1990; R CALIMANI, *Storia del Ghetto di Venezia*, Milan, 1985; G COZZI, *Gli Ebrei e Venezia*, Milan, 1987; and U FORTIS (ed), *Venezia Ebraica*, Rome, 1979.

3 B PULLAN, *Rich and Poor in Renaissance Venice*, Oxford, 1971, especially 'Foundations of the Ghetto', pp476–509.

4 *Ibid*, p 477; SANSOVINO and MARTINIONI, *Venetia*, Vol 1, p368.

5 CHAMBERS and PULLAN, *Venice*, pp338–9.

6 *Ibid*, pp326–7.

7 GIANIGHIAN, *Dietro i palazzi*, pp186–91.

8 CURIEL and COOPERMAN, *The Venetian Ghetto*, pp43–55, 57–68 and 81–90.

9 PULLAN, *Rich and Poor*, pp510–37. For the Senate decree see; CHAMBERS and PULLAN *Venice*, p 344; see also COZZI, *Gli Ebrei*, pp211–60.

10 CURIEL and COOPERMAN *The Venetian Ghetto*, pp125–43.

11 MARETTO, *La Casa*, pp318–21; and BELLAVITIS and ROMANELLI, *Venezia*, p104.

12 PULLAN, *Rich and Poor*, pp510–11, 537 and 538–78. See also C ROTH, *A History of the Marranos*, Philadelphia, 1932.

13 SANSOVINO and MARTINIONI, *Venetia*, Vol 1, p368.

CHAPTER 7

1 For the origins of the market, see CALABI, *Il Mercato*, pp63–6; the book also contains comparative studies of markets in Paris, Seville, Augsburg, London, Florence, Antwerp etc. See also CESSI and ALBERTI, *Rialto*; D CALABI and P MORACHIELLO, *Rialto:le fabbriche e il ponte*, Turin, 1987, pp5–15.

2 BELLAVITIS and ROMANELLI, *Venezia* p28; DORIGO, *Venezia:Origini*, pp456–60.

3 CALABI and MORACHIELLO, *Rialto*, p17; CESSI and ALBERTI, *Rialto*, pp25–6; and BELTRAMI, *Storia della popolazione*.

4 For trading voyages, see F C LANE, *I mercanti di Venezia*, Turin, 1982, especially pp123–41.

5 CALABI, *Il mercato*, pp81–5; CALABI and MORACHIELLO, *Rialto*, pp16–40; and for the various government departments located here, see also SANUDO, *La città*, pp 249, 251, 253, 263,273 etc.

6 SANUDO, *La città*, pp29–31. See also CHAMBERS and PULLAN, *Venice*, pp11–14. For another impression, see P CASOLA, *Viaggio a Gerusalemme*, 1494, Milan, 1855, pp7–9.

7 CALABI and MORACHIELLO, *Rialto*, pp28–37; also LANE, *I mercanti*, pp219–36, and CESSI AND ALBERTI, *Rialto*, p32.

8 CALABI and MORACHIELLO, *ibid*, pp91–117 ('Le chiese dell'insula'). See also FRANZOI AND DI STEFANO, *Le chiese*, pp13–18.

9 Mc ANDREW, *Venetian architecture* pp434–48; also H SIMONSFELD, *Der Fondaco dei Tedeschi in Venedig*, 2 Vols, Stuttgart, 1887. For the frescos see G VASARI, *Lives of the Painters*, 1st complete English edn, translated by J FOSTER, 5 Vols, London, 1879, Vol 2, pp398–9.

10 For the fire, see CALABI and MORACHIELLO, *Rialto*, pp41–9; Sanudo's eyewitness account is in his *Diarii*, R FULIN et al eds, Venice 1879–1903, Vol XVII, cols 458–69.

11 For debates on reconstruction, see CALABI and MORACHIELLO, *Rialto*, pp50–60.

12 *Ibid*, pp52–5; for the Fabbriche Vecchie; *ibid*, pp61–78. One of the proposals was by Fra Giocondo: see R BRENZONI, *Fra Giocondo veronese*, Florence, 1960, pp47–57.

13 CALABI, *Il mercato*, pp164–7.

14 McANDREW, *Venetian Architecture*, pp505–27; P PAOLETTI, *L'architettura e la scultura del Rinasci- mento in Venezia*, 2 Vols, Venice, 1897, Vol 2, p260; and CALABI and MORACHIELLO, *Rialto* pp79–90.

15 HOWARD, *Jacopo Sansovino*, pp47–61; M TAFURI, *Jacopo Sansovino e l'architettura del' 500 a Venezia*, Padua, 1969; and CALABI and MORACHIELLO, *Rialto*, pp42–59.

16 For early chronicles relating to the timber bridge, see refs in CALABI and MORACHIELLO, *Rialto*, p174; see also CESSI and ALBERTI, *Rialto*, pp163–5.

17 CALABI and MORACHIELLO, *ibid*, pp196–206, 207–18; also HOWARD, *Jacopo Sansovino*, pp53–4.

18 HOWARD, *Jacopo Sansovino*, pp60–1.

19 For Palladio's designs, see PUPPI, *Andrea Palladio*, pp140–4; CALABI and MORACHIELLO, *Rialto*, pp219–34. For Palladio's second project, see his *I Quattro Libri dell'Architettura*, Venice 1570; new facsimile edn, Milan, 1968, Lib III, pp25–7; and O BERTOTTO SCAMOZZI *Le fabbriche e i disegni di Palladio*, Vicenza, 1796; new facsimile edn, London, 1968, Lib IV, pp77–9. See also G G ZORZI, *Le chiese e i ponti di Andrea Palladio*, Vicenza, 1966, p225.

20 HOWARD, *Jacopo Sansovino*, pp60–1.

21 For the 1580s *renovatio*, see TAFURI, *Venice and the Renaissance*, pp161–96.

22 SANSOVINO and MARTINIONI, *Venetia*, Vol 1, p365. CALABI and MORACHIELLO, *Rialto*, pp235–59. Guglielmo de'Grandi's final attempt to get his own design accepted was on 23 December 1587. His description is cited in; CHAMBERS and PULLAN, *Venice*, pp404–5.

23 For all the above see CALABI and MORACHIELLO, *Rialto*, pp283–300.

24 SANSOVINO and MARTINIONI, *Venetia*, 1, pp364–5.

25 The sculptures are by Tiziano Aspetti and Agostino Rubini. A plaque also records the names of the three *provveditori*, 'Aloysio Georgio, Proc, M Antonio Barbaro, Eq et Proc; Iacobo Foscareno Eq et Proc.'

CHAPTER 8

1 SANUDO, *La città*, pp33–4; translated in CHAMBERS AND PULLAN, *Venice*, pp16–17.

2 MARANINI, *La costituzione, passim*. For an accessible summary history, see LANE, *Venice*, Chps 8, 9 and 13; also CESSI, *Storia di Venezia*, Vol 2; for a contemporary account, SANUDO, *ibid*, p85, et seq; also DE QUELLER, *Il Patriziato veneziano: la realtà contro il mito*, Rome, 1987; translation of *The Venetian Patriciate: Reality versus Myth*, Chicago, 1986; also; SANUDO, *ibid*, pp145–52.

3 MARANINI, *ibid*, Vol 1, pp172–206; *ibid*, Vol 2, pp273–383; SANUDO, *ibid*, p96.

4 MARANINI, *ibid*, Vol 2, pp387–472.

5 There is a concise summary of these, and all other government posts and offices, in; SANUDO, *La città*, esp pp92 and 127–8.

6 All of the important, though meagre surviving documents on the construction were published by G LORENZI, *Monumenti per servire alla storia del Palazzo Ducale di Venezia*, Venice, 1869.

7 SANSOVINO and MARTINIONI, *Venetia*, Vol 1, p 319.

8 For the Palazzo della Ragione in Padua, see; G A MOSCHINI, *Il Palazzo della Ragione di Padova*, Venice, 1963.

9 For the Molo wing generally, see E ARSLAN, *Venezia gotica*, Milan, 1970, esp, pp137–50.

10 W WOLTERS, *La scultura veneziana gotica*, 2 Vols, Venice, 1976, Vol 1, pp40–8, 173–9; also; J POPE-HENNESSEY, *Italian Gothic Sculpture*, 3rd edn, London, 1979, pp47–8 and 219–22.

11 For the window, see ARSLAN, *Venezia gotica*, pp149–50; also PAOLETTI, *L'architettura*, Vol 1, pp2–3.

12 See especially N HUSE and W WOLTERS, *The Art of Renaissance Venice*, Chicago and London 1990, p303 et seq.

13 S ROMANO, *The Restoration of the Porta della Carta*, translated by A CLARKE AND P RYLANDS, Venice, 1979, *passim*; also *ibid*, WOLTERS, Vol 1, pp281–4; *ibid*, POPE-HENNESSEY, pp49–5, 222 & 284; ARSLAN, *Venezia gotica*, pp242–4.

14 A M SCHULZ, *Antonio Rizzo, Sculptor and Architect*, Princeton, 1983, esp, pp32–8 & 152–5; also D PINCUS, *The Arco Foscari: The Building of a Triumphal Gateway in 15th Century Venice*, New York, 1976, *passim*.

15 SCHULZ, *ibid*, pp27–38, 82–113 and 190–202.

16 HUSE and WOLTERS, *The Art of Renaissance Venice*, pp27–9, where the attribution to Codussi of both the canal and courtyard facades is made.

17 F CESSI, *Alessandro Vittoria, scultore (1525–1608)*, 2 Vols, Trento, 1961–2.

18 The ducal apartments were also connected to a large banqueting hall by a passageway. This hall now forms part of the Palazzo Patriarcale.

19 P FORTINI BROWN, *Venetian Narrative Painting in the Age of Carpaccio*, New Haven & London, 1988.

20 CHAMBERS and PULLAN, *Venice*, pp400–1, for the themes and iconographic programme.

21 SANSOVINO and MARTINIONI, *Venetia*, Vol 1, 337.

22 L PUPPI, *Andrea Palladio*, Milan 1973,pp266–9.

23 For the prisons, see U FRANZOI, 'Le prigioni' in Samona, *Piazza*, pp173–5; also TAFURI, *Venice and the Renaissance*, pp182–3.

24 For the Procurators, see SANUDO, *La città*, pp104–6.

25 For the Torre, see PUPPI and PUPPI, *Mauro Codussi*, pp208–14; L ANGELINI, *Le opere in Venezia di Mauro Codussi*, Milan 1945, pp54–66; McANDREW, *Venetian Architecture*, pp378–96. The relevant documents were published in L ERIZZO, *Relazione storico-artistica della Torre dell'Orologio di San Marco in Venezia*, Venice 1860.

26 For the costs and specification of the clock, see CHAMBERS and PULLAN, *Venice*, pp394–6.

27 SAMONA, *Piazza*, pp143–9; McANDREW, *Venetian Architecture*, pp400–25.

28 HOWARD, *Jacopo Sansovino*, pp17–28; SANSOVINO AND MARTINIONI, *Venetia*, Vol 1, pp308–12.

29 *Ibid*, HOWARD; *ibid*, SANSOVINO, Vol 1, pp308– 14; G B STEFINLONGO, 'La libreria di San Marco' in Samona, *Piazza*, pp161–71; M TAFURI, *Jacopo Sansovino e l'architettura del '500 a Venezia*, Padua, 1969, p54 et seq.

30 HOWARD, *ibid*, pp28–35.

31 HOWARD, *ibid*, pp38–47; G SCATTOLIN, 'La Zecca' in SAMONA, *Piazza*, pp151–8; SANSOVINO and MARTINIONI, *Venetia*, Vol 1, pp314–5.

32 U FRANZOI, 'Le trasformazioni edilizie' in SAMONA, *Piazza*, pp56–7.

33 T TEMANZA, *La vita di Vincenzo Scamozzi vicentino architetto*, Venice, 1770; also T TALAMINI, 'Le Procuratie Nuove' in SAMONA, *Piazza*, pp177–84.

34 For Longhena, see BASSI, *Architettura*, pp108–10.

35 CALABI and MORACHIELLO, *Rialto*, p22–3, 28&31.

36 BASSI, *Architettura*, pp110, 158 and 160.

CHAPTER 9

1 G BRUSIN, 'Aquileia e Grado' in *Storia di Venezia*, Vol 2, Venice, 1957; C COSTANTINI *Aquileia e Grado*, Milan 1916.

2 FRANZOI and Di STEFANO, *Le chiese*, ppIX–XX.

3 F GILBERT, 'Venice in the crisis of the League of Cambrai' in HALE, *Renaissance Venice*, pp274–92.

4 SARPI was a prolific writer, see his *Opere*, eds G AND L COZZI, Milan and Naples, 1969.

5 A succinct guide to Grado's churches is S TAVANO, *Grado: guida storica e artistic*, Udine, 1976.

6 M BRUNETTI et al,*Torcello*, Venice, 1940; G LORENZETTI, *Torcello, la sua storia, i suoi monumenti* Venice 1939; R POLACCO, *La cattedrale di Torcello*, Venice 1984. There are particularly fine baptisteries at Florence, Pisa, Parma & Ravenna.

7 Cf the Dome of the Rock in Jerusalem. See also 'The religious symbolism of centralised churches' in WITTKOWER, *Architectural Principles*, pp38–40.

8 ZANETTI, *Guida*, pp133–54; V ZANETTI, *La basilica dei SS Maria e Donato di Murano*, Venice 1873; F CORNER, *Notizie storiche*.

9 The essential bibliography for San Marco must include: O DEMUS, *The Mosaics of San Marco in Venice*, 4 Vols, Dumbarton Oaks, 1984; a more accessible summary is O DEMUS, *The Mosaic Decoration of San Marco, Venice*, Chicago, Dumbarton Oaks and London, 1988, ed H KESSLER. See also L MARANGONI, *La basilica di San Marco in Venezia*, Rome, 1910; S BETTINI, *L'architett-ura di San Marco*, Padua, 1945; G MARIACHER AND T PIGNATTI, *La basilica di San Marco a Venezia*, Venice, 1950. Also refer to general bibliography.

10 For comparative plans, see also PEROCCO and SALVADORI, *Civiltà*, Vol 1, pp132–4.

11 For the reconstruction of the facade, see *ibid*, Vol 1, p141; also DEMUS, *The Mosaic Decoration*, p88.

12 M PALLOTTINO et al, *The Horses of San Marco*, translated by J and V WILTONELY, Milan, 1977.

13 DEMUS, *The Mosaic Decoration*, pp7– 14, 39–54 and 127, *passim*.

14 W F VOLBACH, *Il tesoro di San Marco: 1: La Pala d'Oro*, Florence, 1965.

15 POPE-HENNESSEY, *Italian Gothic*, pp49 and 221; WOLTERS, *La scultura*, Vol 1, pp276–8.

16 For rituals, see esp SANSOVINO and MARTINIONI, *Venetia*, Vol1, p406 et seq.

17 SANUDO, *La città*, pp40–5.

18 FRANZOI and DI STEFANO, *Le Chiese*, pp66–8, 69–73, 190–93 and 278–9.See also; G COSTANTINI, *La chiesa di San Giacomo dell'Orio*, Venice, 1912.

19 FRANZOI and DI STEFANO, *Le Chiese*, pp13–14.

20 FRANZOI and DI STEFANO, *Le Chiese*, pp33–46; C ESSER, *Origins of the Franciscan Order*, Chicago, 1970; G FOGOLARI, *Chiese veneziane: I Frari i SS Giovanni e Paolo*, Milan, 1931.

21 R GOFFEN, *Piety and Patronage in Renaissance Venice: Bellini, Titian and the Franciscans*, New Haven and London, 1986.

22 SANSOVINO and MARTINIONI, *Venetia*, Vol 1, pp56 and 187.

23 FRANZOI and DI STEFANO, *Le Chiese*, pp333–4; A NIERO, *La chiesa di S Stefano in Venezia*, Padua, 1978.

24 A CLARKE and P RYLANDS, *The Church of the Madonna dell'Orto*, London, 1977.

25 For all of the above, see FRANZOI AND Di STEFANO, *Le Chiese*, pp89, 129–131, 149, 177–181, 216–23 and 534.

26 A M SCHULZ, *Antonio Rizzo, Sculptor and Architect*, Princeton, 1983, pp43–65, and cat no 16; and pp191–4, and cat no 25. Schulz rejects the attribution of the Cappello relief to Rizzo, and ascribes it instead to Nicolo di Giovanni Fiorentino. See also McANDREW, *Venetian Architecture*, pp62–81.

27 There is no comprehensive monograph on Pietro Lombardo, but for stylistic analyses of the three tombs see McANDREW, *Venetian Architecture*, pp118–33.

28 For the Miracoli, see R LIEBERMAN, 'The Church of S Maria dei Miracoli in Venice' (PhD Dissertation, Univ of New York, 1972); FRANZOI AND Di STEFANO, *Le Chiese*, pp162–7; McANDREW, *Venetian Architecture*, pp150–81.

29 PUPPI and PUPPI, *Mauro Codussi*, *passim*, esp pp177–83, with docs. See also ANGELINI, *Le Opere*, pp29–38; McANDREW *Venetian Architecture*, pp236–61.

30 For Gambello at San Zaccaria, see McANDREW, *ibid*, pp24–37; for Codussi, *ibid*, pp268–81; ANGELINI, *ibid*, pp40–6; PUPPI and PUPPI, *ibid*, pp48–61, 134–9 and 190–95.

31 McANDREW, *ibid*, pp282–301; ANGELINI, *ibid*, pp51–4; PUPPI AND PUPPI, *ibid*, pp164–70 and 206–8.

32 For San Giovanni Crisostomo, see PUPPI and PUPPI, *ibid*, pp131–4 and 260–71; McANDREW *ibid*, pp302–19. For San Felice and Santa Maria Mater Domini, see FRANZOI and DI STEFANO, *Le Chiese*, pp60–1 and 144–5. For centralized church plans, see WITTKOWER, *Architectural Principles*, pp16–40.

33 For Scarpagnino, see FRANZOI and Di STEFANO, *Le Chiese*, pp16–17, 182 and 322. For San Salvador, see McANDREW, *Venetian Architecture*, pp449–55; TAFURI, *Venice*, pp17–31; and for the Vendramin monument, McANDREW, *ibid*, pp462–9.

34 For Sansovino's churches, see HOWARD, *Jacopo Sansovino*, pp64–87; for Zorzi's theories, see WITTKOWER, *Architectural Principles*, pp104–7; TAFURI, *Venice*, pp59–64. For Francesco Sansovino on his father's churches, see *Venetia*, Vol 1, pp34, 48, 109 and 126.

35 The Palladio bibliography is very extensive; for the churches, see esp. PUPPI, *Palladio*; BERTOTTI SCAMOZZI, *Le fabbriche*; B BOUCHER, *Andrea Palladio: The Architect in his Time*, London, New York and Paris, 1994; G G ZORZI, *Le chiese e ponti di Andrea Palladio*, Venice, 1966.

36 See note 35 above; also E BASSI, *Il convento della Carità*, Vicenza, 1971; ANDREA PALLADIO, *Quattro Libri*, II, pp29–32.

37 PUPPI, *Palladio*, pp187–9; WITTKOWER, *Architectural Principles*, pp89–96; BOUCHER, *Andrea Palladio*, pp176–80.

38 FRANZOI and DI STEFANO, *Le Chiese*, pp366–83; BERTOTTI SCAMOZZI, *Le fabbriche*, IV, pp16–19. See also note 35 above.

39 PUPPI, *Palladio*, pp262–6; BERTOTTI SCAMOZZI, *Le fabbriche*, IV, pp11–15; BOUCHER, *Andrea Palladio*, pp192–200.

40 BASSI, *Architettura*, pp86–108; FRANZOI AND DI STEFANO, *Le Chiese*, pp242–56. For the ducal procession see SANSOVINO AND MARTINIONI, *Venetia*, Vol 1, pp525–6.

41 For Longhena's other churches see BASSI, *Architettura*, pp110, 112, 118–22, 188–92 and 204–5; FRANZOI AND Di STEFANO, *Le Chiese*, pp98–9 and 444–50.

42 For Sardi's career, see BASSI, *Architettura*, pp185–205.

43 For Tremignon, see BASSI, *Architettura*, pp233–6.

44 For Gaspari's work, see FRANZOI and DI STEFANO, *Le Chiese*, pp337–42 and 418–20; BASSI, *Architettura*, pp246–63.

45 BASSI, *Architettura*, pp207–32.

46 For Tirali, see BASSI, *Architettura*, pp269–94; FRANZOI AND Di STEFANO, *Le Chiese*, pp80–4. For Scalfarotto, see BASSI, *ibid*, pp335–8; FRANZOI, *ibid*, pp77–8. For Temanza, FRANZOI, *ibid*, pp120–22.

47 For Massari, see BASSI, *ibid*, pp295–334.

48 For Selva, see FRANZOI and DI STEFANO, *Le Chiese*, pp329–32.

CHAPTER 10

1 The essential bibliography for the Scuole Grandi includes PULLAN, *Rich and Poor*; MacKENNEY, *Tradesmen and Traders*; P SOHM, *The Scuola Grande di San Marco 1437–1550*, London and New York 1982. Also, SANSOVINO AND MARTINIONI, *Venetia*, Vol 1, p281 et seq.

2 PULLAN, *Rich and Poor*, pp33–62 and 84–131.

3 SOHM, *The Scuola Grande*, esp, pp50–60.

4 Cited in CHAMBERS and PULLAN, *Venice*, p214, translated by R MacKENNEY.

5 For the Carità Church, see GOY, 'To the Glory of God', *Architectural History*. For the scuola, see SOHM, *The Scuola Grande*, pp297–308; SANSOVINO and MARTINIONI, *Venetia*, Vol 1, pp281–2.

6 SOHM, *ibid*, *passim*; P PAOLETTI, *La Scuola Grande di San Marco*, Venice 1929; U STEFANUTTI, *La Scuola Grande di San Marco*, Venice 1955.

7 McANDREW, *Venetian Architecture*, pp182–93 and 358–63; PUPPI and PUPPI, *Mauro Codussi*, pp73–89 and 196–203; SANSOVINO and MARTINIONI, *Venetia*, Vol 1, pp286–7.

8 SOHM, *The Scuola Grande*,pp72–5;G LORENZETTI, *La Scuola Grande di San Giovanni Evangelista a Venezia*, Venice 1929.

9 McANDREW, *Venetian Architecture*, pp364–77; SOHM, *The Scuola Grande*, pp197–207; PUPPI and PUPPI, *Mauro Codussi*, pp93–110 and 218–21.

10 BROWN, *Venetian Narrative Painting*, especially pp266–8.

11 SOHM, *The Scuola Grande*, pp309–13.

12 HOWARD, *Jacopo Sansovino*, pp96–112; SANSOVINO and MARTINIONI, *Venetia*, Vol 1, pp285–6; TAFURI, *Venice*, pp81–2 and 93–5.

13 SOHM, *The Scuola Grande*, pp207–21; McANDREW, *Venetian Architecture*, pp519–24; A MAZZUCATO, *La Scuola Grande e la chiesa di*

San Rocco in Venezia, Venice, 1953; PAOLETTI, l'Architettura, Vol 2, pp289–90.

14 SOHM, ibid, pp207–21 and 324–54; TAFURI, Venice, pp84–6 and 96–101.

15 C RIDOLFI, The Life of Tintoretto (1st edn, Venice, 1642; new edn translated by C and R ENGGASS, University Park and London, 1984) pp30–7; H TIETZE, Tintoretto, London, 1958; E NEWTON, Tintoretto, London, 1952.

16 For some of the housing developments of the Scuola Grande, see GIANIGHIAN, Dietro i Palazzi, pp80–3, 92–5 and 132–5.

17 PULLAN, Rich and Poor, pp63–83.

18 G SCATTOLIN, La Scuola Grande di San Teodoro in Venezia, Venice, 1961.

19 A NIERO, La Scuola Grande dei Carmini, Venice, 1963.

20 MacKENNEY, Tradesmen, pp10–16 and 44–65.

21 See bibliography to Ch 6, note 2; especially CURIEL AND COOPERMAN, The Venetian Ghetto; and CALIMANI, Storia del Ghetto.

22 For a new general survey, see H MEEK, The Synagogue, London, 1994.

23 The Greeks petitioned the Republic in 1498 and again in 1511, see CHAMBERS and PULLAN, Venice, pp333–6.

24 BASSI, Architettura, pp168–73.

25 T PIGNATTI, Le scuole di Venezia, Milan, 1981, pp89–118.

26 For the painting cycles in the hall, see BROWN, Venetian Narrative Painting, especially pp287–90.

CHAPTER 11

1 Cited in CHAMBERS and PULLAN, Venice, pp303–6.

2 G BENZONI, 'La stenta vita' in GIANIGHIAN AND PAVANINI, Dietro i Palazzi, pp27–31.

3 PULLAN, Rich and Poor, pp197–215; FRANZOI AND DI STEFANO, Le Chiese, pp481–7.

4 PULLAN, Rich and Poor, pp216–38 and 287–326; FRANZOI and DI STEFANO, ibid, pp181,226,232 and 444. For the Derelitti and Incurabili, see CHAMBERS and PULLAN, Venice, pp308–12; for the Pietà, ibid, pp313–4.

5 HOWARD, Jacopo Sansovino, pp112–9.

6 For an accessible modern survey, see H C ROBBINS LANDON and J J NORWICH, Five Centuries of Music in Venice, London, 1991, p119, et seq.

7 C De BROSSES, Lettres familieres sur l'Italie, Paris, 1931, Vol 1, p239.

8 HOWARD, Jacopo Sansovino, pp88–95.

9 BASSI, Architettura, pp164–9 and 313–8.

10 For an exhaustive survey of housing types, see P MARETTO's encyclopedic La casa veneziana nella storia della città, Venice, 1986.

11 Ibid, passim. See also GOY, Venetian Vernacular, pp163–7 (for city centre examples) and pp251–85 (Burano).

12 TRINCANATO, Venezia Minore,esp pp267 & 272.

13 GOY, Venetian Vernacular, pp150–63.

14 TRINCANATO, Venezia Minore, p256 et seq; ARSLAN, Venezia gotica pp28 and 33; MARETTO, La casa, passim.

15 GOY, Venetian Vernacular, Chp 11 (Murano) and Ch 13 (Pellestrina).

16 MARETTO, La casa, pp353–433; and TRINCANATO, Venezia Minore, pp136–45.

17 GIANIGHIAN and PAVANINI, Dietro i Palazzi, pp68–9, 76–83 and 136–7; and TRINCANATO, Venezia Minore, pp310–13.

18 GIANIGHIAN and PAVANINI, Dietro i Palazzi, pp74–5 and 84–7.

19 Ibid, pp88–91, 96–7, 110–13 and 140–5.

20 For the fights or pugni, see R C DAVIS, Shipbuilders, pp135–49.

21 O LOGAN, Venezia: Cultura e società 1470–1790 Rome, 1980, pp103–36.

22 UNESCO, Venice Restored 1966–86 Milan, 1991, pp147–9.

23 PEROCCO and SALVADORI, Civiltà, Vol 3, pp922–35.

24 H E REDLICH, Claudio Monteverdi, Life and Works, Oxford, 1952; W WEAVER, The Golden Century of Italian Opera: from Rossini to Puccini, London, 1980.

25 ROBBINS LANDON and NORWICH, Five Centuries, p156 et seq.

26 C GATTI, Verdi, Milan, 1931; and ROBBINS LANDON and NORWICH, Five Centuries, pp167–74.

CHAPTER 12

1 A ZORZI, Venetian Palaces, New York, 1989, pp42–7.

2 Ibid, pp48–59; and MARETTO, L'edilizia, p63.

3 For analyses of this group, with plans, see MARETTO, L'edilizia, pp59–62.

4 ARSLAN, Venezia gotica, pp13–30; MARETTO, La casa, pp75–96.

5 ARSLAN, ibid, pp30–5, 160 and 230; ZORZI, Venetian Palaces, pp118–21.

6 ZORZI, ibid, pp122–9; ARSLAN, ibid, pp92–6, 157–8 and 163; and MARETTO, La casa, pp131–7.

7 GOY, Venetian Vernacular, pp42–4; and MARETTO, L'edilizia, pp48–50.

8 Ibid, GOY, pp129–35; ARSLAN, Venezia gotica, p 236–50 and 317–31; and MARETTO, La casa, esp pp142–58.

9 R J GOY, 'Architectural taste and style in early quattrocento Venice: the facade of the Cà d'Oro and its legacy' in War, Culture and Society in Renaissance Venice, eds; D S Chambers, C H Clough and M E Mallett, London and Rio Grande, 1993, pp173–90.

10 GOY, House of Gold, passim; ZORZI, Venetian Palaces, pp148–63.

11 ZORZI, ibid, pp164–9; ARSLAN, Venezia gotica, pp246–8, 320 and 324; and MARETTO, L'edilizia, pp102–5.

12 ZORZI, ibid, pp170–7; MARETTO, L'edilizia, p98; ARSLAN, Venezia gotica, pp319–20.

13 ARSLAN, Venezia gotica, p321; MARETTO, La casa, pp277–8.

14 GOY, House of Gold, pp37–40; LANE, I mercanti, passim.

15 On rustication, see McANDREW, Venetian Architecture, pp12–14; BASSI, Palazzi, p38 et seq. Filarete (Antonio Averlino) was born in Florence in c1400; he visited Rome and in 1449 was in Venice. He went to Milan at Francesco Sforza's behest and, on the recommendation of Piero de' Medici, he stayed in Milan until 1465. In 1461–4 he wrote the Trattato di architettura in twenty-five 'books'. The first such treatise in Italian, it included his development of the ideal city of Sforzinda. He visited Venice many times in the employment of Sforza.

16 McANDREW, Venetian Architecture: for Cà Dario, see pp215–21; for Cà Gussoni pp221–5. See also TRINCANATO, Venezia Minore, pp176–8.

17 PUPPI and PUPPI, Mauro Codussi, pp154–64, 183–5 and 247–54; BASSI Palazzi, p558–9; ANGELINI, Le opere, pp89–92; McANDREW, Venetian Architecture, pp349–53; and ZORZI, Venetian Palaces, pp234–7.

18 Ibid, PUPPI and PUPPI, pp161–4 and 203–6; Ibid, McANDREW, pp351–3; and ibid, BASSI, pp386–91.

19 Ibid, PUPPI and PUPPI, pp196–8 and 200–2; ANGELINI, Le opere pp92–100; ZORZI Venetian Palaces, pp238–47; and SANSOVINO, Venetia, Vol 1, p387.

20 Ibid, PUPPI and PUPPI, pp236 and 241–2; and BASSI, Palazzi, pp242–3, 493 and 496. For Buora, see McANDREW, Venetian Architecture, p488 et seq; for Spavento, ibid, pp426–55.

21 Ibid, PUPPI and PUPPI, pp231–8 and 271 (where the attribution to Codussi is rejected): BASSI, Palazzi pp94–6, 382 and 386; and ANGELINI, Le opere, pp105–8.

22 SANSOVINO and MARTINIONI, Venetia, Vol 1, p 385; ibid, PUPPI and PUPPI, pp236 and 240–41; ibid, BASSI, pp493–7 (Pal Bembo), pp228–35 (Pal Grimani). The attribution to Sanmicheli was first made by T TEMANZA in Vite dei più celebri z.

23 S SERLIO, Libro primo d'architettura di Sebastiano Serlio, Venice, 1559; Tutte le opere d'architettura di nuovo aggiunto ... raccolto da Gio Dom Scamozzi, Venice, 1584. The five books were first published in English as The Five Books of Architecture of Sebastian Serly (sic), translated by R Peake, London, 1611.

24 See especially D COSGROVE, The Palladian Landscape, passim; P HOLBERTON, Palladio's Villas, passim.

25 SANSOVINO and MARTINIONI, Venetia, Vol 1, p388.

26 VASARI, Lives, Vol V, p421; HOWARD, Jacopo Sansovino, pp126–32; BASSI, Palazzi, pp154–9.

27 Ibid, HOWARD, pp132–46; for Sansovino's Cà Corner, see also BASSI,Palazzi, pp88–93; for Sanmicheli's at San Polo ibid, pp334–7; see also ZORZI, Venetian Palaces, pp264–71.

28 VASARI, Lives, Vol V, p437; P GAZZOLA, Michele Sanmicheli, Venice, 1960, pp168–70.

29 Ibid, VASARI, Vol V, p437; ibid, GAZZOLA, pp172–5; SANSOVINO and MARTINIONI, Venetia, Vol 1, p 387; BASSI, Palazzi, pp146–53.

30 PALLADIO, Quattro Libri, II, pp72–3; BERTOTTI SCAMOZZI, Le fabbriche, IV, pp53–4.

31 GOY, Venetian Vernacular, pp216–27; BASSI, Palazzi ,p 528 et seq; G M URBANI De'GHELTOF, Il palazzo di Camillo Trevisan a Murano, Venice, 1890.

32 Ibid, BASSI, pp124–30 and 140–44; BASSI, Architettura, p86; and ZORZI, Venetian Palaces, pp302–13.

33 For the Murano villa, see GOY, Venetian Vernacular, pp185–250.

34 Ibid, pp171–5, 208 and 225; BASSI, Palazzi, pp524–7.

35 Serlio, too, had offered examples for the modernization of older, asymmetrical palace facades. See Tutte le Opere, VII, pp157 and 171; and BASSI, Palazzi, pp224–7.

36 BASSI, Palazzi, pp104–8 and 261–3; BASSI, Architettura, pp86, 150 and 178; and SANSOVINO and MARTINIONI, Venetia, Vol 1, p392.

37 Ibid SANSOVINO, Vol 1, p393; Zorzi, Venetian Palaces, pp384–5; Bassi, Architettura, pp136 and 143–4.

38 Ibid, BASSI, pp146–54; BASSI, Palazzi, pp114–23; ZORZI, Venetian Palaces, pp400–23; G LORENZETTI, Cà Rezzonico, Venice, 1936; G ROMANELLI AND F PEDROCCO, Cà Rezzonico, Milan, 1986.

39 ZORZI, ibid, pp392–9; BASSI, Palazzi, pp174–89; BASSI Architettura, pp124–36.

40 BASSI, Palazzi, pp185–203, 220–3, 293–5 and 300–1; TEMANZA, Vita, p52; SANSOVINO and MARTINIONI, Vol 1, p393.

41 Ibid, SANSOVINO, Vol 1, p393; BASSI, Palazzi, pp204–10; and ZORZI, Venetian Palaces,pp448–71.

42 Ibid, BASSI, pp348–53; ibid ZORZI, pp338–47; and BASSI, Architettura, pp250–4.

43 Ibid, ZORZI pp190–205,222–31,438–47, 482–9.

44 Ibid, ZORZI, pp494–503; and BASSI, Architettura, pp324–9.

CHAPTER 13

1 See especially BELLAVITIS, Venezia, pp159–93.

2 SAMONA, Piazza San Marco, pp187–97.

3 BELLAVITIS, Venezia, pp177–8.

4 Ibid, pp180–81 and 189; and PEROCCO AND SALVADORI, Civiltà, Vol 3, pp1222–6.

5 Ibid, BELLAVITIS, pp221–4.

6 Ibid, BELLAVITIS, pp225–8.

7 Ibid, BELLAVITIS, pp202 and 210–12; PEROCCO AND SALVADORI, Civiltà, Vol 3, pp1228–33.

8 Ibid, BELLAVITIS, pp213–7.

9 A DONAGGIO, Biennale di Venezia: un secolo di storia, Art Dossier, Florence, 1988, esp pp8–11. See also R BAZZONI, 60 anni della Biennale di Venezia, Venice, 1962; P RIZZO and E DI MARTINO, Storia della Biennale, Milan, 1982; for the pavilions, see especially M MULAZZANI, I padiglioni della Biennale, Venezia 1887–1988, Milan, 1988.

10 For the Gregotti project, see Rassega, No 22, Bologna, June 1985, pp35–7. The same issue, titled 'Venezia, città del moderno' also has articles on early twentieth-century housing and several unexecuted 'grandiose schemes'.

11 For Carlo Scarpa, see F Dal CO AND G MAZZARIOL, Carlo Scarpa 1906–1978, Milan, 1984; and A F MARCIANO Carlo Scarpa, Bologna, 1984.

Biographical notes on the architects of Venice

BARTOLOMEO BON (c1410 – c1467)

Bon was a native Venetian, who succeeded to the workshop of his father Zane (*c*1355–1442), another notable master. Bartolomeo became the leading sculptor-mason of the last or 'florid' Gothic period of Venetian architecture, in which figure sculpture is integrated with richly carved architectural elements. There are many attributions to both Bon, but the following are documented: Palazzo Barbaro at San Vidal (1420s); the Cà d'Oro (1423–31); the Scuola Vecchia della Misericordia (1440s); Santa Maria della Carità (1441–*c*1450); the Porta della Carta at the Palazzo Ducale (1438–*c*1442); Cà del Duca (later 1450s); main portal of Santi Giovanni e Paolo (1458); and the main portal of the Madonna dell'Orto (1450s and later).

ANTONIO RIZZO (c1430 – c1499)

Born in Verona, Rizzo moved to Padua and then on to Venice in *c*1460. His early career was as a sculptor, he was influenced by Donatello. His first documented Venetian works are three altars in San Marco (*c*1463–9), commissioned by Doge Cristoforo Moro; he probably carved some of the statues for the Arco Foscari at the Palazzo Ducale, and the figures of Adam and Eve, carved in 1476, are among his finest works. Other generally accepted works include: the Tomb of Doge Nicolo Tron at the Frari (1476–80) and the Tomb of Vettor Cappello at Sant'Elena (early 1470s). In 1483 he was appointed *proto* (chief surveyor) in the reconstruction of the east wing of the Palazzo Ducale after a fire. He completed the Scala dei Giganti and the lower part of the wing before fleeing the city in 1499.

PIETRO LOMBARDO or SOLARI (c1435 – 1515)

From Carona in Lombardy, Lombardo became the head of an important and prolific workshop, together with his two sons, Tullio (d 1532) and Antonio (d *c*1516). Pietro's style is characterized by rich, refined relief decoration, and the application of panels of rare marbles on to wall surfaces. He was an important catalyst in bringing Florentine Renaissance forms to Venice, where they were adapted to the Venetian taste and environment. His chief works are the Monuments to Doge Pasquale Malipiero (1470s), Doge Pietro Mocenigo (*c*1481) and Doge Nicolo Marcello (1481–5), all in Santi Giovanni e Paolo; the completion of San Giobbe (*c*1472); the choir screen in the Frari Church (1475); entrance screen and parts of the Scuola di San Giovanni Evangelista (after 1481); Santa Maria dei Miracoli (1480–8); part of the Scuola Grande di San Marco (1489–90); completion of the east wing of Palazzo Ducale (1498–1515). Most of these works incorporated contributions from one or both of his sons. Tullio's chief Venetian works include the completion of much of San Salvador; the monuments to Doges Andrea Vendramin (late 1480s) and Giovanni Mocenigo (after 1495), both in Santi Giovanni e Paolo. He also assisted his father at the Miracoli. Tullio's son Sante (1504–60) was also an architect, and the church of San Giorgio dei Greci is ascribed to him (1539–61); he was also proto for a short time at the Scuola Grande di San Rocco.

MAURO CODUSSI sometimes CODUCCI (c1440 – 1504)

Born at Lentina, near Bergamo, but settled in Venice in 1469, Codussi was the most creative and influential of the early Renaissance architects of Venice. He established his reputation with San Michele, and his church interiors show a refined classicism and spatial harmony. His palaces, particularly their facades, illustrate the development of the Renaissance as applied to traditional Venetian forms. Palazzo Loredan is the finest example of this process. Documented or accepted works include: San Michele in Isola (1469–78); Palazzo Zorzi (*c*1480); Campanile of San Pietro in Castello (1482–90); the completion of San Zaccaria (1483–91); the completion of Scuola Grande di San Marco (1490–95); Palazzo Lando Corner-Spinelli (1480s); Santa Maria Formosa (1492–1504); Torre dell'Orologio (1496–1504); San Giovanni Crisostomo (1497–1504); the staircase at Scuola Grande di San Giovanni Evangelista (1498); and Palazzo Loredan Vendramin Calergi (*c*1502–8).

GIORGIO SPAVENTO (c1440 – 1509)

From Lake Como, Spavento was probably an associate and follower of Codussi. Little is known of his life, but in 1486 he was appointed proto of the Procurators of San Marco, and worked with Rizzo at the Palazzo Ducale. In 1489 he designed the bell chamber and roof of the Campanile of San Marco; in 1508 he restored the Ponte di Rialto and from 1505–8 was chiefly responsible for the reconstruction of the Fondaco dei Tedeschi, rebuilt after a fire in 1505. His masterpiece is the church of San Salvador, begun in 1506, and continued by Tullio Lombardo.

ANTONIO ABBONDI SCARPAGNINO (c1475 – 1549)

Initially a disciple of Codussi, Scarpagnino's work was strongly influenced by him, notably at the churches of San Fantin (after 1506), and San Sebastiano, also rebuilt after 1506, in a harmonious, refined style. He is closely associated with the Rialto: he probably designed the portals to the Fondaco dei Tedeschi, and perhaps completed the building after Spavento's death. After the Rialto fire of 1514, Scarpagnino rebuilt San Giovanni Elemosinario, and designed the Fabbriche Nuove and the Palazzo dei Dieci Savi, both in a very simple classical manner. He also designed the grandiose stair at the Scuola Grande di San Rocco and completed its facades (after 1545).

MICHELE SANMICHELI (c1484 – 1559)

Born in Verona, Sanmicheli studied in Rome before fleeing the Sack of the city in 1527, and returning to the Venetian Republic. He was an important influence in spreading the mature Roman Renaissance, and developed a characteristically robust, powerfully modelled style. Sanmicheli built palaces in Verona for the Canossa and Bevilacqua families, and became the official military architect of the Republic, with notable works of fortification including the Porta Nuova and Porta Palio at Verona and fortresses at Zara, in Corfu, Crete and Cyprus. His chief works in Venice are the fortress of Sant'Andrea on the north shore of the Porto di Lido and the palaces for the Corner at San Polo (1545–60) and for the Grimani at San Luca, begun in 1556. The last is his finest work, its noble facade one of the most imposing in Venice.

JACOPO SANSOVINO (1486 – 1570)

Born in Florence, Sansovino moved to Rome, where, like Sanmicheli, he studied the classical monuments and was influenced by Bramante and Sangallo. In 1527 he fled to Venice, where in 1529 he was made proto of the Procurators of San Marco *de supra*, responsible for the buildings on the Piazza. He developed a strong, richly moulded style, elaborating classical forms with Roman Renaissance features. He designed six churches in Venice of which three survive: San Francesco della Vigna (after 1534), San Martino (1540) and San Zulian (1566). He built two major palaces, Palazzo Dolfin-Manin (1538) and Palazzo Corner della Cà Grande (after 1545). His most important work was the transformation of Piazza San Marco, with the Loggetta (1537–40), the Biblioteca Marciana (1537–54) and the Zecca (Mint) (1535–66). Other projects included the great uncompleted Scuola della Misericordia (begun 1532).

ANDREA PALLADIO (1508 – 1580)

Born in Padua, Palladio settled in Vicenza in 1524, where most of his early works were built. He designed palaces for the Vicentine nobility, including those of the Civena (1540), Thiene (1542), Chiericati (1550) and Valmarana (1565); he also built villas in the countryside for the Pisani at Bagnolo (1542), the Thiene at Quinto (1540s), the Cornaro at Piombino (1551), the Barbaro at Maser (1557) and the Foscari at Malcontenta (1559). Palladio became one of the most influential architects in history, partly as a result of the success of these houses, particularly the villas, and partly as a result of the publication of *I quattro libri dell'architettura* in Venice in 1570, in which many of his works were illustrated and described. After *c*1560 he began working in Venice, where his chief buildings are situated: the cloisters at Santa Maria della Carità (1560–1); the refectory (1560–2) and the Church of San Giorgio Maggiore (after 1565); the facade of San Francesco della Vigna (1562); Il Redentore (1577); Le Zitelle (1579–80); and the refurbishment of the halls of the Senate, Collegio and Sala delle Quattro Porte in the Palazzo Ducale. Palladio's churches were extremely influential; their plans ingeniously combined both linear and centralized spatial arrangements, while their facades, with their revolutionary development of the classical portico, became among the most widely adopted and imitated motifs in Western architectural history.

ALESSANDRO VITTORIA (1524 – 1608)

Born in Trento, Vittoria is chiefly known as a sculptor. After 1543 he was a close associate of Sansovino, with whom he collaborated at the Biblioteca Marciana. His decorative work includes the Scala d'Oro at the Palazzo Ducale and the interior of Palladio's Villa Barbaro at Maser. Vittoria was also almost certainly the designer of Palazzo Balbi, with its early Baroque facade.

VINCENZO SCAMOZZI (1552 – 1616)

Born in Vicenza, where his early career was spent designing villas and palaces, Scamozzi arrived in Venice in 1572, and studied the work of Palladio and Sansovino. He developed a rather eclectic style, and in 1613 published a treatise, *Dell'idea dell'architettura universale.* He extended Sansovino's Biblioteca Marciana, and built the first stage of the Procuratie Nuove. He also produced two unsuccessful designs for the Rialto bridge, and worked on the new Venetian fort-town of Palmanova, where he may have designed the cathedral. In Venice Scamozzi designed the churches of the Tolentini (later altered) and the Celestia, later rebuilt.

THE CONTINI

A 'clan' of architects and masons, originally from Lugano, some of whom moved to Venice in the late sixteenth century. The chief members (with works and attributions) were: Bernardino (d *c*1597) designer of the Palazzo Barbarigo della Terrazza (1568); Tommaso (active 1600 to 1618), who was Bernardino's brother, and completed the Scuola di San Girolamo 1600–1604; Antonio, son of Bernardino (1566–1600), who worked on the Rialto Bridge 1588–91, the Scuola di San Girolamo and the Ponte dei Sospiri (Bridge of Sighs) at the Palazzo Ducale, 1602; Francesco (active 1618; d before 1675), also son of Bernardino, who was responsible for the Church of the Angelo Raffaele, 1618 and the Church of S Maria del Pianot 1647–59.

BARTOLOMEO MONOPOLA or MANOPOLA (active 1597 – 1623)

Very little is known of his life, but he was elected proto at the Palazzo Ducale in 1597; he designed the north facade to the central courtyard, with the Clock Tower, as well as many internal works in the Palazzo Ducale. Monopola was also architect for the first stage of Palazzo Pisani at Santo Stefano (*c*1615) and Palazzo Ruzzini-Priuli (*c*1600–10) at Santa Maria Formosa. His style is monumental and essentially Palladian, although with fairly restrained Baroque touches.

BALDASSARE LONGHENA (1598 – 1682)

A native Venetian and follower of Scamozzi, Longhena became the dominant figure in Venetian architecture in the seventeenth century. His career encompassed the entire period of the development of the mature Baroque and his output was prolific. His first major work was the cathedral at Chioggia (1624–74); there followed several Venetian palaces, including the Widmann, Giustinian-Lolin, Papadopoli and Belloni-Battagia, most of them built in *c*1625–35. In 1630 he won a competition for the Salute church, his greatest work, only completed after his death, in 1687. The Salute combines a highly original plan with a monumental classical interior and a uniquely powerfully modelled exterior, dominated by its great dome. After 1634 he completed the Procuratie Nuove, and in 1635 the Spanish Synagogue. In the 1640s he built the library and the great staircase at San Giorgio Maggiore, as well as high altars in several churches. Palazzo da Lezze was begun in *c*1654, and Santa Maria, known as the Scalzi Church, two years later. His work after *c*1660 is even more powerful in style, as shown by the facade of Santa Maria dei Derelitti, called the Ospedaletto (1666–72), the Pesaro Monument in the Frari (1669) and his two great palaces, Cà Rezzonico (begun 1667) and Cà Pesaro, the two finest Baroque palaces in Venice and whose facades were begun in 1676. Other works include the Scuola dei Carmini (1668) and the Greek complex on Rio dei Greci, after 1678.

GIUSEPPE SARDI (c1621 – 99)

Probably the most important Baroque architect after Longhena, Sardi's early work is comparatively modestly detailed but his later buildings are far more strongly modelled Baroque works. From 1649–63 he designed the facades of San Salvador and the adjacent Scuola Grande di San Todaro, both fairly restrained. The later facades of the Scalzi Church (1672–80) and that of Santa Maria del Giglio (1680–3) are far more ornate and are his finest works. He designed at least three substantial palaces, Palazzo Savorgnan (before 1663), Palazzo Flangini (1664–82) and Palazzo Surian (complete 1663). In 1689 he was appointed proto of San Marco *de supra*, responsible for the church and the buildings on the Piazza.

ANDREA TIRALI (1657 – 1737)

Son of a native builder, Tirali spent forty years in public service firstly as proto of the Magistrato alle Acque, and then of San Marco, building the Ponte dei Tre Archi in Cannaregio, and repaving the Piazza San Marco and the Piazzetta in 1722–35. His wide range of building works included Palazzo Grassi and the Trinità Church, both in Chioggia (1703–14) and the Palazzi Diedo, Priuli and Emo in Venice, all between c1720–37. Other works include the Scuola dell'Angelo Custode (1713), the facade of San Vidal, and the monastery of San Giovanni Laterano.

ANTONIO GASPARI (c1660 · c1720)

Gaspari was a close follower of Longhena, but his fluidity of style also shows the influence of Bernini. Among his chief works are: Este Cathedral (1690–1708); the triumphal arch in the Sala dello Scrutinio in the Palazzo Ducale (1696); Palazzo Zenobio (1700); Palazzo Giustinian at Murano (1708); the completion of Longhena's Cà Pesaro (1710); and the Churches of San Vidal (after 1700) and Santa Maria della Fava (after 1705). The last is his finest Venetian work, although the facade remained unbuilt.

GIORGIO MASSARI (1687 – 1766)

The last great native architect, whose career spanned both the late Baroque and the Neoclassical periods. A follower of Tirali, Massari also collaborated frequently with the painter Giambattista Tiepolo. Massari's extensive work on the Terraferma included villas at Vicenza and churches at Brescia, Castelfranco and Udine. Of his Venetian churches the Gesuati (Santa Maria del Rosano) (after 1726) is the most important; he also built the Orphanage of Santa Maria Pietà (1735–55), San Marcuola and the 'hospital' Catecumeni. His lay works included the completion of Longhena's Cà Rezzonico, including the great stair and ballroom (1750–66) and Palazzo Grassi (1748–70), the last great palace built before the fall of the Republic. After 1737 he was proto at San Marco.

GIANANTONIO SELVA (Venice 1753 – 1819)

A pupil of the Neoclassical Tommaso Temanza, whose legacy he developed, Selva was also a close friend of the sculptor Antonio Canova; Selva designed a studio for Canova on the Zattere, although it was never built. His work was prolific, and there are examples over much of the Veneto, as well as in Venice itself. His chief work in Venice was the Teatro alla Fenice, built in 1790–2, although later altered internally; other major works include San Maurizio, where he collaborated with Leopoldo Cicognara and Antonio Diedo (1806–28); Selva also designed the first layout of the Napoleonic Gardens in Castello (begun 1810). On the Terraferma, his works include the cathedral at Cologna Veneta (1805–27).

CARLO SCARPA (1906 – 78)

Scarpa has a unique role in the history of Venetian architecture; he was one of the most outstanding truly modern Italian architects of the twentieth century, but at the same time his work reflects the ancient traditions of fine craftsmanship and understanding of materials. Almost all of his work is in Venice and the Veneto, and much consists of the sensitive remodelling of historic buildings. Among a number of museums and art galleries remodelled, the most important are: Palazzo Abbatelli, Palermo; the Gipsoteca Canoviana, at Possagno, Treviso (1956–7); Palazzo Querini-Stampalia, Venice (1959); Museo Civico Correr, Venice (1959); Castelvecchio, Verona (1964); Galleria Franchetti at the Cà d'Oro, Venice (1972). Other projects included the Brion Cemetery, near Verona; Olivetti showrooms, Piazza San Marco, Venice (1959); the Italian Pavilion in the Biennale Gardens, Venice (1968); and Villa Ottolenghi, Bardolino, Verona (1974).

Glossary of terms

A NOTE ON VENETIAN TERMINOLOGY

The Venetian dialect remains as robustly independent of modern standard Italian as the history of the Republic differs from that of the rest of the peninsula. The dialect is an integral part of the city's history and was written and spoken by all classes of Venetians, from gondoliers to doges. Many Italian words have quite different Venetian equivalents, while the particular environment of the lagoon and the unique constitution both gave rise to specialized vocabularies. Venetian terms in widespread usage have been used in the text.

ABBREVIATIONS
(Heb): Hebrew, (It): Italian, (Ven): Venetian

ABBAINO (Ven)
A dormer in the roof of a Venetian house.

ALBERGO (Ven)
In its historic sense an inn or place of shelter; also more particularly applied to the small hall on the upper floor in a scuola (qv), where the governing board met and where the scuola's treasury was kept.

ALTANA (Ven)
A timber roof terrace, reached by stairs from the uppermost storey.

ANDRONE (Ven)
The principal ground floor hall of a Venetian palace; also applied to the lower hall of the Scuole Grandi (qv).

ARSENALE (Ven/It)
The state shipyards of the Republic in eastern Castello; by extension, the naval bases of other cities; *arsenalotto*: a craftsman who works at the Arsenale.

ARTE (Ven)
One of the trade crafts or guilds of the city.

ARON (Heb)
The cupboard in a synagogue containing the scrolls of the Law.

ATRIUM
The colonnaded entrance to a basilica or other early Christian church.

BASILICA
The colonnaded hall that formed the most widespread form of the early Christian church, especially in Rome. San Marco, although often so called, is not strictly a basilica.

BARENA (It)
A sand or mudbank, exposed at low tides.

BARBACANE (Ven)
The projecting timber beam forming the jetty carrying an upper storey; or a large section timber set on to a column to reduce the span of the principal beams; widespread in the Scuole Grandi and other larger public buildings.

BARCHESSA (Ven)
The side wing of a Venetian Terraferma villa (qv), usually lower than the villa itself, and containing ancillary farm accommodation.

BARCO (Ven)
The upper gallery in a church, almost always at the west end, and usually occupied by monastic choirs.

BECCARIA (Ven/It)
A retail meat market; there was one in Venice at the Rialto and another on the Molo at San Marco until the sixteenth century.

BROCCATELLO (Ven)
A hard reddish marble from Verona, widely used in Venice for decorative sculpture, wellheads, paving etc.

BORDONAL (Ven)
A massive timber beam used to support the floor of a scuola or other great hall.

BUCINTORO (Ven)
The ducal state barge.

CÀ (Ven)
The general abbreviation for casa (house); in Venice it is also frequently applied to the most notable palaces, as an abbreviation for *casa da stazio*, principal family seat. Other derivations and related usages: *casa di delizie*: a pavillion or other retreat used by the Venetian nobility; *casa padronale*: one of the substantial farm houses on the lagoon islands; and *casa a schiera*: a house forming part of a terrace.

CALLE (Ven)
The usual word for a street in Venice and the lagoons; diminutive *calesella*.

CAMINO (It)
A chimney.

CAMPANILE (It)
A bell tower.

CAMPO (Ven)
In Italian, literally a field, in Venice the usual name for a square; diminutive *campiello*.

CANALAZZO (Ven)
The Grand Canal (literally, 'the big canal').

CANEVA (Ven)
A small boathouse.

CANNAREGIO
One of the six districts or *sestieri* (qv) of Venice.

CASADA (Ven)
One of the noble clans or extended families that formed the Republic's ruling class.

CASINO (Ven)
A pavilion for entertaining, usually attached to a noble palace.

CASTELLO
One of the six districts or sestieri (qv) of Venice.

CASTRUM
A fortified group of buildings similar to a castle, but less well integrated.

CAVANNA (Ven)
An inlet of water.

CIVITAS
The Renaissance concept of the city and its cultural life as the hub of civilized living; this could be expressed in many ways, but chiefly, in the context of the present work, in the beautification of the urban form itself.

COLLEGIO (Ven)
The innermost circle of government of the Venetian Republic, or the Cabinet, chaired by the doge. Also known as the Serenissima Signoria.

CONTADO (It)
The rural territory around a town; its adjacent, dependent lands, usually occupied by farms.

CORTE (Ven)
The term usually given to a development of houses around a common open space.

COTTO (It)
Brickwork.

CONSIGLIO DEI DIECI (Ven)
The Council of Ten, the supreme organ of state security of the Venetian Republic, and the highest court of appeal.

CORTILE (It)
A courtyard; in Venice usually the private courtyard attached to a palace.

DIECI SAVI SOPRA LE DECIME (Ven)
The Venetian magistracy responsible for collecting tithes.

DOGADO (Ven)
The original nucleus of the Venetian Republic's mainland territories, a coastal strip of land extending from Chioggia to Grado.

DOGE (Ven)
The elected head of state of the Venetian Republic.

DUCAT (Ven)
The principal element of the Venetian monetary system, a gold coin very similar in size and value to the Florentine florin.

DOGANA (It)
A customs-house.

DORSODURO
One of the six *sestieri* of the city of Venice.

ERBERIA (It)
A vegetable market.

FANTE (Ven)
An apprentice in one of the city's crafts or guilds.

FINESTRA (It)
A window; *finestrone*: a large window, usually of several lights.

FONDACO or FONTEGO (Ven)
A warehouse or storage building; also applied to the trading bases of the foreign communities in the city, eg those of the Germans, Turks and Persians.

FONDAMENTA (Ven)
A public quay along a canal.

GHETTO (Ven)
The island in Cannaregio where all Venice's Jews were ordered to reside, by a Republican decree in 1516; by extension, the quarter of any city where Jews lived.

GIUSTIZA VECCHIA (Ven)
A department of the Republic's government responsible (among other duties) for the registration and supervision of the trade guilds.

GOTICO FIORITO (Ven)
Literally 'florid gothic'; the last stage of the indigenous Venetian Gothic style, after c1400, characterized by a stylized flower carved above the head of the windows.

LIDO (Ven)
One of the long narrow islands that divide the lagoons of the Venetian littoral from the Adriatic Sea; usually qualified as, for example, Lido di Venezia or Lido di Iesolo. By extension, after the development of the Lido di Venezia into a resort, the term has come to mean any similar sandy shoreline developed in this manner, pl.*lidi*.

LIBRO D'ORO (Ven)
The 'Golden Book', the register containing the names of all the Venetian nobility, who collectively governed the Republic. A similar *Libro d'Argento* (Silver Book) contained the names of the Republic's citizen families.

LOGGIA (It)
A covered colonnade open on at least one side; in Italy frequently found in a town or city's principal public square, to serve as a meeting place for the merchants of nobility.

LUNETTE
A crescent shaped or semicircular gable above a doorway or on the top of a facade; in Venice frequently decorated with relief sculptures.

MAGAZEN (Ven; It MAGAZZINO)
A warehouse or place for bulk storage.

MAGGIOR CONSIGLIO (Ven)
The Great Council, the assembly of all eligible adult male nobles, which formed the foundation of the constitution of the Republic.

MAGISTRATO ALLE ACQUE (Ven)
The Venetian government agency respon-sible for the maintenance of the lagoon, the littoral, canals and sea defences.

MARANGONO (Ven)
A carpenter.

MARIEGOLA (Ven)
The statutes or governing regulations of a trade guild or *arte*.

MATRONEO (It)
A Women's gallery in a church or synagogue.

MAR, IMPERO DA (Ven)
The overseas territories of the Venetian Re-public, including Crete, Cyprus, Corfu and the lesser Greek islands.

MEZÀ (Ven)
The mezzanine floor of a palace, usually used for the storage of traded goods.

MURER, MURATORE (Ven, It)
A builder.

OCIO or OCCHIO (Ven, It)
An 'eye', the circular window often found on the facades of medieval churches.

OLIVOLO
The island at the extreme eastern and of Venice where the bishopric was based, today known as San Pietro in Castello.

ORTO (It)
An orchard.

PALAZZO (It)
A palace; in Venice usually refers to the houses of the nobility; diminutive: *palazzetto*; a *palazzata* is a contiguous group of such houses.

PALIFICATA (Ven)
A grouping of timber piles or stakes used to form a foundation.

PALLADIAN WINDOW
A window consisting of a larger arched central light flanked by two smaller lights usually with square heads; popularized by Andrea Palladio, the form originated with Sebastiano Serlio.

PALUDO (It)
A swamp or marsh.

PATRIARCH
The title given by the Orthodox church based in Constantinople (Byzantium) to the most senior bishops of the Eastern Church; the Venetian patriarchate was originally granted to Aquileia and Grado; it was transferred to Venice in 1131 and permanently established there in 1451.

PENDENTIVE
The curved, sail-like surface below a dome, which joins it to the top of the supporting pier or column.

PESCHERIA / PESCARIA (It, Ven)
A fish market.

PIANO (It)
A storey of a building; the *piano nobile* or principal storey of a Venetian palace is always on the first floor above the *androne*(qv)

PIOVEGO (Ven)
The government department responsible for approval of building works and for the maintenance of streets.

PODESTA (Ven/ It)
In the Republic the title usually given to the governor of Venetian cities or territories, always a Venetian nobleman.

PORTEGO (Ven)
The great hall of a Venetian palace, located on the principal upper storey.

POZZO (It)
A well; *vera da pozzo*: a wellhead.

PREGARDI (Ven)
The Venetian Senate (qv).

PROCURATORS OF SAN MARCO (Ven)
The senior officials responsible for the properties on Piazza San Marco, and for the maintenance and administration of the church of San Marco.

PROTO or MAESTRO (Ven)
A senior salaried master mason or architect employed to organize and supervise the construction of a major building project, or permanently retained by a government body.

PROVVEDITORE (It)
A superintendent or commissioner for some aspect of government policy or works; the Venetian Republic appointed many *provveditori*, some on a permanent basis, others for a particular building project, eg the Rialto bridge.

RIDOTTO
A gaming house; the name was originally applied to the government established official 'Ridotto'; later the name was adopted by the many private gambling houses in the city.

RIO (Ven)
One of the minor canals of the city; a rio terà (rio interrato) is a reclaimed canal; pl. *rii*.

RIVO ALTO (Ven):
A rialto or 'high bank', the earliest name of the Venetian *archipelago*.

RUGA (Ven)
An important street in the city, which is usually primarily commercial.

SALA CAPITOLARE (It)
The chapter hall or great hall of the Scuole Grandi (qv).

SALIZZADA (Ven)
A street that was paved (*selciata*) at an early date, hence an important thoroughfare.

SANDOLO (Ven)
A small boat of very shallow draft, similar to a gondola, used in the city and lagoon.

SCHOLA (Ven)
A Venetian synagogue.

SCUOLA GRANDE (Ven)
One of the senior charitable confraternities of the city; originally three in number, there were eventually seven; *Scuola Piccola*: a minor confraternity, of which there were several dozen.

SENATO (Ven)
The Senate, or Pregadi, was the upper house of the Venetian constitution, elected by the Maggior Consiglio.

SENSA (Ven)
Ascension Day, one of the most important festivals of the Venetian calendar, marked by a great fair in the Piazza of San Marco.

SERLIANA (It)
A composite window formed with a large arched central light, flanked by smaller rectangular lights, often with further small square lights above them. From Sebastiano Serlio's *Five Books of Architecture*, where they are illustrated.

SESTIERE (Ven)
One of the 'sixth parts' into which Venice was divided for administration in 1171: San Marco, San Polo, Santa Croce, Dorsoduro, Cannaregio and Castello. San Marco is in the centre of the city; San Polo and Santa Croce are in the west; Dorsoduro is to the south, facing the Giudecca; and Cannaregio is along the northern shore.

SOTTOPORTEGO (Ven):
A covered colonnade or passageway with accommodation above.

SQUERO (Ven)
A yard for the building and repair of small boats.

STEMMA (It)
A coat of arms or armorial bearing.

SOLAIO, SOLER (It)
A storey or floor of a building.

TAIAPIERA, TAGLIAPIETRA (Ven)
A stonemason.

TAVOLA, TOLA (Ven)
A plank or board of timber, used in building construction.

TEGOLA (It)
A roof tile.

TERRAFERMA (Ven)
The mainland constituent of the Venetian empire, consisting of most of the present-day Veneto, the Friuli and the eastern edge of Lombardy, as far as Bergamo.

TERRAZZO (Ven)
The traditional Venetian flooring, containing a mixture of lime and marble or brick powder, with chips of marble.

TRAGHETTO (It)
A ferry.

TORRE (It)
A tower; in the diminutive, *torresella*, the turret on the corners of Venetian Byzantine palaces.

TERENI NUOVI (Ven)
The large area of reclaimed land that was developed during the sixteenth and seventeenth centuries in the western part of Venice.

VERIER (Ven)
A glass-maker.

VIA, VIALE (It)
A broad street or avenue.

VILLA (It)
A country house built by Venetian and other nobility as a base for the *villeggiatura* (qv).

VILLEGGIATURA (It)
The practice of families (usually noble) transferring from their city palace to their lands in the countryside, most often in summer, for a period of some weeks. These lands were administered from the villa, which was generally surrounded by farm buildings, in the form of *barchesse* (qv).

ZATTARON (Ven)
The heavy timber planks forming a foundation for the walls of a building.

ZATTERA (It)
A raft of timber; in Venice, the rafts brought down to the lagoons from the upland forests, for use in the construction industry and for shipbuilding.

ZECCA (It)
A mint for the production of coinage.

Key to map locations

▪ PALACES

▪ CHURCHES AND MONASTIC HOUSES

▪ SCUOLE GRANDI AND PICCOLE

NB: All the major buildings discussed or related to the text are listed above with the page number on which they are first mentioned, where applicable. It has not been possible to indicate the locations on this map of a small number of these buildings, however, for the sake of consistency, they have been allocated a reference number, and a note of their location is given.

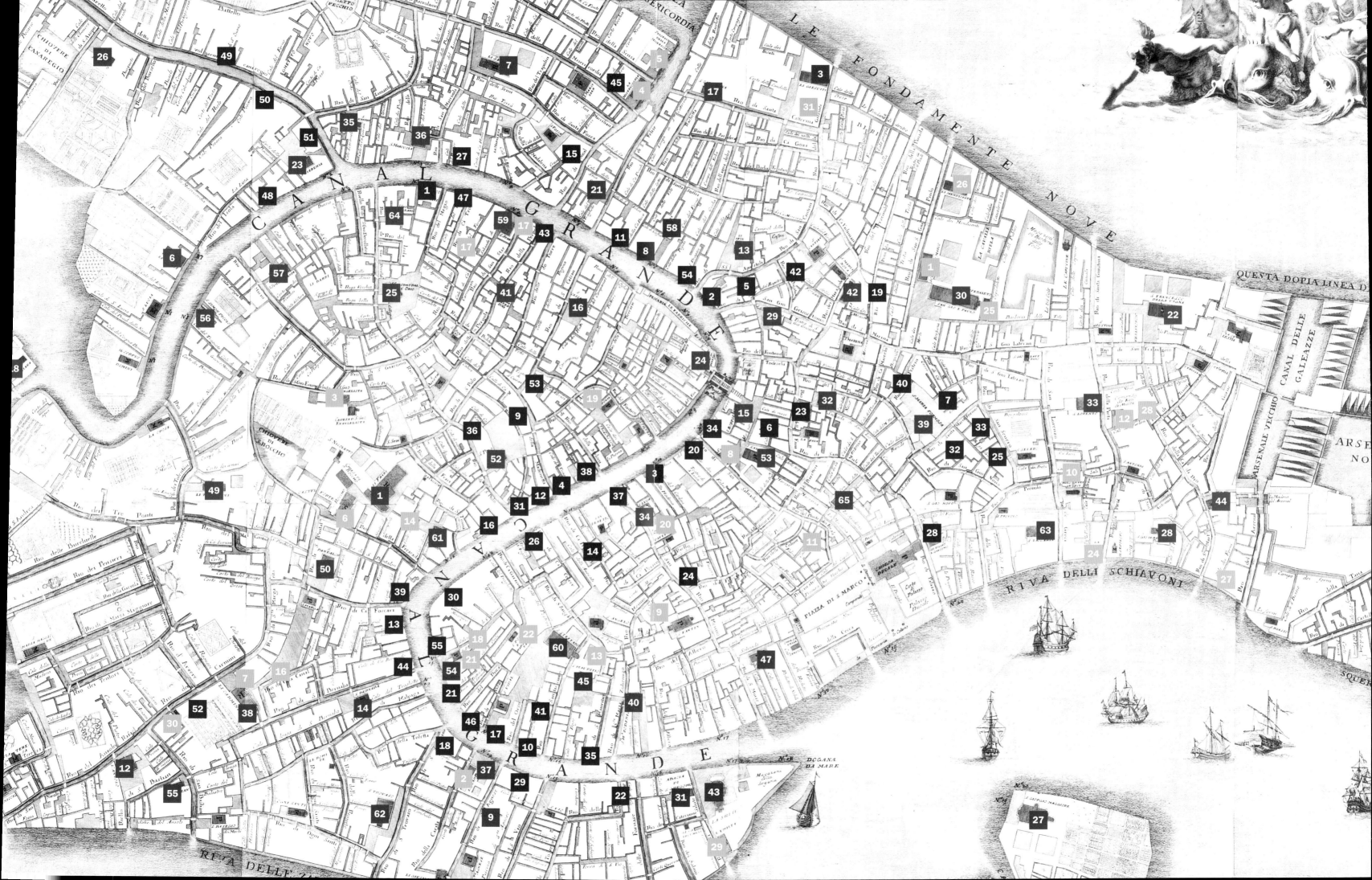

Bibliography

The bibliography on Venice and its architecture is very extensive indeed. In these first paragraphs are summarized some of the most useful general studies, most of them also reasonably accessible. In the bibliography which follows I have tried to provide at least one representative monograph title on each major field of interest, that is, the building types, the styles and periods, and monographs on all the major architects, artists and sculptors.

There is only one general history of the Venetian Republic currently in print in English, and that is; J J Norwich's two-volume work, *Venice: the Rise to Empire* (London, 1977) and *Venice: the Greatness and the Fall* (London, 1981), later reprinted in a single volume. Needless to say, the definitive histories are all in Italian: R Cessi, *Storia della Repubblica di Venezia*, 2 vols (Milan, 1968), is arguably the most authoritative. Also fundamental are: S Romanin, *Storia Documentata di Venezia*, 10 vols (Venice, 1912–21); and P Molmenti, *Storia di Venezia nella Vita Privata*, 3 vols (Bergamo,1906–8). An excellent single volume history, emphasizing trade, shipping and commerce, is F C Lane, *Venice: A Maritime Republic* (Baltimore, 1973).

In course of publication is the multi-volume *Storia di Venezia* (Istituto della Enciclopedia Italiana, Rome); when complete it will comprise eleven chronological volumes and a further eight thematic studies.

On the Venetian constitution, still fundamental is G Maranini, *La costituzione di Venezia*, 2 vols, (reprinted edn, Florence, 1974).

For Venice's imperial era, the following offer an excellent introduction: D S Chambers, *The Imperial Age of Venice 1380–1580*; D S Chambers and B Pullan (eds), *Venice: A Documentary History 1450–1630* (Oxford and Cambridge, Mass, 1992).

Of the many general cultural guides to the city, G Lorenzetti, *Venice and its Lagoon* (Trieste, 1975) remains indispensable, while much incidental detail on the streets, canals and campi is contained in G Tassini, *Curiosità Veneziane* (9th edn, Venice,1988).

On the history of Venetian architecture in general, an authoritative introduction is D Howard, *The Architectural History of Venice* (2nd edn, London, 1987). More recent is the excellent study by Ennio Concina, *Storia dell'architettura di Venezia dal VII al XX secolo* (Milan, 1995).

One of the surprisingly few general cultural histories of the Republic is G Perocco and A Salvadori, *Civiltà di Venezia*, 3 vols (Venice, 1973–6).

On the chief building types, the following works are the most useful: E Arslan, *Venezia Gotica* (Milan, 1970), which concentrates on medieval palaces, but not the ecclesiastical architecture; A Zorzi, *Venetian Palaces* (New York, 1990) offers sumptuous illustrations, including many inaccessible interiors; Renaissance and Baroque palaces are authoritatively covered by E Bassi, *Palazzi di Venezia* (Venice, 1976); for the churches, U Franzoi and D di Stefano, *Le Chiese di Venezia* (Venice, 1976) is comprehensive and very well illustrated. For the Renaissance architecture of the city in general, J McAndrew, *Venetian Architecture of the Early Renaissance* (Cambridge, Mass and London, 1980) covers the period from *c*1450 to the early 1500s with great insight. A more broadly based recent survey, also covering sculpture and painting, is N Huse and W Wolters, *The Art of Renaissance Venice* (Chicago, 1990). For the Baroque and Rococo periods in general, see E Bassi, *Architettura del sei e settecento a Venezia* (Naples, 1962). For monographs of a more specialized nature and for works on individual architects, see the general bibliography that follows.

ACKERMAN, J S *Palladio* (Harmondsworth, 1966).

ALBERTI, L B *De re aedificatoria* (Florence, 1485); published in English as *The Ten Books of Architecture*, translated by Giacomo Leoni, (London, 1726).

ANGELINI, L *Le opere in Venezia di Mauro Codussi* (Milan, 1945).

ARETINO, P *Selected Letters*, translated by G Bull (Harmondsworth, 1976).

ARSLAN, E *Venezia Gotica* (Milan, 1970).

BACCHION, E *The Basilica of St Mark* (Venice, 1972).

BARBIERI, F *Vincenzo Scamozzi* (Vicenza, 1952).

BARBIERI, G *Andrea Palladio e la cultura veneta del Rinascimento* (Rome, 1983).

BASSI, E *GianAntonio Selva, architetto veneziano* (Padua, 1936).

BASSI, E *Architettura del sei e settecento a Venezia* (Naples, 1962).

BASSI, E *Il Convento della Carità*, Corpus Palladianum, Vol 6 (University Park and London, 1971).

BASSI, *Palazzi di Venezia* (Venice, 1976).

BASSI, E AND TRINCANATO, E R *Il Palazzo Ducale nella storia e nell'arte di Venezia* (Milan, 1960).

BELLAVITIS, G *L'Arsenale di Venezia: Storia di una grande struttura urbana* (Venice, 1983).

BELLAVITIS, G AND ROMANELLI, G *Venezia*, Le città nella Storia d'Italia (Rome, 1985).

BELTRAMI, L *Storia della popolazione di Venezia dalla fine del sec.XVI alla caduta della Repubblica* (Padua, 1954).

BERTI, G *L'Architettura a Venezia: Il Rinascimento* (Turin, n d).

BERTOTTI SCAMOZZI, O *Le fabbriche e i disegni di Andrea Palladio* (Vicenza, 1796; facsimile edn, London, 1968).

BOERIO, G *Dizionario Veneziano* (Venice, 1856).

BOLDRIN, G *I pozzi di Venezia* (Venice, 1910).

BOSIO, L *Itinerari e strade della Venetia romana* (Padua, 1970).

BOUCHER, B *Andrea Palladio: the Architect in his Time* (New York, London and Paris, 1994).

BOUWSMA, W J *Venice and the Defense of Republican Liberty* (Berkeley, Cal, 1968).

BRAUDEL, F *The Mediterranean and the Mediterranean World in the Age of Philip II*, translated by S Reynolds, 2 vols (2nd edn, London, 1972).

BROWN, H F *The Venetian Printing Press* (London, 1891).

BROWN, P FORTINI *Venetian Narrative Painting in the Age of Carpaccio* (New Haven and London, 1988).

CALABI, D *Il mercato e la città* (Venice, 1994).

CALABI, D AND MORACHIELLO, P *Rialto: le fabbriche e il Ponte* (Turin, 1987).

CALASANTI, A *L'arte bizantina in Italia* (Milan, 1912).

CALIMANI, R *Storia del Ghetto di Venezia* (Milan, 1985).

CANIATO, G AND Dal BORGO, M *Le arti edili a Venezia* (Venice, 1990).

CASALI, L A *La guerra di Chioggia e la pace di Torino* (Florence, 1866).

CASSINI, G *Piante e vedute prospettiche di Venezia 1479–1855* (Venice, 1971).

CESSI, F *Alessandro Vittoria, Scultore 1525–1608*, 2 vols (Trento, 1961–2).

CESSI, R *Documenti relativi alla storia [...] anteriore al mille* (Padua, 1942).

CESSI, R *Storia della Repubblica di Venezia*, 2 vols (2nd edn, Milan, 1968).

CESSI, R AND ALBERTI, A *Rialto: l'isola [...] il mercato* (Bologna, 1934).

CHAMBERS, D S *The Imperial Age of Venice 1380–1580* (London, 1970).

CHAMBERS, D S AND PULLAN, B (eds) *Venice: A Documentary History 1450–1630* (Oxford and Cambridge, Mass, 1992).

CICOGNA, E A *Delle iscrizioni veneziane, [...]* (Venice, 1824–53).

CICOGNARA, L, DIEDO, A, AND SELVA, G *Le fabbriche più cospicue di Venezia, misurate illustrate e intagliate* (2nd edn, Venice, 1[...]).

CO, F Dal, AND MAZZARIOL, G (eds) *Carlo Scarpa, 1906–1978* (Milan, 1984).

COLE, B *The Renaissance Artist at Work [...]* York and Toronto, 1983).

CONCINA, *L'Arsenale della Repubblica di [...]* (Milan, 1984).

CONCINA, E *Arsenali e città nell'occidente europeo* (Rome, 1987).

CONCINA, E *Pietre, parole, storia: glossario [...] costruzione nelle fonti veneziane* (Venice, [...]).

CONNELL, S *The Employment of Sculptors [and] Stonemasons in Venice in the Fifteenth Century* (London and New York, 1988).

CORNER, F *Notizie storiche delle chiese e monasteri di Venezia e di Torcello* (Padua, [...]).

CORYAT, T *Coryat's Crudities*, 2 vols (London, 1905).

COSGROVE, D *The Palladian Landscape* (Leicester, 1993).

COSTANTINI, C *Aquileia e Grado* (Milan, 1[...]).

COZZI, G *Gli Ebrei e Venezia* (Milan, 1987[...]).

CRACCO, G *Società e stato nel medioevo veneziani* (Venice, 1967).

CRISTINELLI, G *Baldassare Longhena, architetto del 600 a Venezia* (Venice, 1972).

CURIEL, R AND COOPERMAN, B D *The Venetian Ghetto* (New York, 1990).

DAVIS, R *Shipbuilders of the Venetian Arsenal* (Baltimore, 1991).

DEMUS, O *The Church of San Marco in Venice* (Washington DC, 1960).

De VRIES, J *European Urbanization 1500 to [...]* (London, 1984).

DICKENS, C *Pictures from Italy* (London, 18[...]).

DORIGO, W *Venezia: Origini* (Milan, 1983).

EVELYN, J *Diary and Correspondence*, 6 vols (Oxford, 1955).

FANELLI, G *Firenze*, Le città nella storia d'Italia (Rome, Bari, 1980).

FEDALTO, G *Le origini di Venezia* (Bologna, 1978).

FIOCCO, G *Paolo Veronese* (Bologna, 1928).

FIOCCO, G *Guardi* (Florence, 1937).

FONTANA, G *Venezia monumentale: I palazzi* (Venice, 1845–63; new edn Venice, 1967).

FORTIS, U (ed) *Venezia Ebraica* (Rome, 197[...]).

FRANZOI, U *Il Palazzo Ducale di Venezia* (Venice, 1973).

FRANZOI, U AND DI STEFANO, D *Le Chiese [di] Venezia* (Venice, 1976).

GASPARETTO, A *Il vetro di Murano dalle origini ad oggi* (Venice, 1958).

GAZZOLA, P *Michele Sanmicheli* (Venice, 1960).

GIANIGHIAN, G AND PAVANINI, P *Dietro i palazzi: tre secoli di architettura minore a Venezia* (Venice, 1984).

GODFREY, J *1204: The Unholy Crusade* (Oxford, 1980).

GOFFEN, R *Piety and Patronage in Renaissance Venice: Bellini, Titian and the Franciscans* (New Haven and London, 1986).

GOFFEN, R *Bellini, Titian and the Franciscans* (New Haven and London, 1986).

GOFFEN, R *Giovanni Bellini* (New Haven and London, 1989).

GOY, R J *Venetian Vernacular Architecture* (Cambridge, 1989).

GOY, R J *The House of Gold: Building a Palace in Medieval Venice* (Cambridge, 1993).

HALE, J R *Renaissance Venice* (London, 1973).

HOLBERTON, P *Palladio's Villas: Life in the Renaissance Countryside* (London, 1990).

HOWARD, D *The Architectural History of Venice* (2nd edn London, 1987).

HOWARD, D *Jacopo Sansovino: Architecture and Patronage in Renaissance Venice* (2nd edn New Haven and London, 1987).

HUMFREY, P *Painting in Renaissance Venice* (New Haven and London, 1995).

HUSE, N AND WOLTERS, W *The Art of Renaissance Venice* (Chicago, 1990).

LANE, F C *Venice: A Maritime Republic* (Baltimore, 1973).

LANE, F C *I mercanti di Venezia* (Turin, 1982).

LANE, F C *Venetian Ships and Shipbuilders of the Renaissance* (Baltimore, 1934; new edn, Baltimore, 1992).

LANFRANCHI, L *San Giorgio Maggiore*, 2 vols (Venice, 1968).

LAURITZEN, P AND ZIELCKE, A *The Palaces of Venice* (London, 1978).

LIEBERMAN, R *Renaissance Architecture in Venice 1450–1540* (London, 1982).

LOGAN, O *Culture and Society in Venice 1470–1790* (London, 1972).

LORENZETTI, G *Ca Rezzonico* (Venice, 1940).

LORENZETTI, G *Venice and its Lagoon* (Trieste, 1975).

LORENZI, G *Monumenti per servire alla storia del Palazzo Ducale di Venezia* (Venice, 1869).

LUZZATTO, G *Storia economica di Venezia dal XI secolo al XVI secolo* (Venice, 1995).

MARANINI, G *La costituzione di Venezia*, 2 vols (Florence, 1927; new facsimile edn 1974).

MARCATO, U *Storia di Chioggia* (Chioggia, 1976).

MARETTO, P *L'edilizia gotica veneziana* (2nd edn, Venice, 1978).

MARETTO, P *La casa veneziana nella storia della città* (2nd edn, Venice, 1987).

MacKENNEY, R *Tradesmen and Traders: the World of the Guilds in Venice and Europe c.1250–1650* (Beckenham, 1987).

McANDREW, J *Venetian Architecture of the Early Renaissance* (Cambridge, Mass, and London, 1980).

MARIACHER, G *Il Palazzo Ducale di Venezia*, (Florence, 1950).

MARIACHER, G *Il Sansovino* (Milan, 1962).

MARIACHER, G *Ca Vendramin Calergi* (Venice, 1965).

MARTINEAU, J AND ROBISON, A (eds) *The Glory of Venice: Art in the 18th century* (New Haven and London, 1994).

MARZEMIN, G *Le origini romane di Venezia* (Venice, 1937).

MAZZUCCO, G (ed) *Monasteri benedettini nella laguna Veneziana* (Venice, 1983).

MIOZZI, E *Venezia nei secoli*, 2 vols (Venice, 1957).

MOLMENTI, P *Le vere da pozzo di Venezia* (Venice, 1911).

MORASSI, A *Tiepolo*, 2 vols (London, 1958).

MORRIS, J *Venice* (London, 1960).

MORRIS, J *The Venetian Empire: a Sea Voyage* (London, 1980).

MUIR, E *Civic Ritual in Renaissance Venice* (Princeton, 1981).

MURARO, M *Venetian Villas* (New York, 1987).

MURATORI, S *Studi per una operante storia urbana di Venezia* (Rome, 1959).

NICOL, D M *Byzantium and Venice: A Study in Diplomatic and Cultural Relations* (Cambridge, 1988).

NORWICH, J J *Venice: The Rise to Empire* (London, 1977).

NORWICH, J J *Venice: The Greatness and the Fall* (London, 1981).

ONIANS, J *Bearers of Meaning: the Classical orders in Antiquity, the Middle Ages and the Renaissance* (Princeton, 1988).

PAGANUZZI, G B *Iconografia delle 30 Parrocchie di Venezia* (Venice, 1831).

PALLADIO, A *I quattro libri dell'architettura* (Venice, 1570; facsimile edn Milan, 1968).

PALLUCCHINI, R *L'opera completa di Giambattista Tiepolo* (Milan, 1968).

PALLUCCHINI, R *La Pittura Veneziana del Settecento* (Venice, 1960).

PAOLETTI, P *L'Architettura e la scultura del Rinascimento in Venezia*, 2 vols (Venice, 1897).

PEROCCO, G (ed) *The Horses of San Marco*, translated by J and V Wilton-Ely and (Venice and London, 1979).

PEROCCO, G AND SALVADORI, A *Civiltà di Venezia*, 3 vols (Venice, 1973–6).

PERTUSI, A *La caduta di Costantinopoli* (Verona, 1976).

PIAMONTE, G *Venezia vista dall'acqua* (Venice, 1967).

PIGNATTI, T *Piazza San Marco* (Novara, 1956).

PIGNATTI, T *Pietro Longhi* (London and New York, 1969).

PIGNATTI, T (ed) *Le scuole di Venezia* (Milan, 1981).

POPE-HENNESSEY, J *Italian Gothic Sculpture* (London, 1955; 3rd edn, London, 1979).

POPE-HENNESSEY, J *Italian Renaissance Sculpture* (London, 1971).

POPE-HENNESSEY, J *Italian High Renaissance and Baroque Sculpture* (London, 1970).

PULLAN, B *Crisis and Change in the Venetian Economy in the 16th and 17th Centuries* (London, 1968).

PULLAN, B *Rich and Poor in Renaissance Venice* (Cambridge, Mass, and Oxford, 1971).

PULLAN, B *Poverty and Charity in Renaissance Venice* (Oxford, 1981).

PUPPI, L AND PUPPI, L OLIVATO *Mauro Codussi* (Turin, 1977).

PUPPI, L *Andrea Palladio* (Milan, 1973).

PUPPI, L (ed) *Alvise Cornaro e il suo tempo* (Padua, 1980).

QUELLER, D E *The Fourth Crusade: the Conquest of Constantinople* (Philadelphia, 1977).

QUELLER, D E *The Venetian Patriciate: Reality versus Myth* (Chicago, 1986).

RAZZA, D *Storia popolare di Chioggia* (Chioggia, 1898).

RIDOLFI, C *The Life of Tintoretto and of his Children Domenico and Marietta* (1st edn, as *La vita di Giacopo Robusti detto il Tintoretto*, Venice, 1642; new ed translated by C and R Engass, Penn State Univ and London, 1984).

RIZZI, A *Scultura esterna a Venezia* (Venice, 1987).

ROBBINS LANDON, H C AND NORWICH, J J *Five Centuries of Music in Venice* (London, 1991).

ROMANELLI, G *Venezia ottocento* (2nd edn, Venice, 1989).

ROMANELLI, G AND PAVANELLO, G *Palazzo Grassi* (Venice, 1986).

ROMANELLI, G AND PEDROCCO, F *Ca Rezzonico* (Milan, 1986).

ROTH, C *The History of the Jews of Venice* (Philadelphia, 1930).

ROTH, C *A History of the Marranos* (Philadelphia, 1932).

RUNCIMAN, S *A History of the Crusades*, 3 vols (Cambridge, 1951–4).

RUNCIMAN, S *The Fall of Constantinople* (Cambridge, 1965).

RUSKIN, J *The Stones of Venice*, 3 vols (London, 1851–3).

RUSKIN, J *St Mark's Rest* (London, 1877).

SAMONA, G et al *Piazza San Marco: l'architettura, la storia, le funzioni* (Padua, 1977).

SANSOVINO, F *Venetia, città nobilissima et singolare*, 2 vols, (facsimile of the 1663 edn, with the additions of Stringa and Martinioni (Venice, 1968).

SANUDO, M, the Younger *La città di Venetia*, (Laus Urbis Venetae), 1493–1530, ed A C Arico (Milan, 1980).

SANUDO, M, the Younger *I Diarii*, 58 vols, eds R Fulin et al (Venice, 1879–1903).

SCAMOZZI, V *L'idea dell'Architettura universale* (Venice, 1615).

SCHULZ, A M *Antonio Rizzo, Sculptor and Architect* (Princeton, 1983).

SERLIO, S *Architettura* (Venice, 1537–40 and Paris 1545–7; 1st English as *The Five Books of Architecture*, London 1611; facsimile of the latter: New York, 1982).

SIMONSFELD, H *Der Fondaco dei Tedeschi in Venedig*, 2 vols (Stuttgart, 1887).

SOHM, P *The Scuola Grande di San Marco 1437–1550* (London and New York, 1982).

SPENCER, J *Filarete's Treatise on Architecture*, 2 vols (New Haven, 1965).

STEER, J *A Concise History of Venetian Painting* (London and New York, 1970).

TAFURI, M *Venezia e il Rinascimento* (Turin, 1985); English edn translated by J Levine as *Venice and the Renaissance* (Cambridge, Mass, and London, 1989).

TAFURI, M *Sansovino e l'architettura del 500 a Venezia* (Padua, 1969).

TALBOT RICE, D *Byzantine Art* (London, 1954).

TAMASSIA MAZZAROTTO, B *Le feste veneziane* (Florence, 1961).

TASSINI, G *Curiosità veneziane* (Venice, 1863; 9th edn, Venice, 1988).

TEMANZA, T *Antica pianta dell'inclita città di Venezia* (Venice, 1781; facsimile edn, Sala Bolognese, 1977).

TENTORI, C *Della legislazione veneziana* (Venice, 1792).

THORNTON, P *The Italian Renaissance Interior* (London, 1991).

TIETZE, H *Tintoretto* (London, 1948).

TIMOFIEWITSCH, W *The chiesa del Redentore*, Corpus Palladianum, Vol III (Vicenza, 1969).

TIOZZO, I *Chioggia nella storia, nell'arte e nei commerci* (Chioggia, 1920).

TRINCANATO, E R *Venezia minore* (Milan, 1948).

TRINCANATO, E R AND FRANZOI, U *Venise au fil du temps* (Boulogne Billancourt, 1971).

UNESCO *Venice Restored 1966–86* (Milan, 1991).

UNRAU, J *Ruskin and St Mark's* (London and New York, 1984).

VALCANOVER, F *Tutta la pittura di Tiziano*, 2 vols (Milan, 1960).

VALCANOVER, F et al *Tizian* (Venice, 1990).

VASARI, G *Vite de' più eccellenti architetti, scultori e pittori* (Florence, 1550; 2nd edn, Florence, 1568; first English edn as *Lives of the Painters* translated by J Foster, 5 vols, London, 1878).

VENTURI, A *Storia dell'arte italiana*, 23 vols (Milan, 1907–41).

VITRUVIUS (Marcus Vitruvius Pollio) *The Ten Books on Architecture*, translated by M H Morgan (Harvard, 1914; facsimile edn, New York, 1960).

WETHEY, H *The Paintings of Titian*, 3 vols (London and New York, 1969, 1971 and 1975).

WITTKOWER, R *Architectural Principles in the Age of Humanism*, 5th edn (London and New York, 1988).

WOLTERS, W *La scultura gotica veneziana 1300–1460*, 2 vols (Venice, 1976).

WUNDRAM, M et al *Palladio* (Köln, n d).

ZANETTI, V *Guida di Murano e delle celebre fornaci vetrarie* (Venice, 1866; new facsimile edn, Sala Bolognese, 1984).

ZORZI, A *Venezia Scomparsa*, 2 vols (Milan, 1984).

ZORZI, A *Venetian Palaces* (New York, 1990).

ZORZI, A et al *Il Palazzo Ducale di Venezia* (Turin, 1971).

ZORZI, G G *Le opere pubbliche e i palazzi privati di Andrea Palladio* (Venice, 1965).

ZORZI, G G *Le chiese e i ponti di Andrea Palladio* (Venice, 1966).

ZORZI, G G *Le ville e i teatri di Andrea Palladio* (Venice, 1969).

ZUCCOLO, G *Il restauro statico nell'architettura di Venezia* (Venice, 1975).

Index

Acknowledgements

I am delighted to acknowledge thanks to a number of friends and organizations in Venice, without whose kind assistance Michael's excellent photographs would not have been possible. On a personal level, warmest thanks to Giulio Vianello for finding excellent accommodation for both Michael and myself in which to stay; to my very kind friends Nubar Gianighian and Paolina Pavanini for their generous welcomes and invaluable help in 'opening doors'; to Dott Giandomenico Romanelli, Director of the Civici Musei Veneziani; to Professor Dario Calimani at the Comunità Ebraica di Venezia; to the Scuola Grande Arciconfraternità di San Rocco; to Sig Carlo Dri at the Curia Patriarcale; to the staff at the Basilica Cattedrale di San Marco and at Santi Giovanni e Paolo; to Arch Michael Karapetian and Padre Vahan Ohanian for kindly allowing access to Cà Zenobio, home of the Collegio Armeno; to the Soprintendenza per i Beni Ambientali e Architettonici di Venezia; to the Soprintendenza per i Beni Artistici e Storici di Venezia; to the Soprintendenza per i Beni Artistici del Veneto; and to the Director and staff of the Palazzo Ducale.

I have quoted a number of excerpts from Venice: A Documentary History (Oxford, 1992), edited by Brian Pullan and David Chambers; in particular these included extracts from Marin Sanudo's 'Laus Urbis Venetae', translated by David Chambers; and the excerpts from decrees of the Venetian Senate, translated by Brian Pullan, all copyright Blackwell Publishers. I have also cited quotations from Alessandro Caravia's Il Sogno di Caravia, in Richard Mackenney's lively translation. Other brief quotations include: Marcel Proust, A la recherche du temps perdu (Chatto and Windus and Random House); and Italo Calvino, Le città invisibili, 'Invisible Cities' (Giulio Einaudi SpA and Pan Books Picador Ltd).

PHOTOGRAPHIC CREDITS

(l = left, r = right, t = top, b = bottom, c = centre)

GALLERIE DELL' ACCADEMIA, Venice
35, 51

AKG, London
30-31, 36 (l), 40, 72, 73, 81, 123, 124,
125 (l & r) 128 (l) 155, 160 (l & b) 163 (t & b)

ANCIENT ART AND ARCHITECTURE COLLECTION
165, 166, 214, 245, 248, 268

ASHMOLEAN MUSEUM, Oxford
92 (l & c) 145, 146

BIBLIOTECA CORRER, Venice
39, 153, (r) 191

BIBLIOTECA NAZIONALE MARCIANA, Venice
46, 47, 49, 82, 212

MARIA IDA BIGGI
29, 48

OSVALDO BOHM
301 (l) 299 (r)

BRIDGEMAN ART LIBRARY
15, 39, 57, 62 (t) 75 (b) 97, 101, 103, 161,
173, 181, 187 (l) 188 (r) 198 (l) 214, 217, 223,
224 (b, r) 226, 227, 244, 269 (l) 300

BRITISH LIBRARY
50, 67, 80, 95, 138, 222, 245, 269 (b)

BRITISH LIBRARY
37 (t&r), 45 (l, c, r), 52, 62 (b) 63, 83, 87, 96,
98, 99 (t & b), 102, 105, 112 (t&b) 122, 133 (b)
134 (b) 135 (r) 146, 150, 151, 171, 182 (l)
183 (l & b,r) 186, 188 (l & b,r) 189 (r)
190 (b), 195 (r) 198 (r) 199 (all) 202 (t & b)
216 (l) 222, 224 (t & b) 237 (top) 250 (t & b, l)
272 (all) 274 (b) 278 (l) 279 (t, r & b)

CORBIS UK LTD.
38, 68-69

FRATELLI ALINARI
28, 77, 149, 154, 178

GALLERIA QUERINI-STAMPALIA, Venice
67 (l) 246

MICHAEL HARDING
2-3, 4-5, 12-13, 22, 23, 24 (r) 25, 26, 27, 42,
58-9, 71 (l) 78 (l) 78 (l & r) 84 (l & r) 85, 86, 88-89,
90, 91, 98, 100, 104, 106, 107 (t & b) 108,
109, 110, 113, 114 (l & r) 115 (l & r) 116, 117,
18-119, 121, 126, 127, 130, 132, 133, 136 (b)
137, 139, 140-141, 142, 147, 152 (l & r) 156,
157, 159, 162, 168, 170 (l & r), 171 (l) 175,
176 (t & b) 177, 179, 182 (r) 183 (l) 189 (t& b l)
190 (t & l) 194, 195, 203, 206 (t) 207 (l) 208,
210-211, 212, 213, 216 (r) 218, 219, 221,
225, 229, 230, 231, 232, 233, 235, 236, 237,
(b) 241, 252, 254, 255, 256 (r) 257, 258, 259,
261 (r), 262, 263, 264 (l & r) 265 (l & r) 266,
270 (l & r) 271, 273, 276 (r) 278 (l) 283 (l) 286,
287, 288 (r), 290, 291, 295 (l & r)

ANGELO HORNAK
41, 43 (t) 134 (l) 151, 172 (r) 193 (l & r) 196,
201, 261 (l) 292, 294 (r)

INDEX
138, 240, 282

A.F. KERSTING
14, 18, 19, 32, 76, 135 (t, l) 148, 169,
207 (t & b) 185 (r) 187 (r) 204, 205, 206 (b)

LIFE FILE
150

G. PAOLO MARTON
24 (l) 25, 34 (t) 111, 122, 124, 128 (t) 129,
192 (r) 284 (l & r) 285, 288 (l) 289, 293 (l)

MUSEO CIVICO, Venice
103

MUSEO DEL SETTECENTO, Venice
54

MUSEO STORICO NAVALE, Venice
83 (above)

NATIONAL GALLERY, London
55

NATIONAL GALLERY, Ottawa
94

NELSON-ATKINS MUSEUM OF ART, Kansas City
65 (b)

NATIONAL TRUST, Tatton Park, Cheshire
65 (t)

SARAH QUILL, Venice Picture Library
16, 17, 20, 21, 34 (b) 36 (r) 43 (b) 51, 60, 70,
71 (l) 74, 79, 85 (t) 92 (r) 93, 98, 115 (c) 131,
135 (b) 136 (t) 143, 153, 158, 164, 167, 172 (l)
180 (l & r) 197, 192 (l) 209 (t) 215, 220, 228,
238, 239, 242 (t) 243 (r) 247, 253, 256 (r) 260
(r) 267, 274 (t) 275, 276 (t) 277, 279, 288 (r)
294 (l) 296, 297 (l & c) 298, 299 (l & c) 301 (l)

RIBA, London
103

THE ROYAL COLLECTION © Her Majesty The Queen
67 (r)

WOBURN ABBEY, Bedfordshire
75 (t)

Phaidon Press Limited
Regent's Wharf
All Saints Street
London N1 9PA

First published 1997
© Phaidon Press Limited 1997

ISBN 0 7148 3005 4

A CIP catalogue record is available from the British Library

All rights reserved. No part of this publication may be reproduced, stored in a retrieval system or transmitted in any form or by any means, electronic, mechanical, photocopying, recording, or otherwise, without the prior permission of Phaidon Press Limited.

Printed in Hong Kong